Pewter at Colonial Williamsburg

PEWTER
AT COLONIAL WILLIAMSBURG

By John D. Davis

in association with
UNIVERSITY PRESS OF NEW ENGLAND
HANOVER AND LONDON

COLONIAL WILLIAMSBURG DECORATIVE ARTS SERIES

American Coverlets and Their Weavers
Coverlets from the Collection of
Foster and Muriel McCarl
Including a Dictionary of More Than 700 Weavers
by Clarita S. Anderson

Degrees of Latitude
Mapping Colonial America
by Margaret Beck Pritchard and Henry G. Taliaferro

Furnishing Williamsburg's Historic Buildings
by Jan Kirsten Gilliam and Betty Crowe Leviner

The Governor's Palace in Williamsburg
A Cultural Study
by Graham Hood

Southern Furniture 1680–1830
The Colonial Williamsburg Collection
by Ronald L. Hurst and Jonathan Prown

What Clothes Reveal
The Language of Clothing in Colonial and Federal America
The Colonial Williamsburg Collection
by Linda Baumgarten

© 2003 by The Colonial Williamsburg Foundation

All rights reserved. No part of this book may be reproduced or transmitted in any form or by any means, electronic or mechanical, including photocopying, recording, or by any information storage and retrieval system, without the written permission of the publisher, except where permitted by law.

Library of Congress Cataloging-in-Publication Data

Davis, John D., 1938-
  Pewter at Colonial Williamsburg / John D. Davis.
     p. cm. — (Williamsburg decorative arts series)
  Includes bibliographical references and index.
  ISBN 0-87935-218-3 (CW : alk. paper) — ISBN 1-58465-315-9 (UPNE : alk. paper)
  1. Pewter—Great Britain—Catalogs. 2. Pewter—Virginia—Williamsburg—Catalogs. 3. Colonial Williamsburg Foundation—Catalogs. I. Title. II. Series.
  NK8415.G7 D38 2003
  739.5'33'097554252—dc21
                                                2002153031

Published in 2003 by The Colonial Williamsburg Foundation, P. O. Box 1776, Williamsburg, VA 23187-1776, in association with University Press of New England, 37 Lafayette St., Lebanon, NH 03766

www.colonialwilliamsburg.org
www.upne.com

Photography by Hans Lorenz, Delmore Wenzel, and Craig McDougal
Designed by Helen M. Olds
Printed and bound in Singapore

Frontispiece
Covered dish or tureen, pewter, Henry Joseph, London, 1736–1794; Diam. (base) 11 3/16", 2002-39, A&B

Section Openers
Introduction, TC-01-000274; Lighting Devices, TC-01-628; Dining Wares, TC-02-390; Drinking Vessels, TC-91-503; Tea and Coffee Equipage, TC-02-391; Household and Personal Accessories, TC-02-15; Religious Objects, TC-02-19

The Colonial Williamsburg Foundation gratefully acknowledges
Sara Lee Corporation's generous underwriting support for this catalog and
for the Pewter at Colonial Williamsburg *exhibition.*

For

Ginny

Spencer

Trevor and Alana

Emily and Aaron

&

(of course)

Isaac

Contents

viii	Foreword
ix	A Message from Sara Lee Corporation
x	Preface
xi	Acknowledgments
1	Introduction
10	Lighting Devices
30	Dining Wares
184	Drinking Vessels
254	Tea and Coffee Equipage
276	Household and Personal Accessories
288	Religious Objects
306	Pewter Marks
331	Glossary
333	Short-Title List
337	Index

Foreword

British pewter, that serviceable, inexpensive, and respectable metal, was everywhere in Great Britain and her American colonies during the seventeenth and eighteenth centuries. When planter Richard Wake died in 1648 his rural Virginia residence contained dishes, plates, saucers, basins, porringers, candlesticks, chamber pots, flagons, a colander, and "three pye plates," all made of pewter. More than a century later, the kitchen of deceased Williamsburg tavern keeper Henry Wetherburn featured so much of the gray metal that his estate appraisers simply weighed it all and recorded the results: 107 pounds of pewter valued at £5.7 Virginia currency.

Colonial Williamsburg's collections handsomely reflect both the volume and the diversity suggested by the Wake and Wetherburn estates, thanks in significant measure to the matchless eye of John D. Davis. For more than thirty-five years, senior curator Davis has made it his business to build and refine the Foundation's outstanding holdings in period British and American pewter, as well as silver, iron, brass, and other metalwares. Today the largest and perhaps the finest collection of early British pewter outside the United Kingdom is exhibited in Williamsburg's historic houses, taverns, and shops, and its art museums. In writing the present volume, Davis has made that vast body of material and three decades of his own seminal research available to an audience far beyond the bounds of the eighteenth-century town.

The sharing of this important work would not have been possible without the generous assistance of the Sara Lee Corporation and the special interest of retired Chairman John H. Bryan. We gratefully acknowledge their public-spirited support of this project and so many others.

Many people at Colonial Williamsburg also contributed to this production. We are particularly indebted to photographers Hans Lorenz and Craig McDougal, conservator David Blanchfield, and Albert O. Louer. Erin Michaela Bendiner gracefully edited the manuscript, Helen M. Olds designed the striking layouts, and Joseph N. Rountree skillfully managed the publication process. These and other members of the staff deserve manifold thanks.

Finally, we recognize with gratitude the support of the DeWitt Wallace Fund for Colonial Williamsburg, established by the founders of *Reader's Digest*, for making possible the conservation of so many objects in this book, and for enabling us to present them in a special exhibition at Colonial Williamsburg's DeWitt Wallace Decorative Arts Museum in 2003–2004.

Ronald L. Hurst
Carlisle Humelsine Chief Curator
Colonial Williamsburg Foundation

A Message from Sara Lee Corporation

Sara Lee Corporation is committed to being an innovative, dynamic presence in community life. Our mission is to feed, clothe, and care for consumers and their families the world over. Just as our brands provide products at the heart of life, our philanthropic endeavors also seek to address life's most pressing needs.

We believe improving quality of life encompasses not only addressing basic necessities such as food, housing, and employment, but also enriching community spirit through cultural programs. That is why our contributions underwrite artistic endeavors that broaden public accessibility to the arts.

Sara Lee Corporation is pleased to sponsor this catalog and the *Pewter at Colonial Williamsburg* exhibition. The catalog documents Colonial Williamsburg's superb British and American pewter collection and the exhibition opens this exceptional collection to the public for the first time. We are delighted to make it possible for you to study this important collection and, through it, gain further insight into the cultural treasure that is Colonial Williamsburg.

C. Steven McMillan
Chairman, President and Chief Executive Officer
Sara Lee Corporation

Preface

It is difficult today, when pewter is no longer commonly used and has not been since before the American Civil War, to understand how pervasive and integral a part of English and American daily life pewter was in the seventeenth and eighteenth centuries. Even those of modest means owned pewter and not infrequently a respectable group of plates and dishes, mugs and porringers, basins and spoons, and sometimes more specialized forms, such as tankards, teapots, and even soup tureens.

The collection of British pewter at Colonial Williamsburg is remarkable for its breadth and detail. It illustrates the development of basic forms and types of decoration from the first decades of the seventeenth century through those of the nineteenth century. The collection also includes a complementary admixture of American examples, which often exhibit readily identifiable regional and individual preferences. This catalog is divided into sections based on use, including dining wares, drinking vessels, and religious objects. This organization allows for the juxtaposition of related forms and for the appreciation of their chronologies and development.

This volume makes more accessible the important Colonial Williamsburg Collection that has been formed over the past seventy-five years to aid in the historical re-creation of colonial Williamsburg. It highlights the many purposes pewter served in early American history, assisting in the transfer of culture from Europe and in the shaping of distinctive American attitudes and artifacts. It is also illustrative of the broad distribution of British wares, especially apparent in Virginia and the lower Chesapeake region, where there were relatively few practicing pewterers and where there was a decided dependence on imported pewter. It is also hoped that this catalog will encourage the publication of other books about public and private collections of early pewter.

Acknowledgments

I was fortunate to have been a graduate student at the Winterthur Museum when Charles F. Montgomery was its director. One of the greatest authorities on American pewter of his generation, he was its enthusiastic evangelist. He would not simply introduce students to a few well-chosen examples, but he would actively seek response. On a trip to Vermont, we talked at length about differences in intent and perception between the surfaces of silver and pewter objects and the influence of materials and technologies. John J. Evans, Jr., noted collector of American pewter, was also at Winterthur then. He was especially patient with the endless questions of a novice.

In the intervening years, I have benefited greatly from the knowledge and advice of many others, in matters both great and small. I am particularly grateful to Christopher Bangs, John Barden, Brian Beet, John Bivins, Claude Blair, Michael Boorer, Richard L. Bowen, George Broadbent, Thomas C. Campbell, Edwin A. Churchill, Gordon W. and Genevieve A. Deming, John A. Douglas, Nancy Goyne Evans, Dean F. Failey, Donald L. Fennimore, Jan A. Gadd, Rupert and Belinda Gentle, Philippa Glanville, Gayle Glinn, Price and Isobel Glover, Thomas A. Gray, Shawn Holl, Peter R. G. and Jennifer Hornsby, Robert Hunter, John A. Hyman, Brand Inglis, Michael A. Kashden, Henry J. Kauffman, William Kayhoe, A. S. Law, David W. J. Little, James Lomax, Ann Smart Martin, Foster and Muriel McCarl, Jr., Cyril C. Minchin, Richard Mundey, Ivor Noël Hume, William Pittman, Sumpter T. Priddy, John F. Richardson, Ian D. Robinson, Quincy J. Scarborough, Jr., Susan Shames, Timothy Schroder, H. H. Standidge, Jr., Charles V. Swain, Joseph Ternbach, John Carl Thomas, Thomas D. and Constance R. Williams, Melvyn D. and Bette Wolfe, and Philip Zea.

I have also been fortunate to work at the Colonial Williamsburg Foundation for a number of years. It has not only splendid collections, but also a selection of historic trades that are practiced as they were in the eighteenth century. Pewter is one of the metals worked at the James Geddy Foundry in Williamsburg. I am grateful for all that I have learned from a remarkable cast of characters: master founders Dan Berg and Doc Hassell, journeymen Mike A. Noftsger and Roger L. Hohensee, and apprentice Suzie Dye.

I have also been the beneficiary of ample ideas and information regarding this book and its contents from most of my curatorial and many of my conservation colleagues. I particularly want to acknowledge the support given me to enlarge the pewter collection by the chief curators I have worked under, John M. Graham II, Milo M. Naeve, Graham S. Hood, John O. Sands, and Ronald L. Hurst. Graham Hood strongly encouraged me to write this catalog, and he was instrumental in securing funding from Sara Lee Corporation, to whom I am especially grateful for its generous corporate support. In particular, the interest of retired Chairman John H. Bryan made this catalog possible. I am also grateful to Robert Lauer, retired vice president for public affairs, and Robin Tryloff, executive director—community relations, for their roles in Sara Lee Corporation's support for this project.

Many individuals have directly assisted in the production of this catalog. Hans Lorenz and the late Delmore Wenzel provided the superb photographs of the objects and their marks, which Craig McDougal processed and printed so handsomely. David S. Moulson read the manuscript and made many useful and necessary suggestions. Erin Michaela Bendiner edited the manuscript and, in turn, was assisted by Tami Carsillo, John B. Ogden, and Cathy Swormstedt. Velva Heneger and Patricia Bare handled the many secretarial functions with ability and aplomb. Last and far from least, I am particularly grateful to Helen M. Olds who designed this visually lucid and elegant volume.

INTRODUCTION

Pewter is no longer a part of daily life, and it is impossible to comprehend how ubiquitous it once was in English and American homes, commercial establishments, taverns and clubs, schools, and churches. Immense quantities of pewter were sent from English ports to America, where demand greatly outstripped local production. Few pewterers are known to have worked in Virginia, unlike more densely settled areas to the north, so most Virginians ate and drank from imported pewter plates and vessels. The Colonial Williamsburg Collection illustrates the diversity of pewter forms used in the Chesapeake region.

Selection of English pewter

PEWTER OBJECTS HAVE BEEN A MAINSTAY of European material culture since antiquity. By the time of early settlement of America in the first half of the seventeenth century, pewter was the metal of choice for household goods. Its bright appearance, easy and safe transport, and durability recommended its use. The trade prospered in the absence of undue competition from base-metal and ceramic producers. This lack of competitive challenge allowed the English pewter industry to reach its maximum size in the last decades of the seventeenth century, with an estimated total of twenty-five hundred to thirty-five hundred masters, journeymen, apprentices, and servants.[1] At the same time, the English had an estimated thirty thousand tons of pewter in use.[2] Although pewter maintained its viability for another century, strong competition from an emerging brass industry was evident by 1700. For dining table and tea table, it would not be much longer before refined white-bodied ceramic services, initially of white salt-glazed stoneware and eventually of lead-glazed creamware and pearlware, would capture the market and sweep pewter aside. By century's end, inexpensive earthenware with colorful decoration had largely replaced pewter as the fashionable choice for tableware in most parts of Britain and her former colonies.

Fine pewter consists mainly of tin, often exceeding 90 percent, with varying small amounts of copper and antimony for strength and durability, and/or lead, which in small amounts aids the flow of hot metal within the molds. Because of pewter's low melting point, it is invariably cast, usually in reusable brass or bronze molds. Such molds represented a sizable percentage of a pewterer's investment in tools and shop equipment. Pewterers made plates, dishes, basins, and spoons in single castings, while they had to assemble more complex forms with separate handles, bases, covers, and spouts from various parts and castings. They finished circular bodies and components, when possible, on a lathe, hammered the short convex sides of the wells, or booges, of plates and dishes in orderly rows to compress the metal and strengthen the object, and scraped, filed, and burnished other areas and features. A 1427 inventory of the shop of a London pewterer contains at that early date all the basic tools needed. Included are "seventeen bronze moulds for casting a variety of plates and dishes from four inches to twenty inches in diameter, a lathe and turning tools, anvils, hammers, files, soldering irons, clipping shears, clamps, burnishers, bellows, casting pans, scales and weights and marking irons."[3]

The English pewter industry grew up under the supervision of The Worshipful Company of Pewterers of London. Granted its initial royal charter in 1473/4, it consolidated the power and influence of the guild that had been in existence since at least the middle of the previous century and established it as one of the City Livery Companies, occupational guilds that presently number one hundred. The Pewterers' Company oversaw apprenticeship and training, use of appropriate alloys, maintenance of standards of workmanship, and the regular marking of wares. It was empowered to search shops throughout the country and to seize substandard goods.

Qualified pewterers were required to register their touchmarks on touch plates at Pewterers' Hall. The original touch plates, in use from at least the middle of the fifteenth century, were destroyed in the Great Fire of 1666. The surviving five London Touch Plates, in use from 1667/8 to 1821, contain the impressions of the marks of 1,090 makers. The London Touch Plates are reproduced in Howard Herschel Cotterell's book, *Old Pewter, Its*

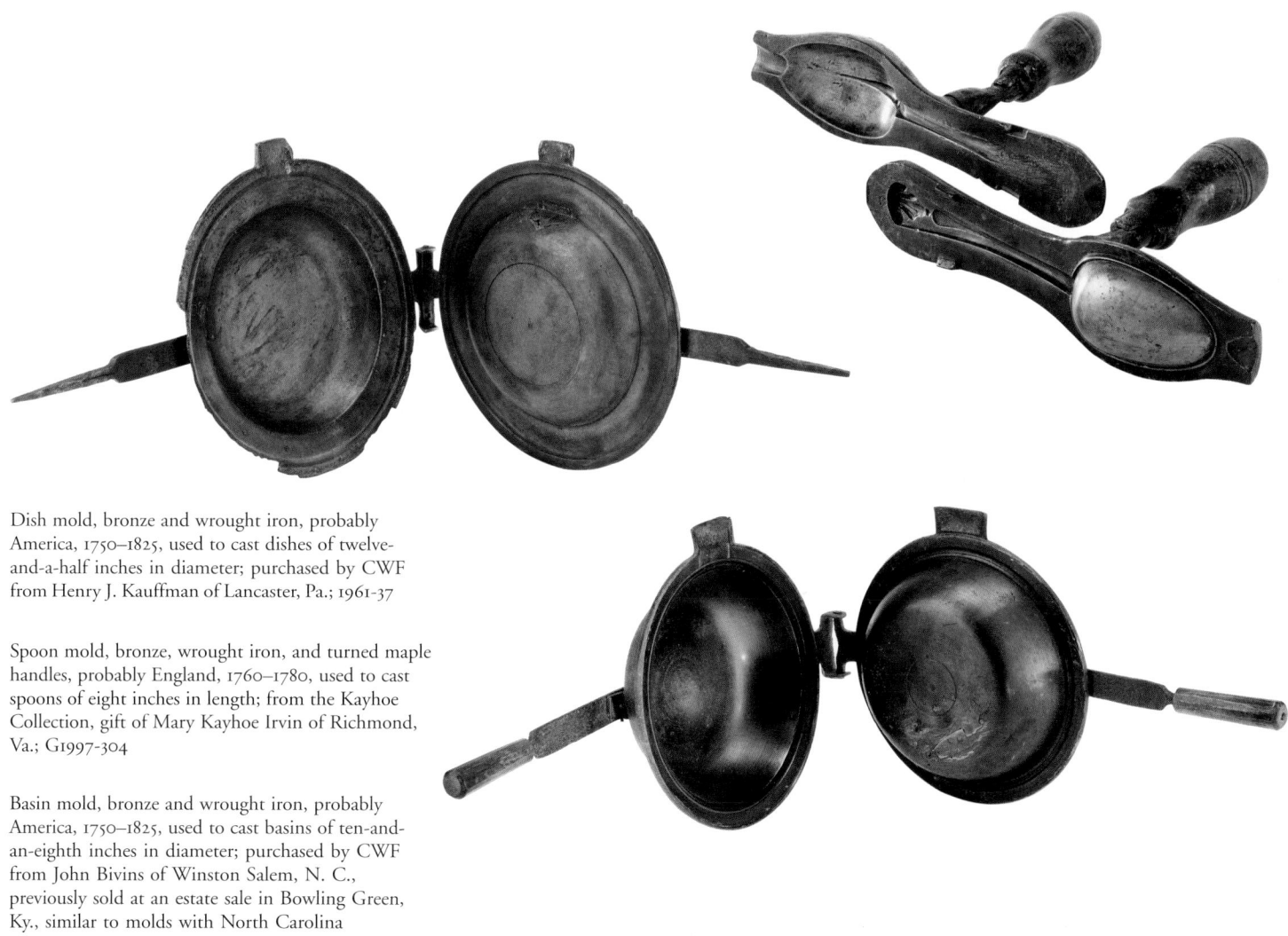

Dish mold, bronze and wrought iron, probably America, 1750–1825, used to cast dishes of twelve-and-a-half inches in diameter; purchased by CWF from Henry J. Kauffman of Lancaster, Pa.; 1961-37

Spoon mold, bronze, wrought iron, and turned maple handles, probably England, 1760–1780, used to cast spoons of eight inches in length; from the Kayhoe Collection, gift of Mary Kayhoe Irvin of Richmond, Va.; G1997-304

Basin mold, bronze and wrought iron, probably America, 1750–1825, used to cast basins of ten-and-an-eighth inches in diameter; purchased by CWF from John Bivins of Winston Salem, N. C., previously sold at an estate sale in Bowling Green, Ky., similar to molds with North Carolina associations; 1985-176

INTRODUCTION 3

Selection of American pewter

Makers and Marks. The plates have been immensely useful to collectors and students alike in attributing and dating marks of London makers. They also illustrate the evolving design of such marks over time.

Other marks are sometimes found on English pewter. A row of pseudo hallmarks, usually four in number and emulating those on assayed silver items, are relatively common in the period from 1630 to 1770. A variety of secondary marks draws attention to the quality of the metal, the location of manufacture, or status as an export piece. These may appear in decorative reserves that relate to the maker's touch, or in label form. The simple *X* with crown above, struck with a raised letter stamp, certified quality when introduced in the seventeenth century, only to lose its specialness through its commonness in the eighteenth century. American pewterers, in turn, often based the general design of their marks on English precedent.

Immense quantities of pewter were sent from English ports to America, where demand greatly outstripped local production. Many substantial firms, especially in London and Bristol, specialized in the production of export wares. Some of the popular export forms, such as pear-shaped teapots, porringers, and eight-inch plates of single-bead type, were tailored specifically to American preferences. These exports rose steadily. By the 1760s, more than three hundred tons of pewter articles were shipped annually. This amount is the equivalent of almost one million eight-inch plates or two hundred fifty thousand quart tankards.[4] Unlike more densely settled areas to the north, few pewterers are known to have worked in Virginia, so most Virginians ate and drank from imported plates and dishes. Many of the simple and predictable forms that were made by export makers and collected in this country through the third quarter of the last century, although uninscribed and without a known history, could very well have been owned here for a long time. This widespread use of imported pewter in the Chesapeake region has determined the character of the Colonial Williamsburg (CWF) Collection.

From an early date, many Virginians owned significant amounts of pewter. For instance, the 1668 inventory of the estate of Major Joseph Croshaw, a substantial planter who lived only a few miles from present-day Williamsburg, Va., included the following pewter: two candlesticks, forty-two dishes, four porringers, thirty-six spoons, one bedpan, and one still. Some of his flagons, tankards, plates, saucers, salts, basins, and chamber pots, although unspecified as to material, undoubtedly were made of pewter.[5]

Pewter maintained a presence in some Virginia homes, especially in rural areas, into the second quarter of the nineteenth century. John Jay Janney (1812–1907) was raised in a Quaker family on a farm in Loudoun Co., Va. In the final year of his life, he wrote down recollections of his youth before he had moved West in 1831. Of particular interest is his appreciation of the use of pewter and its relation to other tablewares. He writes:

> On the kitchen shelves were the table ware, including pewter plates and dishes, and mugs, the spoons lying in notches along the edge of a shelf.
>
> Travelling tinkers were not strangers. They would come at frequent intervals and mend the tinware and

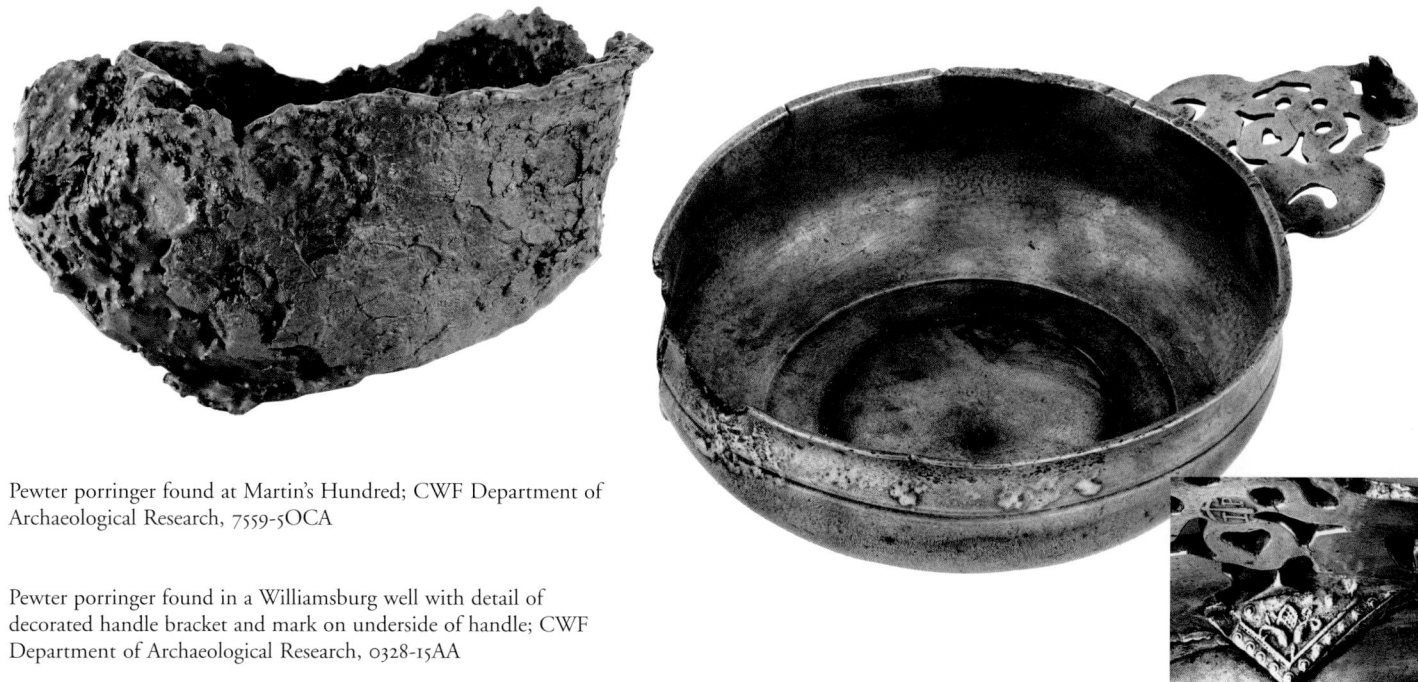

Pewter porringer found at Martin's Hundred; CWF Department of Archaeological Research, 7559-5OCA

Pewter porringer found in a Williamsburg well with detail of decorated handle bracket and mark on underside of handle; CWF Department of Archaeological Research, 0328-15AA

remould the broken pewter spoons. Tin pedlars were common with a load of tin cups, buckets, coffee pots and such. The "earthen ware" included milk pans, pie dishes, pitchers, jars and jugs were bought at the store.

We had silver spoons, both table and tea, but they were not used by the family, only when visitors or strangers were present, and there was a china tea pot, sugar bowl, and teas to match, which were only used on special occasions. In every day use we had pewter spoons and dishes, among the dishes some platters twelve to fifteen inches in diameter.[6]

Pewter objects are much more commonly found by sleuthing in written records than by excavating archaeological sites. The high value of the metal relative to initial cost of the object and the ease with which one could recycle it precluded intentional burial. If a piece of pewter happened to find its way into the ground, a mixture of substances would usually hasten deterioration. Two porringers in the archaeological collections of CWF are rare instances of hollowware survivals recovered from sites in the Williamsburg vicinity. The earlier example with a cup-shaped bowl is of a rare type and dates from about 1625. It is from Martin's Hundred, on the present site of Carter's Grove in James City Co., Va.[7] The more intact porringer by Joseph Pickard of London dates from about 1720. Its handle features a triangular bracket on its underside with relief-cast decoration. This porringer was found in a Williamsburg well. Locations, such as the silt of the Thames River, where there is an absence of oxygen, have

Selection of candlesticks

6   PEWTER AT COLONIAL WILLIAMSBURG

for long periods of time preserved articles such as the splendid half-pint mug, apparently deposited shortly after it was made about 1720 (no. 279) and the rare punch strainer of similar date (no. 296).

The collection of British pewter at CWF is one of the finest of its kind in this country. It illustrates, in breadth and detail, the development of basic forms and types of decoration during the colonial and early Republican periods, that is, from about 1610 until about 1820. This collection also includes a complementary admixture of American examples, often exhibiting regional preferences in form and detail. The catalog is divided into sections based on the major areas of use: lighting devices, dining wares, drinking vessels, tea and coffee equipage, household and personal accessories, and religious objects.

Candlesticks are one of the glories of seventeenth-century English pewter. This collection contains a number of uncommon examples that show the variety and complexity of patterns during the last four decades of the century. Most representative of this early date are those with tall cylindrical or pillar stems, often combined with polygonal bases. In the 1680s, Huguenot émigré silversmiths introduced a new form of candlestick with a baluster stem. Brass founders quickly adopted the new model and pre-empted the market for base-metal candlesticks.

The largest category of early pewter, with the greatest number of pieces in the CWF Collection, is that associated with dining. Almost all are plates and dishes, which are distinguished from one another by size and function. Plates measure less than ten inches in diameter. Except for a few rare exceptions, dishes are flat forms

INTRODUCTION 7

of ten inches or more in diameter. While individuals ate from plates, dishes performed the various tasks of transport and service. Occasionally, plates and dishes received decoration for presentation and display purposes. There are a limited number of other forms used in eating. Principal among these forms are bowls and basins, salvers and soup tureens, salts and sauceboats, and porringers and spoons.

Pewter vessels for serving and consuming alcoholic beverages constitute another traditionally important category. Most of the activities related to this group were masculine pursuits. They involve not only those of convivial association, but also the assertion of individual and class position and privilege. This collection is particularly rich in tankards and related mugs that date from the late seventeenth century until the beginning of the nineteenth century. It also contains a broadly representative group of British measures that illustrate basic English, Scottish, and Channel Island types. Rarities include a church tankard of 1679 with acanthus and palm leaf chasing and religious symbolism in its decoration (no. 234), a magnificent wine cup of about 1620 with cast decoration that was probably made for the use of Charles I when Prince of Wales (no. 288), and a splendid two-handled cup with alternate cast flutes and gadroons (no. 290).

In contrast to pewter mugs and tankards for quaffing beer and ale, pewter wares for drinking tea and coffee were relatively late arrivals. The earliest English pewter teapots are extremely rare, and they date from the first half of the eighteenth century (nos. 333–334). English ceramic manufacturers were efficient in producing a plethora of teapots for every taste and pocketbook that effectively pushed most competition aside. The numerous pear-shaped ones in pewter were not produced for English use but for the American market (nos. 335–338). English and American pewterers turned out significant quantities of teapots and related forms in the neoclassic style, both in cast pewter and sheet Britannia metal. Pewter coffeepots survive in considerably fewer numbers than their counterparts for tea.

A variety of pewter household and personal accessories were involved in the daily activities of most individuals. Shaving and wash basins and sundials aided in rising and starting the day. Pewter chamber pots stored under the bed and commode pots for commode chairs and close stools had a convenient presence. People fed and administered medicine to the very young and the infirm with modest papboats. Individuals used rectangular inkstands of treasury type with covers hinged down the center for their personal correspondence and commercial accounts. Gentlemen kept their tobacco fresh in lidded canisters or carried it in a smaller box for convenience and on occasion smoked tobacco in pewter pipes. Gleaming buttons and buckles could complete one's dress for social occasions or church attendance.

Pewter communion vessels were commonly used in less wealthy church congregations that could not afford costly ones in silver. It is difficult to know in some instances, especially of an early date, whether a flagon was intended for church or domestic use, for they often appear before 1720 in household inventories. There are distinctive regional and national types of flagons and chalices, including English, Scottish, Irish, and American. The considerable number of flagons and matching chalices made by Johann Christoph Heyne (1715–1781) of Lancaster, Pa. (nos. 403–404), have an appearance all their own, and they are one of the great monuments in American pewter of the colonial period.

Although the collecting of pewter began at CWF in 1930, it was not until the arrival of John M. Graham II as chief curator in 1950 that the medium received professional advocacy. While at the Brooklyn Museum, he had organized an exhibition of American pewter. After coming to CWF, Graham secured the collection of English and American pewter that Dr. Percy E. Raymond of Lexington, Mass., had formed. Graham enlisted the assistance of Capt. A. V. Sutherland-Graeme, English authority and writer on pewter, to find representative examples for the re-creation at Colonial Williamsburg. Toward this end, he also acquired considerable pewter from Thomas D. and Constance R. Williams of Litchfield, Conn., and Carl and Celia Jacobs of Southwick, Mass. He also purchased many pieces of particularly fine English pewter from A. H. Isher & Son of Cheltenham, Eng. Graham succeeded in acquiring a sizable body of appropriate pewter objects to furnish exhibition buildings and to create a collection broadly representative of its medium. It was the firm basis on which his successors have built. This remarkable collection continues to grow, with a greater understanding of pewter objects and their place in the material culture of the lower Chesapeake.

1. John Hatcher and T. C. Barker, *A History of British Pewter* (London, 1974), p. 141.
2. *Ibid.*, p. 292.
3. Ronald F. Homer, "The Pewterers of London," in Peter R. G. Hornsby, Rosemary Weinstein, and Ronald F. Homer, *Pewter: A celebration of the craft, 1200–1700* (London, 1989), p. 12.
4. Charles F. Montgomery, *A History of American Pewter* (New York, 1973), p. 8.
5. Inventory of the estate of Joseph Croshaw, York Co., Va., Deeds, Orders, Wills, Etc. no. 4 (1668), pp. 190–191.
6. Asa Moore Janney and Werner L. Janney, eds., *John Jay Janney's Virginia: An American Farm Lad's Life in the Early 19th Century* (McLean, Va., 1978), p. 18.
7. Ronald F. Michaelis classifies this form of bowl as type II and illustrates a similar example with a distinctive shell-shaped ear or handle in "English Pewter Porringers: Their evolution over three hundred years. Part II," *Apollo*, L (August 1949), pp. 46–47, fig. VIII. A drawing of the excavated example is illustrated in Ivor Noël Hume and Audrey Noël Hume, *The Archaeology of Martin's Hundred. Part II: Artifact Catalog* (Williamsburg, Va., 2001), pp. 358, 360, fig. 43, no. 8. Mentioned is a further porringer of this bowl type with a ring handle in the Museum of London and another with a shell handle that was recovered from the ruins of Port Royal, Jamaica.

Detail from *A Rake's Progress* (plate three), William Hogarth, designer and engraver, London, June 25, 1735, black-and-white line engraving, 1967-566, 3

Lighting Devices

Candlesticks are among the most distinctive and ambitious forms in English pewter of the seventeenth century. The Colonial Williamsburg Collection contains a number of uncommon examples that show the variety and complexity of patterns used during the last four decades of the century. In the early eighteenth century, brass founders largely preempted the market for base-metal candlesticks. Pewter became the metal of choice in the nineteenth century for the many oil lamps produced by American artisans.

I

1 Pair of Candlesticks

Maker unidentified
London, 1660–1680

MARKS: Indistinct touchmark incorporating, in part, an *S* within a small beaded circle on face of one stem at rim; removable nozzles unmarked

INSCRIPTIONS: Unimpaled arms of the Glanville family engraved within a lozenge on face of both bases for an unmarried lady of the Glanville family

DIMENSIONS: OH. (with nozzle) 9 7/8", Diam. (base) 8 1/16", Diam. (nozzle) 4 9/16"

PROVENANCE: Glanville and Edgcumbe families by descent (sold at Sotheby's in 1956 and purchased by Ronald F. Michaelis, Newhaven, Eng.); purchased from Cyril C. Minchin, Bucklebury, Eng., by CWF; 1977-264, 1–2

PUBLISHED: Sales cat., Sotheby's, June 1, 1956, p. 10, lot 37, ill.; Michaelis, "Early Stuart Pewter," pp. 32–34, fig. 3; *Exhibition of Pewter,* no. 13, pl. 1; *Exhibition of British Pewterware,* p. 19, nos. 70–71; Ullyett, *Guide for Collectors,* frontis.; Hornsby, *Pewter of the Western World,* p. 313, fig. 1063; Neish, "Supreme Candlesticks," pp. 213–216, fig. 3; Gadd, "Famous Old Candlesticks," pp. 14–16, fig. 7; Gadd, "Candlesticks of the Baroque Period," pp. 19–20, 38, 39, figs. 6–7; Gadd, "Disc-base Candlesticks," p. 29, fig. 2

EXHIBITED: Exhibition of Pewter, City of Lincoln Usher Gallery, Lincoln, Eng., Sept. 29–Oct. 27, 1962; Exhibition of British Pewterware through the Ages from Romano-British Times to the Present Day, Reading Museum and Art Gallery, Reading, Eng., Sept. 20–Oct. 31, 1969

One of the glories of British pewter and particularly of this collection is the array of ambitious candlesticks from the second half of the seventeenth century. England's fledgling brass industry had just begun to pose a threat to the continued production and popularity of pewter candlesticks, which eventually led to the dominance of brass ones and to the virtual exclusion of those of pewter by the end of the first quarter of the eighteenth century.

The extensive research of collector Jan Gadd has established that a relatively small coterie of London pewterers in the second half of the seventeenth century, often related by training, made and exported a considerable number of pewter candlesticks to Norway, Sweden, and the American colonies.[1] Principal among these were Benjamin Cooper, Francis Lea, Hugh Quick, and Richard Withebed.

This pair of candlesticks, according to Gadd, is from a relatively small group that are characterized by pillar stems, either plain or clustered, punctuated by midbands with pronounced central fillets, or bandings, over circular drip trays above broad circular bases with a trumpet-shaped section over an outward-flaring rim. The edges of the drip trays, the shoulders of the bases, and the edges of the bases are usually trimmed with the same type of rope border.[2]

Other known English examples of this type include a pair marked by Lea that were inscribed in 1668 for a wedding that took place two years earlier at the Church of Saint Nicholas in Stockholm, Sweden.[3] That pair, now in the Gadd Collection, purports to be the earliest dated English pewter candlesticks in the baroque style. They feature clustered columnar stems. That their drip trays and bases are of identical size and design to those of the CWF pair prompted Gadd to suggest that they were also the work of Lea.[4] The fragmentary presence of another pewterer's touchmark contradicts this possibility. Unfortunately, when these candlesticks were marked, the maker stamped his touch on one of the pair at the very end of its stem. When he flared out the edge of the stem for strength and to support the removable nozzle, he obliterated most of the touchmark. At the rim of the other candlestick of the pair, a short section, approximately half the stem's circumference, has been replaced, perhaps removing the touchmark from this candlestick.

The closest parallels to the CWF candlesticks are a pair that Gadd discovered in the Nordic Museum in Stockholm, Sweden, in 1998.[5] Although unmarked, they are of identical design and detailing, but they measure an inch and a half taller.

Two related pairs of candlesticks at York Minster Cathedral in England have the same combination of clustered columnar stems and circular drip trays and bases with rope edges that the Lea

1.1 Unimpaled arms of the Glanville family

Lighting Devices 13

1.2 Threaded female fittings

1.3 Original removable nozzles

candlesticks of 1668 have. Both pairs are marked, and they are believed possibly to be the work of Francis Lucas I and Richard Booth, both of York.[6]

The CWF candlesticks are engraved with the arms of the Glanville family, and they descended in the Glanville and Edgcumbe families until they were sold at auction in 1956. The arms are displayed within a lozenge, or diamond, which is the customary shape of reserve for the arms of an unmarried lady. The fact that they are unimpaled, that is, not marshaled with those of a husband, is usually indicative of maidenhood. Writers have speculated about the identity of the unmarried lady. There has been the stubborn belief that the arms are those of Mary Glanville, second daughter of Sir John Glanville of Broad Hinton, Wiltshire, and that the candlesticks would accordingly have to antedate her marriage in 1636 to Piers Edgcumbe.[7] It seems clear from evidence that these candlesticks date from the third quarter of the century and that a subsequent lady in the Glanville family owned them.

Pillar and columnar candlesticks are often constructed so that they are open through their bases and stems to the bottoms of their sockets. Larger examples, such as these, sometimes have threaded female fittings on the undersides of their sockets to enable the maker to secure the assembled candlestick firmly to the lathe for final finishing.

1. Jan Gadd, "Famous Old Candlesticks," *Journal of the Pewter Society*, XI (spring 1998), pp. 9–24; Jan Gadd, "English Pewter Candlesticks of the Baroque Period," *Journal of the Pewter Society*, XIV (autumn 2000), pp. 17–41.
2. Gadd, "Candlesticks of the Baroque Period," pp. 19–21.
3. *Ibid.*, pp. 20–21, figs. 9a and b.
4. *Ibid.*, p. 20.
5. *Ibid.*, pp. 19–20, fig. 5.
6. Gadd, "Famous Old Candlesticks," pp. 9–11, figs. 1–2.
7. This notion was first advocated in Ronald F. Michaelis, "Early Stuart Pewter from Cotehele, Co. Cornwall," *Antique Collector*, XXX (February 1959), pp. 31–34. It was largely accepted until Gadd questioned it within a broader context in "Famous Old Candlesticks," pp. 14–15.

2 PAIR OF CANDLESTICKS

Hugh Quick
London, 1674–1685

MARKS: Touchmark of a cross formée with fleurs-de-lis at the ends of the vertical arms and with *H* to the left, *Q* to the right, *16* above, and *74* below within a beaded circle on underside of each base (London Touch Plate I, 231; Cotterell, *Old Pewter*, 3806; Peal, *More Pewter Marks*, 3806)

INSCRIPTIONS: None

DIMENSIONS: OH. 9 1/2", OW. (bases) 7 7/8"

PROVENANCE: John M. Graham II, Williamsburg, Va., and Mentone, Ala. (purchased from A. H. Isher & Son, Cheltenham, Eng.); purchased from Graham by CWF with funds provided by Mr. and Mrs. William H. Murdoch, Jr., Brielle, N. J.; G1974-670, 1–2

PUBLISHED: Sutherland-Graeme, "British Pewter in American

2

Collections," p. 3, figs. 1–2; *Art Treasures Exhibition,* no. 233, ill.; Michaelis, *Old Domestic Base-Metal Candlesticks,* pp. 91–94, fig. 135; Hornsby, *Pewter of the Western World,* p. 315, fig. 1068; Gadd, "Famous Old Candlesticks," pp. 18–20, fig. 11; Gadd, "Candlesticks of the Baroque Period," pp. 27, 39, fig. 23b

EXHIBITED: Art Treasures Exhibition, Parke Bernet Galleries, New York, N. Y., 1967; Recent Accessions to the Colonial Williamsburg Collection, Allen-Byrd House, Williamsburg, Va., 1974

These magnificent candlesticks of imposing size and scale relate directly to a small group of London silver candlesticks from the 1670s. The silver ones are, in large part, the work of the German émigré silversmith Jacob Bodendick. The CWF pair are particularly close to Bodendick's splendid parcel-gilt pair of 1675/6 from Harthill Church in Yorkshire, Eng.[1] They share the same deep sockets of clustered columnar type, bound top and bottom by conforming moldings. The central sections of the stems of both are of inverted baluster form with octagonally paneled sides. The octagonal theme is further extended by the broad vestigial drip trays and bases of octagonal plan that they have in common.

Until 1998, the CWF pair were thought to be the only surviving examples of such candlesticks in English pewter. In that year, Gadd discovered an identical pair by Quick in the Museum of Applied Art in Oslo, Norway.[2] Those are engraved on the exterior of their bases with a wedding inscription of 1678, which not only documents Quick's production of such complex candlesticks just four years after he received his freedom and entered his touchmark at Pewterers' Hall in London, but also aids in the dating of this pair.

Gadd relates how candlesticks such as the CWF pair and related examples were introduced to replace those with more fragile bases, such as no. 1. Featured is a more complex assembly of elements for strength and a closer emulation of stylish prototypes. Instead of the soldered assembly of a few large cast elements such as stems, drip trays, and bases, this new approach involved the vastly more complex soldering together of many smaller parts, both cast and cut from sheet. Sturdier construction not only made larger candlesticks more durable, but also permitted more intricate detail and greater variety.[3]

A single candlestick of clustered columnar form with a stem, drip tray, and base of square plan, also marked by Quick, has a Connecticut history and is in the collections of the Wadsworth Atheneum in Hartford, Conn. It is believed to be "A Pewter Candlestick" valued at seven shillings in the inventory of the estate of Phineas Wilson, a Hartford merchant, taken in 1692.[4]

1. Charles Oman, *English Church Plate, 597–1830* (London, 1957), p. 242, pl. 142; Ronald F. Michaelis, *Old Domestic Base-Metal Candlesticks from the 13th to the 19th Century* (Woodbridge, Eng., 1978), p. 93, fig. 136.
2. Gadd, "Candlesticks of the Baroque Period," p. 27, figs. 23 a and c.
3. *Ibid.,* pp. 21–30.
4. Gerald W. R. Ward and William N. Hosley, Jr., eds., *The Great River: Art & Society of the Connecticut Valley, 1635–1820* (Hartford, Conn., 1985), pp. 306–308, ill.; Gadd, "Candlesticks of the Baroque Period," p. 16, no. 19, ill.

3 CANDLESTICK

Unmarked
England, 1675–1690

MARKS: None

INSCRIPTIONS: Indistinct probable owner's initials stamped on underside of base at edge

DIMENSIONS: OH. 8 13/16", OW. (base) 7 5/16"

PROVENANCE: Purchased from A. H. Isher & Son, Cheltenham, Eng. (said by vendor to have come from Durham Co.); 1958-563

PUBLISHED: Michaelis, *Old Domestic Base-Metal Candlesticks,* p. 90, fig. 134

This candlestick and nos. 4–5 are of the most common baroque type in English pewter. They represent a simplified and consequently less expensive alternative to complex candlesticks, such as no. 2 by Hugh Quick. They all feature a base of polygonal plan with a molded edge and short, concave sides rising to a flat, circular plateau with a trumpet-shaped transition to a drip tray. Stems are either composed of a large central knop below a

3.1 Relief-cast decoration on shoulder of base

3

4

generous socket, as in this example, or of variously detailed pillar forms, as in the succeeding examples.[1]

Some candlesticks of this type, including this one, have narrow relief-cast borders of naturalistic ornament at the angled shoulder of their bases. Such decoration usually appears on candlesticks with knopped stems.[2] One infrequently finds a candlestick with a pillar stem and a band of this decoration on its base.[3]

The same casting was sometimes used in different forms. Such decorative bands also appear in rare instances on the bases of large polygonal salts or on the trumpet-shaped bases of some early salvers, or footed plates.[4]

1. A very similar candlestick, formerly in the Cooper and Bradshaw Collections, is presently in the Little Collection. *Journal of the Pewter Society,* IV (autumn 1983), front cover ill.; Peter R. G. Hornsby, *Pewter of the Western World, 1600–1850* (Exton, Pa., 1983), p. 316, fig. 1070. Hornsby also illustrates a similarly decorated candlestick with a knopped stem and an unusually large ball knop replacing the customary drip tray. *Ibid.,* fig. 1069.
2. The Pewterers' Company owns a pillar candlestick of this type. *The Worshipful Company of Pewterers of London: Supplementary Catalogue of Pewterware, 1979* (London, 1978), p. 74, no. S6/603, p. 78, ill. A similar pillar example by the same maker, formerly in the Cooper Collection, is illustrated in A. V. Sutherland-Graeme, "Seventeenth Century Pewter Candlesticks," *Connoisseur,* CXXXVII (May 1956), p. 183, fig. 6.
3. Peter R. G. Hornsby, Rosemary Weinstein, and Ronald F. Homer, *Pewter: A celebration of the craft, 1200–1700* (London, 1989), p. 74, no. 65, ill.
4. *Ibid.,* p. 98, no. 122, ill.

4 PAIR OF CANDLESTICKS

William Allen
London, 1674–1695

MARKS: Touchmark of an acorn under a crown with *W* to the left and *A* to the right within a beaded octagon on face of each stem below rim (London Touch Plate I, 240; Cotterell, *Old Pewter,* 61)

INSCRIPTIONS: None

DIMENSIONS: OH. 9 3/16", OW. (base) 6 9/16"

PROVENANCE: Purchased from Charles Casimir, The Old Pewter Shop, London; 1954-765, 1–2

PUBLISHED: Sale ad, The Old Pewter Shop, *Connoisseur,* CXXXI (June 1953), p. xivi, ill.; sales cat., Grosvenor House, June 10–25, 1953, p. 68, ill.; Michaelis, *Old Domestic Base-Metal Candlesticks,* pp. 88–89, fig. 128; Hornsby, *Pewter of the Western World,* p. 314, fig. 1067; Gadd, "Candlesticks of the Baroque Period," p. 33, fig. 39

A candlestick of this same pattern, also by Allen, descended in the Buell family of Connecticut. Katharine Prentis Murphy acquired it in the last century from Dr. Charles Turkington of Litchfield, Conn., who, in turn, had purchased it from the Buell family. It is in the Bayou Bend Collection, Houston, Tex.[1]

Gadd illustrates a similar pair marked by Hugh Quick that were apparently exported to Norway in the last decades of the seventeenth century. They have a history of church use and are currently in the custody of the Norwegian Museum of Cultural History in Oslo, Norway.[2]

1. Joseph T. Butler, *Candleholders in America, 1650–1900* (New York, 1967), p. 19, fig. 6.
2. Gadd, "Candlesticks of the Baroque Period," p. 32, figs. 37–38.

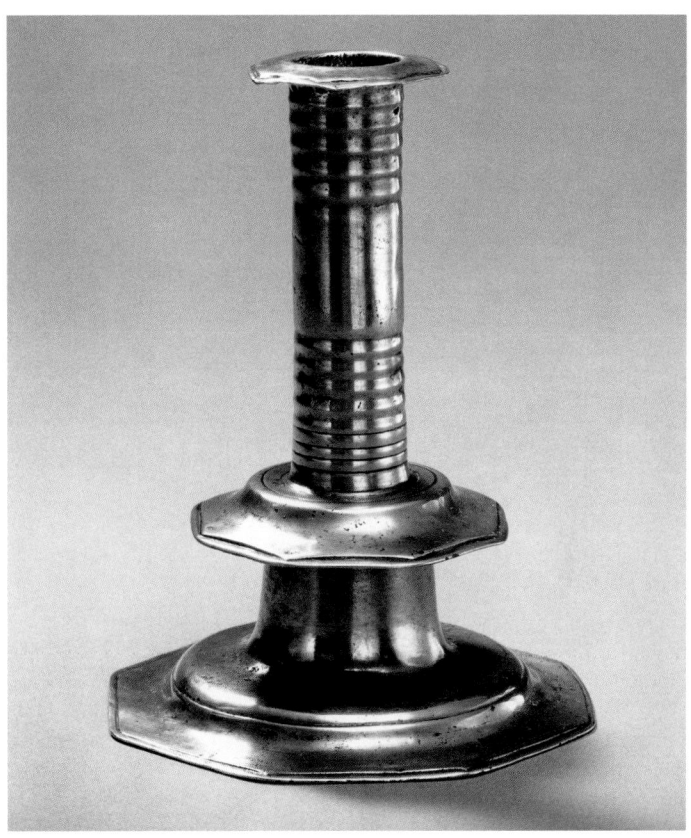

5

5 CANDLESTICK

Unmarked
England, 1675–1690

MARKS: None

INSCRIPTIONS: Indistinct probable owners' initials *F, M,* and *E* within separate shields stamped on underside of base at edge

at consecutive corners

DIMENSIONS: OH. 6 9/16", OW. (base) 5"

PROVENANCE: Purchased from A. V. Sutherland-Graeme, London; 1954-81

Pillar candlesticks of this type and size form the largest group of surviving pewter candlesticks from the seventeenth century. A similar example with a long New England history is in the Pilgrim Hall Museum in Plymouth, Mass.[1]

1. Butler, *Candleholders in America*, p. 18, fig. 5; Jonathan L. Fairbanks and Robert F. Trent, eds., *New England Begins: The Seventeenth Century,* II (Boston, Mass., 1982), p. 252, no. 238, ill.

6 PAIR OF CANDLESTICKS

Unmarked
England, 1685–1710

MARKS: None

6

INSCRIPTIONS: None

DIMENSIONS: OH. 7 1/2", OW. (bases) 4 1/2"

PROVENANCE: Purchased from Carl and Celia Jacobs, Southwick, Mass.; 1961-215, 1–2

PUBLISHED: Michaelis, *Old Domestic Base-Metal Candlesticks*, p. 83, fig. 119; Gordon, *Candlestick Maker's Bawle,* p. 56, no. 28, ill.

This pair of candlesticks and nos. 7–10 are usually referred to as ball-knopped candlesticks. Of modest size and simple construction, these candlesticks are characterized by a pillar stem of simple tubular design above a prominent knop of compressed spherical form supported on a round or polygonal base. Collector Kenneth Gordon, in his monograph on candlesticks of this type, discusses forty-one examples. Since silver prototypes do not exist and most pewter ones are unmarked, it is difficult to date this group precisely. Most examples, like those in the CWF Collection, appear to date between 1685 and 1710, although records of the Pewterers' Company refer to "Candlesticks with bawles" as early as 1612/3.[1] The gadrooning of this pair's knops and bases also suggests this period when gadrooning appeared on a variety of forms.

1. Kenneth G. Gordon, *Pewter: The Candlestick Maker's Bawle 'A Family Portrait'* (Congleton, Eng., 1994), p. 18.

7 CANDLESTICK

Unmarked
England, 1685–1705

MARKS: None

INSCRIPTIONS: None

DIMENSIONS: OH. 6 3/8", OW. (base) 3 7/8"

PROVENANCE: Purchased from A. H. Isher & Son, Cheltenham, Eng.; 1958-597

PUBLISHED: Gordon, *Candlestick Maker's Bawle,* p. 46, no. 18, ill.

This modest ball-knopped candlestick has no silver prototype. Other copper alloy examples are even less common than those in pewter. The diminutive brass example (fig. 7.1) appears to date from the late seventeenth century. It is crudely and heavily cast with vertical seams on opposite sides of the knop clearly visible.

20   PEWTER AT COLONIAL WILLIAMSBURG

7.1 Brass candlestick, England, 1685–1705, OH. 4 3/4", OW. (base) 2 3/4", formerly in the Lear Collection; 1999-6

LIGHTING DEVICES 21

8

8 CANDLESTICK

Unmarked
England, 1685–1705

MARKS: None

INSCRIPTIONS: None

DIMENSIONS: OH. 6 3/8", Diam. (base) 3 7/8"

PROVENANCE: Purchased from A. H. Isher & Son, Cheltenham, Eng.; 1966-297

PUBLISHED: Michaelis, *Old Domestic Base-Metal Candlesticks*, p. 90, fig. 132; Gordon, *Candlestick Maker's Bawle*, p. 52, no. 25, ill.

Some three hundred candlesticks of eight different patterns are listed in a 1716 inventory of the stock of John Shorey I of London. These include "26 pairs large knurled/ 12 pairs mid ditto/ 12 pairs small ditto/ 14 pairs large diamond/ 29 pairs small ditto/ 12 pairs mid HB [possibly high bell] candlesticks weight 18 lbs/ 20 pairs small ditto/ 5 water candlesticks."[1] Since knurled usually indicates having a gadrooned or similar edging or banding, Gordon questioned whether the inventory refers to ball-knopped candlesticks with gadrooning, such as this example, although such candlesticks are thought out of fashion by this date. Ball-knopped candlesticks with gadrooned, or repeated rib, decoration certainly survive in greater numbers than gadrooned candlesticks with inverted baluster stems.[2]

1. Ronald F. Homer to Gordon, in Gordon, *Candlestick Maker's Bawle,* pp. 54–55. Records indicate that Shorey and his son had a large and successful business. From the listing of molds in the 1716 inventory, they appear to have specialized in the production of flatwares. It enumerates 30 molds for dishes up to 24 inches in diameter as well as for various plates and saucers. The molds in 1716 weighed just over a ton and the aggregate weighed 3,200 pounds in 1719. See Ronald F. Homer, "John Shorey senior and junior," *Journal of the Pewter Society,* VIII (autumn 1991), p. 54.
2. Gordon, *Candlestick Maker's Bawle,* pp. 54–55.

9

10

9 CANDLESTICK

Unmarked
England, 1685–1705

MARKS: None

INSCRIPTIONS: None

DIMENSIONS: OH. 7 1/8", Diam. (base) 4 3/16"

PROVENANCE: Purchased from A. V. Sutherland-Graeme, London; 1960-316

PUBLISHED: Sutherland-Graeme, "Some British Pewter," p. 365, fig. 5; Michaelis, *Old Domestic Base-Metal Candlesticks*, p. 83, fig. 118; Gordon, *Candlestick Maker's Bawle*, p. 40, no. 12, ill.

10 PAIR OF CANDLESTICKS

Unmarked
England, 1685–1705

MARKS: None

INSCRIPTIONS: None

DIMENSIONS: OH. 7", Diam. (base) 4 5/8"

PROVENANCE: Purchased from A. H. Isher & Son, Cheltenham, Eng. (vendor noted that the candlesticks came from Wales); 1960-794, 1–2

PUBLISHED: Michaelis, *Old Domestic Base-Metal Candlesticks*, p. 83, fig. 117; Hornsby, *Pewter of the Western World*, p. 317, fig. 1072; Gordon, *Candlestick Maker's Bawle*, pp. 61–62, nos. 35–36, ill.

The knops of the stems of hemispherical shape are an unusual feature.

LIGHTING DEVICES 23

II

11 CANDLESTICK

Maker unidentified
London, 1690–1710

MARKS: Touchmark *AR* within a rectangle on underside of base

INSCRIPTIONS: Owners' initials *E/D•B* engraved on upper face of base

DIMENSIONS: OH. 8 5/16", OW. (base) 5 7/8"

PROVENANCE: Gilbert L. D. Hole, Edinburgh, Scot.; acquired from Hole by Cyril C. Minchin, Bucklebury, Eng.; purchased from Minchin by CWF; 1981-179

PUBLISHED: Cotterell, *Old Pewter,* p. 93, pl. XXVC; Cotterell, *Pewter down the Ages,* pp. 138–139, fig. 95; Michaelis, *Antique Pewter of British Isles,* pl. XVI, fig. 48; Ullyett, *Guide for Collectors,* color ill. opp. p. 80; Gadd, "Candlesticks of the Baroque Period," p. 30, fig. 32c

Candlesticks, such as this large one of bold design with an inverted baluster as the principal element of the stem, were first introduced by Huguenot silversmiths into London in the mid-1680s. By the early years of the eighteenth century, examples in silver and brass had, in large part, replaced those with pillar stems. Brass candlesticks, in turn, had virtually supplanted those of pewter at this time. Consequently, many more candlesticks survive from the second half of the seventeenth century than from the first half of the eighteenth century.

Pewter candlesticks with baluster stems are rare. A less robust example was formerly in the Cooper Collection.[1] Two matching bases by Benjamin Cooper of London, similar in size and design to the base of the CWF candlestick, were excavated at Port Royal in Jamaica. These date from 1692 or earlier.[2] Gadd illustrates two candlesticks of more modest size, both with gadrooned bases. One with a square base with clipped corners was marked by Hugh Quick of London and was formerly in the Gordon Collection and now in the Neish Collection.[3] The other with a circular base was also marked by Quick and is in the Neish Collection at the Museum of British Pewter, Harvard House, in Stratford-upon-Avon, Eng.[4]

1. H. J. L. J. Massé, *The Pewter Collector: A guide to British Pewter, with some references to foreign work,* rev. ed. with additions by Ronald F. Michaelis (London, 1971), pls. 15, 16a.
2. Robert F. Marx, *Silver and Pewter Recovered from the Sunken City of Port Royal, Jamaica, May 1, 1966–March 31, 1968* (Kingston, Jamaica, 1971), figs. 68–69. A stem that is similar to the stem on the CWF example was also found at Port Royal, yet Marx claims that it does not fit either of the bases. The bases are also illustrated in Gadd, "Candlesticks of the Baroque Period," p. 30, figs. 32a and b.
3. Hornsby, *Pewter of the Western World,* p. 317, fig. 1074; Gadd, "Candlesticks of the Baroque Period," p. 34, fig. 41.
4. Gadd, "Candlesticks of the Baroque Period," p. 34, fig. 40.

11.1 Owners' initials engraved on upper face of base

12 CANDLESTICK

Probably John Trapp
London, 1715–1725

MARKS: Maker's touch *JT* within a rectangle on exterior of socket

INSCRIPTIONS: None

DIMENSIONS: OH. 7 1/4", OW. (base) 4 3/4"

PROVENANCE: Purchased from Cyril C. Minchin, Bucklebury, Eng.; 1983-203

PUBLISHED: Minchin, "Some Uncommon Examples," pp. 23–24, fig. 9; Hornsby, *Pewter of the Western World,* p. 323, fig. 1090; Gadd, "Candlesticks of the Baroque Period," p. 34, fig. 42

This pattern of polygonal candlestick with a domed base with a flanged edge is more commonly found in silver and brass than in pewter. Only one other pewter example is recorded, a virtually identical candlestick in the Maihaugen Open Air Museum in Lillehammer, Norway.[1]

The unrecorded mark on the CWF candlestick is thought to be an early mark of Trapp. Trapp, a native of Stratford-upon-Avon, commenced his apprenticeship in 1688 under Benjamin Cooper of London, a principal maker and exporter of candlesticks. It would appear that Trapp probably served as a journeyman in Cooper's shop after completing his apprenticeship in 1695, for he did not enter his own touchmark until 1720. The fact that the candlestick in the Maihaugen is thought to have a long history in Norway is a further tie with the earlier generation of London makers and exporters of candlesticks.[2]

1. Gadd, "Candlesticks of the Baroque Period," p. 34, fig. 43.
2. *Ibid.*

13 TWO CANDLESTICKS

George Lowes
Newcastle, Eng., 1720–1750

MARKS: Touchmark incorporating a bird on face of each base (indistinct on one and virtually obliterated on the other); secondary mark of an *X* on face of each base

INSCRIPTIONS: Owners' initials *ET* stamped on underside of one base and *P/IM* on underside of other base; these different initials indicate that these candlesticks, although of the same pattern and by the same maker, did not begin as a pair

DIMENSIONS: OH. 6 1/2", Diam. (base) 4 1/8"

PROVENANCE: John L. Grant, East Preston, Eng. (sold after his death by Sotheby's, July 17, 1975); collection numbers *G 36* and *G 37* in white ink on undersides of bases; 1975-158, 1–2

PUBLISHED: Sales cat., Sotheby's, July 17, 1975, lot 173, ill.

The production of this distinctive and uncommon type of candlestick with an inverted baluster stem was based in Newcastle and not in London. The complete circularity of all elements greatly simplified the making of patterns and the finishing of candlesticks. These functions could be accomplished with ease on a lathe.

Lowes was the principal maker associated with this type. Aside from these examples, three others by Lowes were part of the Peal Collection. An additional example of this type marked *RS,* possibly for Robert Sadler of Newcastle, was also in the Peal Collection.[1]

Lowes became a member of the Company of Plumbers, Pewterers, Glaziers, and Painters of Newcastle in 1725, after having served his apprenticeship under the local pewterer, Jacob Watson. When he died at age 70 in 1774, the *Newcastle Courant* noted that Lowes had been for "many years an eminent pewterer on The Side who had acquired a handsome fortune and who had been retired these many years."[2]

1. These four candlesticks are illustrated in Ronald F. Michaelis, *British Pewter* (London, 1969), p. 75. One of the Lowes examples and the one marked *RS* are illustrated in *Exhibition of British Pewterware through the Ages from Romano-British Times to the Present Day* (Reading, Eng., 1969), nos. 162–63; sales cat., Sotheby's, Oct. 6, 1981, p. 13, lot 39; and Hornsby, *Pewter of the Western World,* p. 324, fig. 1095.
2. David Lamb, "Newcastle pewter and pewterers, Part 1 Pewterers—Lowes, Saddler and Hogg," *Journal of the Pewter Society,* VIII (autumn 1992), p. 129.

12

13

14 PAIR OF CANDLESTICKS

James Weekes
New York, N. Y., or Poughkeepsie, N. Y., 1830–1845

MARKS: Maker's touch *J. WEEKES* in incuse letters on underside of one base (Laughlin, *Pewter in America,* II, p. 115)

INSCRIPTIONS: None

DIMENSIONS: OH. 7 3/4", Diam. (base) 4 1/4"

PROVENANCE: Purchased from Louis G. Myers, New York, N. Y.; 1930-582, 1–2

PUBLISHED: Butler, *Candleholders in America,* p. 100, fig. 72

Surviving American pewter candlesticks from the eighteenth century are scarce.[1] They did not become relatively common until after 1830, paralleling the popularity of oil lamps. This pair are representative of their date with their stems being dense stacks of stocky elements supported on domed circular bases. The main sections of their stems derive from the traditional inverted baluster form, but their capping and breadth give them a distinct acorn appearance, as this element is usually described by collectors today.

Weekes was listed in New York City trade directories from 1822 to 1833. He then set up business in Poughkeepsie in the latter year, and his firm of James Weekes & Co. was still listed there as "Britannia Ware Manufacturers" in the *Western Business Directory* for 1842–43. In the mid-1830s, a young Rufus Dunham worked as a journeyman in Weekes's shop before returning to Westbrook, Maine, in 1837.[2] Dunham cast a shorter version of the CWF candlesticks. They are so close in detail and nuance that Dunham may have secured the mold from Weekes by purchase or exchange.[3]

1. These include a set of four monumental church candlesticks in the baroque style by Johann Christoph Heyne of Lancaster, Pa. Two are in the Winterthur Museum, Winterthur, Del. Montgomery, *History of American Pewter,* pp. 90–92, fig. 5-3. Montgomery also illustrates a pair of short pillar candlesticks with bands of reeding that he attributes to Philadelphia, Pa., and dates in the 1790s, fig. 5-4.
2. Ledlie Irwin Laughlin, *Pewter in America, Its Makers and Their Marks,* II, reprint (Barre, Mass., 1969), pp. 115–116; Ledlie Irwin Laughlin, *Pewter in America, Its Makers and Their Marks,* III (Barre, Mass., 1971), p. 193. Edwin A. Churchill, *Hail Britannia, Maine pewter and silverplate: An exhibition of Maine Britannia ware and silverplate, 1829–1941* (Augusta, Maine, 1992), p. 13.
3. A Weekes candlestick of this pattern and the Dunham example, both from the Swain Collection, are illustrated in Hornsby, *Pewter of the Western World,* p. 330, fig. 1123.

14

15 LAMP

Probably Ephraim Capen
West Roxbury, Mass., 1844–1847

MARKS: Touchmark *BROOK FARM* within a curved rectangle on underside of base (Laughlin, *Pewter in America,* II, p. 98)

INSCRIPTIONS: None

DIMENSIONS: OH. 5 3/4", Diam. (base) 5"

PROVENANCE: Purchased from John Carl Thomas, Hanover, Conn., with funds donated by The Antique Collectors' Guild, Richmond, Va., in memory of William Kayhoe, also of Richmond and past president of The Pewter Collectors Club of America; G1987-25

Brook Farm was the site of a short-lived cooperative community of transcendentalists. Situated in West Roxbury, Mass., the community was active from 1841 to 1847. It included, among others, George W. Curtis, Charles A. Dana, Margaret Fuller, and Nathaniel Hawthorne. Aside from agricultural activities, a number of trades were practiced, including the making of pewter

28 PEWTER AT COLONIAL WILLIAMSBURG

15

lamps and teapots. Capen became a member of the community on May 12, 1844. He was the only member to register his livelihood as a pewterer, and he is considered responsible for the manufacture of pewter marked *BROOK FARM*. He left the community in 1847, and between 1848 and 1854 he was in partnership with George Molineux at 132 William St. in New York, N. Y. This partnership specialized in lamps, and it was one of the leading firms in the production of this iconic pewter form of the middle decades of the nineteenth century.[1]

1. Laughlin, *Pewter in America,* II, pp. 98–99; *Ibid.,* III, pp. 178–179. An overview of American pewter lamps is provided in Melvin D. Wolf, "Marked Nineteenth Century American Pewter Fluid Lamps," *Pewter Collectors Club of America Bulletin,* VIII (March 1984), pp. 303–363.

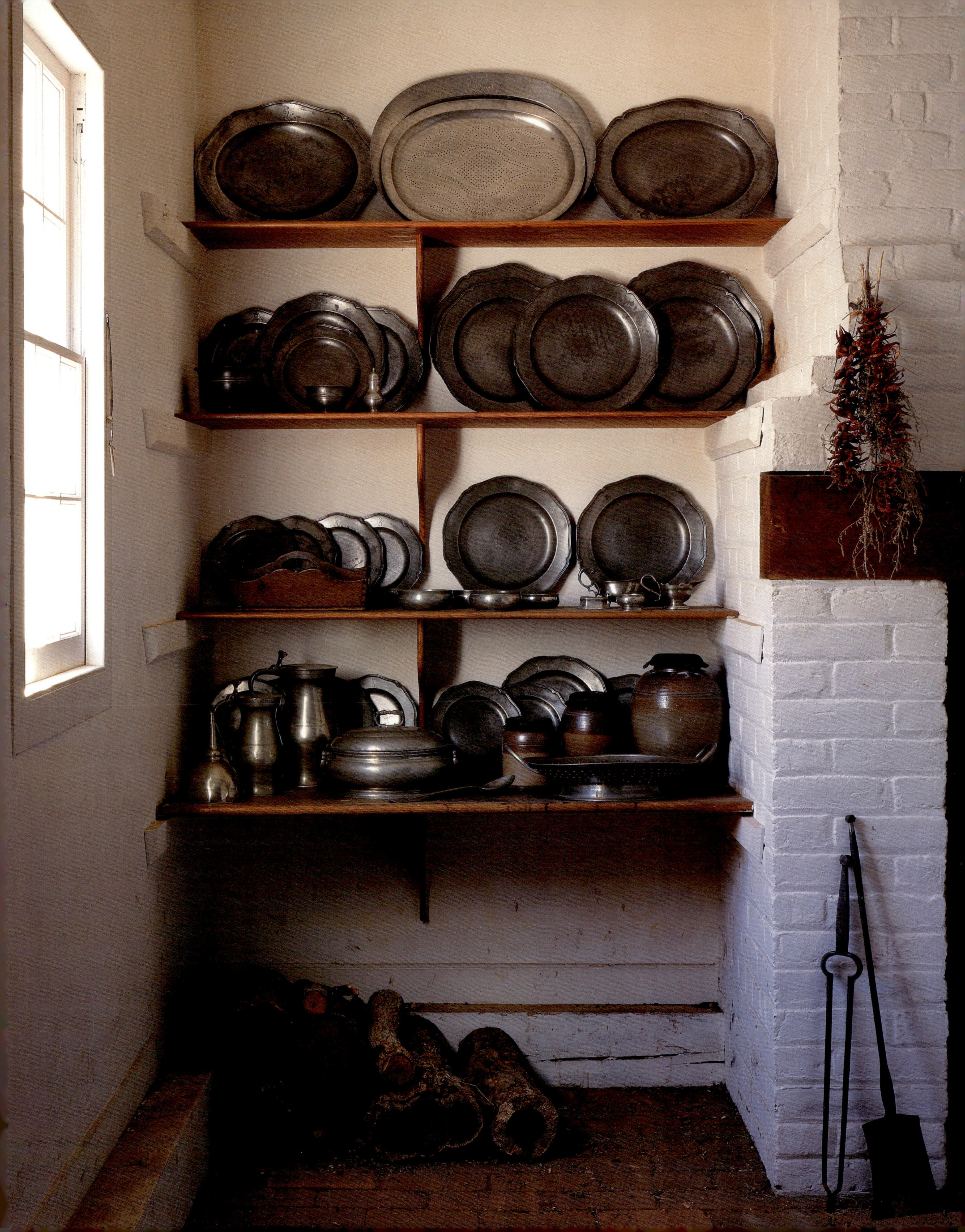

DINING WARES

Polite dining became a highly organized social ritual during the first half of the eighteenth century. The English adopted the French dinner service with its coordinated plates and dishes in graduated sizes and a host of specialized objects. Matched services in pewter are first evident in affluent households of the second quarter of the eighteenth century, yet pewterers found it progressively more difficult to compete with the ready availability of relatively inexpensive and fashionable ceramics and glassware. The Colonial Williamsburg Collection richly represents the range and quality of these pewter dining wares.

DISHES AND PLATES/CENTRAL BOSSES

This category consists mainly of dishes that predate 1700. They are relatively deep and of intermediate size for general usefulness. Coordinated dinner services in the modern sense with matching plates and dishes in graduated sizes did not occur until the first half of the eighteenth century. Some of these earlier dishes, like their more costly counterparts in precious metal, were also used for the washing of hands. The undulation of the well adds to their rigidity and strength.

16 DISH OR BASIN

Possibly John Rebate
Edinburgh, Scot., 1603–1625

MARKS: Touchmark *X* with horizontal bar through center with *I* to the left, *R* to the right below, and *1600* above within a shaped shield on underside of rim (Edinburgh Touch Plate I, 11)

INSCRIPTIONS: Inset brass boss in center with English royal arms, enhanced with colored enamels, with *I* and *R* flanking crest at top for James VI of Scotland and James I of England

DIMENSIONS: OH. (rim) 2 5/8", OW. (rim) 15/16", Diam. 17 3/4"

PROVENANCE: One of a pair owned in 1935 by Prof. D. Dougal, Manchester, Eng.; purchased from Christopher Bangs, London, who had acquired it in the Netherlands; 1996-121

PUBLISHED: Sutherland-Graeme, "Pewter Rose-water Dishes," pp. 329–331, figs. I, IV–V; Shemmell, "Dishes with Enamelled Bosses," pp. 106–107

This example is one of about twenty dishes that are fitted with a central brass boss enameled in polychrome with the English royal arms and the initials of either James VI of Scotland and James I of England or of Charles I of England. The dishes were probably royal gifts and not objects of royal ownership. Rather than having an association with the service of food, larger examples, such as no. 16, were probably intended for display or as a rosewater dish for washing hands during and after meals. Those with long histories of church ownership may have served the clergy in baptism, in cleansing hands before administering the sacrament, or in other clerical functions.[1] In this later circumstance, an accompanying ewer could have provided a convenient source of water.[2]

This dish is certainly among the earliest datable pieces of Scottish pewter. It is rivaled by a pair of dishes fritted with *IR* enameled medallions and marked by Richard Weir of Edinburgh, Scot. One is in the collection of the Museum of Scotland in Edinburgh, and the other is in the Neish Collection at the Museum of British Pewter.[3]

16.1 Inset boss with enamels

1. Stanley Shemmell, "Dishes with Enamelled Bosses of the Royal Arms," *Journal of the Pewter Society,* III (autumn 1982), p. 114.
2. *Ibid.* Shemmell cites three ewers of early seventeenth-century date that may have originally accompanied dishes or basins of this sort. One at Ludlow Castle bears on its handle an enameled medallion with the royal arms. Another with its enameled medallion applied to its body is at the Decorative Arts & History Museum of the National Museum of Ireland in Dublin. The third is owned by the church in Biggar, Scot. Shemmell took his information from A. V. Sutherland-Graeme, "Pewter Rose-water Dishes," *Connoisseur,* VC (June 1935), p. 329. The Ludlow Castle example is clearly illustrated in Hornsby, *Pewter of the Western World,* p. 78, fig. 133.
3. George Dalgleish, "Royal Rosewater Dish Returns to Scotland," *Pewter Collectors Club of America Bulletin,* VIII (September 1981), pp. 139–140, ill.

17–21

17 DISH

Maker unidentified
England, 1610–1640

MARKS: Maker's touch of a bell with *C* to the left and *A* to the right within an outlined and beaded circle on underside of rim

INSCRIPTIONS: Owner's initials *AR* stamped on face of rim

DIMENSIONS: OH. (rim) 1 5/8", OW. (rim) 1", Diam. 10 7/8"

PROVENANCE: Purchased from A. H. Isher & Son, Cheltenham, Eng.; 1963-450

18 DISH

Maker unidentified
England, 1620–1650

MARKS: Indistinct touchmark possibly incorporating a hammer with a plumb bob below left end of head on underside of rim

INSCRIPTIONS: Owner's initial *T* crudely wriggle engraved on underside of well in center and possibly on underside of rim

DIMENSIONS: OH. (rim) 1 7/8", OW. (rim) 1 3/16", Diam. 14"

PROVENANCE: Purchased from A. H. Isher & Son, Cheltenham, Eng.; 1960-458

19 DISH

Probably Ralph Marsh
London, 1630–1660

MARKS: Touchmark of a sheaf of wheat with *R* to the left and *M* to the right within an outlined circle on underside of rim (related to London Touch Plate I, 37; Cotterell, *Old Pewter,* 5791; Peal, *More Pewter Marks,* 3079)

INSCRIPTIONS: Owner's initials *MP* stamped on face of rim

DIMENSIONS: OH. 1 7/8", OW. (rim) 1 1/4", Diam. 13 7/8"

PROVENANCE: Purchased from A. H. Isher & Son, Cheltenham, Eng.; 1958-595

Ralph Marsh died of the plague the day after his election as master in 1665.[1]

1. Howard Herschell Cotterell, *Old Pewter, Its Makers and Marks in England, Scotland, and Ireland; An Account of the Old Pewterer & His Craft,* reprint (Rutland, Vt., 1963), p. 262, no. 3079.

20 DISH

Thomas Ford
Wigan, Eng., 1680–1700

MARKS: Indistinct touchmark incorporating, in part, a rose framed by crossed palm fronds within an outlined inner circle framed by *THOMAS•FORD* within a beaded outer circle on underside of rim (Peal, *More Pewter Marks,* 1721); indistinct pseudo hallmarks stamped on face of rim

INSCRIPTIONS: None

DIMENSIONS: OH. (rim) 2 1/8", OW. (rim) 1 13/16", Diam. 14 1/4"

PROVENANCE: A. V. Sutherland-Graeme, London; 1960-900

21 DISH

Possibly John Cave I
Banbury, Eng., 1650–1680

MARKS: Maker's touch of three lions passant within a beaded shield on underside of rim; pseudo hallmarks (1) leopard's head, (2) *I•C,* (3) lion passant, and (4) acorn and sprig, each within a serrated reserve on face of rim (Cotterell, *Old Pewter,* 857 with some variation)

INSCRIPTIONS: None

DIMENSIONS: OH. (rim) 1 3/4", OW. (rim) 1 13/16", Diam. 14 13/16"

PROVENANCE: Purchased from A. H. Isher & Son, Cheltenham, Eng.; 1960-457

The Pewterers' Company searched the shops in Banbury of John Cave I in 1674, 1676, and ca. 1690 and John Cave II in 1689 and ca. 1690.[1]

1. Ronald F. Homer, "A List of the Names and Locations of All Those Provincial Pewterers Whose Shops Were Searched by the Searchers of the Worshipful Company of Pewterers 1474–1723," *Journal of the Pewter Society,* XI, Additional Issue (summer 1998), p. 57.

22 SAUCER

Maker unidentified
England, 1600–1640

MARKS: Touchmark of an acorn with sprig of leaves below, mullet above, *S* to the left, and *R* to the right within an outlined circle on underside of well

INSCRIPTIONS: Owner's initials *H* and *W* stamped on opposite sides of rim on face

DIMENSIONS: OH. (rim) 1/2", OW. (rim) 9/16", Diam. 3 15/16"

PROVENANCE: Purchased from Robin Bellamy Antiques, Witney, Eng. (acquired by that firm at Sotheby's, 1984); 1984-140

PUBLISHED: Sales cat., Sotheby's, May 17, 1984, lot 14, ill.

Pewter saucers in the form of small plates or basins have survived in England from as early as the late thirteenth century.[1] This example, like others dating from the first half of the seventeenth century, measures approximately four inches in diameter and follows in design contemporary basins or dishes with plain rims and domed centers.

1. Anthony North and Andrew Spira, *Pewter at the Victoria and Albert Museum* (London, 1999), p. 38.

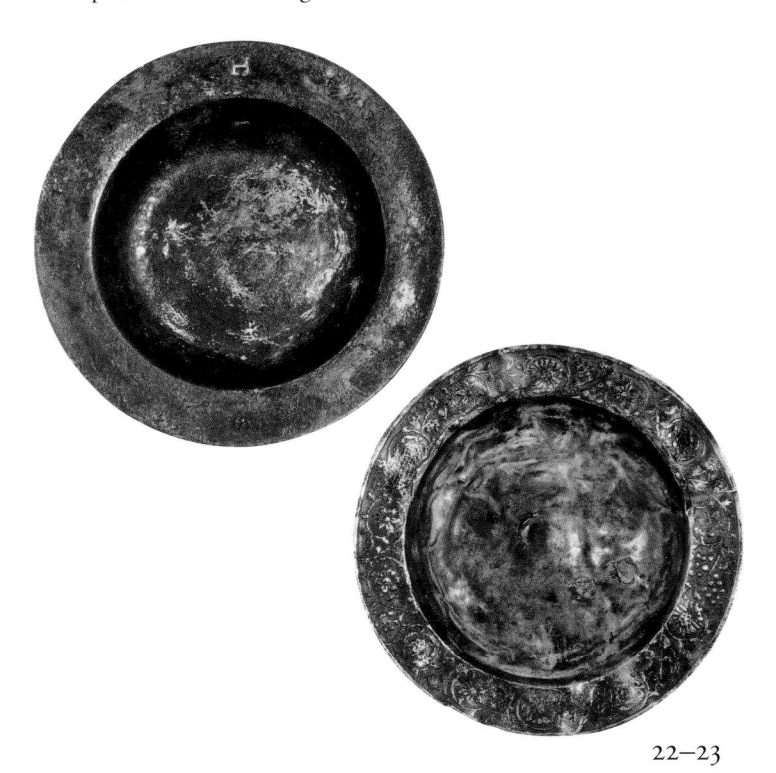

23 SAUCER

Maker unidentified
England, 1605–1625

MARKS: Touchmark incorporating, in part, [?]•*M* within a beaded circle on underside of well in center

INSCRIPTIONS: None

DIMENSIONS: OH. 7/16", OW. (rim) 1/2", Diam. 3 3/4"

PROVENANCE: Excavated near Hampton Court Palace; purchased from Richard Mundey, London; 1983-58

PUBLISHED: Hall, "Four saucers," p. 55

This saucer, found in crushed condition, has been drastically straightened. Originally, the well may have had a more domed appearance. It is from a small group of objects, principally drinking vessels and saucers, with relief decoration created by the maker's cutting these designs into the casting molds. These early examples, dating from the first quarter of the seventeenth century, usually feature borders of a naturalistic character. This decorative technique returned to favor toward the end of the century and into the early years of the eighteenth century.

Very few saucers of this approximate size and date with cast decoration on the faces of their rims survive. They include an example with two winged cherub heads, a crown, and a pierced heart, placed on a conventional running floral decoration, in the British Museum; one with running floral decoration on its rim that is marked by an unidentified maker with the initials *IC;* and another with running floral decoration in the Neish Collection at the Museum of British Pewter. An even more elaborate example with a similarly decorated rim but with a relief-cast central boss and intermediate wreathed border is in the Museum of London.[1]

1. Ronald F. Homer, "Pewter in the British Museum," *Journal of the Pewter Society,* VI (autumn 1988), pp. 121–122, fig. 8; David Hall, "Four saucers," *Journal of the Pewter Society,* VII (autumn 1989), p. 55, fig. 4; David Hall, "Early plates at Leamington," *Journal of the Pewter Society,* X (spring 1995), pp. 30–31, fig. 1; Ronald F. Homer and Stanley Shemmell, *Pewter: A Handbook of selected Tudor and Stuart pieces* (London, 1983), p. 22, back cover ill.

22–23

24 Two Probable Marriage Dishes

Maker unidentified
Probably England, 1620–1640

MARKS: Touchmark of a rose with crown above, *H* to the left, and *M* to the right within a conforming reserve on underside of each rim (Peal, *More Pewter Marks,* 5774a)

INSCRIPTIONS: Owner's initials *GH/SL* stamped on the face of one rim and *HP/BL* on the face of the other

DIMENSIONS: OH. (rims) 3 3/4", OW. (rims) 2 3/4", Diam. 14 3/4"

PROVENANCE: Purchased from A. H. Isher & Son, Cheltenham, Eng.; 1958-593, 1–2

English pewterers have occasionally used small punches, or stamps, to form decorative borders, mainly on the rims of dishes, from as early as the late sixteenth century. Three punches were used to decorate these dishes. The first punch is repeated to form a continuous border of outward-facing ellipses with the appearance of drapery swags that are stamped just inside the molded edges of the rims. Then a second punch with a small bifurcated device is stamped on the inner sides where the ends of each ellipse meet those of the next. These serve as a transition to a triad of acorns of the third punch that visually form an inner border. These dishes are part of a small group of punch-decorated examples dating from the last quarter of the sixteenth century and the first half of the seventeenth century.[1] Although aspects of their form, edging, and marking have Continental parallels, they are probably of English origin.

1. This group is discussed in Ronald F. Michaelis, "Decoration on English Pewterware, Part II: 'Punched' Ornamentation," *Antique Collector,* XXXV (February 1964), pp. 20–22. The two earliest dishes, both stamped with the date 1585, belong to the British Museum and to the Pewterers' Company, respectively. The latter was in the Jaeger Collection when Michaelis published it. The closest example to no. 24 is the one in the Homer Collection, *ibid.,* p. 22, fig. 3. Another dish of the same size and by the same maker, although undecorated, is owned by David S. Moulson, Alcester, Eng.

24.1 Stamped owner's initials and decoration on dish at left

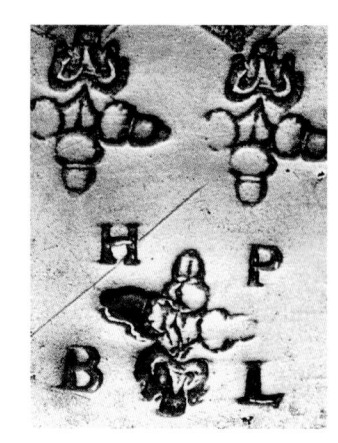

24.2 Stamped owner's initials and decoration on dish at right

36 PEWTER AT COLONIAL WILLIAMSBURG

Dishes and Plates/Broad Rims

The broad rim is the noblest in proportions of all dish and plate types in English pewter. In most circumstances, the width of the rim measures between one-fifth and one-sixth of the total diameter. First introduced about 1640, they continued to be made until about 1680. Pseudo hallmarks are invariably stamped on the face of the rim opposite stamped initials of owners and other proclamations of ownership.

25 DISH

Probably Samuel Jackson
London, 1640–1660

MARKS: Touchmark of a paschal lamb with stars above, *S* to the left, and *I* to the right within an outlined and corded circle on underside of rim (London Touch Plate I, 11; Cotterell, *Old Pewter*, 5741; Peal, *More Pewter Marks,* 5741; Peal, *Addenda,* 5741)

INSCRIPTIONS: Coat of arms of the Beauchamp family engraved within a wreath on face of rim; owner's initials *B/EM* stamped on face of rim opposite coat of arms

DIMENSIONS: OW. (rim) 7", Diam. 34 3/8"

PROVENANCE: A. T. Isher, Cheltenham, Eng. (sold after his death by Bruton Knowles in 1976); purchased from Richard Mundey, London; 1976-422

PUBLISHED: Sales cat., Bruton Knowles, Apr. 27, 1976, lot 188; Robinson, "Big Chargers," p. 5; Robinson, "Big Chargers (Followup)," p. 18; Mundey, "Great Dish," pp. 203, 208–209

This great dish, or charger, measuring almost a yard in diameter, is among the largest surviving English pewter dishes. It was probably intended more as a central focal point in a garnish or display of large dishes in a hall or early dining space than as an object of service or practical use. Most surviving large dishes were made in London with examples in excess of thirty inches in diameter being extremely rare. The maker of this dish, probably Jackson of London, apparently worked most of his career before the Great Fire of London in 1666. After this event, in which the touch plates at Pewterers' Hall were destroyed, active pewterers were required to restrike their touchmarks on new touch plates. The maker of this dish was the eleventh pewterer to do so.

25.1 Coat of arms

26.1 Wriggle-engraved sunburst and stamped owner's initials

26 DISH

Maker unidentified
London, ca. 1662

MARKS: Touchmark of an eagle displayed with *H* to the left and *R* to the right within an outlined and beaded circle on underside of rim (Cotterell, *Old Pewter,* 5972B; Peal, *More Pewter Marks,* 5972b); pseudo hallmarks (1) fleur-de-lis, (2) leopard's head, and (3) lion passant stamped within separate shaped shields on face of rim

INSCRIPTIONS: *Vivat Rex Carolus Secundus Beati Pacifici* [Long Live Charles II, Blessed Peacemaker] *1662* engraved on face in booge; owner's initials *N/IE* and *O/IE* stamped on either side of large sunburst on face of rim at top

DIMENSIONS: OW. (rim) 4", Diam. 20 1/2"

PROVENANCE: R. W. Cooper, Woodborough, Eng. (purchased from Richard Mundey, London, prior to 1955); sold after his death by Sotheby's on July 25, 1974, to CWF; 1974-176

PUBLISHED: Michaelis, *Antique Pewter of British Isles*, pl. XXXIII, fig. 77; Michaelis, "'Wriggled' Decoration on Pewter," pp. 197–198, fig. 2; *Exhibition of British Pewterware*, p. 20, no. 87, ill.; sales cat., Sotheby's, July 25, 1974, p. 30, lot 140, ill.

38 PEWTER AT COLONIAL WILLIAMSBURG

26

EXHIBITED: Exhibition of British Pewterware through the Ages from Romano-British Times to the Present Day, Reading Museum and Art Gallery, Reading, Eng., Sept. 20–Oct. 31, 1969

This dish is one of a small and highly important group of fewer than twenty large dishes made to celebrate the marriage of Charles II to Catherine of Braganza in 1662. The well of each is filled with the Stuart coat of arms engraved within the collar of the Garter (a clasped belt or garter of circular configuration bearing the motto *HONI SOIT QUI MAL Y PENSE*) framed by an elaborate wriggle-engraved surround with crest, supporters, motto, and various leafed and scrolled embellishments. A fairly broad rocker tool was walked back and forth to create the distinctive zigzag line of the wriggle engraving. The booge, or the short, curved sides of the well, of no. 26 and other examples bid tribute to Charles II, and the lion supporter is rendered with his crowned likeness. Their rims are often engraved with running naturalistic decoration, usually featuring royal symbols such as roses and acorns. It is difficult to give a precise count of how many of these dishes have survived because their rarity and desirability to collectors and institutions have prompted a number of fakes.

These dishes are among the earliest and principal exemplars of wriggle engraving. Most examples of this decorative engraving date from the decades immediately before and after the turn of the eighteenth century.

26.2 Wriggle-engraved lion supporter as King Charles II

27 DISH

Maker unidentified
England, 1650–1680

MARKS: No touchmark apparent; three indistinct pseudo hallmarks stamped on face of rim

INSCRIPTIONS: Owner's initials *I/S✶M* engraved on underside of rim

DIMENSIONS: OW. (rim) 3 11/16", Diam. 21 7/8"

PROVENANCE: Purchased from Dr. Percy E. Raymond, Lexington, Mass.; 1950-783

PUBLISHED: Raymond, "Ancestral Pewter," pp. 9–10, fig. 1

This dish, according to the last owner, was found in New Hampshire, and descended in the Morse family. Its engraved owner's initials (*I/S✶M*) may be for members of that family.

27.1 Engraved owner's initials

28 DISH

Thomas Drinkwater
London, 1665–1680

MARKS: Touchmark of a castle tower with *T* to the left and *D* to the right within an outlined and beaded circle on underside of rim (London Touch Plate I, 146; Cotterell, *Old Pewter,* 5556; Peal, *More Pewter Marks,* 1448a); pseudo hallmarks (1) lion passant within a serrated rectangle, (2) leopard's head crowned within a shaped shield, (3) buckle within a shaped shield, and (4) *TD* within a shaped shield, on face of rim (Cotterell, *Old Pewter,* 5556)

INSCRIPTIONS: Owner's initials *F/IM* and *F/MP* stamped on face of rim

DIMENSIONS: OW. (rim) 2 7/8", Diam. 16 1/4"

PROVENANCE: Purchased from Thomas D. and Constance R. Williams, Litchfield, Conn.; 1956-54

27–34

30.1 Engraved inscription on underside of rim

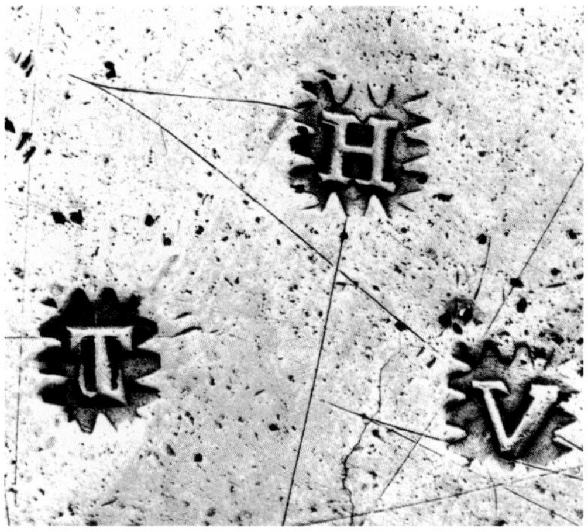

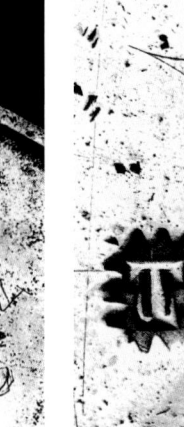

30.2 Stamped owner's initials on face of rim

29 DISH

Maker unidentified
England, 1650–1680

MARKS: Indistinct touchmark on underside of rim; pseudo hallmarks of lion passant (1 and 3) and leopard's head (2 and 4), all within shaped shields, on face of rim

INSCRIPTIONS: Owner's initials *W/IM* stamped on face of rim opposite pseudo hallmarks

DIMENSIONS: OW. (rim) 3 13/16", Diam. 20 1/4"

PROVENANCE: Purchased from A. H. Isher & Son, Cheltenham, Eng.; 1960-470

30 DISH

Jonathan Inglis
London, ca. 1679

MARKS: Touchmark of a pair of clasped hands with *II* above and *1670* below within an outlined and beaded circle on underside of rim (London Touch Plate I, 170; Cotterell, *Old Pewter*, 2525); pseudo hallmarks (1) lion passant within a serrated rectangle, (2) leopard's head crowned within a shield, (3) horse's head within a shield, and (4) a buckle within a shield, on face of rim

INSCRIPTIONS: Owner's initials *H/TV* within separate serrated rectangles on face of rim opposite pseudo hallmarks; *T✶H/V✶H* and *A SON IOHN BORN/1679* engraved on underside of rim

DIMENSIONS: OW. (rim) 2 15/16", Diam. 14"

PROVENANCE: Purchased from Thomas D. and Constance R. Williams, Litchfield, Conn.; 1954-444

The inscription indicates that this dish commemorates the birth or christening of a son.

31 DISH

Thomas Haward
London, 1650–1680

MARKS: Touchmark of a crown over a heart with *T* to the left, *H* to the right, and palm fronds at the sides and crossing below within a beaded vertical oval on underside of rim (London Touch Plate I, 5; Cotterell, *Old Pewter*, 2214); pseudo hallmarks (1) *TH* with two pellets above and one below within a shield, (2) leopard's head within a serrated rectangle, (3) buckle with two pellets above and one below within a shield, and (4) lion rampant within a serrated rectangle, on face of rim (Cotterell, *Old Pewter*, 2214)

INSCRIPTIONS: Owner's initials *M/IM* stamped on face

DIMENSIONS: OW. (rim) 3 1/2", Diam. 18 1/4"

PROVENANCE: Purchased from A. H. Isher & Son, Cheltenham, Eng.; 1960-471

32 DISH

Daniel Ingole
London, 1670–1690

MARKS: Touchmark *DI* with recumbent lion and lamb below within a beaded and outlined circle on underside of well (London Touch Plate I, 52; Cotterell, *Old Pewter,* 2538); pseudo hallmarks (1) lion rampant with two pellets above within a shield, (2) flower or sun with two pellets above within a shield, (3) possible buckle within a shield, and (4) indistinct hallmark on face of rim (Peal, *More Pewter Marks,* 2538)

INSCRIPTIONS: Owner's initials *D/IS* stamped on face of rim opposite pseudo hallmarks

DIMENSIONS: OW. (rim): 2 5/8", Diam. 15"

PROVENANCE: Purchased from Dr. Percy E. Raymond, Lexington, Mass.; 1950-806

PUBLISHED: Raymond, "Ancestral Pewter," pp. 9–10, fig. 1

This dish, according to the last owner, was found in the Connecticut River Valley, and descended in the Nims family.

33 DISH

Maker unidentified
England, probably London, 1670–1690

MARKS: Touchmark of an indistinct cipher with coat of arms with lion and unicorn supporters to left and right above and *LONDON* in curved arrangement below within a shaped vertical oval on underside of rim (Cotterell, *Old Pewter,* 5464; Peal, *More Pewter Marks,* 5464, 5977); pseudo hallmarks (1) *SB,* (2) lion passant, (3) leopard's head, and (4) buckle, within separate shaped shields on face of rim (Peal, *More Pewter Marks,* 5977)

INSCRIPTIONS: Owner's initials *H* and *O* within separate serrated rectangles stamped on face of rim

DIMENSIONS: OW. (rim) 4 1/8", Diam. 20 1/2"

PROVENANCE: Purchased from A. H. Isher & Son, Cheltenham, Eng.; 1960-456

34 DISH

Christopher Raper
London, 1670–1685

MARKS: Two castle towers with dagger between over a third with *CHRIS*✻*RAPER* within a curved reserve above and palm fronds at the sides and crossing below within a circle on underside of rim (London Touch Plate I, 140; Cotterell, *Old Pewter,* 3839); pseudo hallmarks (1) lion passant within a serrated rectangle, (2) leopard's head crowned within a shield, (3) buckle within a shield, and (4) *CR* within a shield, on face of rim

INSCRIPTIONS: Owner's initials *G/D+A* engraved above pseudo hallmarks on face of rim

DIMENSIONS: OW. (rim) 3 7/8", Diam. 23 7/8"

PROVENANCE: Purchased from A. H. Isher & Son, Cheltenham, Eng.; 1960-455

35.1 Engraved crest on face of rim

35 PLATE

Thomas Haward
London, 1650–1670

MARKS: Touchmark of a heart with crown above, *T* to the left, and *H* to the right within a beaded circle on underside of rim (Peal, *More Pewter Marks,* 2214); pseudo hallmarks (1) leopard's head within a serrated rectangle, (2) lion passant with two pellets above and below within a serrated rectangle, (3) buckle with two pellets above and one below within a shaped shield, and (4) *T•H* with crown above and heart below within a lozenge, on face of rim

35

35.2 Engraved arms on face of rim

INSCRIPTIONS: Crest and coat of arms of a descendant of Sir Francis Drake engraved within separate palm frond surrounds opposite one another on face of rim

DIMENSIONS: OW. (rim) 2 1/4", Diam. 10 1/16"

PROVENANCE: Norton Asner, Baltimore, Md. (sold after his death by Weschler's, Washington, D. C., June 5, 1992); 1992-93

PUBLISHED: Sales cat., Weschler's, Washington, D. C., June 5, 1992, lot 241, ill.

This fine plate is handsomely engraved on opposite sides of the rim with the arms and crest that Elizabeth I granted to Sir Francis Drake on his return from circumnavigating the globe in 1581. The engravings are particularly evocative. The crest depicts the arm of God reaching through the clouds to grasp lines attached to the bow of the *Golden Hind* to guide it in its voyage around the globe. A banner is aptly labeled *XILI⁰*[AUXILIO]•*DIVIN⁰* [By divine assistance]. Likewise, the arms are divided in the middle by a wavy fess, or serpentine bar, reminiscent of the ocean, with a large pole star above and below. Although Drake married twice without any descendants, the family continued to use these arms long after his death in 1596. A small crescent moon cadency mark is included in the coat of arms, which indicates that the arms are those of a second son in that generation of the Drake family. Cadency marks are used in heraldry to distinguish between branches of a family by indicating numerically to which son the arms belong.

Another plate from the same set was exhibited at the Museum of London in 1989/90 and is in the Little Collection.[1]

1. Hornsby, Weinstein, and Homer, *Celebration of the craft*, p. 96, no. 120, ill.; Hornsby, *Pewter of the Western World*, p. 71, fig. 120.

36 PLATE

James Taudin I
London, 1660–1680

MARKS: Maker's touch of a rose within a shield with palm fronds to the sides and crossing below with *E:SONNANT* and *I:TAUDIN* within curved reserves with intervening scrolls and bosses above, all within an oval on underside of rim (London Touch Plate I, 16; Cotterell, *Old Pewter*, 4650); pseudo hallmarks (1) *I*[?] *RT* with mullet above and below within a lozenge, (2) unicorn passant within a serrated rectangle, (3) leopard's head within a serrated rectangle, and (4) indistinct, on face of rim

INSCRIPTIONS: English royal arms engraved on face of rim opposite pseudo hallmarks; owner's initials *HW* engraved on underside of well

DIMENSIONS: OW. (rim) 2 7/16", Diam. 10 1/8"

PROVENANCE: A. T. Isher, Cheltenham, Eng. (sold after his death by Bruton Knowles in 1976); purchased from Jellinek & Sampson, London; 1976-362

PUBLISHED: Sales cat., Bruton Knowles, Apr. 27, 1976, p. 27, lot 148

This splendid plate is the only recorded English pewter plate from the seventeenth century that is engraved with the royal arms. It may have been occasioned by the remarkable relationship between Taudin, the maker, and King Charles II. Members of the Pewterers' Company harassed Taudin, trying to discourage him

36.1 Engraved English royal arms on face of rim

36

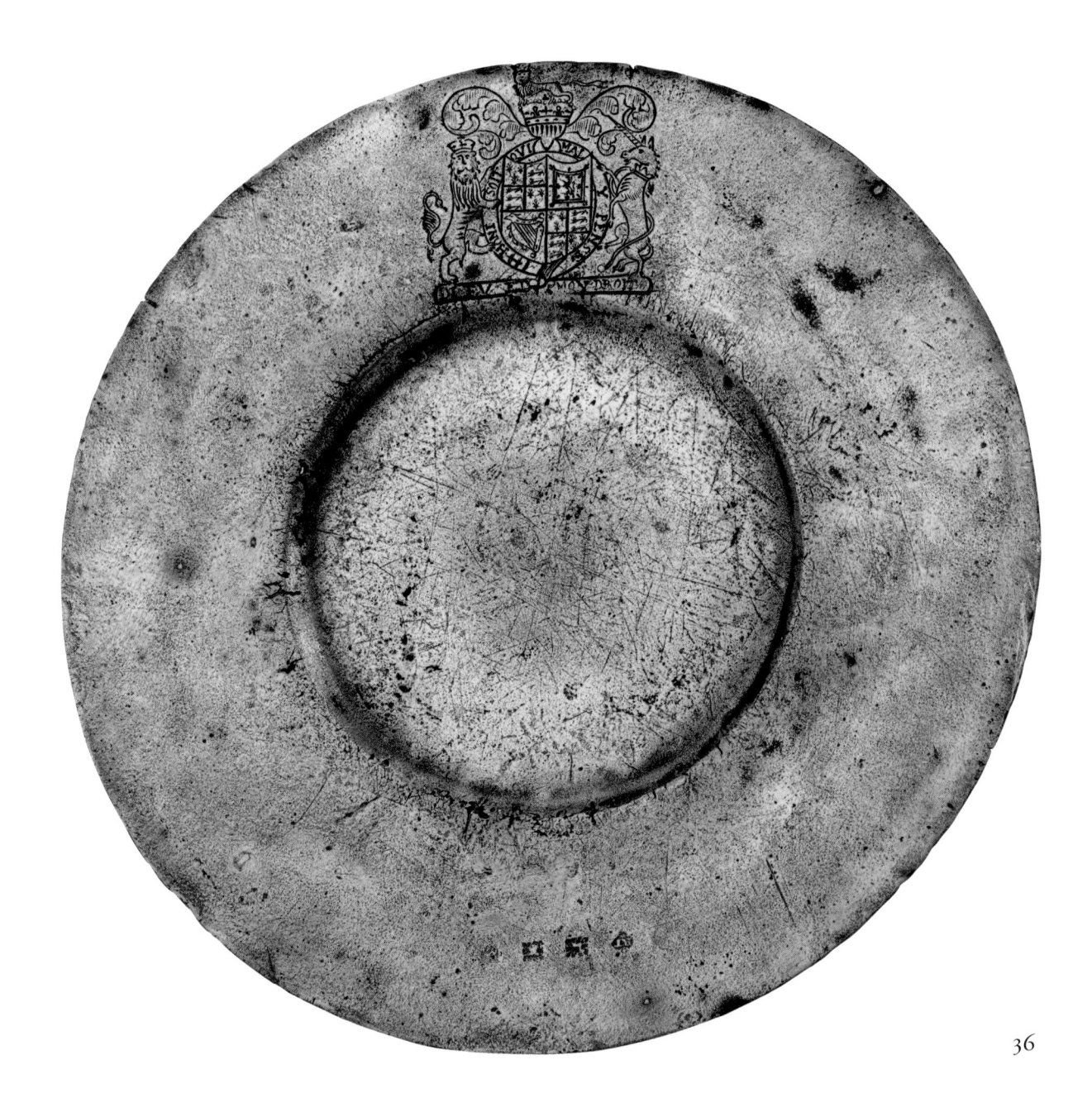

from practicing his trade, ever since his arrival from France in the 1650s. They forcibly entered his house to damage and seize more than eighteen hundred pounds of pewter. Taudin petitioned Cromwell, and the Pewterers' Company was forced to accept him as a member. When he was further harassed, an angry Charles II sent a blunt letter to the company, dated Nov. 7, 1668. The king wrote, in part, "We expect you will look on the said James Taudin as Our Servant and that he shall not have any occasion given him from you or any of you to complain at any time of his being so admitted into your Corporation or to seek relief from Us against any hard usages he may receive from you. We shall not doubt your Compliance."[1]

Homer has suggested that the king's reference to Taudin as "Our Servant" indicates that he made pewter by appointment to the king. This relationship to the Crown was not an unknown distinction, for Homer cites William Hurstwaight's having been referred to as "pewterer to the king" in 1526, and James Durand, a successor to Taudin, as "Pewterer to his Majesty" in 1763.[2]

1. Ronald F. Homer, "The story of James Taudin," *Journal of the Pewter Society*, IV (autumn 1984), pp. 118–122. A full transcript and illustration of the letter appears in Hornsby, Weinstein, and Homer, *Celebration of the craft*, p. 13.
2. Hornsby, Weinstein, and Homer, *Celebration of the craft*, p. 14.

37 Plate

Edward Everett
London, 1655–1665

MARKS: Indistinct touchmark incorporating, in part, an anchor with a crown above the pointed end on the right side within a beaded circle on underside of rim (Peal, *More Pewter Marks,* 5565; Peal, *Addenda,* 1598); pseudo hallmarks (1) indistinct, (2) lion passant within a serrated rectangle, (3) possible leopard's head within a serrated rectangle, and (4) *EE* with pellets below within a shaped shield (Peal, *More Pewter Marks,* 1598, 5565; Peal, *Addenda,* 1598, 5565)

INSCRIPTIONS: Crest and coat of arms framed by crossed ostrich plumes engraved on opposite sides of face of rim for the Jenison family; owner's initials *TI,* presumably for a member of the Jenison family, stamped on underside of well

DIMENSIONS: OW. (rim) 2 3/8", Diam. 11 13/16"

PROVENANCE: A. V. Sutherland-Graeme, London (sold at

37.1 Engraved crest of the Jenison family on face of rim

Sotheby's, 1965); Kenneth W. Bradshaw, Lincoln, Eng. (sold at Sotheby's, 1977); 1977-219

PUBLISHED: Sutherland-Graeme, "Pewter Church Flagons," pp. 94–95, fig. xiii; Sutherland-Graeme, "Some British Pewter," p. 364, fig. 2; Thomas, *American and British Pewter*, p. 25; Ramsey, "Notable Private Collection," p. 12, fig. 7; sales cat., Sotheby's, June 3, 1965, p. 17, lot 60; sales cat., Sotheby's, June 13, 1977, p. 12, lot 49, ill.

This object appears to be an unusually large plate rather than a small dish.

37.2 Engraved coat of arms of the Jenison family on face of rim

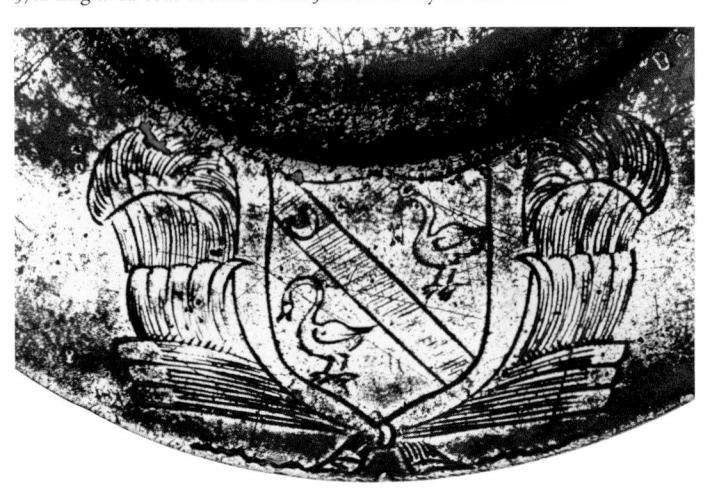

38 PLATE

Maker unidentified
England, ca. 1674

MARKS: Touchmark of the arms of the Pewterers' Company with *SB* with a mullet to either side barely visible above and scrolls at the sides within a vertical oval (Cotterell, *Old Pewter*, 5463); partially indistinct pseudo hallmark of a lion passant within a rectangle repeated four times on face of rim (Cotterell, *Old Pewter*, 5463)

INSCRIPTIONS: *THE GIFT IS SMALL THE LOVE IS ALL 1674* engraved on interior face of booge

DIMENSIONS: OW. (rim) 1 15/16", Diam. 9 9/16"

PROVENANCE: A. T. Isher, Cheltenham, Eng. (sold after his death by Bruton Knowles, 1976); purchased from Jellinek & Sampson, London; 1981-210

PUBLISHED: Sales cat., Bruton Knowles, Apr. 27, 1976, p. 27, lot 148

This inscribed plate, decorated with a unicorn with a cupid's bow and arrow in the clouds above, was intended as a keepsake, perhaps at the time of marriage, rather than as an object for daily use. The rim is pierced with a small hole for hanging and display.

A broad-rim dish of the same year and by the same maker, inscribed in large letters *SAINT GEORGE FOR ENGLAND* and engraved with Saint George and the Dragon, was formerly in the Bradshaw Collection.[1]

1. Sales cat., Sotheby's, June 13, 1977, p. 31, lot 98, ill.

39 PLATE

William Matthews
Pseudo hallmarks of Thomas Haward
London, 1674–1680

MARKS: Touchmark of a crown with *W* beneath a pellet to the left and *M* under a pellet to the right over a heart with a palm frond and intervening pellet to either side within a corded vertical oval on underside of rim (London Touch Plate I, 203; Cotterell, *Old Pewter*, 3141); pseudo hallmarks of Thomas Haward of London (1) *TH* with two circles above and one below within a shaped shield, (2) leopard's head within a serrated rectangle, (3) buckle

48 PEWTER AT COLONIAL WILLIAMSBURG

38

with two circles above and one below within a shaped shield, and (4) lion rampant within a serrated rectangle on face of rim (Cotterell, *Old Pewter,* 2214, 3140)

INSCRIPTIONS: Owner's initials *W*/*/WE within crossed palm fronds engraved on face of rim opposite pseudo hallmarks

DIMENSIONS: OW. (rim) 1 3/4", Diam. 9 3/8"

PROVENANCE: Purchased from Richard Mundey, London; 1980-72

This plate is from a distinguished set, of which at least nine plates survive. Aside from this one, a single example is in the collections of the Pewterers' Company.[1] Six plates from the set were formerly in the Bradshaw Collection.[2] The ninth, formerly in the Isher Collection and presently belonging to the Cheltenham Art Gallery and Museum, has a sentimental association. Antonio de Navarro, the noted collector and benefactor of the Fitzwilliam Museum in Cambridge, presented Howard Herschel Cotterell with a plate from this set as a momento of Cotterell's first visit to de Navarro's Worcestershire home. Cotterell wrote, "It is one of the very rarest of English pewter plates, a fact which enhances a hundredfold both the generosity of the giver and the pleasure of its present owner."[3]

1. *Supplementary Catalogue of Pewterware, 1979,* p. 14, no. SI/107, ill., p. 20.
2. Bradshaw purchased them at Sotheby's on Mar. 28, 1980, as lot 76 and sold them at Sotheby's on Mar. 18, 1997, as lot 401. Also illustrated in David Hall, "The Bradshaw Collection," *Journal of the Pewter Society,* XI (autumn 1997), p. 49, fig. 24; Mark Stephen, "British Pewter Plates, Dishes and Chargers, A Guide to Identification," *Antique Collecting,* XXXV (September 2000), p. 31, fig. 5.
3. This quotation first appeared in Howard Herschel Cotterell, "National Types of Old Pewter, Part V," *The Magazine Antiques,* V (March 1924), p. 123. These plates have been illustrated and discussed by Antonio de Navarro, *Causeries on English Pewter* (London, 1911), pl. LXI; Howard Herschel Cotterell, *Pewter down the Ages, from Mediæval Times to the Present Day, with Notes on Evolution* (London, 1932), pp. 107–108, fig. 63; Howard Herschel Cotterell, Adolphe Riff, and Robert M. Vetter, *National Types of Old Pewter,* rev. ed. with new introduction by Charles V. Swain (Princeton, N. J., 1972), p. 24, fig. 130.

Dishes and Plates/Multiple Reeds

Dishes and plates of this type are characterized by incised or relief-cast multiple reeds, or moldings, at the edges of their rims. The rims of dishes tend to be of moderate width, while those of many of the plates are distinctly narrow. Pseudo hallmarks are common on plates and dishes of this type. They invariably appear, as with broad rims, on the face of the rim, usually opposite stamped owner's initials and other identifications of ownership. More than any other type, these plates and dishes are consistently decorated, either hammered in decorative patterns or wriggle engraved with naturalistic, patriotic, or commemorative designs.

40

40 Dish

Richard White
London, 1689–1710

MARKS: Touchmark of a pelican in its piety, that is, in a self-vulned posture, with *89* above framed by *RICHARD* above and *WHITE* below within separate curved reserves and a plumed cartouche to either side on underside of rim (London Touch Plate II, 448; Cotterell, *Old Pewter,* 5097); secondary mark of a rose with crown above, *R* to the left, and *W* to the right within a conforming reserve on underside of rim (Cotterell, *Old Pewter,* 5097); pseudo hallmarks (1) black letter *R,* (2) black letter *W,* (3) pelican in its piety, and (4) leopard's head crowned, each within a separate shaped shield on face of rim (Cotterell, *Old Pewter,* 5097)

INSCRIPTIONS: Owner's initials *AL* stamped on face of rim opposite pseudo hallmarks

DIMENSIONS: OW. (rim) 2 7/8", Diam. 22 3/8"

PROVENANCE: Purchased from Dr. Percy E. Raymond, Lexington, Mass.; 1950-784

It is in this category that one occasionally encounters plates and dishes with their entire surfaces hammered in a regular pattern of concentric circles, not just the customary hammering of the booge. This hammering not only immeasurably enhanced their decorative effect and appeal, but also compressed and strengthened the metal, which lent added strength to these sometimes quite broad, flat forms.

41 Dish

Maker unidentified
England, 1680–1700

MARKS: Touchmark of a spinning wheel distaff and bobbin with •*I* to the left and *I*• to the right and two pellets both above and below within an outlined and beaded circle on underside of rim (Cotterell, *Old Pewter,* 5724; Peal, *More Pewter Marks,* 5724); pseudo hallmark of an eagle displayed within a shaped shield stamped four times on face of rim (Cotterell, *Old Pewter,* 5724; Peal, *More Pewter Marks,* 5724)

INSCRIPTIONS: Owner's initials *C/WE* within separate shaped shields stamped on face of rim opposite pseudo hallmarks

DIMENSIONS: OW. (rim): 2 3/16", Diam. 15 1/8"

PROVENANCE: Purchased from A. H. Isher & Son, Cheltenham, Eng.; 1960-802

41

British pewter, by and large, is undecorated. Its makers relied on pleasing design, proportions, and the use of good metal for its appeal and success. The largest exception to this rule was the popularity of wriggled engraving, particularly in the period between 1680 and 1740, as exemplified by this dish. A fairly broad rocker tool was walked back and forth to create its distinctive zigzag line. Naturalistic motifs predominate with a lesser number of patriotic portraits of reigning sovereigns. In this regard, wriggle engraving is analogous to delft with similar naturalistic and patriotic decoration that was intended for a comparable clientele.

1. The same touchmark and pseudo hallmarks that appear on the CWF dish are also present in a larger dish of this type in the Gadd Collection. "Marks," *Journal of the Pewter Society*, XVIII (autumn 2002), p. 50.

42 DISH

Dx. Roe
England, 1688–1700

MARKS: Touchmark of a rose with crown above, *8* to the left, and *8* to the right framed by *DX+ROE* within a curved reserve above and by crossed palm fronds at the sides and below within a shaped vertical oval on underside of rim (Peal, *More Pewter Marks,* 4007a); pseudo hallmarks (1) buckle, (2) leopard's head, (3) lion rampant, and (4) *DR* with indistinct devices above and below, each within a separate shield on face of rim (Peal, *More Pewter Marks,* 4007a)

INSCRIPTIONS: Owner's initial *A* stamped on face of rim opposite pseudo hallmarks

DIMENSIONS: OW. (rim) 2 1/8", Diam. 15 1/16"

PROVENANCE: Purchased from A. H. Isher & Son, Cheltenham, Eng.; 1958-592

43–45

43 DISH

Probably Richard Smith
London, 1680–1700

MARKS: No apparent touchmark; pseudo hallmarks (1) lion passant within a serrated rectangle, (2) leopard's head crowned within a shaped shield, (3) rose within a shaped shield, and (4) indistinct, on face of rim (Cotterell, *Old Pewter*, 4374)

INSCRIPTIONS: Owner's initials *RE* stamped on face of rim opposite pseudo hallmarks

DIMENSIONS: OW. (rim) 3", Diam. 20"

PROVENANCE: Gift of David Pleydell-Bouverie, New York, N. Y.; G1951-45

The pseudo hallmarks on this dish match those on a similar dish of the same size in the collections of The Worshipful Company of Pewterers of London.[1] The attribution of no. 43 to Smith of London stems from this visual similarity.

1. *A short history of The Worshipful Company of London and a catalogue of pewterware in its possession* (London, 1968), p. 19, no. 10. The pseudo hallmarks are illustrated in *Supplementary Catalogue of Pewterware, 1979*, p. 120, no. 10B.

44 DISH

John Greenbank II
Worcester, Eng., 1680–1700

MARKS: Touchmark of a lion rampant on a wreath bar with palm fronds to the sides and crossing below within an outlined and beaded vertical oval on underside of rim (Cotterell, *Old Pewter,* 5619; Homer and Hall, *Provincial Pewterers,* 26); secondary mark of a rose with a crown above with palm fronds to the sides and crossing below within an outlined and beaded vertical oval on underside of rim (Cotterell, *Old Pewter,* 5619; Homer and Hall, *Provincial Pewterers,* 26); pseudo hallmarks (1) indistinct, (2) lion passant, (3) rose, and (4) *IG* with a pellet above and below, each within a separate shaped shield on face of rim (Cotterell, *Old Pewter,* 5619; Homer and Hall, *Provincial Pewterers,* 26)

INSCRIPTIONS: Owner's initials *E* [an arrangement of five pellets] *A* engraved on face of rim opposite pseudo hallmarks

DIMENSIONS: OW. (rim) 2 11/16", Diam. 20 1/8"

PROVENANCE: Purchased from Thomas D. and Constance R. Williams, Litchfield, Conn.; 1956-73

The Greenbank family was involved with pewter in Worcester

54 PEWTER AT COLONIAL WILLIAMSBURG

46–48

from the late sixteenth century. The maker of this dish, who died in 1700, was from the fourth of six generations of the family to earn livelihoods as pewterers. Eleven members of the family are known to have worked at this trade between 1570 and the 1730s.[1]

1. Ronald F. Homer and David W. Hall, *Provincial Pewterers: A Study of the craft in the West Midlands and Wales* (London, 1985), pp. 43–45.

45 DISH

Adam Banks
Milngate, Eng., or Wigan, Eng., 1690–1716

MARKS: No apparent touchmark; secondary mark of a rose with crown above within a conforming reserve on underside of rim (Cotterell, *Old Pewter,* 222A); pseudo hallmarks of a bird within a shaped rectangle alternating with *AB* within a shaped rectangle on face of rim (Cotterell, *Old Pewter,* 222A)

INSCRIPTIONS: None

DIMENSIONS: OW. (rim) 2 5/8", Diam. 20 3/16"

PROVENANCE: Purchased from A. H. Isher & Son, Cheltenham, Eng.; 1967-428

Members of the Banks family began their long tradition as pewterers in Wigan in the middle years of the sixteenth century. They reestablished themselves in Bewdley after Christopher Banks I moved there in 1697.[1] Little is apparently known of Adam Banks, Christopher's uncle, aside from his surviving work and that his will was proved in Chester in 1716.[2]

1. Homer and Hall, *Provincial Pewterers,* pp. 64, 72–74.
2. Cotterell, *Old Pewter,* p. 154, no. 222A. Confirmed by Homer and Hall, *Provincial Pewterers,* p. 73.

46 DISH

Maker unidentified
England, dated 1695

MARKS: Indistinct touchmark incorporating, in part, a heart superimposed on an anchor within a beaded circle on underside of rim; pseudo hallmark of a thistle within a shaped shield stamped four times on face of rim

INSCRIPTIONS: Owner's initials *I* and *H* within separate shaped shields repeated above one another on face of rim opposite pseudo hallmarks; *1695* engraved on face of rim below pseudo hallmarks

DINING WARES 55

46.1 Stamped owner's initials on face of rim

DIMENSIONS: OW. (rim) 1 1/2", Diam. 18 1/4"

PROVENANCE: Purchased from Thomas D. and Constance R. Williams, Litchfield, Conn.; 1956-71

47 DISH

Maker unidentified
England, dated 1698

MARKS: Indistinct touchmark incorporating, in part, a heart superimposed on an anchor within a beaded circle on underside of rim; pseudo hallmark of a thistle within a shaped shield stamped four times on face of rim

INSCRIPTIONS: Owner's initials *WH/16*98/AH* within a foliate wreath engraved on face of rim opposite pseudo hallmarks

DIMENSIONS: OW. (rim) 2 9/16", Diam. 18 5/16"

PROVENANCE: Purchased from Thomas D. and Constance R. Williams, Litchfield, Conn.; 1956-72

48 DISH

Daniel Ingole
London, 1680–1691

MARKS: Touchmark of a recumbent lion and lamb with *DI* flanked by leafed branches above within a corded vertical oval on underside of rim (Cotterell, *Old Pewter,* 2538); secondary mark of a rose with crown above within a conforming reserve on underside of rim; pseudo hallmarks (1) lion rampant, (2) sun face or leopard's head with two pellets, (3) buckle, and (4) *DI* with mullet below, each within a shaped shield on face of rim (Peal, *More Pewter Marks,* 2538)

INSCRIPTIONS: Owner's initials *N*[or *H*]/*TE* stamped on face of rim above pseudo hallmarks; later owner's initials *SP* in large script letters with foliate flourishes engraved on underside of well

DIMENSIONS: OW. (rim) 2 5/8", Diam. 18 1/4"

PROVENANCE: Purchased from Dr. Percy E. Raymond, Lexington, Mass.; 1950-785

This dish dates before Ingole's death on July 16, 1691.[1] Its touch is a variant of that entered about 1670 on London Touch Plate I, no. 52.

1. Cotterell, *Old Pewter,* p. 241, no. 2538.

47.1 Engraved owner's initials and date

48.1 Later engraved owner's initials

49 DISH

Christopher Baldwin
Wigan, Eng., 1690–1710

MARKS: Touchmark of an animal's head erased with scrolls to the sides and +CHRIS+BALDWIN+ within a curved reserve below, all within a circle stamped twice on underside of rim (Cotterell, *Old Pewter,* 210; Peal, *More Pewter Marks,* 210); secondary mark C•BALDWIN within a rectangle on underside of rim below touchmark (Cotterell, *Old Pewter,* 210); pseudo hallmarks C•B with a shaped rectangle stamped four times on face of rim (Cotterell, *Old Pewter,* 210)

INSCRIPTIONS: Owner's initials *S* and *W* within separate conforming reserves stamped on face of rim opposite pseudo hallmarks

DIMENSIONS: OW. (rim) 2 1/4", Diam. 18 1/4"

PROVENANCE: Purchased from Dr. Percy E. Raymond, Lexington, Mass.; 1950-786

Cotterell notes that Baldwin's will was proved in Chester in 1725.[1]

1. Cotterell, *Old Pewter,* p. 153, no. 210.

50–51

50 DISH

William Ellwood I
London, 1696–1710

MARKS: Indistinct touchmark incorporating, in part, *ELLWOOD* in a curved reserve at bottom on underside of rim (probably London Touch Plate II, 540; Cotterell, *Old Pewter*, 1553); indistinct secondary mark incorporating, in part, a rose with crown above with fronds to either side and crossing below on underside of rim; pseudo hallmarks (1) lion passant within a shaped shield, (2) leopard's head crowned within a circle, (3) bust within a shaped shield, and (4) *WE/97* with a fleur-de-lis flanked by a pellet to either side above within a rectangle with canted corners, on face of rim

INSCRIPTIONS: Owner's initials *W/RE* stamped on face of rim opposite pseudo hallmarks

DIMENSIONS: OW. (rim) 2 5/8", Diam. 18 5/16"

PROVENANCE: Purchased from William Bozarth, Williamsburg, Va.; 1955-14

Ellwood entered this touch at Pewterers' Hall in London on Mar. 23, 1696.[1]

1. Cotterell, *Old Pewter*, p. 203, no. 1553.

51 DISH

John Baskerville
London, 1691–1702

MARKS: Touchmark of a stemmed flower, half rose and half thistle, with *IOHN* above and *BASKERVILLE* below within separate curved cartouches, all contained within a vertical oval on underside of rim (London Touch Plate II, 474; Cotterell, *Old Pewter*, 290); pseudo hallmarks (1) black letter *I*, (2) black letter *B*, (3) combination rose and thistle, and (4) crown, each within a shaped rectangle on face of rim (Cotterell, *Old Pewter*, 290)

INSCRIPTIONS: Owner's initials *M/[?]* stamped on face of rim opposite pseudo hallmarks

DIMENSIONS: OW. (rim) 2 1/4", Diam. 16 1/2"

58   PEWTER AT COLONIAL WILLIAMSBURG

52–53

PROVENANCE: Purchased from Dr. Percy E. Raymond, Lexington, Mass.; 1950-801

Baskerville entered this touch on Dec. 14, 1691, and it appears as no. 474 on London Touch Plate II. He was buried on Aug. 24, 1702, at Saint Vedast, Foster Lane, London.[1]

1. Cotterell, *Old Pewter*, p. 156, no. 290.

52 DISH

John Greenbank II
Worcester, Eng., 1680–1700

MARKS: Touchmark of a lion rampant on a wreath bar with fronds to either side and crossing below within an outlined vertical oval on underside of rim (Cotterell, *Old Pewter*, 5619; Homer and Hall, *Provincial Pewterers*, 26); secondary mark of a rose with crown above with fronds to either side and crossing below within an outlined vertical oval on underside of rim (Cotterell, *Old Pewter*, 5619; Homer and Hall, *Provincial Pewterers*, 26); pseudo hallmarks (1) shell with two pellets above and one below, (2) lion passant, (3) rose, and (4) *IG* with a pellet above and one below, each within a shaped shield on face of rim (Cotterell, *Old Pewter*, 5619; Homer and Hall, *Provincial Pewterers*, 26)

52.1 Engraved owner's initials on face of rim

INSCRIPTIONS: Owner's initials */*E*E*/* stamped on face of rim opposite pseudo hallmarks

DIMENSIONS: OW. (rim) 2 1/4", Diam. 16 5/8"

PROVENANCE: Purchased from Frances M. Healey, Norfolk, Va.; 1970-144

The Greenbanks were one of the leading pewter-making families of Worcester. They can boast of no fewer than six generations of pewterers. The maker of this dish rose to the rank of city alderman in 1683, and he died in 1700.[1]

1. Homer and Hall, *Provincial Pewterers*, pp. 43–45.

DINING WARES 59

54 DISH OR STAND

Richard Webb
London, 1687–1710

MARKS: Touchmark of a seated sovereign with a palm frond to either side and *RICHARD* above and *WEBB* below within curved reserves on underside (London Touch Plate II, 458; Cotterell, *Old Pewter,* 5007); secondary mark of a rose with crown above with a palm frond to either side and *LONDON* below within a curved reserve on underside (Cotterell, *Old Pewter,* 5007); pseudo hallmarks (1) *RW* with pellets above and below within a shaped shield, (2) leopard's head crowned within a shaped shield, (3) black letter *C* with two pellets above and one below within a shaped shield, and (4) lion passant within a rounded rectangle, on face near rim (Cotterell, *Old Pewter,* 5007)

INSCRIPTIONS: Owner's initials *I/IW* within separate serrated rectangles on face opposite pseudo hallmarks

DIMENSIONS: OW. (rim) 9/16", Diam. 15 1/8"

PROVENANCE: Purchased from F. H. Foxall, Ludlow, Eng. (acquired at auction in Brighton, Eng.); 1947-222

PUBLISHED: Sutherland-Graeme, "British Pewter in American Collections," p. 4, figs. IV, V

Flat plates of this size with a molded edge, such as nos. 54 and 55, are sometimes described as scale plates. It is more likely that they are either cake plates or some other type of specialized stand or dish for the presentation and service of food. Examples from this date range with multiple-reeded edging are rare.

54.1 Stamped owner's initials on face

54

53 DISH

Edward Leapage I
London, 1699–1710

MARKS: Touchmark of a sheaf of wheat and a rabbit in a shield with *EDW:LEAPIDGE* and *LONDON* in curved reserves above and fronds to either side and crossing below within a vertical oval on underside of rim (Cotterell, *Old Pewter,* 2893; London Touch Plate II, 568); secondary marks (1) *LONDON* within a serrated rectangle, and (2) a rose with crown and *LONDON* in a curved reserve above and fronds to either side and crossing below within a shaped vertical oval, both on underside of rim (Cotterell, *Old Pewter,* 2893); pseudo hallmarks (1) *EL,* (2) sheaf of wheat, (3) leopard's head, and (4) buckle, each within a shaped rectangle on face of rim

INSCRIPTIONS: None

DIMENSIONS: OW. (rim) 2 1/4", Diam. 16 11/16"

PROVENANCE: Purchased from Thomas D. and Constance R. Williams, Litchfield, Conn.; 1956-70

Leapage entered this touch at Pewterers' Hall in London on Feb. 19, 1699.[1]

1. Cotterell, *Old Pewter,* pp. 255–256, no. 2893.

60   PEWTER AT COLONIAL WILLIAMSBURG

55 Dish or Stand

Jonas Durand I
London, 1700–1716

MARKS: Touchmark of a rose with palm fronds to either side and crossing below with *IONAS/E:SONNANT/1699* within curved reserves above and *DURAND* within a curved reserve below on underside (London Touch Plate II, 557; Cotterell, *Old Pewter*, 1475, with small differences)

INSCRIPTIONS: Arms of Devereux impaling those of Norborne within a lozenge and with a viscount's coronet above for Elizabeth (1678–1742), daughter of Walter Norborne of Calne, Wiltshire, and widow of Edward Devereux, Eighth Viscount Hereford

DIMENSIONS: Diam. 15 3/8"

PROVENANCE: Sold at Sotheby's, 1984; purchased from Robin Bellamy Antiques, Witney, Eng.; 1984-139

55.1 Engraved coat of arms on face

PUBLISHED: Sales cat., Sotheby's, May 17, 1984, lot 17

The engraved arms can be used to date this dish or stand after the death of Elizabeth Norborne's first husband, Edward Devereux, Eighth Viscount Hereford, on Aug. 9, 1700, and before her marriage on Feb. 21, 1716/7, to John Symes Berkeley of Stoke Gifford, Gloucestershire. Her son by her second marriage was Norborne, Baron de Botetourt, who served as the penultimate royal governor of Virginia between 1768 and his death in the Governor's Palace in Williamsburg, Va., on Mar. 15, 1770.

DINING WARES 61

56

56 DISH

Thomas King
London, 1689–1694

MARKS: Touchmark incorporating, in part, a crown with king's name within a curved reserve above and palm fronds to either side below on underside of well; secondary mark of a rose with crown above and *WR* (conjoined) to the left and *MR* (conjoined) to the right within a conforming reserve on underside of well; pseudo hallmarks (1) *TK* with a fleur-de-lis below, (2) anchor, (3) crown, and (4) lion rampant, each within a shield with crown above within well on face (Cotterell, *Old Pewter*, 2752)

INSCRIPTIONS: None

DIMENSIONS: OW. (rim) 1/2", Diam. 13 7/8"

PROVENANCE: Bertram Isher, Cheltenham, Eng. (sold after his death by Bruton Knowles in Cheltenham); purchased from Richard Mundey, London; 1976-123

PUBLISHED: Sales cat., Bruton Knowles, Apr. 27, 1976, p. 34, lot 186

Although narrow-rimmed plates survive in appreciable numbers, narrow-rimmed dishes are quite scarce. They appear not to have been made as large as contemporary dishes with rims of conven-

tional width. The largest recorded example measures only sixteen inches in diameter.[1] The secondary mark on this dish includes the initials of William and Mary flanking the royal crown, which dates this dish during their joint reign between 1689 and 1694.

1. Christopher A. Peal et al., *Pewter of Great Britain* (London, 1983), p. 94, fig. 64.

57 PLATE

Maker unidentified
England, 1688–1702

MARKS: Touchmark of a stemmed and leafed flower with *C* to the left, *B* or *R* to the right, and *1670* below within an outlined circle on underside of well

INSCRIPTIONS: *WR,* for William III, wriggle engraved in large letters to either side of his portrait in center

DIMENSIONS: OW. (rim) 9/16", Diam. 8 1/2"

PROVENANCE: Purchased from Robin Bellamy Antiques, Witney, Eng.; 1982-184

Patriotic and naturalistic motifs were the most popular themes for wriggle-engraved decoration on pewter, particularly during the last quarter of the seventeenth century. Many patriotic decorations relate to William III.

A very similar William III portrait plate by the same pewterer is in the collections of The Worshipful Company of Pewterers of London.[1]

1. This plate is illustrated in sales cat., Sotheby's, Feb. 9, 1978, p. 11, no. 116, pl. I, and in *Supplementary Catalogue of Pewterware, 1979,* pp. 16, 27, no. S1/122.

58 PLATE

Unmarked
England, 1680–1700

MARKS: None

INSCRIPTIONS: None

DIMENSIONS: OW. (rim) 5/8", Diam. 8 5/8"

57

PROVENANCE: Purchased from Robin Bellamy Antiques, Witney, Eng., that, in turn, acquired it from Cyril C. Minchin, Bucklebury, Eng.; 1984-214

The wriggle-engraved decoration on this plate is in an exceptional state of preservation.

58

DINING WARES   63

59–64

59 SET OF FIVE PLATES

Henry Wiggin
London, 1688–1700

MARKS: Touchmark of a dagger with an *8* to either side of the blade framed by *HY•WIGGIN* above and *LONDON* below in curved reserves within a vertical oval on underside of well (Cotterell, *Old Pewter,* 5136 with differences); pseudo hallmarks (1) *HW* with two mullets above and one below within a shaped rectangle, (2) buckle within a shaped shield, (3) leopard's head with pellets above within a shaped shield, and (4) a lion passant within a shaped rectangle, on face of well toward edge (Cotterell, *Old Pewter,* 5136)

INSCRIPTIONS: Owner's initials *AB* stamped on face of well opposite pseudo hallmarks

DIMENSIONS: OW. (rim) 9/16", Diam. 9 1/8"

PROVENANCE: Purchased from H. W. Keil, Broadway, Eng.; 1960-491–495

60 PLATE

Richard Smith
London, 1685–1700

MARKS: No touchmark; secondary mark of a crowned rose with *LON* to the left and *DON* to the right within a conforming reserve on underside of well (Peal, *More Pewter Marks,* 4374); pseudo hallmarks (1) lion passant within serrated rectangle, (2) leopard's head crowned, (3) rose within a shaped shield, and (4) *RS* with pellet below within a shaped shield, on face of rim (Cotterell, *Old Pewter,* 4374; Peal, *More Pewter Marks,* 4374; *Supplementary Catalogue of Pewterware, 1979,* p. 120, 10B)

INSCRIPTIONS: None

DIMENSIONS: OW. (rim) 1/2", Diam. 8 9/16"

PROVENANCE: Purchased from Dr. Percy E. Raymond, Lexington, Mass.; 1950-829

PUBLISHED: Raymond, "Ancestral Pewter," p. 9, fig. 1

61 PLATE

John Greenbank II
Pseudo hallmarks of William Greenbank II
Worcester, Eng., 1680–1700

MARKS: Touchmark of a lion rampant on a wreath bar with fronds to either side and crossing below within an outlined vertical oval on underside of well (Cotterell, *Old Pewter,* 5619; Homer and Hall, *Provincial Pewterers,* 26); partially indistinct secondary mark of a rose with crown above with fronds to either side and crossing below within a beaded circle on underside of well (Cotterell, *Old Pewter,* 5619; Homer and Hall, *Provincial Pewterers,* 26); pseudo hallmarks (1) castle with two rings above and below, (2) fleur-de-lis with two mullets above and a pellet below, (3) animal's head erased with two rings above and a pellet below, and (4) rose, each within a separate shield on face of well toward edge (Cotterell, *Old Pewter,* 1992; Homer and Hall, *Provincial Pewterers,* 27; *Supplementary Catalogue of Pewterware, 1979,* p. 122, 45)

INSCRIPTIONS: Owner's initials *MD* stamped on face of well opposite pseudo hallmarks; the *M* is composed of a *V* with an *I* to either side

DIMENSIONS: OW. (rim) 9/16", Diam. 8 5/8"

PROVENANCE: Purchased from Thomas D. and Constance R. Williams, Litchfield, Conn.; 1956-58

Nos. 44 and 52 are also by John Greenbank II.

62 PAIR OF PLATES

W. Baron
England, 1685–1700

MARKS: No touchmark; pseudo hallmarks (1) rose with crown above, (2) fleur-de-lis with crown above, (3) harp with crown above, and (4) *W:B* with heart below and crown above, each within a separate shield on face of rim (Peal, *More Pewter Marks,* 5487b; Peal, *Addenda,* 5487b, 266c)

INSCRIPTIONS: Owner's initials *M* and *W* within separate serrated rectangles stamped on face of rim opposite pseudo hallmarks

DIMENSIONS: OW. (rim) 5/8", Diam. 9 3/16"

PROVENANCE: Purchased from A. H. Isher & Son, Cheltenham, Eng.; 1960-796, 1960-797

63 PLATE

Maker unidentified
England, 1680–1700

MARKS: Touchmark incorporating, in part, a heart superimposed on an anchor with *E* above left point of anchor within a beaded circle on underside of well; pseudo hallmark of a thistle within a shaped shield stamped four times on face of rim

INSCRIPTIONS: Owner's initials *A, S, T,* and *H* stamped within separate shaped shields on face of rim opposite pseudo hallmarks

DIMENSIONS: OW. (rim) 7/8", Diam. 9"

PROVENANCE: Purchased from Thomas D. and Constance R. Williams, Litchfield, Conn.; 1956-59

A touchmark of similar design, but different size, and the same pseudo hallmarks are on nos. 46 and 47.

63.1 Stamped owner's initials on face of rim

64 PLATE

Erasmus Dole
Bristol, Eng., 1680–1700

MARKS: Touchmark of a rose framed by *ERASMUS DOLE* with decorative breaks within an inner-lined and beaded circle on underside of well (Cotterell, *Old Pewter,* 1410); pseudo hallmarks (1) *ED* with rose below, (2) fleur-de-lis, (3) lion rampant, and (4) tulip, each within a shaped shield on face of rim (Cotterell, *Old Pewter,* 1410)

INSCRIPTIONS: Owner's initials *MF* stamped on underside of well in center; subsequent initials *FFW* scratched on underside of rim

DIMENSIONS: OW. (rim) 13/16", Diam. 9 5/16"

PROVENANCE: Purchased from Thomas D. and Constance R. Williams, Litchfield, Conn.; 1955-287

By the close of the seventeenth century, Bristol had become one of the principal pewter-making centers in provincial England and a major port for the export of pewter wares to the American colonies.[1]

1. Homer and Hall, *Provincial Pewterers,* pp. 115–116.

65 PLATE

Thomas Shakle
London, 1680–1695

MARKS: Indistinct touchmark incorporating, in part, a ducal coronet with devices above and a cross below with leafed fronds to either side and crossing below with first letter *T* of name at top within a vertical oval on underside of well (Peal, *More Pewter Marks,* 4207); indistinct secondary mark incorporating, in part, a rose with crown above with *T* to the left on underside of well (Peal, *More Pewter Marks,* 4207); pseudo hallmarks (1) lion passant within a serrated rectangle, (2) leopard's head crowned, and (3) buckle within a shaped shield on face of rim (Peal, *More Pewter Marks,* 4207)

INSCRIPTIONS: Owner's initials *EW* stamped on face of rim

DIMENSIONS: OW. (rim) 1 1/4", Diam. 9 11/16"

PROVENANCE: Purchased from Dr. Percy E. Raymond, Lexington, Mass.; 1950-863

The marks on this piece are those of Shakle of London, who became a Liveryman of the Company in 1680 and was a prominent maker of plates and dishes for export.[1] He was the master of James Spackman, who worked on his own before becoming a partner with Edward Grant in 1709. The Spackmans remained a leading London pewter-making family into the nineteenth

65–67

century. The use by the Spackmans of a ducal coronet with small crosses and fleurs-de-lis as devices in their marks originated with Shakle. It was not unusual for pewterers to borrow devices from their former master's marks and for these to be passed along.

1. Jan Gadd, "The Crowned Rose as a Secondary Touch," *Journal of the Pewter Society,* XII (autumn 1999), p. 46.

66 PLATE

Benjamin Blackwell
England, 1690–1700

MARKS: Touchmark of a bell with *BENIAMIN* above and *BLACKWELL* below in curved reserves with vestige of a palm frond to either side on underside of well (Cotterell, *Old Pewter,*

DINING WARES 67

437A); secondary mark incorporating, in part, a rose with crown above with a leafed frond to either side and crossing below; pseudo hallmarks (1) lion passant, (2) leopard's head, (3) black letter *D,* and (4) first of two initials *C* or *G* (remainder indistinct) on face of rim

INSCRIPTIONS: Owner's initials *IR* stamped on face of rim below pseudo hallmarks

DIMENSIONS: OW. (rim) 1 1/4", Diam. 9 11/16"

PROVENANCE: Purchased from A. H. Isher & Son, Cheltenham, Eng.; 1958-594, 2

67 PLATE

William Hall
London, 1689–1710

MARKS: Touchmark of a full-length robed figure holding a crooked staff with *WILL•HALL* above and *LONDON* below in curved banners and *16* to the left and *89* to the right within a beaded vertical oval on underside of well (London Touch Plate II, 447; Cotterell, *Old Pewter,* 2093); pseudo hallmarks (1) leopard's head within a shaped shield, (2) lion passant with two pellets above and one below within a serrated rectangle, (3) buckle with two pellets above and one below within a shaped shield, and (4) *I•B* with a pellet above and below within a shaped shield on face of rim

INSCRIPTIONS: Owner's initials *IR* stamped on face of rim below pseudo hallmarks

DIMENSIONS: OW. (rim) 1 5/16", Diam. 9 5/8"

PROVENANCE: Purchased from A. H. Isher & Son, Cheltenham, Eng.; 1958-594, 1

68 PAIR OF PLATES

Alexander Cleeve I
London, dated 1693

MARKS: Touchmark of a hand holding a stemmed rose framed by a palm frond to either side and *ALEX* and *CLEEVE* within curved reserves above and below on underside of well; secondary mark incorporating, in part, a rose with a crown above and a palm frond to either side and crossing below within a beaded vertical oval on underside of well; pseudo hallmarks (1) lion passant within a serrated rectangle, (2) leopard's head

68.1 Stamped owner's initials on face of rim

crowned within a shaped shield, (3) buckle within a shaped shield, and (4) two indistinct initials with a mullet above on face of rim

INSCRIPTIONS: Owner's initials *S* and *G* within separate shaped shields stamped on face of rim opposite pseudo hallmarks; *1693* stamped on face of rim below pseudo hallmarks

DIMENSIONS: OW. (rim) 1 3/16", Diam. 9 1/4"

PROVENANCE: Purchased from A. H. Isher & Son, Cheltenham, Eng.; 1966-301, 1–2

The marks on this pair of plates clearly reflect the close connection between Cleeve and Nicholas Kelk. Cleeve borrowed the device of a right hand holding a long-stemmed rose from the touchmark of Kelk, his former master. He also used a similar, although at that time conventional, secondary mark of a rose with crown above. The pseudo hallmarks are a direct reference to Kelk's. They appear to be of the same design with the same devices. The fourth hallmark even retains Kelk's initials *NK* below a perforated rosette.

69 PLATE

William Burton
London, 1681–1700

MARKS: Touchmark of a hand holding a device, possibly a dagger, with *WILLIAM/BVRTON* in curved reserves above and a palm frond to either side and crossing below within a vertical oval on underside of well (London Touch Plate II, 354; Cotterell, *Old Pewter,* 733); pseudo hallmarks (1) *WB* with rose above within a shaped shield, (2) hand holding a device within an outlined and serrated rectangle, (3) *(P)* within a shaped shield, and (4) lion rampant within an outlined and serrated rectangle on face of rim (Peal, *More Pewter Marks,* 733)

68 PEWTER AT COLONIAL WILLIAMSBURG

68–71

INSCRIPTIONS: Owner's initials *EB* stamped on underside of well

DIMENSIONS: OW. (rim) 1 1/4", Diam. 9 3/4"

PROVENANCE: Purchased from A. H. Isher & Son, Cheltenham, Eng.; 1958-598

Burton was active during most of the second half of the seventeenth century. Apprenticed to Ralph Marsh in 1645, he first entered his mark at Pewterers' Hall in 1653. After the Great Fire of London in 1666, Burton presumably restruck his touch on London Touch Plate I. The mark on this piece, which uses the same device of a hand and dagger, was entered on London Touch Plate II in 1681.

70 PAIR OF PLATES

William Sandys
London, 1690–1710

MARKS: Touchmark of a griffin segreant on a wreath bar with *WILLIAM* above and *SANDYS* below with three fleurs-de-lis on either side at indentations of reserve on underside of both rims (Cotterell, *Old Pewter,* 4110)

INSCRIPTIONS: Owner's initials *H/WS* stamped on underside of both wells in center

DIMENSIONS: OW. (rim) 1 1/4", Diam. 8 15/16"

PROVENANCE: Purchased from A. H. Isher & Son, Cheltenham, Eng.; 1962-246, 1–2

71 PLATE

John Shorey I
London, 1695–1715

MARKS: Indistinct touchmark of a bird facing left and standing on a rose with *IOHN•SHOREY* in a curved reserve above and with a palm frond to either side and crossing below within a vertical oval on underside of well (Cotterell, *Old Pewter,* 4263); indistinct secondary marks (1) a rose with crown above with *LONDON* in a curved reserve above and *GOD PROTECT* below (Cotterell, *Old Pewter,* 4263), (2) *LONDON* within a rectangle (Cotterell, *Old Pewter,* 4263), and (3) *X* crowned, all on underside of well; partially indistinct pseudo hallmarks (1) lion passant within a serrated rectangle, (2) cockerel within a shaped shield, (3) leopard's head crowned within a shaped shield, and (4) *JS* in script within a shaped shield, all on underside of well (Cotterell, *Old Pewter,* 4263)

INSCRIPTIONS: Owner's initials *B/TC* stamped on underside of well

DIMENSIONS: OW. (rim) 1 1/4", Diam. 8 15/16"

PROVENANCE: Kenneth W. Bradshaw, Lincoln, Eng. (sold by him at Sotheby's, June 13, 1977); 1977-221

PUBLISHED: Sales cat., Sotheby's, June 13, 1977, p. 23, lot 79, ill.

Shorey, who entered his first touchmark in 1683, developed a large and thriving business by the early eighteenth century. Shop records dating from 1708 to 1720 indicate just how big it was.[1] He particularly specialized in production of a broad range of plates and dishes. His year-end inventory of finished goods in 1716, for instance, amounted to 12,100 pounds. Included were 2,436 hard metal plates, 1,056 ordinary wrought plates, and 3,096 "ruff" ordinary plates.[2]

Although plates with gadrooned borders were occasionally made throughout the eighteenth century, early examples are particularly rare. The gadroons on this plate are part of the casting, while those on later fancy-rim plates such as no. 141 are invariably applied.

1. Helen Clifford, "Colonel Shorey, citizen and pewterer of London," *Journal of the Pewter Society,* VII (autumn 1990), pp. 130–132; Homer, "John Shorey senior and junior," pp. 51–57.
2. Homer, "John Shorey senior and junior," p. 54.

DISHES AND PLATES/SINGLE BEADS

The moderate width of rims on plates and dishes, still in use today, is first seen in multiple-reeded dishes and plates that date from the last quarter of the seventeenth century. This feature became more standardized with newer plates and dishes with single-beaded edges that first appeared at this same time. This type maintained its popularity into the nineteenth century, offering a more modest and less costly choice than heavier and more pretentious plain and fancy-rimmed alternatives. Single-beaded plates and dishes were particularly popular in the American colonies and during the early Republican period with Americans showing a decided preference for smaller plates, whether made in the United States or imported.

72–73

72 DISH

John Shorey I
London, 1695–1715

MARKS: Touchmark of a bird facing left and standing on a rose with *IOHN•SHOREY* within a curved reserve above and with a palm frond to either side and crossing below within an outlined vertical oval on underside of well (partially indistinct; Cotterell, *Old Pewter,* 4263); secondary marks (1) *LONDON* within a rectangle (Cotterell, *Old Pewter,* 4263), and (2) incorporating, in part, *LONDON* within a larger and more complex mark, both on underside of well; pseudo hallmarks (1) lion passant with two pellets above and one below within a shaped shield, (2) leopard's head crowned within a rectangle with canted corners, (3) standing bird facing within an indistinct reserve, and (4) indistinct, on face of rim (Cotterell, *Old Pewter,* 4263)

INSCRIPTIONS: Owner's initials *AL* stamped on face of rim opposite pseudo hallmarks

DIMENSIONS: OW. (rim) 1 9/16", Diam. 14 1/2"

PROVENANCE: Purchased from A. V. Sutherland-Graeme, London; 1957-195

The flattening of the bead, the hammering of the face of the

DINING WARES 71

rim, and the front-marking of the pseudo hallmarks are all early features associated with single-beaded examples of the pre-1720 period. Further, the size, depth, and proportions of this dish recall early seventeenth-century dishes with bossed centers and narrowed rims (such as nos. 17–21).

Shorey and his son entered into partnership in 1708, and for the next twelve years it was a large and thriving concern. Their sales of flatware (dishes, basins, mazarines, plates, and saucers) were prodigious. The 1716 year-end inventory, for instance, included eight hundred pounds of basins.[1]

1. Homer, "John Shorey senior and junior," pp. 54–55.

73 DISH

John Shorey I or John Shorey II
London, 1705–1720

MARKS: Touchmark of a bird facing left and standing on a leafed frond with *I* to the left, *S* to the right, and *LONDON* in a banner below within a foliated vertical oval on underside of well (Cotterell, *Old Pewter,* 5923A); secondary marks (1) incorporating in part a rose with crown above and palm fronds to either side, and (2) *LONDON* (with *N*s reversed) in a curved and outlined reserve with scrollwork below, both on underside of well; pseudo hallmarks (1) lion passant with two mullets above and one below, (2) leopard's head crowned with two mullets above and one below, (3) wheat sheaf with two mullets above and one below, and (4) indistinct, each within a shield on face of rim (Cotterell, *Old Pewter,* 4263, 5923A)

INSCRIPTIONS: Owner's initials *R* and *H* within separate shaped shields stamped on face of rim opposite pseudo hallmarks

DIMENSIONS: OW. (rim) 2 9/16", Diam. 20 5/16"

PROVENANCE: Purchased from Dr. H. Baines, Harrow on the Hill, Eng.; 1954-645

73.1 Stamped owner's initials on face of rim

The Shoreys' large business was commented on in no. 72. The 1716 year-end inventory lists pewter articles weighing no less than 12,650 pounds. Included was just over a ton of hard metal dishes from eleven to twenty-eight inches in diameter, plus more than three thousand pounds of "ruff" dishes and more than eight hundred pounds of unwrought hard metal dishes.[1]

1. Homer, "John Shorey senior and junior," pp. 54–55.

74 DISH

Maker unidentified
Probably London, 1720–1740

MARKS: None

INSCRIPTIONS: Owner's initials *WE* stamped on face of rim

DIMENSIONS: OW. (rim) 2 1/4", Diam. 18 3/8"

PROVENANCE: John L. Grant, East Preston, Eng.; purchased from Sotheby's; 1973-238

PUBLISHED: Sales cat., Sotheby's, July 25, 1973, lot 115

74.2 Stamped border and owner's initials on face of rim

This dish is one of a small group of approximately a dozen English dishes that were cast as plain examples with their wells then chased using various hammers and punches in a design of a swirl of large gadroons or petals around a central boss. The rims of most of these dishes are decorated with a small-scale running border of repetitive punch work (see no. 24). These dishes were based on Nuremberg brass examples of similar format that were produced in large numbers during the seventeenth and eighteenth centuries. It is not known whether these pewter dishes were used for secular or religious purposes.[1]

1. The most useful article on these dishes is Ronald F. Michaelis, "Decoration on English Pewterware Part II," pp. 20–22.

74

74.1 Underside of dish

75–76

75 DISH

John Aughton
England, 1720–1740

MARKS: Touchmark of a crown over a rose with *IOHN* above and *AVGHTON* below within a beaded vertical oval with a constricted waist on either side stamped twice on underside of well (Cotterell, *Old Pewter,* 149)

INSCRIPTIONS: Owner's initials *IH* stamped on face of rim

DIMENSIONS: OW. (rim) 2 1/4", Diam. 18 1/4"

PROVENANCE: Purchased from William Bozarth, Williamsburg, Va.; 1955-13

76 DISH

John Dolbeare
Ashburton, Eng., 1720–1750

MARKS: Touchmark of a rose with a crown above with a palm frond to either side and crossing below with *I•DOLBEARE* below, all within a conforming reserve stamped twice on underside of well (Cotterell, *Old Pewter,* 1408); pseudo hallmarks (1) *ID,* (2) standing bird with wings raised, (3) Britannia, and (4) lion passant, each within a rectangle with canted or rounded corners on underside of well (Cotterell, *Old Pewter,* 1408)

INSCRIPTIONS: Owner's initials *H/RM* stamped on face of rim

DIMENSIONS: OW. (rim) 2 1/4", Diam. 18 1/4"

PROVENANCE: Gift of Mr. and Mrs. Jess Pavey, Troy, Mich.; G1989-315

77–78

Dolbeare was one of the later members of a notable pewter-making family from the country town of Ashburton in Devonshire. His antecedents from the middle years of the seventeenth century made considerable flatware, ranging from small saucers to large dishes for the Edgcumbe family of nearby Cotehele House.[1] Edmund Dolbeare, one of the makers of the Edgcumbe pewter, left Ashburton about 1670 to become Boston's first pewterer.[2] The maker of this dish died about 1761.[3]

1. Several lots of pewter by the Dolbeares were part of the sale of pewter and other furnishings from Cotehele House that was held at Sotheby's, June 1, 1956. See also Peter Hornsby, "Edmund Dolbeare in England," *Pewter Collectors Club of America Bulletin,* VII (September 1978), pp. 308–311; Webster Goodwin, "5. The Nicholas Dolbeare Dish," *Pewter Collectors Club of America Bulletin,* VII (March 1979), pp. 357–359.
2. Reginald F. French, "The Dolbeares," *Pewter Collectors Club of America Bulletin,* III (May 1954), pp. 57–59; Laughlin, *Pewter in America,* III, pp. 28–31.
3. Cotterell, *Old Pewter,* p. 197, no. 1408.

77 Deep Dish

Thomas Spencer
London, 1705–1720

MARKS: Touchmark of the arms of Spencer within a shield with T✱S above, *1702* below, and a palm frond to either side within an outlined circle on underside of well (Peal, *More Pewter Marks,* 4453); secondary mark incorporating, in part, a rose with crown above with a palm frond to either side on underside of well

INSCRIPTIONS: Owner's initials *RA* stamped on face of rim

DIMENSIONS: OW. (rim) 1 3/4", Diam. 16 3/8"

PROVENANCE: Purchased from the Artisans, Boston, Mass.; 1946-18

DINING WARES 75

78 DEEP DISH

Edward Gregory
Bristol, Eng., 1720–1740

MARKS: Touchmark of a rose framed, in part, by *GREGORY* within an outlined circle stamped twice on underside of well (Cotterell, *Old Pewter,* 2001); pseudo hallmarks (1) *E•G* within a rectangle with outlined and beaded upper and lower borders, (2) Britannia within a shield, (3) lion's head erased within a rectangle with canted corners, and (4) double-headed eagle displayed within a shield, on underside of well (Cotterell, *Old Pewter,* 2002)

INSCRIPTIONS: Owner's initials *M∗L* engraved on face of rim

DIMENSIONS: OW. (rim) 1 9/16", Diam. 17 13/16"

PROVENANCE: Purchased as part of the Glen-Sanders Collection from Robert H. Palmiter, Bouckville, N. Y.; 1964-292

PUBLISHED: *Glen-Sanders Collection,* p. 44, no. 183, ill.

EXHIBITED: The Glen-Sanders Collection from Scotia, New York, Abby Aldrich Rockefeller Folk Art Center, Colonial Williamsburg, Williamsburg, Va., 1966

78.1 Engraved owner's initials on face of rim

This dish descended in the Glen-Sanders families of Scotia, N. Y. The initials *M∗L* engraved on the face of the rim may be for Maria Lansing (d. 1743), first wife of Robert Sanders (1705–1765).

79 DISH

Richard Going
Bristol, Eng., dated 1747

MARKS: Touchmark of a paschal lamb framed by *RICHARD* and *GOING* within curved reserves above and below with vestiges of palm fronds amid scrolls to either side on underside of well (Cotterell, *Old Pewter,* 1909); secondary marks (1) a rose with crown above with vestiges of palm fronds to either side and *BLOCK•TINN* within a curved reserve below on underside of well (Cotterell, *Old Pewter,* 1909), and (2) label *RICHARD:GOING* within a rectangle of scrolled outline on underside of well (Cotterell, *Old Pewter,* 1909)

INSCRIPTIONS: Owner's initials and date *EB/1747/MF* stamped on face of rim

DIMENSIONS: OW. (rim) 2 7/16", Diam. 18 1/8"

PROVENANCE: Purchased from A. H. Isher & Son, Cheltenham, Eng.; 1960-486

79.1 Stamped owner's initials and date

Bristol was a major center throughout the eighteenth and early nineteenth centuries for the export of pewter to America. Going was the most prominent pewterer of that city during the second quarter of the eighteenth century. His output was large and diverse, and a selection of his holloware articles can be seen in his shop window in the painting of Broad Quay, Bristol, by Peter Monamy (1670–1749).[1] That he was a major figure in the export trade is not surprising, since ships could be loaded literally across the street from his shop.

The makers of the following dish and the London firms of John Townsend and of his partnership with Thomas Compton were also deeply involved in the American export trade.

1. Cotterell, *Old Pewter,* p. 21, pl. V; *Journal of the Pewter Society,* XVIII (autumn 2002), front cover.

80 DISH

Robert Bush & Co.
(Robert Bush I, James Curtis, and Preston Edgar I)
Bristol, Eng., 1770–1793

MARKS: Touchmark of cipher *RB* with crest of a goat's head couped on a wreath bar above within an outlined vertical oval stamped twice on underside of well (Peal, *More Pewter Marks,* 739); pseudo hallmarks (1) *B&C^O* within a rectangle with outlined and beaded upper and lower borders, (2) Britannia within a rectangle, (3) lion's head erased within a shield, and (4) rose within a rectangle with canted corners on underside of well (Cotterell, *Old Pewter,* 739)

76 PEWTER AT COLONIAL WILLIAMSBURG

79–80

INSCRIPTIONS: None

DIMENSIONS: OW. (rim) 1 5/8", Diam. 13 7/16"

PROVENANCE: Purchased from the Antique House, Richmond, Va.; X1939-340

81 DISH

John Townsend
London, 1748–1765

MARKS: Touchmark of a lamb passant with a dove with an olive branch in its beak flying above within an outlined vertical oval framed by *IOHN* and *TOWNSEND* within curved reserves above and below and with *17* to one side and *48* to the other on underside of well (Cotterell, *Old Pewter,* 4795); secondary mark of a label with *FENCHURCH/STREET LONDON* within a rectangle with scrolled borders on underside of well (Cotterell, *Old Pewter,* 4795)

INSCRIPTIONS: None

DIMENSIONS: OW. (rim) 1 7/16", Diam. 12 1/16"

PROVENANCE: Purchased from Mrs. Miles White, Jr., Baltimore, Md.; 1933-209

Townsend was the greatest of the export makers. He commenced business in 1748. From 1767 until his death in 1801, he was involved in a succession of partnerships: Townsend & Reynolds (1767–1771), Townsend & Giffin (1771–1778), John Townsend & Co. (1778–1784), and John Townsend and Thomas Compton (1784–1801). Townsend was an active Quaker, and he maintained

DINING WARES 77

81–84

close relations with the Quaker community of eastern Pennsylvania. He visited Philadelphia in 1785, ministering to various meetings there, and in Virginia and North Carolina.[1]

For Americans, Townsend was a major source for finished pewter goods. He and his various partnerships were amazingly productive, and they shipped immense quantities of their wares to these shores. For instance, Daniel Wister, Philadelphia merchant, ordered pewter on a regular basis from Townsend. One of his three orders in 1763 amounted to 12,916 pieces. He requested that part of this shipment should be packed in twenty-four casks. Each containing the same assortment of 256 pieces, they consisted of shallow and deep plates, basins in graduated sizes, tankards, teapots in two sizes, porringers, bottles, and spoons. These, in turn, Wister could wholesale by the barrelful to shopkeepers.[2]

In 1843, John S. Williams, writer and magazine editor on pioneer life, recalled the small house that his family lived in when it arrived in Ohio in 1800:

> In the interior supported on pins driven into the logs, were our shelves. Upon these shelves, my sister displayed in ample order, a host of pewter plates, basins, and dishes, and spoons, scoured and bright. It was none of your new-fangled pewter made of lead, but the best London pewter, which our father himself bought of Townsend, the manufacturer.[3]

The continued importance of pewter in the transmission of culture and manners to less settled parts of the country then and the remembrance and reputation of Townsend is apparent.

This dish is one of a large group of diverse objects that was purchased to furnish the kitchen of the Governor's Palace in Colonial Williamsburg.

1. Charles F. Montgomery, "John Townsend, English Quaker with American Connections," *Pewter Collectors Club of America Bulletin*, V (December 1964), pp. 23–26; Donald M. Herr, *Pewter in Pennsylvania German Churches* (Birdsboro, Pa., 1995), p. 143; Peter Hayward, "The Townsend and Compton Sequence of Businesses," *Journal of the Pewter Society*, XI (autumn 1997), pp. 2–12.
2. Montgomery, "John Townsend, English Quaker," pp. 25–26; Montgomery, *History of American Pewter*, p. 8.
3. Quoted in Montgomery, *History of American Pewter*, p. 16.

82 DISH

John Townsend and Thomas Compton
London, 1780–1801

MARKS: Touchmark of a lamb passant with a dove with an olive branch in its beak flying above within an outlined vertical oval framed by *TOWNSEND* and *& COMPTON* in curved and scrolled reserves on underside of well (Cotterell, *Old Pewter*, 4800); secondary mark of a label with *FENCHURCH/STREET LONDON* within a rectangle with scrolled borders on underside of well (Cotterell, *Old Pewter*, 4800)

INSCRIPTIONS: None

DIMENSIONS: OW. (rim) 1 7/8", Diam. 14 7/8"

PROVENANCE: Purchased from F. J. Van Reeth, New York, N. Y.; 1946-74

83 DISH

John Townsend and Thomas Compton
London, 1780–1801

MARKS: Touchmark of a lamb passant with a dove with an olive branch in its beak flying above framed by *TOWNSEND* and *& COMPTON* within curved reserves above and below on underside of well (Cotterell, *Old Pewter*, 4800); secondary mark of a rose with a crown above framed by *MADE IN* and *LONDON* within curved reserves above and below on underside of well (Cotterell, *Old Pewter*, 4800); pseudo hallmarks (1) arms of the Pewterers' Company, (2) arms of the city of London, (3) lion passant with two pellets above, and (4) *TC* with foliate device below, each within a shaped shield, on underside of well (Cotterell, *Old Pewter*, 4800 with variations)

INSCRIPTIONS: None

DIMENSIONS: OW. (rim) 1 1/4", Diam. 11 15/16"

PROVENANCE: Norton Asner, Baltimore, Md. (sold after his death by Weschler's, Washington, D. C., June 5, 1992); 1992-95

PUBLISHED: Sales cat., Weschler's, Washington, D. C., June 5, 1992, lot 241, ill.

84 Dish

John Townsend and Thomas Compton
London, 1780–1801

MARKS: Touchmark of a lamb passant with a dove with an olive branch in its mouth flying above framed by *TOWNSEND* and *& COMPTON* within curved reserves above and below on underside of well (Cotterell, *Old Pewter,* 4800); secondary mark of a rose with a crown above framed by *MADE IN* and *LONDON* within curved reserves above and below on underside of well (Cotterell, *Old Pewter,* 4800); pseudo hallmarks (1) arms of the Pewterers' Company, (2) arms of the city of London, (3) lion passant with two pellets above, and (4) *TC* with foliate device below, each within a shaped shield, on underside of well (Cotterell, *Old Pewter,* 4800, with variations)

DIMENSIONS: OW. (rim) 1 1/2", Diam. 14 1/2"

PROVENANCE: Gift of Mr. and Mrs. William H. Murdoch, Jr., Brielle, N. J.; G1973-207

85 Dish

Thomas Danforth III
Middletown, Conn., and Wethersfield (Rocky Hill), Conn., 1783–1800

MARKS: Touchmark of a lion rampant on an apparent wreath bar with *T* to the lower left and *D* to the lower right within a shaped vertical oval formed by two cross-hatched C-scrolls on underside of well (Laughlin, *Pewter in America,* I, 364); pseudo hallmarks (1) *T•D,* (2) lion's head erased, (3) Britannia, and (4) dagger, each within a shaped shield, on underside of well (Laughlin, *Pewter in America,* I, 364)

INSCRIPTIONS: None

DIMENSIONS: OW. (rim) 1 1/4", Diam. 11 5/8"

PROVENANCE: Purchased from Mrs. Miles White, Jr., Baltimore, Md.; 1933-212

Danforth was born, raised, and trained in Middletown before moving his family and business to the Rocky Hill section of Wethersfield in 1783. He trained Samuel Kilbourn, the maker of no. 88. Danforth probably learned about business opportunities in Philadelphia from Blakslee Barns, a tinsmith from Berlin, Conn., and maker of no. 86. Danforth opened a Philadelphia shop in 1806/7 and was joined by Barns in 1809. After about 1811, Danforth returned permanently to Connecticut, leaving the Philadelphia shop to his son and others.[1]

1. John Carl Thomas, *Connecticut Pewter and Pewterers* (Hartford, Conn., 1976), pp. 83–86.

86 Dish

Blakslee Barns
Philadelphia, Pa., 1812–1817

MARKS: Touchmark of an American eagle displayed with *B•BARNS* in a curved banner above within a circle on underside of well (Laughlin, *Pewter in America,* II, 551b); secondary mark *B.BARNS/-PHIL^A* stamped with raised letter die on underside of well (Laughlin, *Pewter in America,* II, 558)

INSCRIPTIONS: None

DIMENSIONS: OW. (rim) 1 3/8", Diam. 13 1/8"

PROVENANCE: Gift of Miss Anne Rowland, Williamsburg, Va.; G1983-304

Barns, a tinsmith from Berlin, Conn., formed a close business relationship with Thomas Danforth III. Having worked in Philadelphia, Barns probably persuaded Danforth to set up a second shop in Philadelphia. They shared the same building from 1809, although it is not known whether they ever entered into a formal partnership.[1]

1. Thomas, *Connecticut Pewter and Pewterers,* pp. 84–86.

87 Dish

Jacob Eggleston
Fayetteville, N. C., 1807–1812

MARKS: Touchmark of an American eagle displayed with stars above within a vertical oval with *JACOB* above and *EGGLESTON* below stamped twice on underside of well (Laughlin, *Pewter in America,* I, 386)

INSCRIPTIONS: None

85–88

DIMENSIONS: OW. (rim) 1 1/4", Diam. 11 1/4"

PROVENANCE: Gift of Thomas A. Gray, Winston-Salem, N. C., in memory of John Bivins, Jr.; G2001-826

Eggleston was another Connecticut pewterer who sought a living elsewhere. Born in Middletown, Conn., in 1773, he probably began his apprenticeship with Jacob Whitmore in 1787, and he married Whitmore's daughter, Sarah, in 1792. After several trips south, he purchased property in Fayetteville, N. C., in 1807. He commenced business that year with Daniel Bass, a tinsmith from Berlin, Conn., as his junior partner. They advertised in the *North-Carolina Intelligencer* (Fayetteville), Apr. 17, 1807:

> Eggleston & Bass
> Respectfully inform the Public they have commenced the TIN PLATE WORKING PEWTER and COPPER SMITHS BUSINESS, a few Rods south of the State House, on Person Street, Fayetteville, where they have constantly on hand a large assortment of Pewter, Tin and Japanned Ware, which they will dispose of on the most reasonable terms. To Shopkeepers and others who purchase to sell again, the usual allowance will be made.

The business closed in 1812, and Eggleston died the following year.[1]

1. Thomas, *Connecticut Pewter and Pewterers,* pp. 157–158; Laughlin, *Pewter in America,* III, p. 158; Quincy Scarborough, *Carolina Metalworkers: Coppersmiths, Pewterers, Tinsmiths of North Carolina and South Carolina* (Fayetteville, N. C., 1995), pp. 33–34, 94. Scarborough reproduces the ad as fig. 1.

88 DISH

Samuel Kilbourn
Baltimore, Md., 1814–1839

MARKS: Touchmark of an American eagle displayed with *S.KILBOURN* in a curved banner above and *BALTIMORE* below within a circle of serrated outline (Laughlin, *Pewter in America,* II, 569)

INSCRIPTIONS: None

DIMENSIONS: OW. (rim) 1 3/8", Diam. 13"

PROVENANCE: Gift of Mr. and Mrs. Foster McCarl, Jr., Beaver Falls, Pa.; G1991-651

A native of Wethersfield, Conn., Kilbourn served his apprenticeship there under Thomas Danforth III. He was one of many Connecticut pewterers who sought business opportunities elsewhere. By 1814, he moved with his family to Baltimore, Md., where he plied his trade as a pewterer and tinplate manufacturer until his retirement in 1836.

89 PLATE

Robert Nicholson
London, 1700–1720

MARKS: Touchmark of an eagle displayed with a pellet below each wing standing atop a globe framed by *ROBERT* and *NICHOLSON* within curved reserves above and below and palm fronds to either side on underside of well (Cotterell, *Old Pewter,* 3400); secondary marks (1) label *NICHOLSON* within an outlined rectangle (Cotterell, *Old Pewter,* 3400), (2) rose with crown within scrolls above, a palm frond to either side, and *LONDON* within a curved reserve below (Cotterell, *Old Pewter,* 3400), and (3) *X* crowned for quality, all on underside of well

INSCRIPTIONS: Impaled coat of arms within a lozenge for the widow of an unidentified family engraved within a baroque cartouche on face of rim

DIMENSIONS: OW. (rim) 1 7/16", Diam. 9 3/4"

PROVENANCE: Purchased from Price Glover Inc., New York, N. Y., with funds provided by John A. Hyman, Williamsburg, Va.; G2001-10

89.1 Engraved coat of arms on face of rim

Plates with single-bead edges were popular for a long time in the United States. First achieving prominence in England in the last decade of the seventeenth century, they remained particularly popular in America well into the nineteenth century. This early London example is especially generous in size and in the width of its rim and beaded edge. Engraved coats of arms infrequently appear on plates and dishes of this type. In the eighteenth century, armorial devices are much more readily found on more expensive flatware with plain and fancy rims that more often comprise matched dinner services.

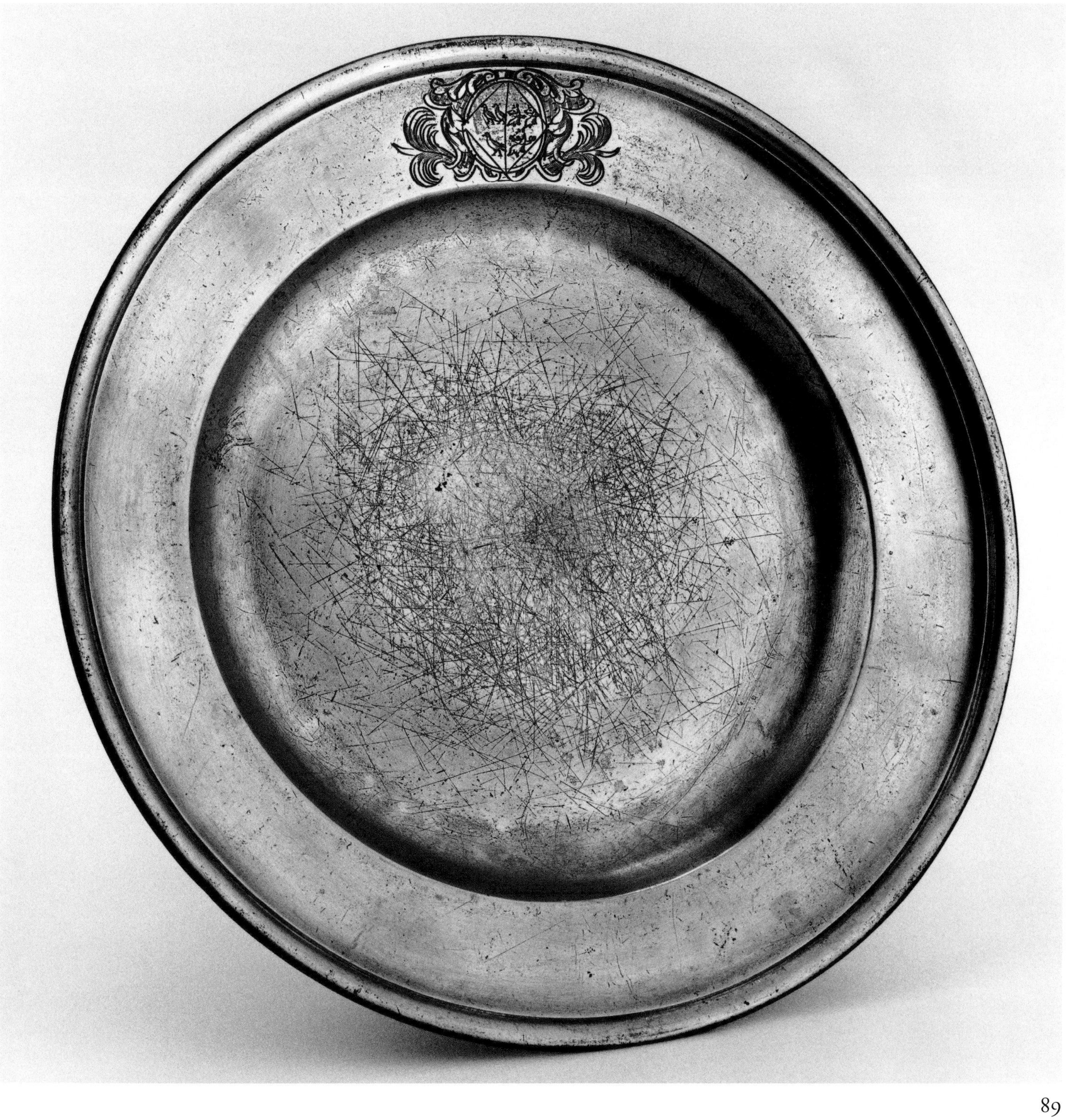

90–91

90 PLATE

Richard Allum
England, 1690–1710

MARKS: Touchmark incorporating, in part, a hand with a pellet to either side with *ALLVM* in a curved reserve below on underside of well (Cotterell, *Old Pewter,* 69); pseudo hallmarks (1) *RA* with pellet above within a serrated rectangle, (2) crown within a shaped shield, (3) hand with two pellets to either side within a serrated rectangle with canted corners, and (4) possible wheat sheaf with two pellets to either side within a shaped rectangle on face of rim (Cotterell, *Old Pewter,* 69)

INSCRIPTIONS: Owner's initials *T/IM* stamped on face of rim opposite pseudo hallmarks and *C/IE* on underside of well in center

DIMENSIONS: OW. (rim) 1 1/4", Diam. 9 1/2"

PROVENANCE: Purchased from Thomas D. and Constance R. Williams, Litchfield, Conn.; 1956-66

The pseudo hallmarks on single-beaded plates and dishes dating before about 1720, such as this example and no. 91, are usually stamped on the face of the rim and on the underside thereafter.

91 PAIR OF PLATES

Stephen Bridges
London, 1700–1720

MARKS: Touchmark of a wheel bordered by *STEPHEN* above and *BRIDGES* below within a beaded circle on underside of each well (Cotterell, *Old Pewter,* 572; Peal, *More Pewter Marks,* 572); secondary marks (1) a rose with crown above and a palm frond to either side and crossing below within a beaded vertical oval on underside of each well (Peal, *More Pewter Marks,* 572), and (2) label *LONDON* within a rectangle of scalloped outline on underside of each well (Peal, *More Pewter Marks,* 572); pseudo hallmarks (1) buckle with pellets above and below, (2) lion passant with pellets above and below, (3) leopard's head crowned, and (4) *SB* with pellets above and below, each within a separate shaped shield, on face of each rim (Peal, *More Pewter Marks,* 572)

INSCRIPTIONS: None

DIMENSIONS: OW. (rim) 1 1/4", Diam. 9"

PROVENANCE: Purchased from Thomas D. and Constance R. Williams, Litchfield, Conn.; 1956-63, 1956-64

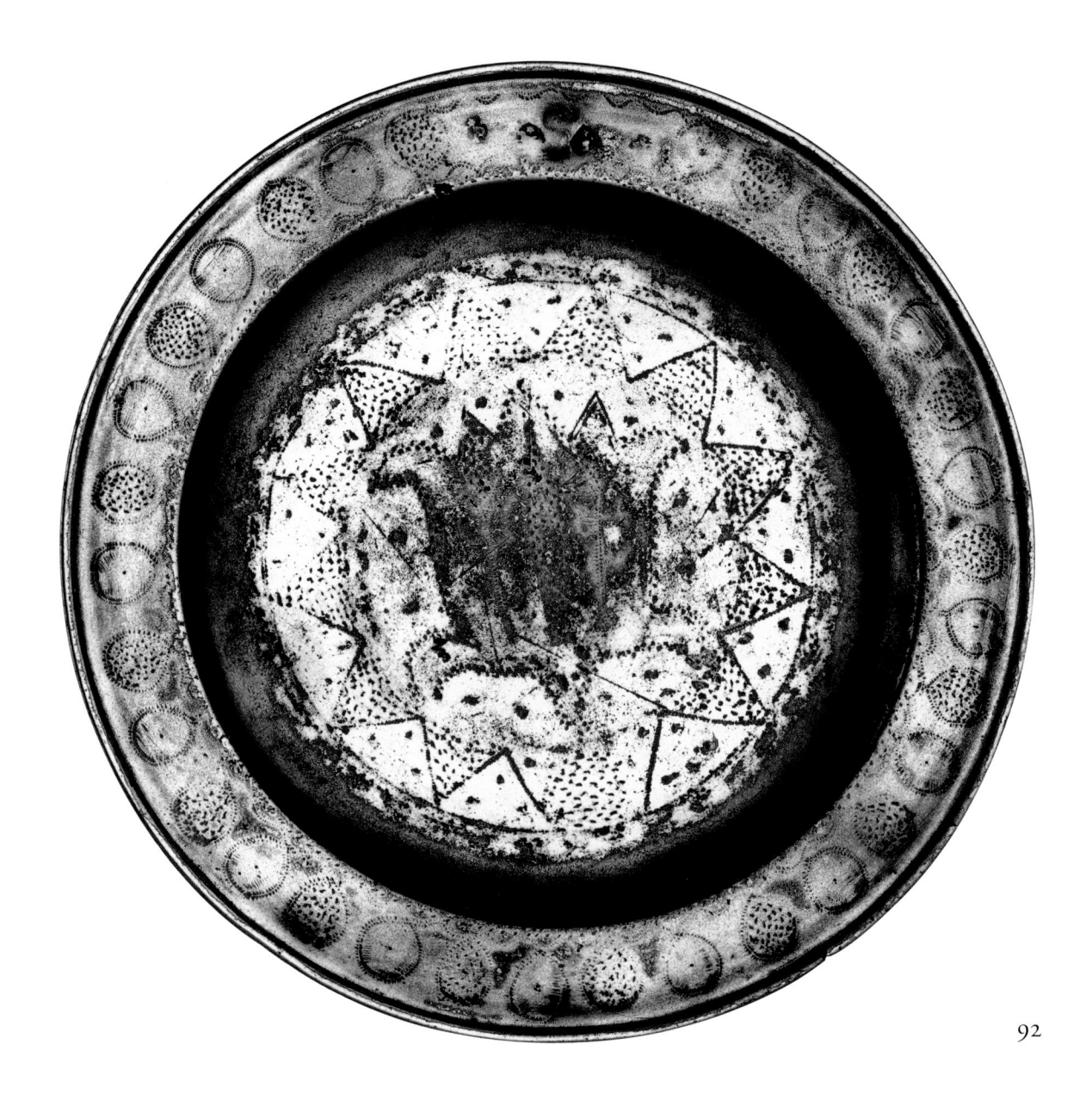

92 PLATE

Probably John Pennington
Tavistock, Eng., 1690–1710

MARKS: Touchmark of a rose with crown above framed by *TAVISTOCKE* within a curved reserve above and scrolls at the sides and below stamped twice on underside of well (Cotterell, *Old Pewter*, 3607); pseudo hallmarks (1) *IP* with a mullet above, (2) an apparent bird with a mullet above, and (3 and 4) indistinct, within variously shaped reserves on face of rim

INSCRIPTIONS: Owner's initial *S* stamped on face of rim between second and third pseudo hallmarks

DIMENSIONS: OW. (rim) 1 1/32", Diam. 8 17/32"

PROVENANCE: Purchased from A. H. Isher & Son, Cheltenham, Eng.; 1966-300

The slightness of its overall dimensions, of the depth of its well, and of the dimensionality of its beaded edge are characteristic of West Country origin. Plates and other products by Pennington are uncommon. A similar plate with a wriggle-engraved bird and flowers is in the Thomas Collection at the Museum of Barnstaple and North Devon in Barnstaple.[1]

1. Ronald F. Homer, *The Stanley E. Thomas collection of pewter in the museum of North Devon, Barnstaple* (London, 1993), p. 36, no. 53, fig. 8, p. 16.

93 Pair of Plates

James Hitchman
London, 1715–1730

MARKS: Touchmark of a lion rampant holding a key with *I•HITCHMAN* in curved arrangement above within a beaded vertical oval on underside of each well (Cotterell, *Old Pewter,* 2340); secondary marks (1) a rose with crown above and *LONDON* below within a beaded vertical oval on underside of each well (Cotterell, *Old Pewter,* 2340), and (2) label incorporating, in part, *I•HITCHMAN/IN•LONDON* in curved arrangement with beaded borders on underside of each well; pseudo hallmarks (1) *I•H* with a pellet above and below, (2) anchor, (3) buckle, and (4) leopard's head within separate shaped shields on underside of each well (Cotterell, *Old Pewter,* 2340)

INSCRIPTIONS: Owner's initials *EW* wriggle engraved on face of each well

DIMENSIONS: OW. (rim) 1 1/8", Diam. 8 1/2"

PROVENANCE: Purchased from A. H. Isher & Son, Cheltenham, Eng.; 1958-588, 1–2

Hitchman is noted for his plates, usually of modest size, that are wriggle engraved with peacocks and flowers. Often made in pairs, the plates are believed to have served as decorative marriage commemorations.

94 PLATE

Fasson & Son
London, 1782–1798

MARKS: Touchmark of a heart within a horseshoe with a dagger above with *FASSON & SON* in curved reserves above and below and scrolls to either side on underside of well; secondary mark of a label *LONDON* within a curved and outlined reserve on underside of well (Cotterell, *Old Pewter,* 1640); pseudo hallmarks (1) golden fleece with two pellets above and one below, (2) lion's head erased, (3) Britannia, and (4) *SE* with two pellets both above and below, each within a separate shaped rectangle on underside of well (Cotterell, *Old Pewter,* 1640)

INSCRIPTIONS: Owner's initials *MD* stamped on face of rim

DIMENSIONS: OW. (rim) 15/16", Diam. 8 1/4"

PROVENANCE: Purchased from Mrs. Miles White, Jr., Baltimore, Md.; 1933-217

Americans favored modest single-bead plates of eight to nine inches in diameter. Plates of this type and size were not only produced in immense number by American artisans, but also specifically supplied to the American market in equally vast quantities by English export makers. The producers of plates through no. 100 all qualify as export makers, and all these examples were acquired from American sources that may suggest long histories of American ownership for at least some.

The hallmarks of Samuel Ellis were used by the succeeding firms of Thomas Swanson, Fasson & Son, and Fasson & Sons. They are also known to have appeared with the touchmark of Richard King.[1] The firm of Fasson & Son consisted of a partnership between John Fasson II and his son, Thomas. It can be documented in business between 1782 and 1798.[2]

1. Herr, *Pewter in Pennsylvania German Churches,* p. 140.
2. Carl Ricketts, *Pewterers of London, 1600–1900* (London, 2001), p. 93.

95 PLATE

Thomas Burford & James Green
London, 1748–1780

MARKS: Touchmark of the arms of Burford (Saint George's cross with two crosslets fitchée) and of Green (three stags trippant, two and one) within separate oval shields in accollé arrangement with *BURFORD* and *& GREEN* in curved reserves above and below on underside of well (London Touch Plate IV, 929; Cotterell, *Old Pewter,* 698); secondary mark of a label with *IN•Y•POULTRY/LONDON* within a curved reserve with scrolled lower edge on underside of well (Cotterell, *Old Pewter,* 698)

INSCRIPTIONS: None

DIMENSIONS: OW. (rim) 15/16", Diam. 7 5/8"

PROVENANCE: Purchased from Dr. Percy E. Raymond, Lexington, Mass.; 1950-879

Burford and Green entered their firm's touchmark on London Touch Plate IV on Oct. 13, 1748. The partnership ended in 1780, when Green retired.[1]

1. Cotterell, *Old Pewter,* p. 171, no. 698.

96 PLATE

Henry Joseph
London, 1760–1785

MARKS: Touchmark of a scallop shell with *HENRY* above and *IOSEPH* below within a shell-shaped reserve on underside of well (London Touch Plate IV, 906; Cotterell, *Old Pewter,* 2686)

INSCRIPTIONS: None

DIMENSIONS: OW. (rim) 15/16", Diam. 7 15/16"

PROVENANCE: Bequest of Grace Hartshorn Westerfield, Camden, Maine; G1974-621

97 PLATE

John Griffith
Bristol, Eng., 1740–1755

MARKS: Touchmark of a griffin passant with a column to either side with *JOHN* with two stars to either side and *GRIFFITH* above and below within a rectangle stamped twice on underside of well (Cotterell, *Old Pewter,* 2021); pseudo hallmarks (1) rose within an octagon, (2) dragon's head erased within a shield, (3) harp within a shield, and (4) *J•G* within a rectangle with

DINING WARES 87

94–97

outlined and beaded upper and lower borders on underside of well (Cotterell, *Old Pewter*, 2021)

INSCRIPTIONS: Owner's initials *P+L* with tree above engraved on underside of well

DIMENSIONS: OW. (rim) 1", Diam. 8"

PROVENANCE: Purchased from Mrs. Miles White, Jr., Baltimore, Md.; 1933-215

97.1 Owner's initials and tree

98 PLATE

John Townsend
London, 1748–1765

MARKS: Touchmark on underside of well, with date and without pellet after surname, partially indistinct (Cotterell, *Old Pewter*, 4795); secondary mark of a label with *FENCHURCH/STREET LONDON* within a rectangle with scrolled borders on underside of well (Cotterell, *Old Pewter*, 4795)

INSCRIPTIONS: None

DIMENSIONS: OW. (rim) 15/16", Diam. 8 1/4"

PROVENANCE: Bequest of Grace Hartshorn Westerfield, Camden, Maine; G1974-622

Townsend commenced business in 1748. From 1767 until his death in 1801, he was involved in a succession of partnerships. For Americans, Townsend was a major source for finished pewter goods. He and his various partnerships were amazingly productive, and they shipped immense quantities of their wares to these shores. Surviving wares of their manufacture are still frequently encountered by American collectors.

99 PAIR OF PLATES

John Townsend
London, 1748–1765

MARKS: Touchmark of a lamb passant and a dove with an olive branch in its beak flying above within an outlined vertical oval framed by *IOHN* and *TOWNSEND* within curved reserves above and below, *17* to the left, and *48* to the right on underside of each well (Cotterell, *Old Pewter*, 4795); secondary mark of a hand holding a flower with a radiant sun above framed by *MADE•IN* above and *LONDON* below and a column to either side with a vertical rectangle with an arched top on underside of each well (Cotterell, *Old Pewter*, 4795); pseudo hallmarks (1) lamb passant with dove flying above within a rounded rectangle, (2) leopard's head within a rounded rectangle, (3) Britannia within a rounded rectangle, and (4) *I•T* with two pellets above and below within a shaped shield on underside of each well (Cotterell, *Old Pewter*, 4795)

INSCRIPTIONS: None

DIMENSIONS: OW. (rim) 1 1/8", Diam. 9 1/4"

PROVENANCE: Anonymous gifts; G1971-1162, G1971-1163

100 DEEP PLATE

John Townsend
London, 1748–1770

MARKS: Touchmark of a lion passant and a dove with an olive branch in its beak flying above within a beaded vertical oval framed by *IOHN* and *TOWNSEND* within curved reserves above and below, *17* to the left, and *48* to the right on underside of well (Cotterell, *Old Pewter*, 4795); secondary mark of a label with *FENCHURCH/STREET LONDON* within a rectangle with scrolled borders on underside of well (Cotterell, *Old Pewter*, 4795)

INSCRIPTIONS: Probable owner's or possible retailer's stamp *R•HULL* within a serrated rectangle stamped on face of rim

DIMENSIONS: OW. (rim) 15/16", Diam. 8 3/4"

PROVENANCE: Purchased from Charlotte and Edgar Sittig, Shawnee-on-Delaware, Pa.; 1955-356

100.1 Probable owner's stamp

This deep plate is not of conventional soup plate form. It is of uncommon conformation and probably was intended for an unknown specialized use.

DINING WARES 89

98–100

101 SET OF EIGHT PLATES

Jacob Whitmore
Middletown, Conn., 1758–1790

MARKS: Touchmark of a rose with crown above framed by *JACOB* and *WHITMORE* within separate curved reserves above and below stamped twice on the underside of each well (Laughlin, *Pewter in America*, I, 383)

INSCRIPTIONS: None

DIMENSIONS: OW. (rim) 1 1/8", Diam. 7 15/16"

PROVENANCE: Louis G. Myers, New York, N. Y. (sold in 1931 to the Yale University Art Gallery); sold by the Yale University Art Gallery to the Morris House, Stamford, Conn.; 1966-356, 1–8

PUBLISHED: Myers, *Some Notes on American Pewterers,* p. 68, ill.; ninth plate in this set, belonging to the York University Art Gallery, appears in Hood, "American Pewter, Garvan," p. 14, no. 12

When Louis G. Myers acquired these plates, then nine in number, in Boston, Mass., Whitmore had not been identified as an American maker. Myers was able to do so from his knowledge of Whitmore's association with Thomas Danforth II that began in Middletown, Conn., in the late 1750s. He knew that Danforth died in 1782 with 260 pounds of his molds that were jointly owned with Whitmore. Pieces survive that were cast from the same mold but in some instances were marked by Danforth and in others by Whitmore.[1]

These plates have survived remarkably preserved with their skimming lines still clearly evident.

1. Louis Guerineau Myers, *Some Notes on American Pewterers* (Garden City, N. Y., 1926), pp. 67–68; Thomas, *Connecticut Pewter and Pewterers,* pp. 69, 148–149.

102 PLATE

Love touch
Pennsylvania, 1770–1800

MARKS: Touchmark of two birds facing one another under a crown with *LO* to the left and *VE* to the right within a beaded circle on underside of well (Laughlin, *Pewter in America,* III, 868); secondary marks (1) label *LONDON* within a curved and serrated rectangle on underside of well (Laughlin, *Pewter in America,* III, 868), and (2) *X* crowned quality mark on underside of well (Laughlin, *Pewter in America,* III, 869)

INSCRIPTIONS: None

DIMENSIONS: OW. (rim) 1 1/8", Diam. 7 7/8"

PROVENANCE: Purchased from Carl Jacobs, Southwick, Mass.; 1950-38

The Love touch, found on a considerable quantity of southeastern Pennsylvania pewter, was attributed during most of the last century to Abraham Hasselberg (active 1750–1779) and to his son-in-law, John Andrew Brunstrom (active 1781–1793).[1] It is now believed that a larger number of pewterers from the Philadelphia area used this touchmark over a longer period of time, from about 1760 to 1820.[2]

1. Laughlin, *Pewter in America,* II, pp. 55–56; Laughlin, *Pewter in America,* III, pp. 130–132, 134–136, pl. CIX, figs. 867–871.
2. Herr, *Pewter in Pennsylvania German Churches,* pp. 133–134.

103 PLATE

Thomas Danforth III
Philadelphia, Pa., 1807–1813

MARKS: Touchmark of an eagle with spread wings holding an olive branch in its right talon and standing on an outlined horizontal oval enclosing *TD,* all within an outlined circle on underside of well (Laughlin, *Pewter in America,* I, 366); secondary mark of a label *T.DANFORTH/PHILAD*[A] within a double rectangle on underside of well (Laughlin, *Pewter in America,* I, 372)

INSCRIPTIONS: None

DIMENSIONS: OW. (rim) 1 1/8", Diam. 7 3/4"

PROVENANCE: Purchased from F. J. Van Reeth, New York, N. Y.; 1946-64

Danforth (1756–1820) was the eldest son of the third generation of the remarkable Danforth family of pewterers. No fewer than nineteen members in five generations practiced the trade. They not only defined Connecticut pewter but also greatly influenced the production, marketing, and use of pewter throughout this country well into the nineteenth century. That this plate bears Danforth's Philadelphia mark is indicative of the continual expansion into new markets by Connecticut's enterprising makers. For a period of time after 1806/7, Danforth maintained businesses in both Philadelphia and Wethersfield, Conn.

101–104

104 PLATE

George Lightner
Baltimore, Md., 1806–1815

MARKS: Touchmark of an American eagle displayed with a vertically striped and starred shield superimposed on its body and holding an olive branch in its right talons and a cluster of arrows in its left talons with *G•LIGHTNER* above and *BALTIMORE* below within a serrated circle stamped twice on underside of well (Laughlin, *Pewter in America,* II, 567)

INSCRIPTIONS: None

DIMENSIONS: OW. (rim) 1 1/8", Diam. 8 3/4"

PROVENANCE: Purchased from John Carl Thomas, Hanover, Conn.; 1993-79

Lightner (1749–1815) was a tavern keeper and carpenter in his early years. He first advertised his tin and pewter manufactory in a Baltimore newspaper on Nov. 21, 1806. His pewter business appears to have been substantial. The 1815 inventory of his estate lists more than 1,500 pounds of finished pewter and 323 pounds of old pewter. His "Pewter Casting Moulds" weighed 419 pounds. He is principally known by collectors for his flatware, that is, plates, dishes, and basins.[1]

1. Laughlin, *Pewter in America,* II, pp. 78–79.

105–107 THREE SMALL PLATES OR SAUCERS

Makers unidentified
America, 1760–1820

MARKS: None

INSCRIPTIONS: None

DIMENSIONS: OW. (105 rim) ¾", Diam. 6", OW. (106 rim) ⅝", Diam. 5⅛", OW. (107 rim) ⅝", Diam. 4 11/16"

PROVENANCE: Purchased from Dr. Percy E. Raymond, Lexington, Mass.; 1950-899 (105); 1950-898 (106); 1950-897 (107)

These small plates are descendants of the traditional saucer. Collectors sometimes refer to them as spice plates.

105–107

DINING WARES 93

Dishes and Plates/Plain rims

Although rare examples of plates of this type from the last decade or so of the seventeenth century are known, such as no. 108, it was not until 1730 that plain-rim plates and dishes became a standard pattern. This pattern was always more popular in England than in America, where the more modest and less costly single-bead type was preferred into the early nineteenth century.

108

108 Plate

Richard Fletcher
London, 1678–1702

MARKS: Touchmark of a windmill with *R* to the left and *F* to the right within a beaded circle on underside of rim (London Touch Plate I, 312; Cotterell, *Old Pewter*, 1697); secondary marks incorporating, in part, a rose framed by crossed palm fronds within an apparent circle on underside of rim and quality mark *X* above pseudo hallmarks on underside of rim; pseudo hallmarks (1) lion passant with mullet below and pellets above, (2) buckle with mullet below, (3) leopard's head with mullet below, and (4) *RF*, each within a shaped shield on underside of rim opposite touchmark and principal secondary mark (Cotterell, *Old Pewter*, 1697)

INSCRIPTIONS: Unidentified impaled arms within a shield with plumed mantling engraved on face of rim

108.1 Engraved coat of arms on face of rim

DIMENSIONS: OW. (rim) 1 3/8", Diam. 9 5/16"

PROVENANCE: Kenneth W. Bradshaw, Lincoln, Eng. (sold by him at Sotheby's, June 13, 1977); 1977-218

PUBLISHED: Sales cat., Sotheby's, June 13, 1977, p. 8, lot 26, ill.

This example dates several decades before the customary production of plain-rim plates.[1] It may reflect the plain rims of moderate width that had been used on basins throughout the seventeenth century rather than late broad rims or multiple reeds that were in vogue when this plate was made. Fletcher struck the mark on this plate on London Touch Plate I in 1678. Although he worked into the first years of the eighteenth century, the style of the engraved armorials would suggest a date early in his working career.

1. Vanessa Brett illustrates details of the armorial engraving from another plate in the set in *Phaidon Guide to Pewter* (Oxford, Eng., 1981), pp. 38, 48, ill. David Hall illustrates a further plate of this type with front-marked pseudo hallmarks and armorials of seventeenth-century appearance by William Greenbank II (1674–1714) of Worcester, Eng., in "Some Worcester Pewter," *Journal of the Pewter Society*, XII (spring 1999), p. 33, fig. 37. Hornsby illustrates a front-marked example without armorials, also of probable late seventeenth-century date, in *Pewter of the Western World*, p. 130, fig. 330.

109 DINNER SERVICE

Four dishes
Twelve dinner plates
Twelve soup plates

Alexander Cleeve II
London, 1729–1750

MARKS: Marked with varying degrees of completeness and clarity; touchmark of a stemmed rose framed by *ALEX* within a curved reserve above, a pilaster on a plinth to either side, and *CLEEVE* within a rectangle below on the undersides of wells (Cotterell, *Old Pewter*, 961); secondary marks (1) a rose with crown above framed by *MADE•IN* within a curved reserve above, a pilaster on a plinth to either side, and *LONDON* within a rectangle below on undersides of wells (Cotterell, *Old Pewter*, 961), and (2) quality mark *X* with crown stamped above touchmark and principal secondary mark on underside of each well; pseudo hallmarks (1) lion passant with two pellets above and one below, (2) leopard's head crowned, (3) black letter *F*, and (4) *AC* with two pellets above and one below, within separate shaped shields on undersides of wells (Peal, *More Pewter Marks*, 960)

INSCRIPTIONS: Crest of a peacock in his pride engraved on face of each rim for an unidentified family

DIMENSIONS: OW. (rims larger dishes) 2 1/4", Diam. (larger dishes) 18 1/8", OW. (rims smaller dishes) 2", Diam. (smaller dishes) 16 1/2", OW. (rims plates) 1 1/4", Diam. (plates) 9 1/2"

PROVENANCE: The following plates and dishes were purchased from A. V. Sutherland-Graeme, London; 1955-423, 1–2 (larger dishes); 1955-424, 1–2 (smaller dishes); 1955-421, 1–12 (dinner plates); 1955-422, 1–12 (soup plates)

During the first half of the eighteenth century, a revolution took place in English dining habits. Polite dining increasingly became a highly organized social ritual and means of genteel expression. The English adopted the French dinner service with matching plates and dishes in graduated sizes and a host of specialized objects to be placed in various symmetries in the formalized sequence of dinner courses. Pewter services are first evident during the second quarter of the century, at the same time that matched services of white salt-glazed stoneware were first produced. The presence of large numbers of pewter plates and dishes in gentry households is indicative of its use, in part, for formal meals that required numerous plates for the various courses. At the time of his death in 1745, Sir Robert Walpole owned no fewer than 558 plates (see no. 113).

The maker of this service was, like his father, a supplier of pewter to the Hudson's Bay Company, both as stores for company use and as merchandise for trade goods. Most of the pewter that he supplied between 1729 and 1737 was for company use at Fort Albany, Fort York, Fort Churchill, and Moose River, and for use aboard ships. Included are plates, dishes, basins, porringers, salts, spoons, inkstands, chamber pots, bedpans, a quart tankard, and a gallon measure. Spoons were the customary commodity Cleeve supplied for trade goods.[1]

Cleeve's son, Richard, was also involved in trade with the Hudson's Bay Company. In 1759, George Washington purchased from him a pewter dinner service consisting of "2 dozen assorted

DINING WARES 95

Superfine hard mettle dishes and 6 dozen of the very best Plates." They weighed 183 pounds at a cost of 13 pence a pound. Washington, in gentry manner, had each of the plates and dishes engraved with his crest at threepence each.[2] Examples of the plates and dishes from this service are at Mount Vernon and in private collections.

1. Red Smith, "The Hudson Bay Company and the 18th Century London Pewterers; and Mathew Rice, Journeyman Pewterer with the Hudson's Bay Company," *Journal of the Pewter Society,* XIII (spring 2000), pp. 17–24.
2. Montgomery, *History of American Pewter,* p. 13. The quoted description of the pieces was taken by Montgomery from the "Invoice of Sundry Goods Shipped by Robert Cary and Company . . . on the account and risque of Col. George Washington," Mount Vernon Archives.

109.1 Engraved crest on face of plate rims

109.2 Engraved crest on face of dish rims

96   PEWTER AT COLONIAL WILLIAMSBURG

110 SET OF FOUR DISHES

Alexander Cleeve II
London, 1730–1750

MARKS: Touchmark partially indistinct incorporating, in part, an open hand holding a stemmed rose with palm fronds to either side and *CLEEVE* below on underside of wells; secondary marks (1) a rose with crown above, scrolls to the sides, and *LONDON* within a curved reserve below, all within a beaded circle on underside of wells, (2) label with *A.CLEEVE* within a rectangle on underside of wells, and (3) quality mark *X* stamped on underside of wells; pseudo hallmarks (1) possible lion passant, (2) leopard's head crowned, (3) black letter *F*, and (4) indistinct, within separate reserves on underside of wells (possibly Peal, *More Pewter Marks*, 960)

110.1 Engraved crest on face of dish rims

INSCRIPTIONS: Crest engraved on face of each rim probably for a member of the Harvey family

DIMENSIONS: OW. (rims 50–51) 2 11/16", Diam. 20 1/4", OW. (rims 52–53) 2 7/16", Diam. 18 1/8"

PROVENANCE: Purchased from Thomas D. and Constance R. Williams, Litchfield, Conn.; 1956-50–53

111–112

111 DISH

John Duncumb
Wribbenhall, near Bewdley, Eng., ca. 1702–1745

MARKS: Touchmark of the arms of Duncumb (a chevron engrailed among three talbots' heads erased) within a shield with scrolled and foliate decoration framed by *IOHN•DUNCUMB•FREEMAN•OF* within a vertical oval on underside of well (Cotterell, *Old Pewter,* 1465); secondary marks (1) a rose with crown above with a palm frond to either side and crossing below within a vertical oval on underside of well to right of touchmark (Cotterell, *Old Pewter,* 1465), and (2) label *LONDON* in arched arrangement within a curved and outlined reserve with pendant scrolls at either end on underside of well below and between the touchmark and the principal secondary mark (Cotterell, *Old Pewter,* 1465)

INSCRIPTIONS: None

DIMENSIONS: OW. (rim) 2 9/16", Diam. 20 1/4"

PROVENANCE: Purchased from Dr. Percy E. Raymond, Lexington, Mass.; 1950-787

Duncumb (ca. 1684–1745), after completing his apprenticeship with William Wood II of Birmingham, commenced a large business in the early years of the eighteenth century, first in Birmingham and after 1720 in Wribbenhall and across the Severn River in Bewdley. A surviving account book (1718–1724) gives an idea of the extent of the business. It shows that Duncumb produced no less than twenty tons of pewterware annually, mostly plates and dishes like no. 111. This amount is equivalent to about fifty thousand common dinner plates a year. Homer and Hall have estimated that Duncumb probably employed twenty or so workers.[1]

1. Homer and Hall, *Provincial Pewterers,* p. 64. See also Ronald F. Homer and David W. Hall, "The Duncumbs; pewterers of Wribbenhall," *Journal of the Pewter Society,* IV (autumn 1984), pp. 128–132.

112 DISH

John Jupe
London, 1737–1760

MARKS: Touchmark of a rose with a fleur-de-lis and *IOHN* above, *IUPE* below within curved reserves, and with a vestigial palm frond to either side on underside of rim (London Touch Plate IV, 878; Cotterell, *Old Pewter,* 2693); secondary marks (1) a rose with crown above with *MADE IN* above and *LONDON* below within curved reserves and with a vestigial palm frond to either side on underside of rim (Cotterell, *Old Pewter,* 2693), (2) quality mark *X* with crown above stamped on underside of rim between touchmark and principal secondary mark, and (3) label *SUPERFINE/HARD METAL* within an oblong scrolled cartouche on underside of rim opposite other marks (Cotterell, *Old Pewter,* 2693)

INSCRIPTIONS: Crest of an unidentified family engraved on face of rim

DIMENSIONS: OW. (rim) 2 7/16", Diam. 20 1/4"

PROVENANCE: Purchased from Dr. Percy E. Raymond, Lexington, Mass.; 1950-788

112.1 Engraved crest on face of rim

113 SIX PLATES

Thomas Ridding (1)
John Carpenter (2–6)
London, 1726–1745

MARKS: Touchmark (1) of a pelican in her piety with her young before her flanked by a palm frond to either side and crossing below with *THOMAS* and *RIDDING* in curved reserves above and below on underside of rim (Cotterell, *Old Pewter,* 3942); secondary mark of a quality mark *X* with crown above on underside of rim opposite touchmark; touchmark (2–6) of a globe with a pair of dividers spread above with *IOHN* and *CARPENTER* in curved reserves above and below and decorative scrollwork at sides on underside of each well (London Touch Plate III, 718; Cotterell, *Old Pewter,* 810)

INSCRIPTIONS: Crest within the collar of the Order of the Garter for Sir Robert Walpole (1676–1745), First Earl of Orford, of Houghton, Norfolk, engraved on the face of each rim

DIMENSIONS: OW. (rim 1) 1 3/8", Diam. 9 9/16", OW. (rims 2–6) 1 7/16", Diam. 9 13/16"

PROVENANCE: Purchased from Carl and Celia Jacobs, Southwick, Mass.; 1958-231, 1–6

These plates are from an immense service that was made for and engraved with the crest of Sir Robert Walpole (1676–1745), First Earl of Orford, of Houghton, Norfolk, who served as First Lord of the Treasury, Chancellor of the Exchequer, and Prime Minister. Each of the plates, and other surviving articles from the service, is engraved with his crest within the collar of the Order of the Garter, the most prestigious of the royal orders. The service probably dates after his appointment by the king to this order.

It would appear that Walpole may have used these plates and their matching dishes, at least, in part, for large entertainments at Houghton. No fewer than "Forty six Dozen and half of Pewter Plates" were listed in the "Store Room" there in the 1745 inventory of his estate. A 1792 inventory records, "In the

113.1. Engraved crest enclosed within the Garter collar

DINING WARES 99

113

press in the Maid's Room 49 round Pewter dishes 18 round ditto . . . 4 old round dishes . . . 36 Doz & 9 Meat Plates."[1] When the service was sold at auction in 1994, it consisted then of only two dozen dinner plates and six matching circular dishes in three sizes, all by Thomas Ridding of London.[2]

1. Sales cat., Christie's, Dec. 8, 1994, lot 121.
2. *Ibid.,* lots 121–125.

114 SIX PLATES

Hellier Perchard
London, 1709–1759

MARKS: Touchmark of an anchor with *17* to the left and *09* to the right framed by *HELLIER* within a curved reserve above, a pilaster on a plinth to either side, and *PERCHARD* within a rectangle below on underside of each well (Peal, *More Pewter Marks,* 3611); secondary mark of a label *MADE IN/LONDON* within an oblong scrolled cartouche on underside of each well; pseudo hallmarks (1) *W.^{M}/* [rosette] */D$_E$J,* (2) eagle displayed, (3) leopard's head, and (4) lion passant, within separate shaped shields on underside of each well (Peal, *More Pewter Marks,* 1349)

114.1 Engraved owner's initial on underside of rim

INSCRIPTIONS: Owner's initial *S* engraved on underside of each rim

DIMENSIONS: OW. (rim) 1 1/4", Diam. 9 5/8"

PROVENANCE: Purchased from Carl and Celia Jacobs, Southwick, Mass.; 1959-246, 1–6

A native of the Isle of Guernsey, Perchard lived and worked in London from the beginning of his apprenticeship under Charles Johnson in 1702 until his death in 1759.

DINING WARES 101

115 Plate

Maker unidentified
Probably London, ca. 1757

MARKS: No apparent touchmark; secondary marks (1) label *SUPER•FINE/HARD•METAL* within a double rectangle with zigzag outlining and pendant scrollwork and central mask, and (2) quality mark *X* with crown above on underside of each well

INSCRIPTIONS: *Success to the/E.C./KING of PRUSSIA/1757/and His Forces* engraved on face of well; owner's initials *T/IS* stamped on underside of well

DIMENSIONS: OW. (rim) 1 3/16", Diam. 9 1/8"

PROVENANCE: Purchased from Jellinek & Sampson, London; 1974-676

This plate reflects England's alliance with Prussia during the Seven Years' War (1756–1763). Plates supporting the Prussian cause are much more common in various English ceramics than in pewter.

116 Plate

Maker unidentified
Virginia or Maryland, 1740–1770

MARKS: Touchmark *EW:VIRGINIA* cast in the mold on underside of rim (Laughlin, *Pewter in America,* III, 885)

INSCRIPTIONS: None

DIMENSIONS: OW. (rim) 1 3/8", Diam. 9 1/8"

PROVENANCE: Oliver and Marion Deming, Connecticut collectors, acquired this plate and a similar example in Frederick, Md., in the 1940s; Charles F. Montgomery, Wallingford, Conn., purchased this plate from them and gave it to CWF; G1949-216

This plate is one of a very small group of similar examples that bears the cast mark *EW:VIRGINIA* under the rim. These few plates are the only known pieces to carry this mark. In place of a more likely candidate, this mark has long been associated with the pewterer Edward Willett of Upper Marlboro, Md. Willett died in 1745, and Laughlin argues cogently that Willett probably did not acquire a new plate mold in his seventies when plates of this type became fashionable.[1]

Aside from this plate and a similar one with the same mark, a further plate from this group was owned in 1949 by Melville T. Nichols of Medford, Mass. Nichols records that he bought it on Nov. 28, 1940, from M. B. Dean, an antiques dealer from Winchester, Va., and Damariscotta, Maine. Dean had purchased the plate from Mrs. Luther Pannett, widow of the sheriff of Frederick Co., Va.[2] These plates were found within approximately fifty miles of one another, which may be useful to the eventual identification of their maker.

There are scattered references in Virginia documents to pewter plates and dishes of local manufacture. The will of Edmund Bayley of Accomack Co., dated 1751, contains "1 dozen of Virginia made Pewter plates."[3] The 1776 inventory of the estate of Phillip Ludwell Lee of Stratford, Westmoreland Co., lists "20 old virg'a pewter plates" as in the kitchen, along with "2 Doz London Plates shallow, 1 doz. Ditto deep."[4] The "3 do [shallow] Country cast do. [pewter dishes]" are part of the pewter stored in the dairy in the 1781 inventory of the estate of Richard Mitchell of Lancaster Co.[5]

1. Laughlin, *Pewter in America,* III, pp. 148–150.
2. Melville T. Nichols to Eleanor L. Duncan, Dec. 12, 1949, CWF acc. file G1949-216.
3. Will of Edmund Bayley, Mar. 26, 1751, Accomack Co., Va., Records, Wills, and Administrations, 1749–1752, p. 347.
4. Inventory of the estate of Phillip Ludwell Lee, Mar. 20, 1776, Westmoreland Co., Va., Records, Inventories, and Accounts, 6, 1776–1790, p. 174.
5. Inventory of the estate of Richard Mitchell, September 1781, Lancaster Co., Va., Records, Wills, Etc., 20, 1770–1783, p. 215.

117 PLATE

Thomas Bacon
London, 1730–1760

MARKS: No apparent touchmark; secondary marks (1) *THO:BACON/THE MAKER* within outlined compartments within an oblong rectangle with a serrated edge on underside of rim (Peal, *More Pewter Marks,* 181), (2) rose with crown above with *MADE IN* and *LONDON* within curved reserves above and below on underside of well (Cotterell, *Old Pewter,* 181; Peal, *More Pewter Marks,* 181), and (3) quality mark *X* with crown above stamped on underside of well

INSCRIPTIONS: Owner's cipher *VR* doubled and reversed for a member of the Van Rensselaer family of New York engraved on face of rim

DIMENSIONS: OW. (rim) 1 1/4", Diam. 9 11/16"

PROVENANCE: Purchased from Dr. Percy E. Raymond, Lexington, Mass., who had purchased it many years before in a shop in Hudson, N. Y.; 1950-869

PUBLISHED: Raymond, "Ancestral Pewter," pp. 10–11, figs. 4 and 4a

Percy Raymond, the plate's last owner, felt that it may have been owned originally by Colonel Johannes Van Rensselaer of Fort Crailo in Greenbush, N. Y. Raymond called it his Yankee Doodle plate, since the words to the song were supposedly written in the garden of this house in 1758.[1]

117.1 Engraved owner's cipher on face of rim

1. Percy E. Raymond, "Ancestral Pewter," *American Collector,* XVI (August 1947), p. 10.

118 PLATE

Samuel Ellis I
London, 1718–1765

MARKS: Touchmark of the golden fleece with annulets above and below with *SAMUEL* and *ELLIS* in curved and outlined reserves above and below within a vertical oval on underside of well (Cotterell, *Old Pewter,* 1547); secondary marks (1) a rose with crown above with *LONDON* within a curved reserve above and flanked by a palm frond to either side and crossing below on underside of well (Cotterell, *Old Pewter,* 1547), and (2) label *S:ELLIS/LONDON* in curved arrangement with scrolls below on underside of well (Cotterell, *Old Pewter,* 1547); pseudo hallmarks (1) golden fleece with two pellets above and one below, (2) lion's head erased, (3) Britannia, and (4) *SE* with two pellets above and one below, each within a separate shaped shield on underside of well (Cotterell, *Old Pewter,* 1547)

INSCRIPTIONS: Owner's initials *ND* stamped on face of rim

DIMENSIONS: OW. (rim) 1 1/8", Diam. 8 3/4"

PROVENANCE: Purchased from Thomas D. and Constance R. Williams, Litchfield, Conn.; 1956-57

DINING WARES 103

119 Four Plates

John Townsend
London, 1748–1766

MARKS: Touchmark on the underside of each indistinct but of the type used by this maker with *17* on the left and *48* on the right (Cotterell, *Old Pewter,* 4795); secondary marks (1) label *MADE IN/LONDON* within an outlined oblong with canted lower corners and scrolled top (Cotterell, *Old Pewter,* 4795), (2) label *SUPERFINE/HARD METAL* in curved arrangement within an outlined reserve with central scrolled pendant (Cotterell, *Old Pewter,* 4795), and (3) quality mark *X* with crown above, all on underside of each well

119.1 Engraved owner's cipher on face of rim

INSCRIPTIONS: Ornamented cipher *STM* engraved on the face of each rim

DIMENSIONS: OW. (rim) 1 1/2", Diam. 9 7/8"

PROVENANCE: Purchased from Mrs. Miles White, Jr., Baltimore, Md.; 1933-243, 1–4

120 Six Plates

Maker unidentified
Probably London, 1750–1780

120.1 Engraved owner's crest on face of rims

MARKS: No apparent touchmark; secondary marks (1) a rose with crown above with *MADE IN* and *LONDON* within curved reserves above and below, (2) quality mark *X* with crown above stamped on either side of previous mark, and label *SUPERFINE/HARD METAL* within an oblong reserve of scrolled outline, all on underside of each well

INSCRIPTIONS: Unidentified crest of a bishop's miter engraved on the face of each rim

DIMENSIONS: OW. (rim) 1 3/8"; Diam. 9 13/16"

PROVENANCE: Purchased from A. V. Sutherland-Graeme, London; 1956-447, 1–6

These plates may have belonged to a bishop or a religious group. Hellier Perchard of London made two dozen similar plates about 1740 for Edward Chandler, Bishop of Durham. These latter plates are also engraved with a bishop's mitre, although issuing from a coronet. Pewter known to have been made for the domestic use of important clerics is uncommon.[1]

1. David Moulson, "Rare 'Durham' plates," *Journal of the Pewter Society,* VIII (autumn 1991), pp. 66–67.

104 PEWTER AT COLONIAL WILLIAMSBURG

121 TWELVE PLATES

Joseph & James Spackman
London, 1782–1800

MARKS: Touchmark of a ducal coronet with a fleur-de-lis and two crosses formée above and a cross formée over crossed palm fronds below with *JOS^H & JA^S* above and *SPACKMAN* below in curved reserves on underside of each base (London Touch Plate IV, 1045; Cotterell, *Old Pewter,* 4442); secondary marks (1) a rose with crown above with *MADE IN* above and *LONDON* below in curved reserves (Cotterell, *Old Pewter,* 4442), and (2) label *CORNHILL/LONDON* in curved arrangement within an outlined reserve with central scrolled pendant (Cotterell, *Old Pewter,* 4442), both on underside of each well; pseudo hallmarks (1) arms of the Pewterers' Company, (2) leopard's head crowned, (3) lion passant with two mullets above and one below, and (4) *I•S* with a bellflower above and below, all within separate shaped shields on the underside of each base

INSCRIPTIONS: None

DIMENSIONS: OW. (rim) 1 1/4", Diam. 9 1/4"

PROVENANCE: Purchased from Thomas D. and Constance R. Williams, Litchfield, Conn.; 1956-544, 1–12

122 PLATE

Richard Pitt & Edward Dadley
London, 1780–1800

122.1 Engraved crest on face of rim

MARKS: Touchmark of a hare courant with *PITT* above and *& DADLEY* below within curved reserves on underside of rim (London Touch Plate IV, 1043; Cotterell, *Old Pewter,* 3694); quality mark crowned *X* stamped on underside of rim to either side of touchmark

INSCRIPTIONS: Unidentified crest of a demilion rampant holding an uncertain object in its forepaws engraved on face of rim

122–123

DINING WARES 105

DIMENSIONS: OH. 1 1/4", OW. (rim) 1 1/2", Diam. 9 5/8"

PROVENANCE: Purchased from Dr. Percy E. Raymond, Lexington, Mass.; 1950-873

This plate is of soup plate depth.

123 SMALL PLATE OR SAUCER

Maker unidentified
England, 1740–1760

MARKS: None

INSCRIPTIONS: None

DIMENSIONS: OW. (rim): 7/8", Diam. 6 5/8"

PROVENANCE: Purchased from A. H. Isher & Son, Cheltenham, Eng.; 1960-464

This small plate is an unusual size. It was probably intended for uses similar to those of a saucer.

124 DISH

John Townsend & Thomas Giffin
London, 1768–1778

MARKS: Indistinct touchmarks (1) a lamb passant with dove with an olive branch in its bill flying above framed by *IOHN* in a curved reserve above, *17* to the left and *48* to the right, and *TOWNSEND* within a curved reserve below, and (2) a crown over a heart pierced by a sword with three mullets to either side with *THOMAS* and *GIFFIN* within curved reserves above and below, and a large *&* within a shaped reserve stamped between touchmarks, all on underside of well (Cotterell, *Old Pewter*, 4801)

INSCRIPTIONS: Face of rim deeply engraved in script with ornamented first letters *Hanna* [prancing deer] *Feeshel* and *In* [foliate pinwheel] *Shepherds Town* [foliate pinwheel] *Anno Domine 1782* separated on either side by long cartouches outlined with zigzag borders and containing voluted and ruffled C-scrolls at ends with extending foliated scrolls

DIMENSIONS: OH. 1 13/16", OW. (rim) 1 1/2", Diam. 12"

PROVENANCE: Dr. and Mrs. Henry P. Deyerle, Harrisonburg, Va.; purchased at an estate auction conducted by Sotheby's in Charlottesville, Va., May 26, 1995; 1995-90

PUBLISHED: Sales cat., Sotheby's, May 26, 1995, lot 622, ill.; Davis, "Metals for fashion-conscious consumer," p. 225, pl. XI

This dish, originally plain, was boldly engraved in 1782 for Hanna Feeshel of Shepherdstown (then in Virginia, now in West Virginia). The design and technique of its deeply cut engraving are the work of a local gunsmith who transformed this English dish into a highly individual piece of pewter from the Virginia backcountry.

125 FISH STRAINER AND DISH

John Wynne
London, 1750–1770

MARKS: Touchmark of a lion rampant with three mullets and scrollwork above and scrollwork below enclosed within a tabernacular frame; tabernacular frame consisting of *IOHN* on face of arched upper member, a fluted column or pilaster on either side surmounted by a globular teapot facing inward, and *WYNNE* on face of base member on underside of well of both strainer and dish (London Touch Plate IV, 923; Cotterell, *Old Pewter*, 5331); secondary marks (1) label *SUPER•FINE/HARD METAL* within an oblong reserve of scrolled outline (Cotterell, *Old Pewter*, 5331), and (2) quality mark *X* with crown above, both stamped on underside of well of both strainer and dish

INSCRIPTIONS: Owner's initials *H/IM* stamped on underside of well of both strainer and dish

DIMENSIONS: OL. (strainer) 18", OW. 13 3/4", W. (rim of strainer) 7/8", OL. (dish) 20 7/8", OW. 16 1/2", W. (rim of dish) 2 1/8"

PROVENANCE: Purchased from Thomas C. Campbell, Hawleyville, Conn.; acquired by vendor from a dealer in Maine; 1994-104, A&B

PUBLISHED: Ad of Thomas C. Campbell, *Maine Antique Digest* (July 1994), p. 33-A, ill.

During the second quarter of the eighteenth century, London silversmiths introduced pierced plates, usually oval in outline, as a refinement to the dinner service. These strainers were meant to

124

125

rest above the well of corresponding dishes to permit drainage in the service of fish. These pierced plates are sometimes referred to as mazarines in the period. This name is not without ambiguity, for it was used in regard to other types of dishes at an earlier date.

Most pewter fish strainers date from the second half of the eighteenth century. Surviving strainers with their matching dishes are uncommon. These latter ensembles include examples by Samuel Ellis I or II of London at Independence National Historical Park in Philadelphia, one by an unacknowledged maker that was sold at auction in Shrewsbury in 1995, and a further one by John Townsend and Thomas Compton, also sold at auction in 1995. Alex Neish illustrates an oval and a circular example without their dishes, presumably from his own collection, in a brief article on the form. A highly distinctive early circular one, pierced with a large central flower and an outer border of hearts and crowns, bears the touch of Richard Grunwin of London and is in the Neish Collection.[1]

The 1770 inventory of the contents of the Governor's Palace in Williamsburg lists "1 pewter fish Strainer" along with "21 Pewter Dishes & 15 plates" in the kitchen.[2] The arrival in Charleston from London of "pewter oval fish dishes" is advertised in the *South-Carolina Gazette* for Oct. 9, 1749.[3]

1. John C. Milley, ed., *Treasures of Independence: Independence National Historical Park and Its Collections* (New York, 1980), p. 86, fig. 80; D. W. Hall, "An Unknown Garnish," *Journal of the Pewter Society,* X (spring 1996), pp. 115–116, figs. 18, 20; sales cat., Skinner Inc., Boston, Mass., Aug. 13, 1995, p. 74, lot 379, ill.; Alex Neish, "Mazarines or straining dishes," *Journal of the Pewter Society,* IX (autumn 1993), pp. 58–59; Hornsby, *Pewter of the Western World,* p. 136, fig. 361; *Journal of the Pewter Society,* IX (spring 1994), front cover ill.
2. Inventory of the estate of Norborne Berkeley, Lord Botetourt, Oct. 24, 1770, Botetourt Papers, Library of Virginia, Richmond, Va.; Graham Hood, *The Governor's Palace in Williamsburg: A Cultural Study* (Williamsburg, Va., 1991), p. 310.
3. *South-Carolina Gazette* (Charleston), Oct. 9, 1749, p. 2, col. 1.

126 Fish Strainer and Dish

John Townsend & Robert Reynolds
London, 1767–1777

MARKS: Touchmark of a lamb passant with a dove with an olive branch in its bill flying above framed by *I•TOWNSEND &* and *R•REYNOLDS* above and below within curved reserves and with a small intervening shell to either side on underside of well of both strainer and dish (London Touch Plate IV, 1012; Cotterell, *Old Pewter,* 4797); secondary marks (1) label *SUPERFINE/HARD METAL* in curved arrangement within an outlined oblong reserve with a central scrolled and foliated pendant (Cotterell, *Old Pewter,* 4795), (2) label *MADE IN/LONDON* within an outlined rectangular reserve with scrolled upper edge and canted lower corners, and (3) quality mark *X* with crown above, all stamped on underside of well of both strainer and dish

INSCRIPTIONS: Owner's cipher *MRH* engraved on face of both rims

DIMENSIONS: OL. (strainer) 20 7/16", OW. 14 7/8", W. (rim of strainer) 1 1/16", OL. (dish) 22 1/2", OW. 17 1/8", W. (rim of dish) 2 1/8"

PROVENANCE: Purchased from Price Glover Inc., New York, N. Y.; 1979-9, A&B

PUBLISHED: Hornsby, *Pewter of the Western World,* p. 136, fig. 362

The originality of the strainer to the dish is confirmed by the same marks and engraved cipher on both pieces.

126.1 Engraved cipher on rim of strainer and dish

DINING WARES 109

127 PLATTER

Thomas Alderson
London, 1821

MARKS: Touchmark of a demilion rampant regardant holding a small object between its paws and issuing from a mural crown with a pellet to the left and a mullet to the right framed by *THOMAS* and *ALDERSON* within curved reserves above and below on underside of well (Cotterell, *Old Pewter,* 40); secondary marks (1) a label *LONDON/SUPERFINE* in curved arrangement in an oblong reserve of scalloped outline on underside of well (Cotterell, *Old Pewter,* 40), and (2) quality *X* to left of touchmark on underside of well

INSCRIPTIONS: *GR* in ornamented script enclosing *IV* with royal crown above for King George IV engraved on face of rim

DIMENSIONS: OL. 15 13/16", OW. 12 3/8", W. (rim) 1 5/16"

PROVENANCE: Purchased from Sumpter Priddy III, Inc., Alexandria, Va.; 1956-49

Alderson, noted for his dinnerware, is particularly remembered for supplying the large pewter service for the coronation banquet of George IV, of which this platter is a piece. The *Observer* for July 30, 1821, described the banquet held at Westminster Hall:

> As soon as His Majesty had risen and passed through the avenue behind the throne, accompanied by the great officers of State and his Royal brothers, the gathering crowd, by a simultaneous rush, in a moment surrounded the Royal table. For a few seconds delicacy, or a disinclination to be the first to commence the scene of plunder, suspended the projected attack, but at last a rude hand having been thrust through the first ranks, and a golden fork having been seized, this operated as a signal to all and was followed by a general snatch. In a short time all the portable articles were transferred into the pockets of the multitude . . . .
>
> The individuals in the galleries, who had hitherto remained passive spectators to the operations beneath, and many of whom had, for some unfortunate omission in the regulations prescribed by the Lord Great Chamberlain, remained the whole of the day without refreshment, poured down the different stairs and passages to the festive board,

127.1 Engraved royal monogram with crown on face of rim

which having been vacated by the Peers and other guests who had long before satiated their appetites, was attacked with a vigour only in proportion to the actual exhaustion of the assailants. A raging thirst was the first want to be satisfied, and in a very few moments every bottle on the board was emptied of its contents . . . .

While some were thus occupied, others still pursued the work of plunder. Arms were everywhere seen stretched forth breaking and destroying the table ornaments, which were of themselves too cumbrous to remove, for the purpose of obtaining some trophy commemorative of the occasion, . . . and finally the plates and dishes. These last were of pewter, engraved with the Royal arms and the letters "Geo. IV" [actually "G IV R" in ornamented script with royal crown above], and were therefore greatly coveted.[1]

A soup tureen and cover, a sauceboat, a salt, soup and sauce ladles, dinner and soup plates, and oval dishes, all a part of the coronation service, are in the collections of the Pewterers' Company.[2]

A further oval dish of immense size, also by Alderson, which measures no less than thirty-six inches in length, was part of the centerpiece on the same day for another banquet. The elaborate inscription engraved in its well informs that *On The Day of the Coronation of King George the fourth/19th July 1821/A Baron of Beef Wt 200 lbs/Was served upon this Dish as part of an Entertainment./Given to 700 children in/Kingston Market Place.* This great dish is in the Kingston Museum and Heritage Service, near London.[3]

1. Quoted in *Short history of The Worshipful Company,* p. 89.
2. *Ibid.,* pp. 90–99, nos. 561–574, fig. 53.
3. John Richardson, "Interesting and Unusual Pieces; Pewter and the Coronation of George IV," *Journal of the Pewter Society,* XI (autumn 1998), pp. 50–52.

128 PLATTER

Thomas Alderson
London, 1796–1832

MARKS: Touchmark of a demilion rampant regardant holding a small object between its paws and issuing from a mural crown with a pellet to the left and a mullet to the right framed by *THOMAS* and *ALDERSON* within curved reserves above and below on underside of well (Cotterell, *Old Pewter,* 40); secondary marks (1) a label *LONDON/SUPERFINE* in curved arrangement in an oblong reserve of scalloped outline on underside of base (Cotterell, *Old Pewter,* 40), and (2) quality mark *X* with crown above on either side of touchmark on underside of base

INSCRIPTIONS: None

DIMENSIONS: OL. 19 11/16", OW. 15 9/16", W. (rim) 1 3/4"

PROVENANCE: Purchased from Thomas D. and Constance R. Williams, Litchfield, Conn.; 1956-49

Plain-rim platters, somewhat more heavily proportioned than nos. 125–127 with their strainer plates, continued to be popular throughout the first half of the nineteenth century.

129 PLATTER

William Scott
Edinburgh, Scot., 1795–1815

MARKS: Touchmark *W.SCOTT* within a rectangle on underside of well; secondary marks (1) label *SUPER FINE/HARD METAL* within an oblong rectangle with scrolled outline, and (2) quality mark *X* with crown above, both stamped on underside of well

INSCRIPTIONS: None

DIMENSIONS: OL. 20 3/4", OW. 15 3/4", W. (rim) 2 5/16"

PROVENANCE: Purchased from Dr. Percy E. Raymond, Lexington, Mass.; 1950-846

DINING WARES 111

128–131

130 Platter

Thomas Compton
London, 1801–1817

MARKS: Touchmark *COMPTON/LONDON* within a horizontal oval contained within a combined rectangle and diamond with hatching radiating from central oval on underside of well (Cotterell, *Old Pewter,* 1063); secondary marks (1) label *SUPERFINE/HARD METAL* within an oblong rectangle of scrolled outline (Cotterell, *Old Pewter,* 1063), and (2) quality mark *X* with crown above, both stamped on underside of well

INSCRIPTIONS: None

DIMENSIONS: OL. 20 3/4", OW. 15 1/4", W. (rim) 2"

PROVENANCE: Gift of David Pleydell-Bouverie, New York, N. Y.; G1951-39

131 Platter

Joseph Spackman & Co.
London, 1790–1815

MARKS: No touchmark apparent; three secondary marks in the form of oval labels on underside of rim (possibly Cotterell, *Old Pewter,* 4443)

INSCRIPTIONS: None

DIMENSIONS: OL. 11 7/16", OW. 8 13/16", W. (rim) 1 3/8"

PROVENANCE: Purchased from Percy E. Raymond, Lexington, Mass.; 1950-866

132 HOT-WATER PLATE

Jonas Durand I or II
London, 1730–1760

MARKS: Touchmark of a rose with palm fronds to either side and crossing below with *IONAS:/E:SONNANT/1699* within curved reserves above and *DURAND* within a curved reserve below on underside of rim (London Touch Plate II, 557; Cotterell, *Old Pewter,* 1475)

INSCRIPTIONS: Unidentified coat of arms within a rococo cartouche engraved on face of rim

DIMENSIONS: OH. 1 11/16", OW. 9 9/16", W. (rim) 7/8", Diam. (top and base) 8 5/8"

PROVENANCE: Purchased from Dr. Percy E. Raymond, Lexington, Mass.; 1950-838

This hot-water plate is an early example of this type of dining accessory for keeping dinner plates and their food warm. The tops and bottoms of most examples are a pair of dinner plates with a narrow connecting sleeve between them that forms short, straight sides. The top is often fitted with a small, hinged flap for filling the interior with hot water. The bold shaping of the pendant handles and the engraved rococo coat of arms are indications of its early date.

132.1 Engraved coat of arms on face of rim

133 PAIR OF HOT-WATER PLATES

John Birch & William Villers
Birmingham, Eng., 1772–1786

MARKS: Touchmark of an eagle issuing from a coronet beneath a radiant sun within a baluster-shaped reserve with scrolled accents on underside of well (Cotterell, *Old Pewter,* 430; Homer and Hall, *Provincial Pewterers,* 6); secondary marks (1) quality mark *X* with crown above stamped over touchmark on underside of well, and (2) label *LONDON* within an outlined oblong rectangle stamped

132–135

DINING WARES 113

below touchmark on underside of well (Cotterell, *Old Pewter,* 430; Homer and Hall, *Provincial Pewterers,* 6); pseudo hallmarks (1) arms of three griffins' heads erased with a chevron between within an outlined shield, (2) crest of a griffin's head erased on a wreath bar within an outlined shield, (3) star within an outlined circle, and (4) *B&V* within an outlined shield, all on underside of well (Cotterell, *Old Pewter,* 430; Homer and Hall, *Provincial Pewterers,* 6)

INSCRIPTIONS: None

DIMENSIONS: OH. 1 3/4", OW. 10 1/8", W. (rim) 1 1/4", Diam. 9 5/16"

PROVENANCE: Gift of Miss Julia Sully, Richmond, Va.; this pair of hot-water plates came to CWF with an unspecified tradition of ownership in the Dandridge family of Virginia; G1932-127, 1–2

134 Hot-Water Dish

John Watts
London, 1740–1760

MARKS: Touchmark of a globe with stand with *IN⁰ WATTS* within an outlined rectangle below on underside of well (London Touch Plate III, 801; Cotterell, *Old Pewter,* 4991); secondary marks (1) a rose with crown above and *LONDON* below within a conforming reserve on underside of well, and (2) label with *WITHOUT/ALDGATE* within curved reserve with pendant shell on underside of well (Cotterell, *Old Pewter,* 4991); pseudo hallmarks (1) *IW* within a shaped shield, (2) globe on stand within a shaped rectangle, (3) lion passant within a shaped rectangle, and (4) leopard's head within a shaped rectangle on underside of well (Cotterell, *Old Pewter,* 4991)

INSCRIPTIONS: None

DIMENSIONS: Diam: 14 3/4"

PROVENANCE: Purchased from F. H. Foxall, Ludlow, Eng.; 1947-502

Listed in the kitchen in the 1770 inventory of the contents of the Governor's Palace in Williamsburg are "2 large pewter water dishes." These dishes were undoubtedly helpful in keeping food warm after it had been cooked in and transported from a separate kitchen building. These dishes are listed after "21 tin meat covers," also useful in maintaining warmth and in protection from insects.[1]

1. Inventory of the estate of Botetourt; Hood, *Governor's Palace in Williamsburg,* p. 293.

135 Pair of Hot-Water Plates

John Yates, Thomas Rawlins Birch & Lucas Spooner
Birmingham, Eng., 1829–1839

MARKS: Touchmark of an eagle issuing from a coronet beneath a radiant sun within a baluster-shaped reserve with scrolled accents stamped twice on underside of each well (Cotterell, *Old Pewter,* 5347); secondary marks (1) quality mark *X* with crown above stamped over touchmarks on underside of each well, and (2) label *BIRMINGHAM* within an oblong rectangle on underside of each well; pseudo hallmarks (1) prancing dog within a shaped reserve, (2) *YB&S* within a shaped reserve, (3) *X,* and (4) pinwheel below touchmarks on underside of each base

INSCRIPTIONS: None

DIMENSIONS: OH. 1 7/8", OW. 10 3/16", W. (rim) 1 3/16", Diam. 9 1/2"

PROVENANCE: Purchased from Franz Middelkoop, New York, N. Y.; 1932-41, 1–2

136 Hot-Water Dish

George Alderson
London, 1810–1826

MARKS: Touchmark of a demilion rampant holding a small object between its forepaws and issuing from a mural crown with a crescent moon to the left of the lion's head and a mullet to the right with *GEORGE* and *ALDERSON* within curved reserves above and below on underside of well (London Touch Plate V, 1084; Cotterell, *Old Pewter,* 38); secondary mark of a label *LONDON/SUPERFINE* in curved arrangement within an oblong of scalloped outline on underside of well (Cotterell, *Old Pewter,* 40)

INSCRIPTIONS: None

DIMENSIONS: OL. 22 1/2", OW. 17 1/4", W. (rim) 2 1/4"

PROVENANCE: Purchased from Richard Mundey, London; 1979-373

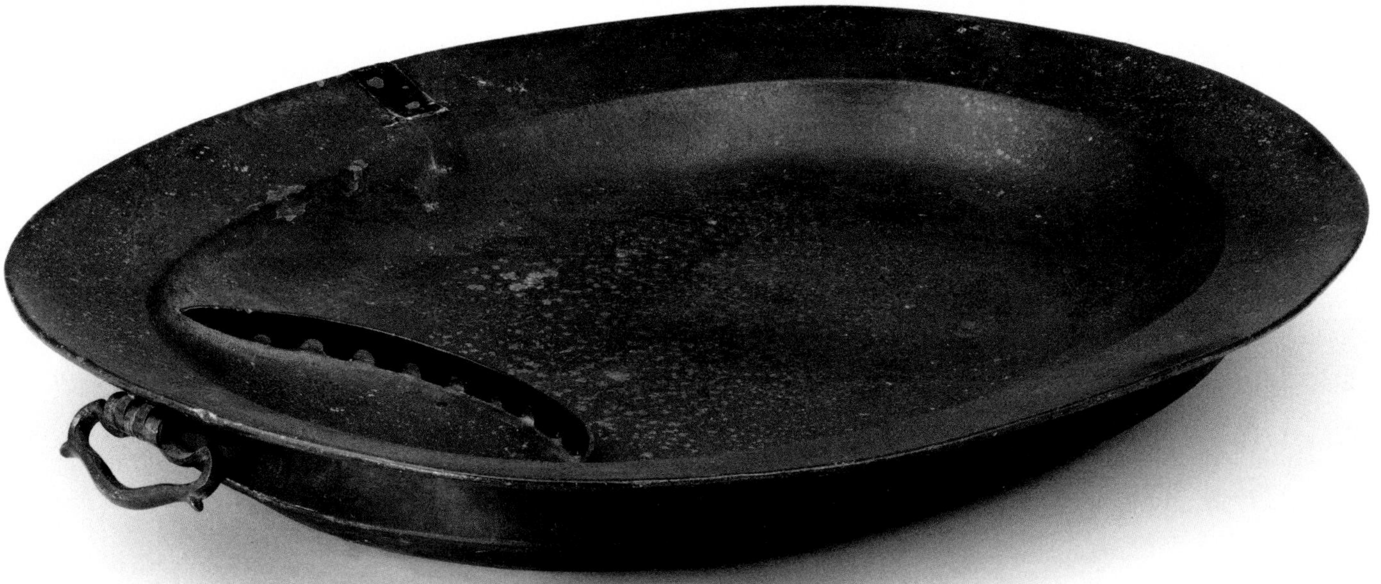

136

Dishes and Plates/Fancy Rims

English pewter wavy-edge and polygonal plates and dishes were most directly influenced by French pewter styles and the styles of English white stoneware and refined earthenware and not by silver or porcelain precedent. It is during the middle decades of the eighteenth century that one first encounters these new shapes and their production in coordinated dinner services. Fancy-rim pewter examples were more expensive than comparable plates and dishes of single-bead or plain-rim types. This greater cost was due to their more complicated fabrication and finishing. Most examples were cast in plain circular molds with their edges cast separately and applied. Only then was the edge of the plate or dish trimmed to its final shape. Fancy-rim plates and dishes were most popular from 1765 to 1785.

137.1 Plate

137 Dinner Service

Twenty-three plates
Twelve circular dishes in five sizes
Three oval dishes

Thomas Burford & James Green
London, 1748–1780

MARKS: Touchmark of the arms of Burford (a cross, with two crosslets fitchée) and Green (three stags trippant, two and one) with separate shields with *BURFORD* and *& GREEN* within curved reserves above and below and scrolls to either side on underside of each rim (London Touch Plate IV, 929; Cotterell, *Old Pewter*, 698)

INSCRIPTIONS: Unidentified owner's crest engraved on face of each rim

DIMENSIONS: W. (rim plates 1–23) 1 1/2", Diam. 9 3/4", W. (rim dish 24) 1 1/2", Diam. 10 3/4", W. (rim dishes 25–26) 1 5/8", Diam.

116 Pewter at Colonial Williamsburg

137.2 Circular dishes in five sizes

12", W. (rim dishes 27–29) 1 3/4", Diam. 13 1/4", W. (rim dishes 30–32) 1 7/8", Diam. 14 3/4", W. (rim dishes 33–35) 2", Diam. 16 1/4", OL. (dishes 36–38) 18 1/2", OW. 14 1/4", W. (rim) 2 1/8"

PROVENANCE: Purchased from G. E. Mays, London (arranged by Ian D. Robinson, Auburndale, Mass.); 1979-90, 1–38

137.4 Engraved crest on face of each rim

137.3 Oval dish

Survival, date, and ownership confirm and make reasonable that a greater percentage of fancy-rim plates and dishes was once part of coordinated dinner ensembles, if not services. Further, as John Douglas has commented in his useful article on such wares, they more often feature armorial engravings than plainer alternatives.[1] This observation is confirmed by the plates and dishes at CWF.

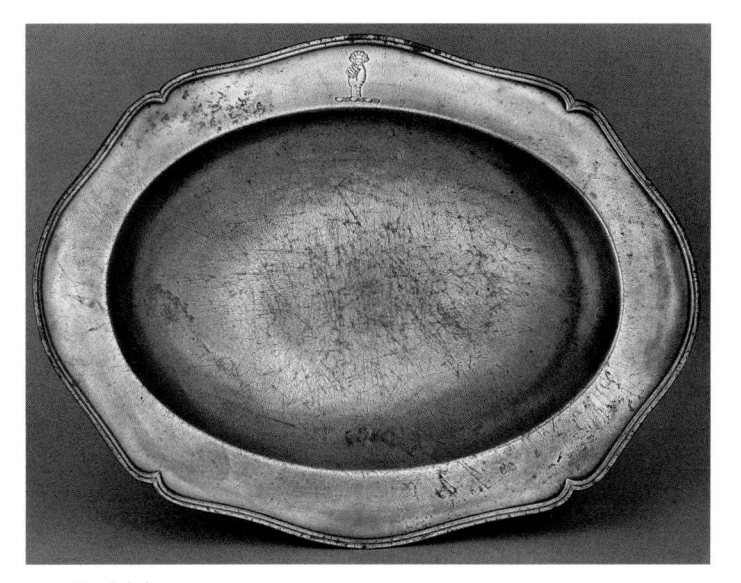

1. John A. Douglas, "Non circular British plates," *Journal of the Pewter Society,* V (autumn 1985), p. 42.

DINING WARES 117

138 Platter

John Carpenter
London, 1717–1747

MARKS: Touchmark of a pair of dividers with a globe below framed by *IOHN* and *CARPENTER* in curved reserves above and below and foliated scrolls on either side on underside of well (London Touch Plate III, 718; Cotterell, *Old Pewter,* 810); secondary mark of an *X* for quality stamped above touchmark

INSCRIPTIONS: Arms within an elaborate baroque cartouche with motto below of the Parker family engraved on face of rim with crest of the Parker family on opposite side of rim

DIMENSIONS: OL. 18 9/16", OW. 14 1/8", W. (rim) 2"

PROVENANCE: Purchased from Price Glover Inc., New York, N. Y.; 1977-303

138.1 Engraved coat of arms on face of rim

138.2 Engraved crest on face of rim

139 SET OF FOUR PLATTERS

Joseph Spackman & Co.
London, 1764–1784

MARKS: Touchmarks (1) a ducal coronet with two crosses paty and a fleur-de-lis above and a cross paty over crossed palm fronds below framed by *IOSEPH* and *SPACKMAN* within curved reserves above and below and scrolls to either side on underside of well (London Touch Plate IV, 982; Cotterell, *Old Pewter,* 4440) and (2–4) *SPACKMAN/CORNHILL/LONDON* within a surround of scrolls within an outlined horizontal oval on underside of each rim (Cotterell, *Old Pewter,* 4443); secondary marks (1) a label *CORNHILL/LONDON* in curved arrangement within an outlined reserve with a central scrolled pendant on underside of well (Cotterell, *Old Pewter,* 4442) and (2–4) royal arms with *BY•HIS•MAJESTY'S•PATENT* above within an outlined oval on underside of each rim and *PATENT OVAL* within a surround of scrolls within an outlined horizontal oval, also on underside of each rim (Cotterell, *Old Pewter,* 4443)

INSCRIPTIONS: Crest and motto of the Tucker family of Coryton, Eng., engraved on face of each rim

DIMENSIONS: OL. (1) 23 11/16", OW. 17 3/4", W. (rim) 2 3/8", OL. (2) 18 11/16", OW. 14 5/8", W. (rim) 2 1/8", OL. (3) 12 5/8", OW. 9 5/8", W. (rim) 1 3/8", OL. (4) 11 3/8", OW. 8 11/16", W. (rim) 1 3/8"

PROVENANCE: Purchased from A. V. Sutherland-Graeme, London; 1958-523, 1–4

The firm of Joseph Spackman & Co. was particularly noted for its patented oval dishes. It secured a patent on Dec. 5, 1764, for the production of oval dishes by turning them on a special lathe. Robert Bush I of Bristol advertised in the Aug. 17, 1765, issue of *Felix Farley's Bristol Journal*:

PATENT OVAL PEWTER DISHES
By His Majesty's Royal Letters Patent bearing date December 5th 1764, Joseph Spackman, late of Fenchurch Street, but now of Cornhill, London, pewterer, having

139

DINING WARES 119

invented a method entirely new of turning ovals in Pewter, English China, and other earthenware, has obtained Letters Patent as above for the term of 14 years within the kingdom of England & the Dominion of Wales, Town of Berwick upon Tweed and the plantations abroad, by virtue thereof he is now making and is ready to serve Merchants and others, with Oval Pewter Dishes, of superior Hard Metal, far superior, both in beauty and strength, to anything hitherto performed in the oval way. The above are the Silver Fashion Egg Oval and are to be sold by Robert Bush, Pewterer, Brazier and Brass-Founder in High Street, Bristol, who is the only person in that city to sell them; and who will render them at 25 per cent under the old price.[1]

1. Alyson Marsden and Mike Marsden, "Burgum and Catcott, Pewterers of Bristol," *Journal of the Pewter Society,* XVI (autumn 2001), p. 27.

139.1 Engraved crest on face of each rim

140 PLATE

Probably George Stafford
London, 1740–1760

MARKS: None

INSCRIPTIONS: Unidentified owner's coat of arms engraved within an elaborate rococo cartouche on face of rim

140.1 Engraved coat of arms on face of rim

DIMENSIONS: OW. (rim) 1 1/2", Diam. 9 5/8"

PROVENANCE: Purchased from Price Glover Inc., New York, N. Y.; 1984-275

This particularly rich and stylish example features a handsomely gadrooned border with unusual mask and foliate breaks at regular intervals. Although this plate is unmarked, it can be attributed to Stafford, for other matched plates and dishes from this service with his marks are known.

141.1 Engraved crest on face of rim

141 PLATE

Robert & Thomas Porteus
London, 1762–1768

MARKS: Touchmark of an ostrich standant regardant framed by *ROB: & THO* and *PORTEUS* above and below within curved reserves on underside of well (London Touch Plate IV, 999; Cotterell, *Old Pewter,* 3732); secondary marks (1) label *GRACE CHURCH/STREET•LONDON* within an oblong reserve of scrolled outline on underside of well (Cotterell, *Old Pewter,* 3732), and (2) quality mark *X* stamped on underside of well

INSCRIPTIONS: Face of rim engraved with an unidentified crest of an apparent scallop shell flanked on either side by an eagle with wings addorsed

DIMENSIONS: OW. (rim) 1 9/16", Diam. 9 3/4"

PROVENANCE: Purchased from Price Glover Inc., New York, N. Y.; 1984-276

The ostrich in the touchmark acknowledges that Robert and Thomas Porteus succeeded Richard King of London, whose principal device was also the ostrich. Another fancy-rim plate with the same very distinctive decorative rim is marked by Stynt Duncumb of Bewdley.[1]

1. Brett, *Phaidon Guide to Pewter,* p. 49, ill.

120 PEWTER AT COLONIAL WILLIAMSBURG

140

141

142

142 SIX PLATES

James Tisoe
London, 1750–1770

MARKS: Touchmark of a portcullis framed by *IAMES* and *TISOE* within curved reserves above and below and scrolls to either side on underside of each rim (London Touch Plate IV, 854; Cotterell, *Old Pewter,* 4755; Peal, *More Pewter Marks,* 4754); secondary mark of a shaped vertical oval containing *FINE/BG* [script] */BRITISH/BP* [script] */METAL* on underside of each rim (Cotterell, *Old Pewter,* 4755; Peal, *More Pewter Marks,* 4754)

INSCRIPTIONS: Arms of the Adair family of Ballymena, Antrim Co., engraved within a rococo cartouche on face of each rim

DIMENSIONS: OW. (rim) 1 7/16", Diam. 9 7/8"

PROVENANCE: R. S. Campkin, Hassocks, Eng. (sold at Sotheby's, 1974); 1974-46, 1–6

PUBLISHED: *Exhibition of Pewter,* no. 211; sales cat., Sotheby's, Feb. 11, 1974, p. 14, lot 130, pl. III

The edgings on fancy-rim plates and dishes were generally cast separately and applied, as in this handsome set of plates. A pair of identical plates with the same engraved arms, although in a more worn condition, is also at CWF.[1]

1. This pair is illustrated in the sales brochure of Robin Bellamy Antiques, Witney, Eng., 1974, p. 6, ill.

142.1 Engraved arms on the face of each rim

143

143 DISH

James Tisoe
London, 1750–1770

MARKS: Touchmark of a portcullis framed by *IAMES* and *TISOE* within curved reserves above and below and scrolls to either side on underside of rim (London Touch Plate IV, 854; Cotterell, *Old Pewter,* 4755; Peal, *More Pewter Marks,* 4754); secondary mark of a shaped vertical oval containing *FINE/BG* [script] */BRITISH/BP* [script] */METAL* on underside of rim (Cotterell, *Old Pewter,* 4755; Peal, *More Pewter Marks,* 4754)

INSCRIPTIONS: Arms of the Adair family of Ballymena, Antrim Co., engraved within a rococo cartouche on face of rim

DIMENSIONS: OW. (rim) 2 1/16", Diam. 16 9/16"

PROVENANCE: Purchased at Sotheby's in 1975; 1975-184

PUBLISHED: Sales cat., Sotheby's, July 17, 1975, p. 16, lot 140, ill.

144 TWELVE PLATES

Thomas Chamberlain
London, 1750–1770

MARKS: Touchmark of the Prince of Wales feathers with royal crown above framed by *THOMAS* and *CHAMBERLAIN* within curved reserves above and below on underside of each rim (Cotterell, *Old Pewter,* 873); secondary mark of a label *CHAMBERLAIN* within an oblong rectangle with beaded upper and lower edges on underside of each rim opposite touchmark (Cotterell, *Old Pewter,* 873)

INSCRIPTIONS: Arms with supporters, motto, and baron's coronet of Baron Edgcumbe of Mount Edgcumbe, Devon, engraved on the face of each rim; the arms are those of either

144–145

DINING WARES   125

144.1 and 145.1 Engraved coat of arms on face of rims

(1) Richard Edgcumbe (d. 1758), First Baron Edgcumbe, (2) his son Richard Edgcumbe (d. unmarried in 1761), Second Baron Edgcumbe, or (3) his brother George Edgcumbe (d. 1795), Third Baron Edgcumbe, created Viscount Mount Edgcumbe and Valletort in 1781 and the First Earl of Mount Edgcumbe in 1789

DIMENSIONS: OW. (rim) 1 7/16", Diam. 9 11/16"

PROVENANCE: Sold by the trustees of the Seventh Earl of Mount Edgcumbe and purchased by CWF at Sotheby's, 1956; 1956-345, 1–12

PUBLISHED: Sales cat., Sotheby's, June 1, 1956, p. 11, lot 41, ill.

These splendid dinner plates, the following dozen soup plates (no. 145), and a pair of soup tureens (no. 164), are part of a large dinner service that Chamberlain supplied to the Earl of Mount Edgcumbe, whose armorial engraving appears on each piece. When these plates were sold in 1956, eighty-two additional plates, twelve soup plates, and thirty dishes in various sizes, both circular and oval, were also auctioned. It is of interest to note how these and other plates and dishes, not only with fancy rims, but also with shaped faces to their rims and short, pinched creases pointing inward between each serpentine rim section, were made. It becomes clear that they were cast plain with flat rims, then the face of the rim was shaped and creased before the decorative edging was applied in sections and the edges trimmed. This procedure is particularly evident with many of Chamberlain's plates and dishes. Invariably, the large oblong label with his name extends in and out of a crease, which indicates that it was stamped prior to shaping.

145 TWELVE SOUP PLATES

Thomas Chamberlain
London, 1750–1770

MARKS: Touchmark of the Prince of Wales feathers with royal crown above framed by *THOMAS* and *CHAMBERLAIN* within curved reserves above and below on underside of each rim (Cotterell, *Old Pewter,* 873); secondary mark of a label *CHAMBERLAIN* within an oblong rectangle with beaded upper and lower edges on underside of each rim opposite touchmark (Cotterell, *Old Pewter,* 873)

INSCRIPTIONS: Arms with supporters, motto, and baron's coronet of Baron Mount Edgcumbe of Mount Edgcumbe, Devon, engraved on face of each rim; the arms are those of either (1) Richard Edgcumbe (d. 1758), First Baron Edgcumbe, (2) his son Richard Edgcumbe (d. unmarried in 1761), Second Baron Edgcumbe, or (3) his brother George Edgcumbe (d. 1795), Third Baron Edgcumbe, created Viscount Mount Edgcumbe and Valletort in 1781 and the First Earl of Mount Edgcumbe in 1789

DIMENSIONS: OH. 1 1/4", OW. (rim) 1 7/16", Diam. 9 11/16"

PROVENANCE: Sold by the trustees of the Seventh Earl of Mount Edgcumbe and purchased by CWF at Sotheby's, 1956; 1956-49, 1–12

PUBLISHED: Sales cat., Sotheby's, June 1, 1956, p. 12, lot 49, ill.

These soup plates are from the same service as no. 144.

146 TWENTY-TWO PLATES

Thomas Chamberlain
London, 1750–1770

MARKS: Touchmark of the Prince of Wales feathers with royal crown above framed by *THOMAS* and *CHAMBERLAIN* within curved reserves above and below on underside of each rim (Cotterell, *Old Pewter,* 873); secondary mark of a label *CHAMBERLAIN* within an oblong rectangle with beaded upper and lower edges on underside of each rim opposite touchmark (Cotterell, *Old Pewter,* 873)

INSCRIPTIONS: An unidentified crest of a tower with a fleur-de-lis issuing from its battlement on a wreath bar engraved on the face of each rim

146–147

DIMENSIONS: OW. (rim) 1 7/16", Diam. 9 3/4"

PROVENANCE: Sold at Sotheby's, 1970; purchased at Christie's, 1972; 1972-415, 1–22

146.1 and 147.1 Engraved crest on face of rims

PUBLISHED: Sales cat., Sotheby's, July 9, 1970; sales cat., Christie's, Nov. 9, 1972, p. 9, lot 21, ill.

These plates are from the same service and appear to be half of the forty-four plates auctioned in 1970, along with a pair of circular dishes and seven oval dishes in four sizes.[1] The following pair of circular dishes (no. 147) are from the same service.

1. Sales cat., Sotheby's, July 9, 1970, p. 13, lots 39–47, ill.

147 Pair of Dishes

Thomas Chamberlain
London, 1750–1770

MARKS: Touchmark of the Prince of Wales feathers with royal crown above framed by *THOMAS* and *CHAMBERLAIN* within curved reserves above and below on underside of each rim (Cotterell, *Old Pewter,* 873); secondary mark of a label *CHAMBERLAIN* within an oblong rectangle with beaded upper and lower edges on underside of each rim opposite touchmark (Cotterell, *Old Pewter,* 873)

INSCRIPTIONS: An unidentified crest of a tower with a fleur-de-lis issuing from the battlement on a wreath bar engraved on the face of each rim

DIMENSIONS: OW. (rim) 1 5/8", Diam. 11 7/8"

PROVENANCE: Purchased at Christie's, 1972; 1972-416, 1–2

PUBLISHED: Sales cat., Christie's, Nov. 9, 1972, p. 9, lot 22, ill.

These dishes are from the same service as no. 146.

DINING WARES 127

148–150

148 Twelve Plates

Jonas Durand II
London, 1750–1775

MARKS: Touchmark of a rose with palm fronds to either side and crossing below with *IONASW:/E:SONNANT/1669* within curved reserves above and *DURAND* within a curved reserve below on underside of each rim (London Touch Plate II, 557; Cotterell, *Old Pewter,* 1475)

INSCRIPTIONS: Unidentified crest of a falcon with wings extended and inverted on a wreath bar engraved on the face of each rim

DIMENSIONS: OW. (rim) 1 7/16", Diam. 9 5/8"

PROVENANCE: Purchased from Carl and Celia Jacobs, Southwick, Mass.; 1959-12, 1–12

148.1 Engraved crest on face of each rim

This set of plates and the following dozen plates (no. 149) were made by the same maker for the same family. They present two different options in plates and dishes of fancy-rim type. This set has a shaped face to the rims with short creases at intervals and unmounted edges. The other set has rims with flat faces and applied moldings at the edges.

149 Twelve Plates

Jonas Durand II
London, 1750–1775

MARKS: Touchmark of a rose with palm fronds to either side and crossing below with *IONAS:/E:SONNANT/1669* within curved reserves above and *DURAND* within a curved reserve on underside of each rim (London Touch Plate II, 557; Cotterell, *Old Pewter,* 1475)

INSCRIPTIONS: Unidentified crest of a falcon with wings extended and inverted on a wreath bar engraved on the face of each rim

DIMENSIONS: OW. (rim) 1 7/16", Diam. 9 11/16"

149.1 Engraved crest on face of each rim

PROVENANCE: Purchased from A. V. Sutherland-Graeme, London; 1958-20, 1–12

Fourteen additional plates and four circular dishes from the same service as these plates were sold at auction in 1985.[1]

1. Sales cat., Sotheby's, Oct. 31, 1985, lot 22, pl. II.

150 Pair of Plates

Samuel Ellis II
London, 1754–1775

MARKS: Touchmark of the golden fleece framed by *SAMUEL* and *ELLIS* within outlined curved reserves above and below and flowers to either side, all within a vertical oval on underside of each well (Cotterell, *Old Pewter,* 1547)

INSCRIPTIONS: Owner's initials *M/PC* engraved within a rococo cartouche on each rim, and *P•S* engraved on underside of each well

DIMENSIONS: OW. (rim) 1 1/2", Diam. 9 3/4"

PROVENANCE: Purchased from Carl Jacobs, The Old Lamp Post, Southwick, Mass.; 1950-389, 1–2

150.1 Engraved owner's initials on face of each rim

151–154

151 DISH

Richard King II
London, 1750–1770

MARKS: Touchmark of the crest of a demiostrich couped on a wreath bar framed by *RICHARD* above within a curved reserve, a pilaster at either side, and *KING* below on underside of rim (Cotterell, *Old Pewter,* 2750); secondary marks (1) a rose with crown above with *GRACIOUS STREET* probably below within a domed reserve with a pilaster with ball above to either side on underside of rim adjacent to touchmark (partially indistinct; Cotterell, *Old Pewter,* 2750), (2) label *SUPERFINE/ HARD•METAL* within a subdivided and beaded rectangle on underside of rim opposite preceding marks (Cotterell, *Old Pewter,* 2750), and (3) quality *X* with crown above stamped between touchmark and large secondary mark on underside of rim

INSCRIPTIONS: Unidentified arms and crest engraved on face of rim within a rococo cartouche

DIMENSIONS: OW. 13 3/4", W. (rim) 1 3/4"

PROVENANCE: Purchased from A. V. Sutherland-Graeme, London; 1961-127

151.1 Engraved coat of arms and crest on face of rim

Polygonal plates and dishes in pewter, mainly dating from the third quarter of the eighteenth century, clearly derived most directly from and were made to compete with refined earthenware examples. Polygonal pewter ones could not successfully compete with the flood of new lightly potted and gaily decorated ceramic choices.

152 TWELVE PLATES

Thomas Chamberlain
London, 1750–1775

MARKS: Touchmark of the Prince of Wales feathers with royal crown above framed by *THOMAS* and *CHAMBERLAIN* within curved reserves above and below on underside of each rim (Cotterell, *Old Pewter,* 873); secondary mark of a label *CHAMBERLAIN* within an oblong rectangle with beaded upper and lower edges on underside of each rim opposite touchmark (Cotterell, *Old Pewter,* 873)

INSCRIPTIONS: Unidentified coat of arms engraved within a rococo cartouche on face of each rim

DIMENSIONS: OW. 9 1/4", W. (rim) 1 1/8"

PROVENANCE: Purchased at Christie's, 1972; 1972-414, 1–12

PUBLISHED: Sale cat., Christie's, Nov. 9, 1972, p. 9, lot 20, ill.

152.1 Engraved coat of arms on face of rims

153 PLATE

Maker unidentified
England, 1750–1780

MARKS: No touchmark; secondary marks (1) indistinct oblong label on underside of rim, (2) a rose with a crown above framed by *MADE IN* and *LONDON* within curved reserves above and below on underside of well, and (3) quality *X* with crown above stamped twice on underside of well adjacent to touchmark

INSCRIPTIONS: Owner's initials *SB* stamped on underside of well in center

DIMENSIONS: OW. 9 1/2", W. (rim) 1 1/4"

PROVENANCE: Purchased from Dr. Percy E. Raymond, Lexington, Mass.; 1950-868

154.1 Engraved coat of arms on face of rim

154 DISH

Henry Maxted
London, 1750–1770

MARKS: Touchmark of a rose with a radiant sun above and to the right framed by *HENRY* within an outlined oblong rectangle above, a pilaster on a plinth to either side, and *MAXTED* within an outlined oblong rectangle below on underside of rim (London Touch Plate IV, 861; Cotterell, *Old Pewter*, 3150)

INSCRIPTIONS: Unidentified arms engraved on face of rim within a rococo cartouche

DIMENSIONS: OW. 13", W. (rim) 1 9/16"

PROVENANCE: Purchased from A. H. Isher & Son, Cheltenham, Eng.; 1956-395

Another twelve-sided dish by Jonas Durand II of London was sold at auction in 1980.[1]

1. Sales cat., Sotheby's, Mar. 28, 1980, p. 15, lot 59, pl. 2.

155 BASIN

Quart size
Semper Eadem makers
Boston area, Mass., 1750–1800

MARKS: Touchmark of a rose with a crown above framed by *SEMPER* within an arched reserve above supported on a column to either side with *EADEM* within a rectangular reserve below on interior center-bottom of body (Laughlin, *Pewter in America*, I, 290)

INSCRIPTIONS: None

DIMENSIONS: OH. 1 15/16", OW. (rim) 3/8", Diam. (rim) 8"

PROVENANCE: Purchased from John Carl Thomas, Hanover, Conn., with funds given by the Antique Collectors' Guild in memory of William Kayhoe of Richmond, Va., past president of the Pewter Collectors Club of America; G1988-237

Basins are certainly among the most ubiquitous of American pewter hollowware forms during the eighteenth and nineteenth centuries. They served a multitude of purposes. Those of eight inches in diameter and smaller primarily served as individual eating bowls or as waste or slop bowls in the service of tea, while larger examples were most often used as wash basins.[1]

Students of eighteenth-century American pewter have long pondered the identities of the makers from Boston who marked their wares with the Semper Eadem touches. A considerable number of plates, dishes, and basins survive by these still unidentified makers. Various candidates include Robert Bonynge, Thomas Green, John Holyoke, Thomas Simpkins, and John Skinner.

1. Montgomery, *History of American Pewter*, pp. 143–144.

156 BASIN

Quart size
William and Samuel Yale
Meriden, Conn., 1813–1820

MARKS: Touchmark of an American eagle displayed against arrayed background with stars in curved arrangement above and *W•&•S YALE* in opposed arrangement below within a serrated vertical oval on interior center-bottom of body (Laughlin, *Pewter in America,* I, 440)

INSCRIPTIONS: None

DIMENSIONS: OH. 2", OW. (rim) 13/32", Diam. (rim) 8 1/8"

PROVENANCE: Gift of Mr. and Mrs. Foster McCarl, Jr., Beaver Falls, Pa.; G1991-650

William and Samuel Yale, sons of a pewter button maker, set up business in their hometown of Meridan, Conn., in 1813. At that time, they acquired molds from the estate of Jacob Eggleston of Middletown, Conn., who had worked in Fayetteville, N. C., between 1807 and 1812. They probably continued in business until about 1820. Their surviving work is rare.

157 BASIN

Gallon size
Joseph Danforth II
Richmond, Va., 1807–1812

MARKS: Touchmark of an American eagle with spread wings and an olive branch and arrows in its talons and stars above standing on an oval enclosing *J✻D,* all contained within a circle stamped twice on inside of bowl (Laughlin, *Pewter in America,* I, 381); secondary mark of a label containing *RICHMOND/WARRENTED* within a conforming reserve on inside of bowl (Laughlin, *Pewter in America,* I, 379)

INSCRIPTIONS: None

DIMENSIONS: OH. 3", OW. (rim) 5/8", Diam. 11 15/16"

PROVENANCE: Purchased with funds provided by the Antique Collectors' Guild from John Carl Thomas, Hanover, Conn., who acquired it at auction on Cape Cod, Mass.; formerly in the collection of Dr. and Mrs. S. Harris Johnson III; G1989-308

Danforth (1783–1844) was of the fourth generation of his Connecticut family to practice the pewter trade. He is but one of a substantial number of fellow pewterers from the Hartford area who were enterprising enough to seek personal opportunity and more promising markets elsewhere. His setting up business in Richmond, Va., in 1807, was not a random foray into the South but part of a more generalized pattern. Other pewterers from this part of Connecticut moved to the South, including Sylvester Griswold from Meriden, Samuel Kilbourn from Hartford, J. W. Olcott (probably Joel White Olcott) from Litchfield, and James Porter from Middletown, all of whom worked in Baltimore. Thomas Danforth IV from Rocky Hill, John North and Isaiah Rowe from Farmington, and Giles Griswold, probably from Meriden, all opened businesses in Augusta, Ga., while Jacob Eggleston, Jehiel Johnson, William Nott, and probably Thomas S. Derby, all from Middletown, worked in Fayetteville, N. C.

156

DINING WARES 133

157

158 SALVER

Possibly John Batcheler
Possibly Bristol, Eng., 1670–1690

MARKS: Touchmark of a fleur-de-lis with *T* or *I* to the left and *B* to the right within a beaded circle on underside of well within foot (Cotterell, *Old Pewter,* 5468)

INSCRIPTIONS: None

DIMENSIONS: OH. 3 3/4", W. (rim) 1 5/16", W. (base) 4 3/4", Diam. 9 11/16"

PROVENANCE: Purchased from A. H. Isher & Son, Cheltenham, Eng.; 1958-560

In the second edition of his *Grossographia,* published in London in 1661, Thomas Blount defined a salver as "a new fashioned piece of wrought plate; broad and flat, with a foot underneath, and is used in giving Beer, or other liquid thing, to save or preserve the Carpit and Clothes from drops." Most English salvers in pewter were used for the same and additional purposes in the service of food and drink, and they are of this enlarged paten form. It is especially clear that this rare example is nothing more than a standard plate with an applied central foot because the foot was cast in a mold that was also probably used for the lower section of table salts (see no. 169). A salver with the same touchmark is in the collections of Arlington Court near Barnstaple, Eng.[1]

1. "Marks," p. 48. Jan Gadd, in submitting this mark, attributes it to Batcheler.

159 SALVER

Possibly John Stribblehill
London, 1678–1700

MARKS: Indistinct touchmark incorporating, in part, a scrolled reserve containing *IO*[?] at top and a palm frond to either side on underside of well (possibly Cotterell, *Old Pewter,* 4569; London

158–161

DINING WARES 135

Touch Plate I, 300); indistinct secondary mark on underside of well incorporating, in part, a rose with a crown above with a palm frond to either side and crossing below; only the lion passant within a shield, the second of four pseudo hallmarks on underside of well, is distinct

INSCRIPTIONS: None

DIMENSIONS: OH. 3", OW. (rim) 21/32", Diam. 10 5/16", Diam. (base) 4 7/16"

PROVENANCE: Purchased from A. H. Isher & Son, Cheltenham, Eng.; 1958-562

This well-made salver is remarkably similar to one in the Carvick-Webster Collection that Cotterell illustrates.[1] The other example bears the mark of John Stribblehill of London. The vestiges of the touchmark on the CWF salver correspond quite closely to the Stribblehill touchmark as struck on London Touch Plate I. He entered this touch in 1678. Ricketts cites as his latest date for Stribblehill the completion in 1704 of the apprenticeship under him of his nephew, Thomas Stribblehill II.[2]

1. Cotterell, *Old Pewter*, p. 126, pl. LVIII, e–f.
2. Ricketts, *Pewterers of London*, p. 206.

160 SALVER

Thomas Banks
Secondary mark of Robert Banks
Wigan, Eng., 1680–1700

MARKS: Touchmark of the crest of a griffin rampant on a wreath bar with fronds or plumes to either side and crossing below with *THOMAS BANCKS* in curved arrangement below, all within a circle stamped twice on underside of well (Cotterell, *Old Pewter*, 234; Homer and Hall, *Provincial Pewterers,* p. 138, 4); secondary marks (1) label *R+BANCKS* within an oblong rectangle on underside of well below repeated touchmark (Cotterell, *Old Pewter*, 234; Homer and Hall, *Provincial Pewterers,* p. 138, 4), and (2) quality *X* with crown above and an apparent frond to either side within a conforming reserve above and between repeats of touchmark on underside of well

INSCRIPTIONS: Owner's initials *D/WC* with a crown over each stamped on upper face near rim

DIMENSIONS: OH. 3 1/4", Diam. 9 1/4", Diam. (base) 4 5/16"

PROVENANCE: Purchased from Thomas D. and Constance R. Williams, Litchfield, Conn.; 1957-94

Little is known of either maker. Their marks, as they appear on this salver, are usually illustrated together. Homer and Hall have speculated whether Robert Banks, probably of Bewdley, may have on occasion factored the work of Thomas Banks of Wigan.[1]

1. Homer and Hall, *Provincial Pewterers*, p. 138.

158

159

161 SALVER

Edward Leapidge I or II
London, 1700–1730

MARKS: Touchmark of a wheat sheaf with a hare sejant to the right framed by *EDWARD* in an oblong rectangle above, a pilaster to either side, and *LEAPIDGE* in an oblong rectangle below, all within a square on underside of well (Cotterell, *Old Pewter,* 2894); secondary marks (1) label *E:LEAPIDGE/LONDON* within a curved and outlined reserve with boldly scrolled lower edge below touchmark on underside of well (Cotterell, *Old Pewter,* 2894), and (2) quality *X* with crown above stamped over pseudo hallmarks on underside of well; pseudo hallmarks (1) *EL*, (2) sheaf of wheat, (3) leopard's head, and (4) buckle, all within shaped shields on underside of well (Cotterell, *Old Pewter,* 2893, 2894)

INSCRIPTIONS: None

DIMENSIONS: OH. 2 3/4", Diam. 9", Diam. (base) 3 11/16"

PROVENANCE: Purchased from A. V. Sutherland-Graeme, London; 1959-152

161

160

DINING WARES 137

162 Soup Tureen

William Sandys Green
London, 1725–1745

MARKS: Touchmark of a rose with a thistle to either side with their stems joined below and with crown above framed by W^M *SANDYS* within a curved reserve above and *GREEN* within a curved reserve below on underside of body (Cotterell, *Old Pewter*, 1991); cover unmarked

INSCRIPTIONS: None

DIMENSIONS: OH. 8", OL. 13 1/4", L. (base) 9 3/4", OW. 9 5/8", W. (base) 7 1/4"

PROVENANCE: Purchased from A. V. Sutherland-Graeme, London; 1957-104

PUBLISHED: Hornsby, *Pewter of the Western World*, p. 188, fig. 611

Silver soup tureens made their appearance in the 1720s, and they immediately assumed an important place in the dinner service. Early pewter tureens are conspicuously scarce. This particularly early example is a rare survival in the late baroque style.

163 Soup Tureen

Probably Thomas Chamberlain
London, 1755–1775

MARKS: None

INSCRIPTIONS: Arms with supporters, motto, and ducal coronet of Sackville, Dukes of Dorset, engraved on opposite sides of

162

163.1 Engraved crest on cover

body with crest and ducal coronet engraved on opposite sides of cover, probably for Lionel Sackville, Tenth Earl of Middlesex, who became First Duke of Dorset in 1720 and died in 1765; his son Charles, the second duke, died without issue in 1769; his nephew, John, succeeded in 1769 to the title, and he served as the third duke until his death in 1799

DIMENSIONS: OH. 9 3/8", OL. 16 3/8", OW. 9 3/8"

PROVENANCE: Purchased at Sotheby's, 1977; 1977-379

PUBLISHED: Sale cat., Sotheby's, Oct. 13, 1977, p. 12, lot 128, frontis.; Hornsby, *Pewter of the Western World,* p. 188, fig. 612

By the time Chamberlain fashioned this splendid tureen, coordinated pewter dinner services, usually headed by one or a pair of soup tureens and accompanied by both soup and dinner plates and a complement of dishes in graduated sizes, were being produced to compete with those in porcelain, earthenware, and fused silver plate (also called Sheffield plate). Chamberlain was the most notable London maker of fashionable dinner wares of the third quarter of the eighteenth century. When this tureen was auctioned in 1977, it was sold with remnants of its original service, including an oval dish, three soup plates, and ten dinner plates. All the plates and dishes in this service were of royal shape, that is, of serpentine outline, and armorial engravings of the Sackville family with the coronet of the Dukes of Dorset. Knole, their

163.2 Engraved coat of arms on body

residence in Kent, is one of the grandest country houses in Great Britain. Further, these other pieces of the service are all marked by Chamberlain, strengthening the attribution of the soup tureen to him.

This tureen is certainly one of the most felicitous examples in English pewter in the rococo style. Its form and detailing, in substance and nuance, are sensitively adjusted to contemporary silver and silver-plate examples (fig. 163.3). Absent are the awkward contours, the short stiff legs with claw-and-ball feet, and the less articulated rims and handles found on most other pewter tureens by this maker and others of this general date. Just compare this tureen with no. 164. Perhaps the aristocratic client made design requests for this service.

Occasionally, pewter tureens appear in the early records of Williamsburg and Yorktown, usually listed without the full supporting cast of matching plates and dishes. They are included in the inventories of James Shields, Williamsburg tavernkeeper, in 1750/1; William McKenzie, Williamsburg physician, in 1755; James Mitchell, Yorktown tavern keeper and saddler, in 1772; and Alexander Craig, Williamsburg saddler, in 1776.[1]

1. Inventory of the estate of James Shields, Jan. 21, 1750, York Co., Va., Wills & Inventories, Book 20, 1745–1759, pp. 198–200; inventory of the estate of William McKenzie, Aug. 18, 1755, York Co., Va., Wills & Inventories, Book 20, 1745–1759, pp. 364–366; inventory of the estate of James Mitchell, July 20, 1772, York Co., Va., Wills & Inventories, Book 22, 1771–1783, pp. 104–106; inventory of the estate of Alexander Craig, Mar. 2, 1776, York Co., Va., Wills & Inventories, Book 22, 1771–1783, pp. 330–337.

164 PAIR OF SOUP TUREENS

Thomas Chamberlain
London, 1745–1770

MARKS: Touchmark of the Prince of Wales feathers with royal crown above framed by *THOMAS* and *CHAMBERLAIN* within separate curved reserves above and below both on undersides of covers and bodies (Cotterell, *Old Pewter*, 873)

INSCRIPTIONS: Arms with supporters, motto, and baron's coronet of Baron Edgcumbe of Mount Edgcumbe, Devonshire, engraved on one side of each body and cover; the arms are those of either (1) Richard Edgcumbe (d. 1758), First Baron Edgcumbe, (2) his son Richard Edgcumbe (d. unmarried 1761), Second Baron Edgcumbe, or (3) his brother George Edgcumbe (d. 1795), Third Baron Edgcumbe, created Viscount Mount Edgcumbe and Valletort in 1781 and First Earl of Mount Edgcumbe in 1789

DIMENSIONS: OH. 9 1/2", OL. 15 1/4", OW. 8 11/16"

163.3 When this tureen is compared with the one of fused silver plate (Sheffield plate) on the right of about 1770 (CWF G1991-1070), a close correspondence in design is clearly evident

164.1 Engraved coat of arms on one side of each cover and body

164

PROVENANCE: Sold by the trustees of the Seventh Earl of Mount Edgcumbe and purchased by CWF at Sotheby's in 1956; 1956-346, 1–2

PUBLISHED: Sale cat., Sotheby's, June 1, 1956, p. 11, lot 40, ill.; *"Fashionable, Neat, and Good,"* p. 119, ill.

This handsome pair of soup tureens is from a much larger service that Chamberlain produced for Baron Edgcumbe of Mount Edgcumbe, Eng. The pair was sold at auction in 1956 along with ninety-four dinner plates, twenty-four soup plates, ten circular dishes, and eighteen oval dishes, all marked by Chamberlain and engraved with the baron's armorials. CWF acquired twelve of the dinner plates and twelve of the soup plates (nos. 144 and 145).

165 Soup Tureen

Maker unidentified
England, 1770–1800

165.1 Engraved coat of arms, motto, and crest on one side of body

165.2 Engraved crest on one side of cover

MARKS: None

INSCRIPTIONS: Arms, motto, and crest of the Protheroe family engraved on one side of body; crest repeated on one side of cover

DIMENSIONS: OH. 7 5/8", OL. 16", OW. 9 1/2"

PROVENANCE: Purchased from A. V. Sutherland-Graeme, London; 1958-561

Soup tureens of this general pattern remained popular well into the nineteenth century. Those supplied by Thomas Alderson for the coronation banquet of George IV in 1821 are similar to this example.[1] The beading

around the central handle and the rim of the cover and style of the armorial engraving are specific concessions to early neoclassic style, and they suggest a late eighteenth-century date.

1   *Short history of The Worshipful Company,* p. 90, no. 570, fig. 53, p. 91. Another example is illustrated in Donald F. Fennimore and Patricia A. Halfpenny with Kate Duffy and Janice Carlson, *Campbell Collection of Soup Tureens at Winterthur* (Winterthur, Del., 2000), p. 51, no. 23, ill.

166 Soup Tureen

With turned and ebonized wooden handles
Thomas Compton
London, 1801–1817

MARKS: No apparent touchmark; secondary marks (1) label *SUPERFINE/HARD METAL* within an oblong rectangle of scrolled outline, and (2) quality *X* with crown above stamped adjacent to label on underside of body; cover unmarked

INSCRIPTIONS: *TRINITY HOUSE* stamped on underside of body and partially obliterated

DIMENSIONS: OH. 8 1/2", OL. 16, OW. 10 1/8"

PROVENANCE: Purchased by Robin Bellamy Antiques, Witney, Eng., from Sotheby's, 1985; purchased by CWF from Robin Bellamy Antiques; 1985-159

PUBLISHED: Sale cat., Sotheby's, Apr. 25, 1985, lot 38, pl. I; Hornsby, *Pewter of the Western World,* p. 190, fig. 617

166.1 Property stamp on underside of body

This tureen is the same persistent pattern of the form.[1] In this instance, there is later neoclassic detailing to the handles and feet. This particular tureen is inscribed *TRINITY HOUSE* for the Corporation of Trinity House, an association of English mariners. Originally headquartered in

166

DINING WARES   143

Deptford, Eng., the association moved its headquarters from Water Lane, Lower Thames Street, London, to Trinity House, Tower Hill, in 1795.

1. Other soup tureens of this pattern are illustrated in Cotterell, *Old Pewter,* p. 143, pl. LXXV, fig. f (Port Collection); and *The Campbell Museum Collection,* 2nd ed. (Camden, N. J., 1972), no. 37, ill.

167 SAUCEBOAT

Henry Joseph
London, 1750–1780

MARKS: Touchmark *H•I* within a shaped rectangle on underside of base (Peal, *More Pewter Marks,* 2687); secondary mark of an *X* with crown above for quality over touchmark on underside of base

INSCRIPTIONS: Owner's initials *MW* with two crowns above stamped on face of handle grip

DIMENSIONS: OH. 3 3/8", OL. 6 1/4", OW. 3 1/2", Diam. (base) 2 1/2"

PROVENANCE: Purchased from Thomas D. and Constance R. Williams, Litchfield, Conn.; 1988-215

English pewter sauceboats from the eighteenth century are scarce, and most surviving examples are by Joseph of London. Elected a yeoman of the Pewterers' Company in 1736 and having risen to master in 1771, Joseph is noteworthy for the broad range of domestic goods that he produced for the American market.[1]

1. Wayne A. Hilt, "Henry Joseph—Master Pewterer," *Pewter Collectors Club of America Bulletin,* VII (September 1978), pp. 293–300.

168 SAUCEBOAT

Henry Joseph
London, 1760–1780

MARKS: No touchmark apparent

INSCRIPTIONS: None

DIMENSIONS: OH. 4 1/8", OL. 7 7/8"

PROVENANCE: Purchased from Michael Allen Kashden, Edgware, Eng.; 1995-72

Although no touchmark is apparent and the body has sustained considerable wear, the castings of handle and feet on this sauceboat match those of marked examples by Joseph.

169 SALT

Maker unidentified
England, 1670–1685

MARKS: None

INSCRIPTIONS: None

DIMENSIONS: OH. 2 3/8", W (rim). 4 5/16", W (base). 4 7/8"

PROVENANCE: Purchased from Thomas D. and Constance R. Williams, Litchfield, Conn.; 1956-85

EXHIBITED: Carol Reece Museum, East Tennessee State University, Johnson City, Tenn., 1967

This salt stands at the end of a long tradition of ceremonial salts. Larger salts were strong focal points to the well-dressed dining tables and defined the social position of diners by the salts' relative proximity to them. Silver table or master salts were often large and elaborate with scrolled brackets on their rims to support dishes with fruits and sweets to create glamorous centerpieces. By the turn of the eighteenth century, smaller and less formal individual salts replaced these large, pretentious ones. The mold for this salt was probably used during these same years to cast the central feet of salvers and the bases of candlesticks.

170 SALT

Hugh Quick
London, 1674–1690

MARKS: Touchmark of a cross formée with a fleur-de-lis issuing from either end of the vertical arms and with *H* to the left end and *Q* to the right end of the horizontal arms and with *16* above and *74* within a beaded circle on underside of well (London Touch Plate I, 230; Cotterell, *Old Pewter,* 3806)

INSCRIPTIONS: None

DIMENSIONS: OH. 2", Diam. (base) 2 3/8"

PROVENANCE: Purchased from the Old Pewter Shop, London; 1963-143

PUBLISHED: Hornsby, *Pewter of the Western World,* p. 143, fig. 392

This salt is a splendid example of an early bulbous trencher. It is more substantial and, with its octagonal paneling, more articulated than most examples. Quick specialized in elaborate candlesticks, and this salt is reminiscent of the central knop from the stems of his important pair (see no. 2).

171 SALT

Maker unidentified
England, 1690–1710

MARKS: Touchmark *IH* within an ornamented quatrefoil on underside of well for salt

INSCRIPTIONS: Owner's initials *AH* stamped inside base

DIMENSIONS: OH. 1 7/16", Diam. (body) 2 9/16", Diam. (base) 1 7/8"

170–173

PROVENANCE: Purchased from Price Glover Inc., New York, N. Y.; acquired, in part, with funds given by Mr. and Mrs. Robert L. Ashbaugh, Springfield, Va., in memory of Mrs. Thomas H. Seay; G1978-22

172 SALT

Maker unidentified
England, 1690–1710

MARKS: Indistinct touchmark incorporating, in part, *IH* on underside of well for salt

INSCRIPTIONS: None

DIMENSIONS: OH. 1 1/2", Diam. (base) 2 1/2"

PROVENANCE: Purchased from A. H. Isher & Son, Cheltenham, Eng.; 1958-557

A salt of the same design and bearing the same touchmark was formerly in the Bradshaw Collection.[1]

1. Sales cat., Sotheby's, June 13, 1977, p. 6, lot 10, ill.

173 SALT

Maker unidentified
England, 1710–1740

MARKS: None

INSCRIPTIONS: None

146 PEWTER AT COLONIAL WILLIAMSBURG

DIMENSIONS: OH. 1 1/4", OL. 3 1/8", OW. 2 3/8"

PROVENANCE: Purchased from A. H. Isher & Son, Cheltenham, Eng.; 1958-605

Oblong trencher salts with paneled bodies derive from a standard pattern in silver that is particularly associated with the specialist salt maker Edward Wood of London.

174 SALT

Maker unidentified
England, 1680–1700

MARKS: Touchmark *LS* within a serrated rectangle within well for salt

INSCRIPTIONS: None

DIMENSIONS: OH. 2 3/8", Diam. (base) 3 3/16"

PROVENANCE: Purchased from A. H. Isher & Son, Cheltenham, Eng.; 1966-291

Capstan salts, like their namesake, are of a spool form. They come plain or, as in this instance, decorated with bands of gadrooning below the rim of the well and on the shoulders of the base, and bound by a broad midband around a constricted waist. Peal illustrates a similar *LS* touchmark, although within a plain rectangle, on a capstan salt in the Michaelis Collection.[1]

1. Peal, *More Pewter Marks*, p. 88, no. 5938a.

175 SALT

Maker unidentified
England, 1680–1700

MARKS: Touchmark *IB* with device below within a heart within well of salt

INSCRIPTIONS: None

DIMENSIONS: OH. 1 11/16", Diam (base). 2 3/4"

PROVENANCE: Purchased from A. H. Isher & Son, Cheltenham, Eng.; 1963-143

This salt is an unusual abbreviation of the capstan type. Peal appears to record this touchmark from a small salt of about 1705, yet he does not indicate the presence of a probable rosette below the initials.[1]

1 Peal, *More Pewter Marks,* p. 58, no. 5441a.

174–175

176–178

176 SALT

Maker unidentified
England, 1770–1800

MARKS: None

INSCRIPTIONS: None

DIMENSIONS: OH. 2 7/16", Diam. (rim) 3 5/16", Diam. (base) 3 1/4"

PROVENANCE: Purchased from George McMahon, Boston, Mass.; 1930-320

These large and usually unmarked bulbous salts, similar to the CWF example, probably date from the last decades of the eighteenth century.

177 PAIR OF SALTS

Maker unidentified
England, 1740–1770

MARKS: Indistinct touchmark inside well

INSCRIPTIONS: None

DIMENSIONS: OH. 1 5/8", Diam. (rim) 2 1/2", Diam. (base) 2 3/8"

PROVENANCE: Purchased from Dr. Percy E. Raymond, Lexington, Mass.; 1950-909, 1–2

178 SALT

Maker unidentified
England, 1770–1810

MARKS: None

INSCRIPTIONS: None

DIMENSIONS: OH. 3 1/16", Diam. (rim) 3 13/16", Diam. (base) 3 3/8"

PROVENANCE: Purchased from A. H. Isher & Son, Cheltenham, Eng.; 1960-317

Salts of the same type as the CWF one, with a broad hemispherical bowl supported on a pedestal foot, are referred to as cup salts. Made in considerable numbers in pewter, they usually are unmarked and date from the second half of the eighteenth century and into the first decades of the nineteenth century.

179 SPICE POT

Henry Joseph
London, 1750–1780

MARKS: Touchmark *H•I* within a shaped rectangle on underside of base (Peal, *More Pewter Marks,* 2687); cover unmarked

INSCRIPTIONS: Unidentified crest of a lion rampant holding a rose in its forepaws engraved on a wreath bar on face of body

DIMENSIONS: OH. 4 11/16", Diam. (base) 1 13/16"

PROVENANCE: Mr. and Mrs. Gordon Perrin; purchased by CWF from John Carl Thomas, Hanover, Conn.; 1991-591

179.1 Engraved crest on face of body

Small containers with unpierced covers served as spice pots. The earliest examples date from the last quarter of the seventeenth century, and they are characterized by straight-sided bodies and rather low covers. Spice pots continue during the first half of the eighteenth century with bodies assuming a baluster shape and their covers a domed appearance with a pronounced finial and, as in this instance, a screw top.[1] This example, marked by Joseph, the prominent maker of export pewter for the American market, is rare as a marked London example, and it is undoubtedly among the latest examples of this uncommon form known. Its top is finely engraved with a running arcade.

1. K. G. Gordon, "Spice Canisters," *Journal of the Pewter Society,* III (autumn 1982), pp. 137–138; Carl Ricketts, "Lidded Containers—Known as 'Spice Pots,'" *Journal of the Pewter Society,* XI (spring 1997), pp. 27–34.

179

DINING WARES 149

180–183

180 Porringer

Maker unidentified
England, 1620–1640

MARKS: Touchmark *S:F* with an apparent animal below within a beaded circle on underside of bowl

INSCRIPTIONS: Owner's initials *R/IP* stamped on upper face of handle

DIMENSIONS: OH. 1 5/8", OL. 7", Diam. (rim) 5"

PROVENANCE: Excavated on the banks of the Thames River, not far from Hampton Court Palace; purchased from Richard Mundey, London; 1983-202

EXHIBITED: A Toast to the Globe: Drinking Vessels in Shakespeare's Time, Steuben Galleries, New York, N. Y., 1990

By the second quarter of the seventeenth century, the porringer had assumed its immediately recognizable form. The body now consisted of a shallow bowl with inclined, curved sides that was fitted with a single handle, or ear, of shaped triangular plan with openwork designs. Handles on porringers of this date, whether of

150 PEWTER AT COLONIAL WILLIAMSBURG

silver or pewter, are usually of geometric patterns, with diamonds or shields superimposed on trefoils the most popular.[1] The bottom of this example is generally domed, without a delineated central boss, in much the same manner as are some contemporary dishes and bowls.

1. Ronald F. Michaelis published a remarkable study of the development of the English pewter porringer in four parts: "English Pewter Porringers—Part I," *Apollo,* L (July 1949), pp. 23–26; "English Pewter Porringers—Part II," *Apollo,* L (August 1949), pp. 46–48; "English Pewter Porringers—Part III," *Apollo,* L (September 1949), pp. 81–84; and "English Pewter Porringers—Part IV," *Apollo,* L (October 1949), pp. 99–102. These articles were reprinted in the *Pewter Collectors Club of America Bulletin,* VII (February 1976), pp. 115–121, and VII (August 1976), pp. 155–162.

181 PORRINGER

Maker unidentified
England, 1680–1700

MARKS: Touchmark of a stylized shell with three pellets above with *T* to the left and *C* to the right within a cabled circle on underside of handle

INSCRIPTIONS: None

DIMENSIONS: OH. 1 3/4", OL. 8", Diam. (rim) 5 1/16"

PROVENANCE: Purchased from A. H. Isher & Son, Cheltenham, Eng.; 1960-463

Porringers of this type have relatively large handles of intricate scrolled design that are expressive of baroque style. These handles retain a plain central shield, a device found on many porringers throughout the seventeenth century. The attachment of the handle to the body is further strengthened by a wedge-shaped bar with a superimposed central triangular tab on the underside of the handle. Many porringer bodies assumed by 1680 the familiar convex, or bellied, silhouette to the exterior of their bowls. Porringers with bowls of this form were described as "booge porringers" then. The 1681 reference to these words in the records of the Pewterers' Company represents an early use of the phrase.[1] Booge is used more frequently to describe the short, curved sides of the well of a standard plate or dish. Simple compass-drawn pinwheel designs within circles appear on the interior center-bottom and the underside of the body.

A porringer of similar design was buried in the devastating earthquake in 1692 that destroyed Port Royal, Jamaica.[2]

1. Michaelis, "English Pewter Porringers—Part IV," p. 100.

2. Marx, *Silver and Pewter Recovered,* fig. 96; P. Spencer Davies, "Seventeenth Century Pewter from the sunken city of Port Royal, Jamaica," *Connoisseur,* CLXXXVIII (February 1975), pp. 136–141.

182 PORRINGER

Maker unidentified
England, 1660–1680

MARKS: Touchmark *WI* with a fleur-de-lis below within a beaded circle within shield between dolphins on upper face of handle

INSCRIPTIONS: Owner's initial *A* within a serrated rectangle stamped on upper face of handle near touchmark

DIMENSIONS: OH. 1 11/16", OL. 7 15/16", Diam. (rim) 5 3/8"

PROVENANCE: Kenneth W. Bradshaw, Lincoln, Eng.; sold and purchased by CWF at Sotheby's, 1977; 1977-220

PUBLISHED: Sales cat., Sotheby's, June 13, 1977, p. 15, lot 59, ill.; Brett, *Phaidon Guide to Pewter,* p. 50, ill.; Hornsby, *Pewter of the Western World,* p. 154, fig. 452

Archaeological excavations in 1859 near Charlestown, R. I., of the grave of Princess Weunquesh of the Niantic Narragansett tribe yielded two similar pewter porringers with rather straight-sided bowls and dolphin handles, along with other household goods, that had been buried with her after her death about 1686. They bear the marks of Joseph Collier and Timothy Blackwell of London, and they are owned by the Rhode Island Historical Society in Providence and the Roger Williams Park Museum, also in Providence.[1] Although documentation does not exist, one wonders whether these porringers were specifically selected as trade goods with coastal Indians and whether they were valued by their Indian owners and chosen as burial goods because of their zoomorphic handles.

1. Ronald F. Michaelis, "Back from the Dead: English Pewter Porringers from a Red Indian Grave in Rhode Island, U.S.A.," *Apollo,* LII (October 1950), pp. 121–122; Fairbanks and Trent, eds., *New England Begins,* II, p. 245, no. 225.

DINING WARES 151

183 PORRINGER

John Quick
London, 1701–1715

MARKS: Touchmark of a harp with a star above with *I* to the left and *Q* to the right within a beaded circle on underside of handle (London Touch Plate II, 591; Cotterell, *Old Pewter,* 3807)

INSCRIPTIONS: Owner's initials *KD* wriggle engraved on upper face of handle

DIMENSIONS: OH. 2", OL. 7 3/4", Diam. (rim) 5 3/8"

PROVENANCE: Purchased at Sotheby's, 1979; 1979-237

PUBLISHED: Sales cat., Sotheby's, June 11, 1979, p. 11, lot 69, pl. 1; Hornsby, *Pewter of the Western World,* p. 155, fig. 455; Law, "Williamsburg, Virginia—1994," p. 159, ill.

By the time Quick had fashioned this splendid porringer in the first years of the eighteenth century, the booged, or bellied, porringer had largely displaced other types. It was customary for most porringers then to have a raised central boss surrounded by a flat gutter in the bottoms of their bowls. Handles, or ears, were invariably burned on, that is, cast directly against the body. This process achieved a more secure join with the body. Since the point of attachment on the body was partly melted in the procedure, the pewterer used a damp cloth to cool the metal on the inside of the bowl. Consequently, one should expect to see a small textured area inside the bowl opposite the handle. Some collectors will not acquire a porringer purporting to be from the eighteenth or nineteenth centuries without the presence of a reassuring linen mark. By the time this porringer was made, the strengthening bar on the underside of the handle had been discarded with just the triangular tab retained.

This porringer is one of only four known English examples with relief-cast gadrooned decoration, all of which bear the mark of Quick of London.[1]

This handsomely executed decoration is cut into the interiors of the molds. A floral blossom of alternating type on a bifurcated stem is superimposed on the flutes between each of the gadroons. An intricate running border of flowers, bound by beaded borders with a band of cabling above, appears above the gadroons.

One of the main advantages of a piece with relief-cast decoration is that it cannot be cleaned up on a lathe to remove its casting marks. The use of a two-part mold with vertical seams is readily apparent on the front of the body and behind the handle. Where the handle was attached, the maker was not reluctant in removing the seam and the raised decoration in the area in a broad and exuberant manner. This same sensibility in adding handles is also evident in a fine two-handled cup at CWF (no. 290).

1. Another porringer by Quick from the Alfred Yeates bequest to the Victoria and Albert Museum was long thought to be the only recorded example of an English porringer with this type of decoration. North and Spira, *Pewter at Victoria and Albert,* p. 100, no. 120, ill. A matched pair, also by Quick but from a different mold than the other two, surfaced at Sotheby's in 1977, and they were acquired by the Pewterers' Company. Sales cat., Sotheby's, Mar. 16, 1977, p. 9, lot 70, frontis.; *Supplementary Catalogue of Pewterware, 1979,* p. 62, S5/501/33–34, ill. p. 66.

184 Commemorative Porringer and Cover

John Langford I
London, 1719–1730

MARKS: Touchmark of a sleeved arm holding a hammer over a tun with *I* to the left and *L* to the right within an outlined circle on underside of left handle; cover unmarked

INSCRIPTIONS: Owner's initials *S•E* stamped on the upper face of both handles and on top of cover in center

DIMENSIONS: OH. 3 3/4", H. (rim of porringer) 2 3/16", OL. 10 1/16", Diam. (cover) 6 1/4", Diam. (rim of porringer) 6"

PROVENANCE: Purchased from Henry J. Kauffman, Lancaster, Pa.; 1965-96

PUBLISHED: Michaelis, "More English commemorative pewter porringers," pp. 52–53, ill.; *"Fashionable, Neat, and Good,"* p. 118, ill.

One of the most remarkable bodies of work in English pewter is the group of approximately twenty known commemorative porringers from the late seventeenth and early eighteenth centuries. These have a distinctly un-English look to them. They exhibit strong Continental influence in their use of double handles and covers, not to mention the degree of elaborate relief-cast decoration. That they are noticeably larger than English porringers lends them an added sense of difference and importance.

This porringer is but one of three known examples that commemorates the signing of the Treaty of Ryswick in 1697. The cover bears the royal initials *WR* with crown above for King William III, military trophies, celebratory scenes, and four circular medallions with allegorical figures labeled *VALOVR, CONDUCT, CONCORDIA,* and *PEACE*. The center is left vacant for stamped owner's initials. Three standing cockerels are burned onto the cover so that the lid may be inverted to serve as a stand for the bowl. John Churchill, First Duke of Marlborough (1650–1722), prominently appears in heroic dress and pose on the boss in the interior center-bottom of the bowl. He holds in his right hand a flail with its tangled thongs spelling *Ryswick* in intertwined script and in his left, a banner inscribed *To Europe Peace I Give Let Nations Happy Unite.* Small circular eyelets with beaded surrounds have broken off the tips of both handles.

This porringer is marked by Langford, who did not commence work until 1719. Michaelis, in his article on English commemorative pewter porringers, speculated that this porringer was probably sold in 1722 to commemorate Marlborough's death. Either earlier castings were still available or new castings from the molds were produced at this time.[1]

Although the earlier history of this porringer is not known, one of the other two Treaty of Ryswick examples has a long tradition of New England ownership. Believed to have been owned by the Richards family of Boston in the eighteenth century, it was exhibited at the Centennial exhibition in Philadelphia in 1876.[2] Three other commemorative porringers have traditions of American ownership.[3]

1. Ronald F. Michaelis, "More English commemorative pewter porringers," *The Magazine Antiques,* LXXVIII (July 1960), p. 53.
2. C. Malcolm Watkins, "The American past in the modern spirit: the Smithsonian's new hall," *The Magazine Antiques,* LXXI (February 1957), ill. p. 144.
3. Harrold E. Gillingham published examples that belonged to Samuel Brown (1694–1769), who owned property adjacent to Pennsbury, Pa., and to the Harrold family of Bucks Co., Pa., in his article "Philadelphia Pedigreed Porringers," *The Magazine Antiques,* XXXVI (October 1939), pp. 189–190. Another commemorative porringer by John Waite of London descended in the Herrick family of Massachusetts and is presently owned by the Peabody Essex Museum in Salem, Mass. Fairbanks and Trent, eds., *New England Begins,* III, p. 384, no. 387, ill. p. 385.

185 PORRINGER

Maker unidentified
England, 1685–1700

MARKS: Touchmark of an elaborate openwork design of decorative cording with *I* or *T* to the left and *P* to the right within a beaded circle on underside of handle; *TP* in relief-cast letters on face of triangular reinforcing tab of handle attachment

INSCRIPTIONS: Owners' initials *IT/MF* stamped on face of handle

DIMENSIONS: OH. 1 11/16", OL. 7 1/4", Diam. (rim) 4 5/8"

PROVENANCE: Purchased from A. V. Sutherland-Graeme, London; 1959-35

This porringer is an early example of one with a handle of so-called Old English type. The handle has on its underside at the point of its attachment with the bowl a thickening bar of triangular cross-section and a central tab of triangular outline. A raised ridge between the relief-cast initials could be either a relief-cast device or the vestige of earlier conical strengthening devices. The porringer's booged body has a flat bottom without recess. These details, and the character of the touchmark and the initialing of the triangular handle tab, all contribute to its late seventeenth-century date.

186 PORRINGER

Richard Going
Bristol, Eng., 1730–1750

MARKS: Touchmark of a paschal lamb framed by *RICHARD/GOING* within an outlined circle on underside of handle

INSCRIPTIONS: Owner's initials *MR* stamped on face of handle

DIMENSIONS: OH. 1 11/16", OL. 6 15/16", Diam. (rim) 4 9/16"

PROVENANCE: Purchased from A. H. Isher & Son, Cheltenham, Eng.; 1963-145

By the time Going of Bristol made this porringer, few porringers were produced in England for the domestic market. Most were made for export and not in London, but in centers with strong ties to overseas shipping such as Bristol.

185–188

187 Porringer

Maker unidentified
England, 1700–1715

MARKS: None

INSCRIPTIONS: Owner's initials *AD* stamped on face of handle

DIMENSIONS: OH. 7", OL. 7 1/4", Diam. (rim) 5"

PROVENANCE: Purchased from A. H. Isher & Son, Cheltenham, Eng.; 1963-146

188 Two Porringers

Henry Hammerton
London, 1707–1740

MARKS: Touchmark of a crown over a tun with *H* to the left and right and *1707* below within a beaded circle on underside of each handle (London Touch Plate III, 642; Cotterell, *Old Pewter*, 2105)

INSCRIPTIONS: None

DIMENSIONS: OH. (1961-60) 1 7/8", OL. 7 3/16", Diam. (rim) 5", OH. (1961-61) 1 7/8", OL. 7 9/16", Diam. (rim) 5 3/8"

PROVENANCE: Purchased from A. V. Sutherland-Graeme, London; 1961-60, 1961-61

Hammerton produced a large number of porringers. He was one of the principal makers of porringers of this type with a distinctive tall concave collar immediately below the rim of the bowls.[1] Hammerton completed his apprenticeship in 1706 and entered his first mark the following year. He died in 1741.

1. Michaelis classifies this type as VIIc. "English Pewter Porringers—Part II," p. 48.

189 Porringer

Stephen Cox
Bristol, Eng., 1735–1754

MARKS: Touchmark of a rose encircled by *STEPHEN•COX* in a circle on underside of handle (Peal, *More Pewter Marks,* 1189)

INSCRIPTIONS: Owner's initials *D+C* engraved on face of body opposite handle

DIMENSIONS: OH. 1 13/16", OL. 7 7/8", Diam. (rim) 4 15/16"

PROVENANCE: Purchased from Dr. Percy E. Raymond, Lexington, Mass.; 1950-901

Porringers with handles with a ducal coronet over a plain circular reserve for stamped or engraved owner's initials or other designations placed in the center and framed by foliated scrolls first appear in English pewter about 1715.[1] Ian D. Robinson, in his article on porringers of this type, observes that he had never seen an example with a London maker's mark.[2] By far, almost all these porringers come from Bristol and bear the marks of makers whose work was exported to America, such as Cox, the maker of this example, Allen Bright, the maker of no. 190, Burgum & Catcott, Robert Bush I, Richard Going, and Ingram & Hunt. That these porringers were made for the export market is not surprising, since most porringers of this type date after the English had abandoned the form.

1. The most informative article on these porringers is Ian D. Robinson, "English Pewter Coronet Ear Porringers and Related Matters—(Who Was T.B.?)," *Journal of the Pewter Society,* XI (autumn 1998), pp. 27–38.
2. *Ibid.,* p. 32.

190 Pair of Porringers

Allen Bright
Bristol, Eng., 1742–1763

MARKS: Touchmark of a fleur-de-lis framed by *ALLEN•BRIGHT* within a circle on underside of each handle (Cotterell, *Old Pewter,* 574)

INSCRIPTIONS: None

DIMENSIONS: OH. 1 11/16", OL. 6 5/8", Diam. (rim) 4 1/4"

PROVENANCE: Purchased from A. H. Isher & Son, Cheltenham, Eng.; 1963-144, 1–2

PUBLISHED: Robinson, "English Pewter Coronet Ear Porringers," p. 33, fig. 26

Bright entered his own mark in 1742, and he died in 1763.

191 PORRINGER

Edgar, Curtis & Co.
Bristol, Eng., 1793–1801

MARKS: Touchmark of the standing figure of Neptune holding a trident in his right hand and the tail of a dolphin in his left hand framed, in part, with *EDGAR CURTIS & C⁰* within a circle on upper face of handle (Peal, *More Pewter Marks,* 1508)

INSCRIPTIONS: None

DIMENSIONS: OH. 1 7/16", OL. 6 1/4", Diam. (rim) 4 3/8"

PROVENANCE: Purchased from Dr. Percy E. Raymond, Lexington, Mass.; 1950-802

DINING WARES 157

PUBLISHED: Raymond, "American Pewter Porringers," p. 15, fig. 18

This porringer is marked with the larger touchmark of Edgar, Curtis & Co., which often appears on export wares of this firm with New England histories.[1]

1. Christopher A. Peal, *Addenda to More Pewter Marks* (Norwich, Eng., 1977), p. 9, no. 1508.

192 PORRINGER

Gershom Jones
Providence, R. I., 1774–1809

MARKS: Touchmark of a lion rampant facing right on a wreath bar with *G* to the left and *I* to the right within an outlined circle on upper face of handle (Laughlin, *Pewter in America*, I, 341)

INSCRIPTIONS: None

DIMENSIONS: OH. 1 15/16", OL. 7 15/16", Diam. (rim) 5 3/8"

PROVENANCE: Purchased from Dr. Percy E. Raymond, Lexington, Mass.; 1950-916

Although England's mercantile policy encouraged American colonists to export raw materials and to import English finished goods, American artisans produced an amazing array of household furnishings with a distinctive character. Porringers, like

192–194

many other objects in a range of materials, are often recognizable as coming from a particular shop, town, or region. Masters taught their apprentices the way objects were made and how they should appear, and customers acquired objects of a familiar appearance that they wished to live with and knew would meet with social approval. Buying a tried and true porringer pattern could be just as fashionable a choice in its time and place as the purchase of one of a newer design. The use of expensive copper alloy molds also encouraged a reluctance to change popular patterns.

Jones was born in Somers, Conn., in 1751. After completing his apprenticeship, probably with John Danforth of Norwich, he moved to Providence, R. I., in the early 1770s, where he entered into partnership with his brother-in-law, Samuel Hamlin. Jones probably learned of porringers with this handsome type of flowered handle from Hamlin, who is thought to have brought the pattern to Rhode Island from Connecticut in 1773. At the time of Jones's death in 1809, the inventory of his estate contained "30 wine-pint porringers." He is known to have made porringers in four sizes.[1]

1. Ledlie Irwin Laughlin, *Pewter in America, Its Makers and Their Marks,* I, reprint (Barre, Mass., 1969), pp. 97–98.

193 PORRINGER

Samuel E. Hamlin
Providence, R. I., 1801–1856

MARKS: Touchmark of an eagle displayed with a superimposed oval with an anchor and with *HAMLIN* within a curved banner above and *PROVIDENCE* in curved arrangement below within a serrated circle on upper face of handle (Laughlin, *Pewter in America,* I, 337)

INSCRIPTIONS: None

DIMENSIONS: OH. 1 29/32", OL. 7 15/16", Diam. (rim) 5 3/8"

PROVENANCE: Purchased from Mrs. Henry A. Hoffman, Litchfield, Conn.; 1952-262

Hamlin and his father, Samuel Hamlin, are noted for their truly prodigious output of porringers, most having burned-on ears, or handles, of flowered type, such as on this porringer and no. 192 by Gershom Jones. In fact, Rhode Island pewterers, in general, are remembered for their porringers, and their handles of flowered design are often referred to as Rhode Island handles. The younger Hamlin continued his father's business and maintained the quality of its productions before his death in 1864 at age eighty-eight.

194 PORRINGER

Samuel Hamlin
Providence, R. I., 1794–1801

MARKS: Touchmark of an eagle displayed with a vertically striped shield superimposed and holding an olive branch in its right talons and a group of arrows in its left talons with banners and stars above and *HAMLIN* below within a circle on upper face of handle (Laughlin, *Pewter in America,* I, 336)

INSCRIPTIONS: None

DIMENSIONS: OH. 1 1/2", OL. 6 1/4", Diam. (rim) 4 1/8"

PROVENANCE: Purchased from Dr. Percy E. Raymond, Lexington, Mass.; 1950-917

Hamlin probably served his apprenticeship between 1760 and 1767 under Thomas Danforth II and possibly Jacob Whitmore, both of Middletown, Conn. He was involved in a partnership with Danforth that was dissolved late in 1773. Hamlin used Danforth molds after he had moved to Providence, R. I., in 1773, for when Danforth died in 1782, his son Joseph traveled to Providence to recover some of his father's molds from Hamlin.[1]

Hamlin is believed to have introduced into Rhode Island the flowered handle, seen in its full form in nos. 192–193. Hamlin probably brought it in porringer or even mold form from Danforth's or Whitmore's shop.

In the same way that cabinetmakers sometimes carved handles for pewter teapots and coffeepots, they are also known on occasion to have made wooden patterns for the production of metal molds. William, Daniel, and Samuel Proud, cabinetmakers and turners from Providence, did considerable mold work for Hamlin. In 1773, William Proud charged Hamlin, "To making some molds," "To 2 molds, Turning for," "To altering 2 Molds," "To turning 2 partes for an Mold," and "To a mold for a handl." Hamlin, who carried on "the Pewterers and Braziers business . . . near the Great Bridge in Providence," informed his public in the Nov. 23, 1773, issue of the *Connecticut Courant* that "he has nearly completed a set of moulds, of the newest and neatest fashions, and flatters himself that they will upon tryal give universal satisfaction."[2]

1. Laughlin, *Pewter in America,* I, pp. 95–96; Montgomery, *History of American Pewter,* pp. 145–156.
2. Montgomery, *History of American Pewter,* p. 33.

195–196

195 Covered Bowl

Henry Joseph
London, 1760–1780

MARKS: Touchmark *H•J* within a rectangle on underside of base (Cotterell, *Old Pewter*, 5747A); secondary quality mark *X* with crown above on underside of base below touchmark; cover unmarked

INSCRIPTIONS: None

DIMENSIONS: OH. 6 3/4", H. (rim) 4 1/2", Diam. (cover) 6 15/16", Diam. (rim) 6 7/8", Diam. (base) 3 15/16"

PROVENANCE: Collection label of Frederick Jaeger (d. 1966), Dorking, Eng.; gift of Mr. and Mrs. Price Glover III, New York, N. Y.; G1985-105

This bowl is an uncommonly large example of its type. The retention of the original cover is an extremely rare feature. The cover is unusually shaped with the bezel having a curved profile that conforms to the outline of the body just below the rim. An uncovered bowl of similar form and size bears the mark of John Langford of London. It continues to serve in baptisms at the Parish Church of Saint Mary, Martlesham, Eng.[1] The touchmark appears to be the smaller of Henry Joseph's two *H•J* marks.[2]

1. John Tyler, "Pewter in a Suffolk Church," *Journal of the Pewter Society*, XVII (spring 2002), p. 50.
2. Hilt, "Henry Joseph," p. 292, fig. 2. Hilt illustrates a smaller bowl of this type of the conventional size belonging to the Connecticut Historical Society. *Ibid.*, p. 299, fig. 22.

196 Bowl

Richard Going
Bristol, Eng., 1730–1760

MARKS: Indistinct touchmark incorporating, in part, a paschal lamb on interior of bowl in center

INSCRIPTIONS: None

DIMENSIONS: OH. 3 1/16", Diam. (rim) 4 11/16", Diam. (base) 2 3/4"

160   PEWTER AT COLONIAL WILLIAMSBURG

PROVENANCE: Purchased from A. H. Isher & Son, Cheltenham, Eng., 1963-148

Although small, banded bowls of this type are often called broth bowls, they were undoubtedly used in many ways for service and consumption. Homer illustrates a similar example from the Worshipful Company of Clothworkers, which presumably is one of the "24 half-pint butter basins" supplied by Samuel Ellis I of London to the Company in 1735.[1]

1. Ronald F. Homer, "Clothworkers Pewter," *Journal of the Pewter Society*, 1 (spring 1977), pp. 27, 30.

197 COLANDER

John Birch & William Villers
Birmingham, Eng., 1772–1786

MARKS: No touchmark apparent; secondary marks of a label with *LONDON* within an outlined rectangle on interior of bowl in center (Cotterell, *Old Pewter*, 430; Homer and Hall, *Provincial Pewterers*, p. 138, 6) and quality *X* on interior of bowl between pseudo hallmarks; pseudo hallmarks (1) griffin's head erased, (2) *B&V*, and (3) sunburst, each within a shield with ears on interior of bowl in center (Cotterell, *Old Pewter*, 430; Homer and Hall, *Provincial Pewterers*, p. 138, 6)

INSCRIPTIONS: None

DIMENSIONS: OH. 5", Diam. (rim) 11 3/8", Diam. (base) 7"

PROVENANCE: Purchased from I. O. Lane, New York, N. Y.; 1932-22

Pewter colanders appear fairly frequently in Virginia household records of the seventeenth and eighteenth centuries. They range from ones professionally made, such as this footed example with swing handles, not dissimilar to those in design and size found on hot-water dishes. Simple examples were sometimes casually adapted from basins or deep dishes by drilling or punching them with circular holes in basic arrangement, as in no. 198.

Birch & Villers, which stands at the beginning of a succession of partnerships, has been called "the first recorded major firm of Birmingham pewterers."[1]

1. Homer and Hall, *Provincial Pewterers*, p. 79.

198 COLANDER

Maker unidentified
Probably England, 1760–1800

MARKS: None

INSCRIPTIONS: Owner's initials *P/HI* stamped on face of rim

DIMENSIONS: OH. 2 13/16", W. (rim) 1", Diam. (rim) approximately 11 1/8"

PROVENANCE: Purchased from Avis and Rockwell Gardiner, Stamford, Conn.; 1951-449

197–198

DINING WARES 161

199–201

199 Dessert Dish

Robert Nicholson
London, 1690–1710

MARKS: Partially indistinct touchmark of an eagle with spread wings with a pellet below each wing standing atop a sphere framed by *ROBERT* and *NICHOLSON* within separate curved reserves above and below and leafy fronds to either side on underside of well (Cotterell, *Old Pewter,* 3400); secondary mark of a label with *NICHOLSON* within an outlined rectangle on underside of well (Cotterell, *Old Pewter,* 3400)

INSCRIPTIONS: Unidentified coat of arms engraved on upper face in center

DIMENSIONS: OH. 1 3/8", Diam. (rim) 10 1/2"

PROVENANCE: Purchased from A. H. Isher & Son, Cheltenham, Eng.; 1966-294

This fluted dish and the following example are obviously based on a silver prototype. Usually referred to as strawberry dishes, they are much more common in expensive silver than in pewter. Another fluted dish of similar design, unmarked and engraved with a different coat of arms, was formerly in the Minchin Collection. The Minchin dish is the largest of the group, measuring fourteen inches in diameter.[1]

1. For a general discussion on this type of dish, see John Douglas, "An English Strawberry Dish," *Journal of the Pewter Society,* XVIII (autumn 2002), p. 38. The Minchin dish is illustrated in Kenneth Ullyett, *Pewter: A Guide for Collectors* (London, 1973), color pl. facing p. 51.

200 Dessert Dish

Probably Robert Nicholson
London, 1690–1710

MARKS: No marks apparent

INSCRIPTIONS: Unidentified coat of arms engraved on upper face of well in center

DIMENSIONS: OH. 11/16", Diam. 9 11/16"

PROVENANCE: Purchased from A. H. Isher & Son, Cheltenham, Eng.; 1958-559

Although this dish is not marked, it is so similar in every detail to no. 199, with the same coat of arms and from the same original service, that Nicholson must be considered its maker.

199.1 Engraved coat of arms in center

200.1 Engraved coat of arms in center

201 Dessert or Condiment Dish

Maker unidentified
England, 1710–1730

MARKS: None

INSCRIPTIONS: Hebrew letters corresponding to L and R wriggle engraved on underside of well; two paper labels with *Michaelis 241* and *83* applied to underside

DIMENSIONS: OH. 11/16", Diam. (rim) 5 1/8"

PROVENANCE: Ronald F. Michaelis, London (sold after his death in 1973 by Sotheby's); Kenneth W. Bradshaw, Lincoln, Eng. (sold in 1977 at Sotheby's, and purchased by CWF); 1977-217

PUBLISHED: Sales cat., Sotheby's, Nov. 12, 1973, p. 11, lot 64, pl. I; Hornsby, *Pewter of the Western World*, p. 135, fig. 358; Douglas, "English Strawberry Dish," p. 38

There are three fluted dessert dishes of this type at the Jewish Museum of London. All three bear the touch of Joseph Spackman of London, and date from the middle years of the eighteenth century. All have Hebrew letters corresponding to H.B. engraved on their undersides.[1] They may suggest a related function for the CWF dish with similarly inscribed Hebrew letters.

1. Alex Neish, "English Jewish Pewter," *Journal of the Pewter Society,* XI (spring 1998), pp. 42–43, fig. 32.

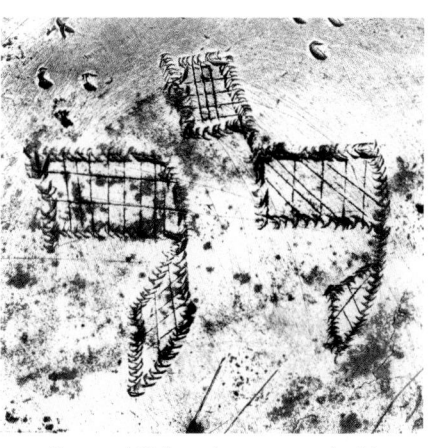

201.1 Engraved Hebrew letters on underside

DINING WARES 163

202 BASKET

James Vickers
Sheffield, Eng., ca. 1787–1800

MARKS: Touchmark *I.VICKERS* partially obliterated on underside of base in center (Scott, *Pewter Wares from Sheffield,* 467)

INSCRIPTIONS: None

DIMENSIONS: OH. 4 9/16", OL. 13 1/2", OW. 9 1/4"

PROVENANCE: Purchased from Mrs. Miles White, Jr., Baltimore, Md.; 1933-256

This handsome basket is not a product of the London pewter trade but of new approaches in the metal trades of Sheffield and of Birmingham. It is a fully representative example of Britannia metal by the individual who established the medium. Not cast in the traditional manner of most pewter, it is fashioned from cold rolled sheets of pewter with the intent of not only using the technology but also re-creating the lightness and designs of fused silver-plated wares. The vertical seam in the center of one side is visible where the sheet was bent into an ellipse and soldered with the base and the edging of the rim and hand holds then applied. The design of this basket is based on a plated prototype, such as the related one that Frederick Bradbury attributes to the Sheffield firm of Daniel Holy Wilkinson & Co.[1] The Williamsburg basket is a particularly rare survival.[2] For this type of rolled-sheet construction, Vickers and other early makers of Britannia wares used an alloy rich in tin with a few percent each of copper and antimony.

1. Frederick Bradbury, *History of Old Sheffield Plate...*, reprint (Sheffield, Eng., 1983), p. 212, ill.
2. Richard Mundey, the London pewter dealer, on viewing this basket in 1980, commented that he had never seen in his long career another Vickers basket of this design.

203 SPOON

Baluster-knop type
Maker unidentified
England, 1560–1600

MARKS: Touchmark *II* with a rayed sun between and enclosed within a beaded circle on face of bowl below juncture with handle (Cotterell, *Old Pewter*, 5717; Price, *Old Base Metal Spoons*, 40; Homer, *Five centuries of base metal spoons*, 56)

INSCRIPTIONS: None

DIMENSIONS: OL. 6 3/8", OW. (bowl) 1 7/8"

PROVENANCE: Found in the Thames River; purchased from Lindsay C. Grigsby, Richmond, Va., who acquired it from Gary Atkins, London; 1988-497

English spoons prior to the third quarter of the seventeenth century are characterized, for the most part, by their narrow, stalklike handles of hexagonal cross-section on a bowl of fig-shaped or related outline. Handles often end in finials of decorative or figural form. Baluster-knop finials differ from seal-top finials by the presence of small peak-shaped projections in the centers of their end.[1] Early English pewter spoons of this general type are most often marked on the face of the bowl, just below its juncture with the handle. This spoon is in remarkable condition, for it survived most of its life in the protective silt of the Thames River. Marks from scraping in the finishing are still clearly evident on the stem.

203.1 Finial

1. Useful guides to base-metal spoon types include F. G. Hilton Price, *Old Base Metal Spoons, with Illustrations and Marks* (London, 1908); Ronald F. Homer, *Five centuries of base metal spoons* (Workingham, Eng., 1975); and David Moulson, "The Development of the Modern Spoon Shape," *Journal of the Pewter Society*, XI (autumn 1998), pp. 2–7.

204 SPOON

Slip-end type
Maker unidentified
London, 1640–1680

MARKS: Touchmark of a hand holding a spoon with *W* to the left and *A* to the right within a beaded circle on face of bowl below juncture with handle (Cotterell, *Old Pewter*, 5402)

INSCRIPTIONS: Owner's initials *W* and *E* within shaped shields on face of bowl to either side of touchmark

DIMENSIONS: OL. 6 3/4", OW. (bowl) 2"

PROVENANCE: Purchased from A. V. Sutherland-Graeme, London; 1956-445

Slip-end spoons are conspicuous for their lack of a finial and the oblique termination of their handle ends, which resemble a gardener's slip. Surviving silver examples date over an extended period from the last decades of the fifteenth century until the third quarter of the seventeenth century.

205 SPOON

Trifid type
Maker unidentified
London, 1676-1690

MARKS: Touchmark *IN* with a fleur-de-lis with *7* to the left and *6* to the right below within a shield with a beaded border on face of bowl below handle (London Touch Plate I, 311; Cotterell, *Old Pewter*, 5814); pseudo hallmarks (1) *IN* with three pellets above within a shaped shield, (2) fleur-de-lis within an outlined lozenge, (3) lion passant with a pellet to the left within a shaped shield (partially indistinct), and (4) buckle within an outlined lozenge, all on underside of handle (nos. 2 and 4, Peal, *More Pewter Marks*, 5814)

INSCRIPTIONS: None

DIMENSIONS: OL. 7 5/16", OW. (bowl) 1 13/16"

PROVENANCE: Ronald F. Michaelis, Newhaven, Eng.; J. R. Franklin, Rowly, Eng.; purchased by CWF from Robin Bellamy Antiques, Witney, Eng.; 1988-403

PUBLISHED: Sales cat., Sotheby's, Nov. 12, 1973, p. 11, lot 67; sales brochure, Robin Bellamy Antiques, Witney, Eng., summer 1988, pl. I, no. 3

205.1 Handle end

203–209

203–209

The trifid spoon, with its broad handle face terrminating in a tripartite top and its oval bowl with level edges and a long rattail on its underside, inaugurates the modern phase of spoon design. It arrived in England in developed form from France about 1660. Skilled artisans cut the molds for spoons enriched with handsome relief-cast decoration with ornamental baroque designs or portraits of reigning sovereigns (see also nos. 206–209).

206 SPOON

Trifid type with portraits of King William III and Queen Mary
Robert Seare
London, 1689–1694

MARKS: Touchmark of a book with *6* to the left, *9* to the right, and *RS* below within an outlined circle on face of bowl below juncture with handle (London Touch Plate I, 165; Cotterell, *Old Pewter,* 4170A); pseudo hallmarks indistinct (1) possible lion passant, (2) buckle within a rectangle, and (3) leopard's head within a rectangle, all on underside of handle

INSCRIPTIONS: None

DIMENSIONS: OL. 7 3/8", OW. (bowl) 1 3/4"

PROVENANCE: Purchased at Phillips, Son & Neale, London, 1980; 1980-168

206.1 Handle end

PUBLISHED: Sales cat., Phillips, Son & Neale, London, June 27, 1980, p. 15, lot 8, pl. III

Patriotic themes, such as the portraits of reigning sovereigns, appear most often on spoons in cast-relief form amid baroque scrolls and naturalistic motifs in the late seventeenth and early eighteenth centuries and only sporadically thereafter. These spoons and other pewter objects with various forms of royal commemoration appealed to the same market as delft with related decoration.

Seventy-two trifid spoons by Stephen Bridges of London with the portrait of King William III on their handles and lace-back decorated bowls were found inside a pewter bottle on the wreck of the *Henrietta Maria,* recovered off the Florida Keys. The ship was reputedly a slaver that sailed from London to Africa and Jamaica in 1699. Presumably, these spoons were used as trade goods.[1] Several trifid spoons with relief-cast portraits of King William III and Queen Mary are among the pewter items found at Port Royal, Jamaica, that had been buried during the earthquake of 1692.[2]

1. Ian Robinson, "William III trifid spoons from a Florida shipwreck," *Journal of the Pewter Society,* VII (spring 1990), pp. 93–95. For additional reading on royal commemorative spoons, see Ronald F. Michaelis, "Royal Portrait Spoons in Pewter: A Mystery Unexplained," *Apollo,* LI (June 1950), pp. 172–173; *Pewterware with Royal Associations* (London, 1974).
2. Shirley Gotelipe-Miller, "The Port Royal pewter collection," *Journal of the Pewter Society,* VI (autumn 1987), p. 54, fig. 10.

207 SPOON

Trifid type with portrait of Queen Anne
Maker unidentified
England, 1702–1714

MARKS: None

INSCRIPTIONS: Initials *ID* cast-in with relief decoration on face of handle; owner's initial *E* within a serrated rectangle stamped on lower face of handle

DIMENSIONS: OL. 7 1/2", OW. (bowl) 1 3/4"

PROVENANCE: Purchased from Robin Bellamy Antiques, Witney, Eng.; 1984-141

There are a considerable number of spoons with a relief-cast portrait of Queen Anne. A number of these bear relief-cast initials. When they are found on a spoon with a touchmark, they would appear to be owner's initials. In this instance, there is no maker's touch, yet there are relief-cast initials *ID* at the base of the relief decoration on the face of the handle. In addition, this spoon bears a stamped *E* within a serrated rectangle further down the face of the stem, and this initial would appear to be unquestionably an owner's stamp. Michaelis raised the question of identities with another Queen Anne spoon (formerly in the Peal Collection). It also has the same cast *ID* initials and the stamped *H* within a serrated rectangle placed lower on the stem.

207.1 Handle end

168 PEWTER AT COLONIAL WILLIAMSBURG

207.2 Probable stamped owner's initial on face of handle

Michaelis offers no identity for the first set of initials, although he does suggest that the *H* within the serrated rectangle probably refers to a later owner.[1] This same spoon or another from the same set is illustrated in the catalog of the 1974 exhibition at Pewterers' Hall.[2] It would seem that these two spoons, which appear to have been cast in the same mold and stamped with different letter dies from the same set, were made by the same maker for different families and that the *ID* relates to their common maker.

1. Michaelis, "Royal Portrait Spoons in Pewter," pp. 172–173, fig. III.
2. *Pewterware with Royal Associations,* p. 10, no. 53, ill.

208 TEASPOON

Trifid type
Maker unidentified
England, 1675–1705

MARKS: None

INSCRIPTIONS: None

DIMENSIONS: OL. 4 1/16", OW. (bowl) 31/32"

PROVENANCE: Ronald F. Michaelis, Newhaven, Eng.; purchased by CWF from Robin Bellamy Antiques, Witney, Eng.; 1982-183

Small pewter spoons, usually called teaspoons, such as this engaging example, were intended for the service not only of tea, but also of coffee and chocolate. Early examples from the last decades of the seventeenth century are of trifid form. They are often covered with cast-relief decoration, in much the same manner as early prototypical silver spoons of this size, which are often gilded and embellished with overall engraving of similar design.

209 PAIR OF SPOONS

Trifid type with portrait of Queen Anne
Maker unidentified
England, 1702–1714

MARKS: None

INSCRIPTIONS: Probable owner's initials *SS* in ornamented script letters cast in relief on underside of each handle

DIMENSIONS: OL. 7", OW. (bowl) 1 11/16"

PROVENANCE: Purchased from A. V. Sutherland-Graeme, London; 1953-1083, 1–2

A considerable number of Queen Anne commemorative spoons, such as no. 207, bear relief initials from their original castings. The cast initials are an embellished *SS* in script on the undersides of the handle ends. Cotterell associated these initials with Simon Sanders, a spoonmaker of Bideford.[1] Michaelis feels quite strongly that these initials and others found on such spoons do not relate to makers. He cites as evidence a Queen Anne commemorative spoon with the relief-cast initials *WP* with crown above on the underside of the handle and the maker's touch of David Heyrich of London in the bowl. Michaelis contends that Anne's coronation in 1702 was the principal occasion for the production of these spoons.[2] Because this pair have been silvered, it is difficult to be confident of their age, especially when they are desirable, decorated examples.

209.1 Handle end

1. Howard Herschel Cotterell, *Bristol and West-Country Pewterers, with Illustrations of their Marks* (Bristol, Eng., 1918), p. 34, no. 175.
2. Ronald F. Michaelis, "Royal Occasions Commemorated in English Pewterware," *Antique Collector,* XXXVII (August–September 1966), pp. 3–5.

209.2 Relief-cast initials on underside of handle

DINING WARES

210–215

210 SPOON

Wavy-end type
Maker unidentified
England, 1690–1725

MARKS: Touchmark of an elaborate openwork design of decorative cording with *I* or *T* to the left and *P* to the right within a beaded circle on underside of handle; possible indistinct pseudo hallmarks on underside of handle

INSCRIPTIONS: None

DIMENSIONS: OL. 7 3/4", OW. (bowl) 1 11/16"

PROVENANCE: Purchased from A. V. Sutherland-Graeme, London; 1953-427

This same touchmark appears on a porringer at CWF (no. 185).

170 PEWTER AT COLONIAL WILLIAMSBURG

210–215

211 SPOON

Wavy-end type
Maker unidentified
England, 1690–1725

MARKS: Possible touchmark with beaded border between quality mark and stamped owners' initials on underside of handle; secondary mark of a quality *X* stamped on underside of handle; indistinct pseudo hallmarks (1) initialled mark incorporating a *W,* (2) apparent crescent, (3) possible lion rampant, and (4) pinwheel or flowerlike device, all on underside of handle

INSCRIPTIONS: Owners' initials *B/TD* stamped on underside of handle

DIMENSIONS: OL. 8 1/4", OW. (bowl) 1 11/16"

PROVENANCE: Purchased from Robin Bellamy Antiques, Witney, Eng.; 1984-144

Wavy-end spoons introduce subtle refinements toward more modern spoon design. The earlier trifid was a somewhat awkward assemblage of separate parts with strange clefts to the handle end, a flatness to the handle face, and an explicit separation between handle and bowl. With the wavy-end spoon, there is a softer, more continuous contour to the handle end, with a handle shank of rounded face and sides of D-shaped cross-section, with a softened and flared transition between the two, to a bowl of elongated oval form that respects a harmonious adjustment of elements. Also, while the trifid spoon, like the contemporary cane-back chair, has a two-dimensional quality with the preferred view that of the front or facade, the wavy-end spoon is more three-dimensional and unified as an object.

Pewter wavy-end spoons, like those in silver, make their appearance in the 1690s, and they continue to be made well after the introduction of the Hanoverian type in the 1720s.[1]

1. One of the earliest datable wavy-end spoons was found at Port Royal, Jamaica, where it was deposited in the earthquake of 1692. Moulson, "Development of Modern Spoon Shape," p. 4.

212 SPOON

Wavy-end type
Maker unidentified
Probably Ireland, 1700–1730

MARKS: No apparent touchmark; secondary mark of a quality *X* stamped on underside of handle; pseudo hallmarks (1 and 3) thistle and (2 and 4) harp, all on underside of handle

INSCRIPTIONS: Owners' initials *P/IM* stamped on face of handle

DIMENSIONS: OL. 8 1/4", OW. (bowl) 1 3/4"

PROVENANCE: Purchased from A. V. Sutherland-Graeme, London; 1953-429

Hall attributes these pseudo hallmarks to an artisan in Ireland but not to any particular maker.[1]

1. Hall, *Irish Pewter,* p. 70.

213 SPOON

Wavy-end type with portrait of George I
Maker unidentified
England, 1714–1727

MARKS: None

INSCRIPTIONS: *GR* for George Rex cast in relief below portrait on face of handle; owners' initials *RE* and *ER* cast in relief on underside of handle

DIMENSIONS: OL. 7 15/16", OW. (bowl) 1 5/8"

PROVENANCE: Purchased from Robin Bellamy Antiques, Witney, Eng., which had acquired this spoon and a matching example from a Nottingham dealer some years ago; 1991-163

This spoon and its mate are the only known spoons with a relief-cast portrait bust of George I in the classical style with a wreath of laurel leaves in his hair, as in his depictions on English coins. The interior of the bowl has been strongly scraped or grated.

213.1 Handle end

213.2 Relief-cast owners' initials

172   PEWTER AT COLONIAL WILLIAMSBURG

214 SPOON

Wavy-end type with Greenwich Hospital medallion
Maker unidentified
England, 1775–1800

MARKS: None

INSCRIPTIONS: Owner's medallion of an anchor with crown and crossed flags above with *G* to the left and *H* to the right within a circle stamped on upper face of handle for Greenwich Hospital; shadow of a former collector's number *220* painted on underside of handle

DIMENSIONS: OL. 8 9/16", OW. (bowl) 1 3/4"

PROVENANCE: Purchased from Robin Bellamy Antiques, Witney, Eng.; 1984-142

Greenwich Hospital spoons are from a later date than is generally realized. Although Cotterell dates an example from the Port Collection about 1700, as does Hornsby one from the Bishop-Vellacott Collection, all examples appear to be cast from the same mold and to date from the late eighteenth century.[1] This later dating is clear from their bowl form (an elongated oval tending toward a pointed egg shape), the short, rounded drop on the undersides of their bowls, and their considerable length.

1. Cotterell, *Old Pewter*, p. 135, pl. LXII, fig. b, no. 25; Hornsby, *Pewter of the Western World*, p. 183, fig. 582.

214.1 Handle end

215 SPOON

Wavy-end type
Maker unidentified
England, 1690–1730

MARKS: No apparent touchmark; secondary mark of a quality *X* on underside of handle

INSCRIPTIONS: Owner's initials *MT* stamped on underside of handle

DIMENSIONS: OL. 6 1/8", OW. (bowl) 1 5/32"

PROVENANCE: Purchased from A. V. Sutherland-Graeme, London; 1953-426

This spoon of unusual intermediate size was probably intended for general utility rather than for more gentrified or specialized use, such as one of a set of dessert spoons. Such distinctions were just being introduced into silver flatware at this time.

216 SPOON

Hanoverian type
John Wyatt
London, 1730–1760

MARKS: Touchmark *IW* with a wheat sheaf flanked by a mullet to either side above and a rose below within a vertical rectangle with an arched top on underside of handle (London Touch Plate III, 739; Cotterell, *Old Pewter*, 5314; Peal, *More Pewter Marks*, 5314); secondary marks (1) label with *LONDON* within an outlined oblong rectangle on underside of handle (Peal, *More Pewter Marks*, 5314), and (2) quality *X* with crown above on underside of handle below touchmark (Peal, *More Pewter Marks*, 5314)

INSCRIPTIONS: Owner's initial *C* engraved on underside of handle

DIMENSIONS: OL. 8", OW. (bowl) 1 13/16"

PROVENANCE: Purchased from A. V. Sutherland-Graeme, London; 1953-1087

Hanoverian spoons had largely replaced wavy-end ones by 1730. The handle end was rounded off and turned upward with the discarded central projection of the handle end replaced by a central

216–224

rib extending down the handle face. Bowls, for the most part, are of elongated oval form with early examples retaining a long rattail. Hanoverian spoons are even more three-dimensional than their antecedents with a more elegant profile, from the thickened and upturned end of the handle through the gradual taper of the stem, to an augmented shank that curves into the heel of the bowl with the long rattail on the underside that conveys and disperses the stress of the handle in the broad metal of the bowl.

217 SPOON

Hanoverian type
Maker unidentified
England, 1720–1770

MARKS: Touchmark *I* [?]•*B* within an outlined circle on underside of handle (Peal, *More Pewter Marks,* 5408b); secondary marks (1) label with *LONDON* within a serrated oblong rectangle on underside of handle, and (2) quality *X* with crown above on underside of handle

INSCRIPTIONS: None

DIMENSIONS: OL. 7 13/16", OW. (bowl) 1 5/8"

PROVENANCE: Purchased from A. V. Sutherland-Graeme, London; 1953-1090

This example is one of a group of spoons that all have a narrow urn-shaped augmentation of the central rib of the handle face. This feature was cut into the mold and is part of the initial

174   PEWTER AT COLONIAL WILLIAMSBURG

216–224

217.1 Handle end    218.1 Handle end

casting of these spoons.

The illustration of the touchmark on this spoon in Peal may very well have come from this spoon, for he comments that his rendering came from "a long bowl spoon, c. 1760" that belonged at one time to Sutherland-Graeme.[1]

1. Peal, *More Pewter Marks,* p. 56, no. 5408b.

218 Spoon

Hanoverian type
George Lowes
Newcastle, Eng., 1740–1765

DINING WARES 175

MARKS: Touchmark of a standing bird with leafed sprig in bill and a mullet over its back framed by *G•LOWES* with crossed fronds below within a double circle on underside of handle (Cotterell, *Old Pewter,* 3001)

INSCRIPTIONS: Owner's initials *DD* stamped on interior of bowl

DIMENSIONS: OL. 7 3/4", OW. (bowl) 1 5/8"

PROVENANCE: Purchased from Robin Bellamy Antiques, Witney, Eng.; 1984-146

Lowes became a member of the Company of Plumbers, Pewterers, Glaziers, and Painters of Newcastle in 1725, after having served his apprenticeship under the local pewterer, Jacob Watson. When he died at age seventy in 1774, the *Newcastle Courant* noted that Lowes had been for "many years an eminent pewterer on The Side who had acquired a handsome fortune and who had been retired these many years."[1]

1. Lamb, "Newcastle pewter and pewterers," p. 129.

219 SPOON

Hanoverian type
Timothy Taylor
London, 1759–1780

MARKS: Touchmark of a crescent framed by *TIMOTHY•TAYLOR* in circular arrangement within an outlined circle on underside of handle (Peal, *More Pewter Marks,* 4675); secondary marks (1) label with *LONDON* within an outlined and serrated oblong rectangle on underside of handle (Peal, *More Pewter Marks,* 4675), and (2) quality *X* with crown above on underside of handle

INSCRIPTIONS: Owner's initials *DS* stamped on underside of handle

DIMENSIONS: OL. 8 3/8", OW. (bowl) 1 3/4"

PROVENANCE: Purchased from A. V. Sutherland-Graeme, London; 1953-1089

Taylor, who specialized in making spoons, was admitted to the Pewterers' Company after completing his apprenticeship in 1759.[1]

1. Ricketts, *Pewterers of London,* p. 211.

220 BASTING OR SERVING SPOON

Hanoverian type
Thomas Leach
London, 1730–1750

MARKS: Touchmark on underside of handle indistinct; secondary mark of a quality *X* with probable crown above on underside of handle; partially indistinct pseudo hallmarks (1) lion passant facing right, (2) arms with a Saint George's cross in center with a sword in the first and second quarters, (3) *T•L* in script, and (4) leopard's head, each within a shaped reserve on underside of handle (Peal, *More Pewter Marks,* 2887)

INSCRIPTIONS: None

DIMENSIONS: OL. 15 1/16", OW. (bowl) 2 9/16"

PROVENANCE: Purchased from Lillian Blankley Cogan, Farmington, Conn.; 1955-269

Large spoons of basic types are not uncommon in silver. They were especially useful in the service of stews, and they were sometimes referred to in Virginia records as ragout spoons.[1]

During at least part of its life, this spoon apparently was used primarily as a basting spoon, for it has a punched hole toward the end of its handle, probably for its convenient hanging in the kitchen.

1. William Byrd III of Westover, Charles City Co., Va., for instance, owned in 1769 "four Ragooe Spoons" with a value of £4. These four spoons would appear to be the "two raguel spoons" and the "two ragoul spoons" listed in the 1813 will of his widow, Mary Willing Byrd. "List of the Plate at Westover August 10th, 1769," ms., Charles City Co., Deeds & Wills, 1766–1774, p. 193, Virginia State Library, Richmond, Va. "The Will of Mrs. Mary Willing Byrd, of Westover, 1813, with a List of the Westover Portraits," *Virginia Magazine of History and Biography,* VI (April 1899), pp. 350–351.

221 SPOON

Hanoverian type
John Vaughan
London, 1760–1780

MARKS: Label touchmark *I•VAUGHAN* within an oblong rectangle on underside of handle (Cotterell, *Old Pewter,* 4863); secondary marks (1) paschal lamb framed by *MADE•IN* within a curved reserve above, a pillar to either side, and *LONDON* below on underside of handle (Cotterell, *Old Pewter,* 4863), and (2) quality *X* with crown above on underside of handle

INSCRIPTIONS: None

DIMENSIONS: OL. 8 3/4", OW. (bowl) 1 3/4"

PROVENANCE: Purchased from A. V. Sutherland-Graeme, London; 1953-1088

It is ironic that Vaughan first registered his touch in 1760, the year in which King George III ascended to the throne and the year before his marriage to Charlotte, since Vaughan is particularly remembered for his handsome royal portrait spoons of these monarchs (see no. 222). He also made a large number of other spoons, such as this straightforward Hanoverian example with a stylish relief-cast shell on the back of its bowl.

222 SPOON

Hanoverian type with portraits of
    King George III and Queen Charlotte
John Vaughan
London, ca. 1761

MARKS: Label touchmark *I•VAUGHAN* within an oblong rectangle on underside of handle (Cotterell, *Old Pewter,* 4863); secondary marks (1) a paschal lamb within an architectural frame with arched top and pillars at sides on underside of handle, (2) label with *LONDON* within a curved rectangle on underside of handle, and (3) quality *X* with crown above on underside of handle

INSCRIPTIONS: None

DIMENSIONS: OL. 8 5/16", OW. (bowl) 1 5/8"

PROVENANCE: Purchased from Robin Bellamy Antiques, Witney, Eng.; 1984-143

Vaughan's King George III and Queen Charlotte portrait spoons are certainly among the most beautiful spoons of Hanoverian type. No other portrait spoons are as technically accomplished in the cutting of their molds. They may very well have been occasioned by George's marriage to Charlotte in 1761. Other spoons of this pattern at CWF are a group of six (1953-1082, 1–6) and a single example

222.1 Handle end

(G1970-136) given by Mr. and Mrs. Derk H. G. van Bergen van der Grijpe of The Hague, the Netherlands, in memory of Mrs. Catherine Aafje Ekama.

223 SPOON

Round end with ears type
John Vaughan
London, 1760–1780

MARKS: Label touchmark *I•VAUGHAN* within an oblong rectangle on underside of handle (Cotterell, *Old Pewter,* 4863); secondary marks (1) paschal lamb framed by *MADE•IN* within a curved reserve above, a pillar to either side, and *LONDON* below on underside of handle (Cotterell, *Old Pewter,* 4863), and (2) quality *X* with crown above on underside of handle

INSCRIPTIONS: None

DIMENSIONS: OL. 8 3/16", OW. (bowl) 1 3/4"

PROVENANCE: Purchased from A. V. Sutherland-Graeme, London; 1953-1091

This spoon is of a strange hybrid type. In many ways, it harkens back to the late seventeenth century. It has a flat handle face with a shank of trapezoidal cross-section. There is an abrupt line of demarcation between stem and bowl. Although the bowl is of relatively narrow and elongated oval outline, like those of most Hanoverian spoons, it has an uncharacteristic early rattail. These features ally it to the trifid examples of the late seventeenth century.

A further spoon of this idiosyncratic type by Vaughan, although with his twin portrait of King George III and Queen Charlotte, usually seen on Hanoverian tablespoons (see no. 222), is part of the Port Collection at the Victoria and Albert Museum, London.[1]

1. North and Spira, *Pewter at Victoria and Albert,* p. 108, no. 138g, ill. p. 106.

224 SPOON

Hanoverian type
Thomas & Townsend Compton
London, 1802–1814

MARKS: Touchmark of a paschal lamb with dove in flight with olive branch in bill above framed by *THOMAS & TOWNSEND COMPTON* within a double vertical oval on underside of handle (Cotterell, *Old Pewter*, 1064); secondary mark of a quality *X* with crown above on underside of handle

INSCRIPTIONS: None

DIMENSIONS: OL. 8 1/16", OW. (bowl) 1 5/8"

PROVENANCE: Gift of John O. Sands, Williamsburg, Va. (acquired at a yard sale in Smithfield, Va.); G1986-261

This spoon shows the survival of the basic Hanoverian type into the early decades of the nineteenth century. It still has the elongated oval bowl with a modified single drop with a pronounced lower lip. This type of drop appears on all the English Hanoverian spoons at CWF, yet it is less common on American spoons of this type.

225–228

225 SPOON

Old English type
Maker unidentified
England, 1770–1790

MARKS: Touchmark *WFB* within a rectangle on underside of handle

INSCRIPTIONS: Owner's initials *HS* stamped on face of handle

DIMENSIONS: OL. 8", OW. (bowl) 1 5/8"

PROVENANCE: Purchased from Robin Bellamy Antiques, Witney, Eng.; 1984-145

Spoons of Old English type are characterized by a handle of continuous loop-shaped outline that turns down at the end. Relatively early examples, such as this one, appropriate the elongated oval bowl with modified single drop from Hanoverian spoons. Introduced about 1770, there is considerable overlap with spoons of Hanoverian type.

225–228

226 SPOON

Old English type with portrait of King George III
Maker unidentified
England, 1800–1820

MARKS: None

INSCRIPTIONS: Initials *I•H* cast in relief on upper face of spoon below portrait of George III

DIMENSIONS: OL. 7 7/16", OW. (bowl) 1 9/16"

PROVENANCE: J. R. Franklin, Rowly, Eng.; purchased from Robin Bellamy Antiques, Witney, Eng.; 1988-402

PUBLISHED: Sale cat., Robin Bellamy Antiques, Witney, Eng., summer 1988, pl. I, no. 9

This spoon depicts an older George III in simple dress as Farmer George. In his later years, George III convalesced in the country, and he was noted for his interest in rural pursuits. As in a number of spoons of this period, the handle is quite flat, neither turning up nor down at the end. It has a rather short single drop on the bowl that was augmented with a superimposed narrow spline to derive some of the same benefit of the earlier rattail. The relief-cast initials *I•H* on the face of the handle appear on other surviving spoons with this portrait, and the question remains as to whom they relate.

225.1 Handle end    226.1 Handle end

227 SPOON

Old English type
George Coldwell
New York, N. Y., 1787–1811

MARKS: Touchmark *G:COLDWELL* within a serrated rectangle on underside of handle (Laughlin, *Pewter in America,* II, 510)

INSCRIPTIONS: None

DIMENSIONS: OL. 7 11/16", OW. (bowl) 1 19/32"

PROVENANCE: Purchased from Mrs. James E. Ingraham, Hamden, Mass.; Mrs. Ingraham and her husband found the spoon in 1965 while they were making repairs to their house (their house was built in 1812); 1966-161

PUBLISHED: Hornsby, *Pewter of the Western World,* p. 183, fig. 585

227.1 Handle end

Coldwell is noted, in part, for his production of spoons with patriotic decoration. He advertised for sale in the *New York Daily Advertiser* for Nov. 22, 1794, "British metal, table, dessert and tea spoons, elegantly ornamented and plain, common pewter table and tea spoons, various sizes, plain and figured," among other things. His decorated spoons are of two basic types: those, such as this example, with feather-edged borders and stamped with crossed flags and a liberty cap atop a pole and a banner lettered *PEACE & AMITY* and others, also with feathered edges, and a circular medallion and the words *FEDERAL CONSTITUTION*.[1]

1. These basic types are illustrated in Laughlin, *Pewter in America,* I, pl. XXV, nos. 173–174. The advertisement of 1794 is quoted on p. 24.

228 SPOON

Old English type
Maker unidentified
Probably New England, 1780–1810

MARKS: None

INSCRIPTIONS: None

DIMENSIONS: OL. 7 7/8", OW. (bowl) 1 1/2"

PROVENANCE: Tradition of descent in the Bailey family, Lynn, Mass.; gift of Mrs. A. E. Alekian, San Francisco, Calif.; G1963-728

PUBLISHED: Hornsby, *Pewter of the Western World,* p. 183, fig. 586

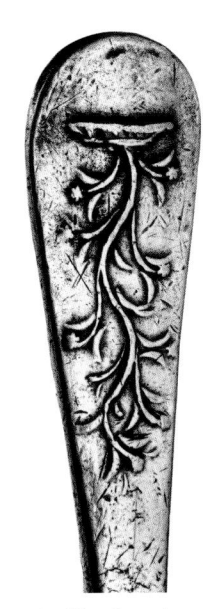

228.1 Handle end

229 SPOON

Old English type
Thomas Yates
Birmingham, Eng., 1849–1882

MARKS: *THOMAS YATES/STEEL WIRE/WIRE TY* within separate oblong reserves on underside of handle (Cotterell, *Old Pewter,* 5346; Homer and Hall, *Provincial Pewterers,* 47)

INSCRIPTIONS: None

DIMENSIONS: OL. 9", OW. (bowl) 1 7/8"

PROVENANCE: Purchased from Robin Bellamy Antiques, Witney, Eng.; 1984-159

Birmingham was a significant center for the production of pewter in nineteenth-century England. In this period of the trade's decline, with the clear choice of consumers for fashionable and inexpensive white-bodied ceramics, the remaining Birmingham pewterers had to be resourceful in exploiting new opportunities, whether for pub mugs and measures, beer machines and bar fittings for public houses, or for blanks for electroplated wares after 1840 and exports to various parts of the empire, in particular, Australia. Prominent among these pewterers was the Yates family.[1]

This late spoon of Old English type is decidedly of nineteenth-century character. Heft has replaced slender grace. The pronounced ridge on the underside of the handle is due to the insertion of an iron-steel wire for strength. The raised drop on the underside of the bowl has greater prominence, and its pierced design is in the gothic style.

1. Homer and Hall, *Provincial Pewterers,* pp. 88–91. For further information on the Yates family, see A. S. Law, "Birmingham pewterers in the 19th Century—the Yates family," *Journal of the Pewter Society,* IV (autumn 1984), pp. 105–109.

230 SPOON

King's pattern
Maker unidentified
England, 1820–1850

MARKS: None

INSCRIPTIONS: None

DIMENSIONS: OL. 9", OW. (bowl) 1 7/8"

PROVENANCE: Purchased from Robin Bellamy Antiques, Witney, Eng.; 1984-160

Some of the most fashionable patterns of spoons in the first half of the nineteenth century use handles of this hourglass outline. The king's pattern, with its elegant scrolled framing accented by shells and anthemia, is the most popular decorative pattern for spoons with handles of hourglass shape. The length of the spoon, at nine inches, is also indicative of its nineteenth-century date.

230.1 Handle end

231 SAUCE LADLE

Plain fiddle type
John Yates
Birmingham, Eng., 1837–1860

MARKS: Maker's touch *JO/HN/YA/TE/S* within a sequence of five rectangles on underside of handle (Cotterell, *Old Pewter,* 5340A; Homer and Hall, *Provincial Pewterers,* 46); secondary mark *VR* in script with royal crown above within a conforming reserve on underside of handle (Cotterell, *Old Pewter,* 5340A; Homer and Hall, *Provincial Pewterers,* 46)

INSCRIPTIONS: None

DIMENSIONS: OL. 7 5/16", Diam. (rim) 2 1/8"

PROVENANCE: Purchased from Robin Bellamy Antiques, Witney, Eng.; 1984-161

232 SPOON

Plain fiddle type
Philip Ashberry
Sheffield, Eng., 1837–1860

MARKS: Maker's or retailer's mark of the royal crown with *V* to the left and *R* to the right with *ASHBERRY'S/BEST METAL/ WARRANTED/FOR USE* below within a shield on underside of handle (Scott, *Pewter Wares from Sheffield,* 25)

INSCRIPTIONS: None

DIMENSIONS: OL. 8 3/8", OW. (bowl) 1 3/4"

PROVENANCE: Purchased from Robin Bellamy Antiques, Witney, Eng.; 1984-158

The most common spoons of the nineteenth century are of this plain fiddle type with a broad spatulate shaping to the end of the handle and narrow angular shoulders, or projections, from the sides of the handle shank immediately above a bowl of egg-shaped outline. Ashberry commenced his career in Sheffield as a

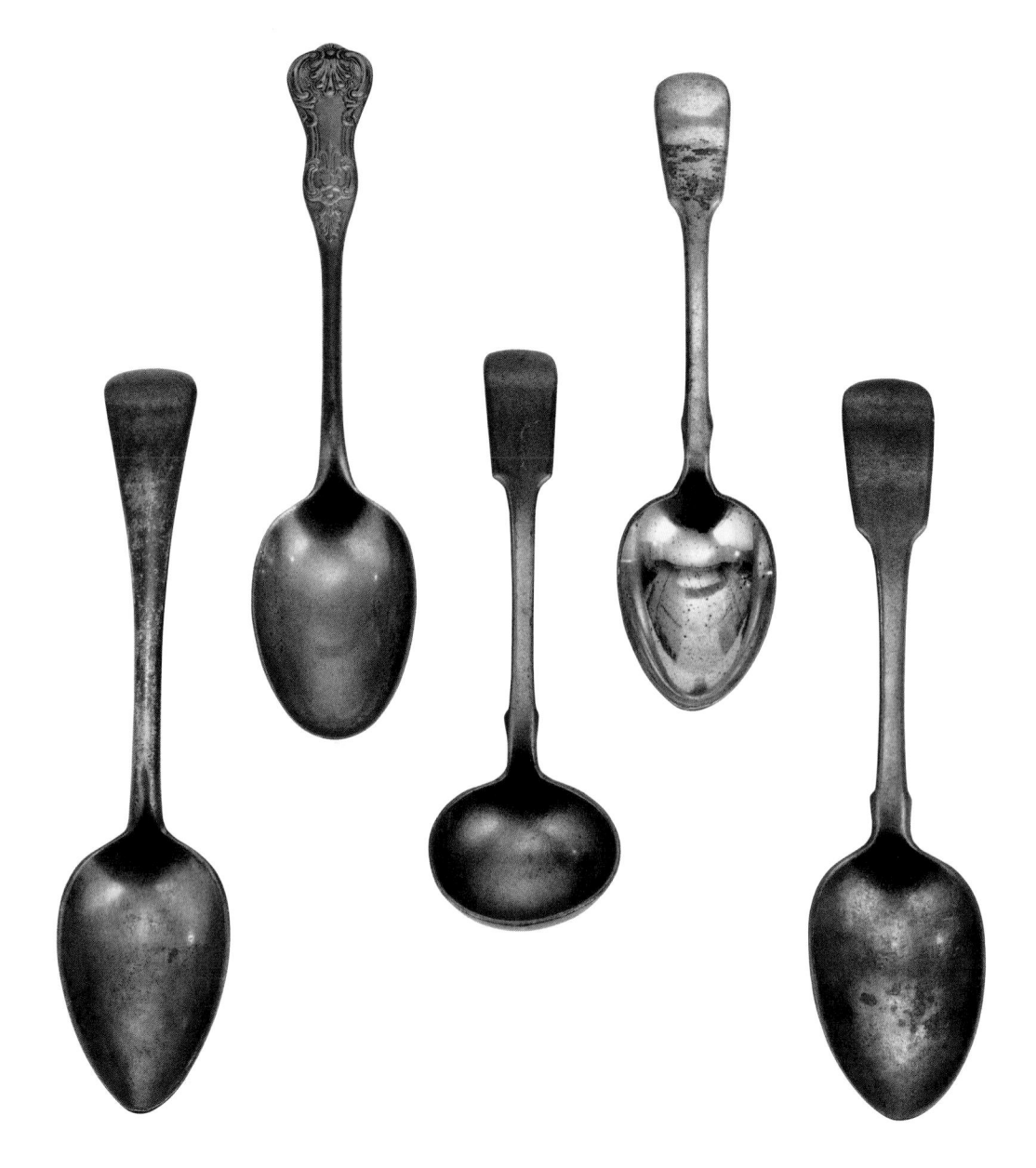

229–233

182   PEWTER AT COLONIAL WILLIAMSBURG

spoonmaker in 1829. During the ensuing decades, he not only produced a broad range of spoons and ladles, but also founded one of England's largest Britannia metal and electroplate manufactories. This spoon also features a wire insert in its stem for strengthening, as in the Thomas Yates spoon (no. 229).

233 SPOON

Plain fiddle type
John Yates
Birmingham, Eng., 1837–1860

MARKS: Maker's touch *JO/HN/YA/TE/S* within a sequence of five rectangles on underside of handle (Cotterell, *Old Pewter,* 5340A; Homer and Hall, *Provincial Pewterers,* 46); secondary mark *VR* in script with royal crown above within a conforming reserve on underside of handle (Cotterell, *Old Pewter,* 5340A; Homer and Hall, *Provincial Pewterers,* 46)

INSCRIPTIONS: None

DIMENSIONS: OL. 9", OW. (bowl) 1 7/8"

PROVENANCE: Purchased from Robin Bellamy Antiques, Witney, Eng.; 1984-157

229–233

THE EMPRESS
OF RUSSIA.
Moll Flanders
TRIO
by
Sigr. Sustenuto
Musick
has
Charms
Voi Amante

DRINKING VESSELS

Tankards and mugs for quaffing of beer and ale constitute the most important category of pewter drinking vessels. They are amply represented by a large number of examples dating from the 1670s to the 1820s. This section of the Colonial Williamsburg Collection, second only to dining wares in size, also contains representative groups of distinctive English, Scottish, and Channel Island measures that were used not only in taverns, but also occasionally in homes. When not used as personal drinking cups or for display, two-handled ones were often passed from one to another in celebratory toasting.

234

234 TANKARD

Maker unidentified
London, dated 1679

MARKS: Indistinct touchmark with the apparent bust-length portrait of Charles II wearing a crown with *I* to the left and *C* to the right within an outlined and beaded circle on interior center-bottom of base (London Touch Plate I, 51; Cotterell, *Old Pewter*, 5504); pseudo hallmarks (1) lion standing guardant within a shield, (2) leopard's head crowned within a circle, (3) black letter *I* within a shield, and (4) black letter *C* within a shield on face of body below rim to right of handle

INSCRIPTIONS: *1679/RH∗WK/Church wardens/of/Englefield* engraved on face of body opposite handle

DIMENSIONS: OH. 6 3/8", Diam. (base) 4 7/8"

PROVENANCE: Church of Saint Mark, Englefield, Eng.; given by the church to a retiring sexton; purchased by Cyril C. Minchin of Bucklebury, Eng., from the sexton's son and by CWF from Mr. Minchin; 1981-177

234.1 Overall view with inscription

234.2 Thumb piece

PUBLISHED: Page and Ditchfield, *Victoria History of Berkshire*, III, p. 412; Ullyett, *Guide for Collectors*, frontis.

This example is certainly one of the most remarkable English pewter tankards to have survived from the seventeenth century. One's eye is immediately drawn to the relief decoration of alternate acanthus and palm leaves that encircles the body just above the base. This form of lush banding was extremely fashionable decoration on silver of this date. That it is chased on silver or created out of the metal of the object through its manipulation with hammer, punch, and other tools made it suitable for silver but not for pewter. In those rare instances of this type of decoration on English pewter, such as the tankard with an inscribed date of 1694 by Peter Duffield of London in the collection of The Worshipful Company of Pewterers and a flagon of about 1690 by William Wood II of Birmingham, the decoration is little more than outlined.[1] The CWF tankard is the only instance in which it is so fully articulated.

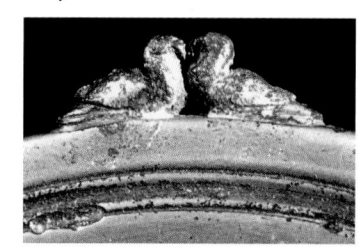

234.3 Rim of cover opposite handle

This tankard appears to have been made specifically for church use. Its thumb piece is in the form of a stylized female pelican with its head turned to the side and pointed downward. This act of self-vulning, in which she pecks blood from her chest to feed her young, symbolizes her piety. The conventional denticulations, or shaped projections, of the cover flange opposite the handle are replaced with a pair of baby birds to represent her young.

1. Cotterell, *Old Pewter*, p. 139, pl. LXXIA; *Short history of The Worshipful Company*, pp. 42, 44, no. 173, fig. 20B; Hornsby, Weinstein, and Homer, *Celebration of the craft*, p. 95, no. 118, ill.

DRINKING VESSELS 187

235 TANKARD

Maker unidentified
England, 1675–1690

MARKS: Indistinct touchmark incorporating, in part, a central device with *T* to the left and *S* to the right within an outlined circle on interior center-bottom of base

INSCRIPTIONS: None

DIMENSIONS: OH. 6 1/16", Diam. (base) 4 5/8"

PROVENANCE: Purchased from The Old Pewter Shop, London; 1966-238

A small number of flat-lid tankards from the 1670s and 1680s display thumb pieces of this twin lovebird type with a voluted cresting, yet perhaps none is more similar to the CWF example than the one by Samuel Billings of Coventry that was formerly in the Peal and Bradshaw Collections.[1]

1. "Treasures from the Bradshaw collection," *Journal of the Pewter Society,* VI (autumn 1987), p. 37, fig. 1; sales cat., Sotheby's, Mar. 18, 1997, p. 30, lot 370, ill. p. 47.

236

236.1 Peripheral view

236 TANKARD

John Donne
London, 1686–1688

MARKS: Touchmark of a hand holding a seal between its thumb and index finger with *I* to the left, *D* to the right, and *1686* above within a beaded circle on interior center-bottom of base (London Touch Plate II, 422; Cotterell, *Old Pewter*, 1415A; Peal, *Addenda*, 1415a)

INSCRIPTIONS: Unidentified coat of arms engraved on shield below hinge on face of handle; allusion to arms engraved on shield-shaped terminal

DIMENSIONS: OH. 7 1/2", Diam. (base) 5 1/4"

PROVENANCE: Purchased from Thomas D. and Constance R. Williams, Litchfield, Conn.; 1959-73

PUBLISHED: Sutherland-Graeme, "British Pewter in American Collections," pp. 3–4, figs. VI–VIII; Michaelis, "Royal Occasions Commemorated," p. 176, fig. 3; *"Fashionable, Neat, and Good,"* p. 117, ill.; Hornsby, *Pewter of the Western World*, p. 259, fig. 876, front cover

This splendid tankard has survived in a remarkable state. It is the only known instance of a portrait of James II on a piece of English pewter. Royal portraits on pewter parallel their more common appearance on a range of delft forms. Both the brevity and the unpopularity of James II's reign (1685–1688) may explain, in part, the scarcity of his likeness.

236.2 Lower hinge plate

236.3 Handle terminal

237

237 TANKARD

William Eddon or Eden
London, 1690–1702

MARKS: Indistinct touchmark on interior center-bottom of base; pseudo hallmarks (1) leopard's head, (2) buckle, (3) lion passant, and (4) indistinct, each within a shaped reserve on top of cover (Cotterell, *Old Pewter*, 1503)

INSCRIPTIONS: Owners' initials *W/IE* within three separate serrated rectangles on underside of cover flange opposite handle; this tankard has a tradition of ownership in the Worthington family, Springfield, Mass.

DIMENSIONS: OH. 7 1/4", Diam. (base) 5 1/8"

PROVENANCE: Purchased from Dr. Percy E. Raymond, Lexington, Mass.; 1950-861

PUBLISHED: Raymond, "Ancestral Pewter," pp. 10–11, figs. 3–3b; Fairbanks and Trent, eds., *New England Begins,* II, pp. 290–291, no. 287, ill.; Robinson, "British Pewter in New England," p. 186, fig. 143

EXHIBITED: New England Begins: The Seventeenth Century, Museum of Fine Arts, Boston, Mass., 1982

There is a sizable group of English pewter with patriotic decoration that was made to commemorate, in particular, the accession of the monarch to the throne or a royal marriage. Such commemorative items, from armorial dishes to portrait spoons and tankards, enjoyed their greatest popularity from the last decades of the seventeenth century through the first quarter of the eighteenth century. This tankard has sustained considerable wear, and its portrait of William III is somewhat faint. He is flanked by wriggle-engraved royal symbols of the rose and lion to the left and of the thistle and unicorn to the right. It is apparent that the thumb piece is a heavy-handed and unconvincing replacement.

This tankard is of particular interest because it has a tradition of ownership in the Worthington family of Springfield, Mass., and stamped owners' initials that purport to be of that family.[1] It is but one of a considerable number of pieces by Eddon with a history in the Connecticut River Valley, prompting speculation of an agent selling his wares in that area.[2] A similarly engraved tankard with the portrait of William III, flanked by the same supporters and emblems, is marked by John Donne of London and is in the New Hampshire Historical Society collection in Concord. It has a history of descent from Hannah (Emerson) Dustin (1657–1736?) of Haverhill, Mass. Indian raiders carried Hannah off in 1697, only

237.1 Owners' initials

237.2 Peripheral view

DRINKING VESSELS 191

for her to escape heroically with ten of their scalps. Cotton Mather recalled later how Hannah and two others who had escaped received not only recompense from the province but also presents of congratulation from individuals. The Dustin tankard is thought perhaps to have been a gift to her from Governor Francis Nicholson of Maryland who, as Mather relates, "sent 'em a very generous token of his favour."[3] Both these tankards document the American ownership at an early date of English examples of this important form with royal portraits.

1. Raymond, "Ancestral Pewter," pp. 10–11.
2. Fairbanks and Trent, eds., *New England Begins,* II, p. 291.
3. Donna-Belle Garvin, "Hannah Dustin tankard donated to the Society," *New Hampshire Historical Society Newsletter,* XXXI (winter 1993–1994), p. 1.

238 TANKARD

Maker unidentified
England, probably West Country, 1685–1700

MARKS: Touchmark of a fleur-de-lis with *L•* to the left and *•A* to the right within an outlined heart on interior center-bottom of base (Cotterell, *Old Pewter,* 5386)

INSCRIPTIONS: None

DIMENSIONS: OH. 6 23/32", Diam. (base) 5 1/8"

238–239

PROVENANCE: Purchased from I. Malcolm Dunn, Williamsburg, Va.; 1960-842

PUBLISHED: "Accessions of Museums, 1960," p. 405, ill. p. 418

This tankard is a particularly handsome example in its conformation and decoration. Its exotic thumb piece and spontaneous relief-cast decoration on lower hinge plate and adjacent handle face are effective complements to its well-conceived wriggle engraving.

239 TANKARD

Maker unidentified
England, 1685–1700

MARKS: Touchmark *GF* within a beaded circle on interior center-bottom of base (Peal, *More Pewter Marks,* 5580c)

INSCRIPTIONS: Owner's initials *MB* scratched on underside of base

DIMENSIONS: OH. 6 1/4", Diam. (base) 4 1/4"

PROVENANCE: Purchased from A. H. Isher & Son, Cheltenham, Eng.; 1963-142

DRINKING VESSELS 193

240–242

240 TANKARD

Maker unidentified
England, 1685–1700

MARKS: Touchmark of a fleur-de-lis with black letter *S* to the left, black letter *B* to the right, and two mullets in corners above within a shaped shield on interior center-bottom of base

INSCRIPTIONS: None

DIMENSIONS: OH. 6 5/16", Diam. (base) 4 3/4"

PROVENANCE: Purchased from A. V. Sutherland-Graeme, London; 1955-318

241 TANKARD

William Wood II
Birmingham, Eng., 1685–1700

MARKS: Indistinct maker's mark of a male head facing left within a beaded circle on interior center-bottom of base (Peal, *More Pewter Marks,* 6032; Homer and Hall, *Provincial Pewterers,* 4); pseudo hallmarks (1) *WW* with a rosette below within a rectangle with canted upper corners, (2) lion's head erased within a rectangle with canted corners, and (3 and 4) lion passant within rectangles on upper face of cover (Peal, *More Pewter Marks,* 6032; Homer and Hall, *Provincial Pewterers,* 44)

INSCRIPTIONS: Owner's initials *ES* engraved on face of handle

DIMENSIONS: OH. 6 7/16", Diam. (base) 4 29/32"

PROVENANCE: Purchased from A. H. Isher & Son, Cheltenham, Eng.; 1956-394

Wood (1645–1726) was the most prominent of the early Birmingham pewterers. His highly productive shop specialized in a broad range of hollowware, whereas John Duncumb, his former apprentice and son-in-law, focused on the large-scale production of plates and dishes. This specific pattern of decorative openwork to the edge of the cover flange opposite the handle, the horizontal

194 PEWTER AT COLONIAL WILLIAMSBURG

ribbing of the thumb piece support, and the voluted handle terminal are particular features of Wood's flat-lid tankards. A helpful further illustration of this touchmark appears in A. S. Law's 1982 article.[1]

1. A. S. Law, "Birmingham Pewterers in the Seventeenth Century," *Journal of the Pewter Society,* III (autumn 1982), p. 132.

242 TANKARD

Maker unidentified
England, 1685–1700

MARKS: None

INSCRIPTIONS: None

DIMENSIONS: OH. 7 3/8", Diam. (base) 5 1/8"

PROVENANCE: Purchased from A. V. Sutherland-Graeme, London; 1957-55

243 TANKARD

John Donne
London, 1686–1700

MARKS: Touchmark of a hand holding a seal between its thumb and index finger with *I* to the left, *D* to the right, and *1686* above within a beaded circle on interior center-bottom of base (London Touch Plate II, 422; Cotterell, *Old Pewter,* 1415A; Peal, *Addenda,* 1415a); pseudo hallmarks (1) black letter *I,* (2) black letter *D,* (3) leopard's head crowned, and (4) lion passant, each within a separate rectangle on top of cover

INSCRIPTIONS: None

243–244

243–244

DIMENSIONS: OH. 6 1/4", Diam. (base) 4 1/4"

PROVENANCE: Purchased from A. H. Isher & Son, Cheltenham, Eng.; 1960-462

It is not surprising that Donne is associated with many fine tankards, for he was described in 1696 as a "pottmaker." He was reported as "Mr Donne pewterer to their late Majesties Queen Anne and King George at the Pewter Dish in Great New Street near Fetter Lane" in the *Daily Journal* for Apr. 29, 1730.[1]

1. Ricketts, *Pewterers of London*, p. 86.

244 TANKARD

William Eddon or Eden
London, 1691–1705

MARKS: Touchmark of an hourglass with *1/W/9* to the left and *6/E/1* to the right and a pellet above and below within a beaded circle on interior center-bottom of base; pseudo hallmarks (1) leopard's head, (2) buckle, (3) lion passant, and (4) indistinct, each within a separate reserve on top of cover (Cotterell, *Old Pewter*, 1503)

INSCRIPTIONS: None

DIMENSIONS: OH. 6 11/16", Diam. (base) 4 7/8"

PROVENANCE: Purchased from Mrs. L. A. Atwood, Watertown, Conn.; 1955-48

Eddon had a long and productive career from 1690 until the late 1740s. He specialized in hollowware, especially tankards, flagons, and cups, and few plates and dishes survive with his marks. He also carried on a considerable export with the American colonies. The body of this tankard, an early example of his work, is handsomely hammered. It is at this time that a number of flatware, plates, dishes, and basins are overall hammered in a decorative way.

245 TANKARD

Unidentified maker
England, probably West Country, 1690–1710

MARKS: Touchmark of a fleur-de-lis within a conforming reserve on interior center-bottom of base (Cotterell, *Old Pewter,* 5385)

INSCRIPTIONS: None

DIMENSIONS: OH. 5 15/16", Diam. (base) 4"

PROVENANCE: Purchased from The Old Pewter Shop, London; 1936-431

245.1 Touchmark of John Smith of London with dome-lidded tankard

The taller, more slender tankard with a domed cover first appears in the 1680s, but it did not largely displace the flat-lidded tankard of squatter proportions until the first years of the next century. Early examples often retain the projecting cover flange with pronounced denticulations opposite the handle and thumb piece forms and boot-heel terminals commonly seen on flat-lidded examples. Most early examples, like this one and no. 246, are of modest size. The earliest depiction of a dome-lidded tankard appears in the illustrated touchmark of John Smith, as struck on London Touch Plate II, no. 420, in 1685.

246 TANKARD

Maker unidentified
England, 1700–1715

MARKS: Indistinct touchmark incorporating an apparent stag on interior center-bottom of base

INSCRIPTIONS: Owner's initials *TV* stamped on upper face of rim opposite handle

DIMENSIONS: OH. 6 1/4", Diam. (base) 4 1/8"

PROVENANCE: Purchased from A. V. Sutherland-Graeme, London; 1954-943

247–248

247 TANKARD

Unidentified maker
England, 1700–1715

MARKS: Indistinct touchmark on interior center-bottom of base

INSCRIPTIONS: None

DIMENSIONS: OH. 7 1/8", Diam. (base) 5 1/8"

PROVENANCE: Purchased from A. V. Sutherland-Graeme, London; 1954-939

This tankard and no. 248 are part of a distinctive group from the first decade or two of the eighteenth century. They are tall in their proportions, aided by their high-domed covers with narrow and inconspicuous flanged rims. They are fitted with late ram's horn thumb pieces with a barred horizontal division and a lower hinge plate of a consistent pointed design with a detached diamond. These lower hinge plates are sometimes described as having a visual similarity to their probable source, which is contemporary decorative appliqués of sheet silver on silver, known as cut-card decoration. A boot-heel handle terminal is customary.

248 TANKARD

Possibly by Thomas Banks III
Wigan, Eng., 1690–1725

MARKS: Touchmark *T•B* within an oblong quatrefoil on interior center-bottom of base (Peal, *More Pewter Marks,* 5466a; Peal, *Addenda,* 5466a)

INSCRIPTIONS: Owner's initial *L* with crown above and an indistinct letter with crown above to either side stamped on face of cover flange opposite handle

DIMENSIONS: OH. 7 3/16", Diam. (base) 4 7/8"

198 PEWTER AT COLONIAL WILLIAMSBURG

PROVENANCE: Purchased from A. V. Sutherland-Graeme, London; 1958-5

Peal notes that this touchmark appears "on a tall dome lid, and on a porringer, both of c. 1700, and also on handle of a dome lid with date '1732.'"[1] Robinson has suggested that this is possibly the touch of the Wigan maker Thomas Banks III, who died in 1724.[2]

1. Peal, *More Pewter Marks,* p. 60, no. 5466a.
2. Robinson, "English Pewter Coronet Ear Porringers," pp. 29–30.

249 TANKARD

John Thomas
London, 1710–1725

MARKS: Touchmark *I*∗*T* with *16* under and *98* over a small device below within a beaded lozenge on interior center-bottom of base (London Touch Plate II, 545; Cotterell, *Old Pewter,* 4709); secondary mark of a quality *X* on face of body above pseudo

DRINKING VESSELS 199

250

hallmarks; pseudo hallmarks (1) lion passant, (2) leopard's head, (3) fleur-de-lis, and (4) indistinct, each within an apparent shaped shield on face of body to right of handle

INSCRIPTIONS: Owner's initials *TP* stamped on upper face of cover flange opposite handle

DIMENSIONS: OH. 6 5/8", Diam. (base) 4 3/4"

PROVENANCE: Purchased from A. V. Sutherland-Graeme, London; 1961-150

During the second decade of the eighteenth century, pewter tankards in the late baroque style assume a more dynamic and resolute appearance than their predecessors. They become squatter and broader in proportions. Their larger handles are more strongly curved and outfitted with expressive scroll thumb pieces and fishtail terminals. The body of this handsome example is lightly hammered.

250 TANKARD

Thomas Carpenter
London, 1725–1740

MARKS: No apparent touchmark; secondary mark of a quality *X* on face of body above pseudo hallmarks; pseudo hallmarks (1) lion rampant within a shield, (2) buckle within a rounded reserve, (3) black letter *T* within a shield, and (4) black letter *C* within a shield on face of body to right of handle (Peal, *More Pewter Marks,* 810)

INSCRIPTIONS: None

DIMENSIONS: OH. 6 5/8", Diam. (base) 4 3/4"

PROVENANCE: Ronald F. Michaelis, Newhaven, Eng. (sold after his death and purchased by CWF at Sotheby's, 1973); 1973-387

PUBLISHED: Michaelis, *British Pewter,* back jacket ill.; sale cat., Sotheby's, Nov. 12, 1973, p. 12, lot 73, pl. IV; Peal, "Great collection dispersed," p. 76, ill.; Mundey, "Sale of Michaelis Collection," pp. 17–18, fig. 3; Hornsby, *Pewter of the Western World,* p. 269, fig. 907

EXHIBITED: Jamestown Festival Park, Jamestown, Va., 1979–1980

This tankard is of an unusual design for an English example. It is obviously taken from a flagon of spire type with its finial, its broad banding with a wide central fillet placed high on its body, and its spreading base. Carpenter was a prominent specialist maker of flagons, particularly of spire type.[1] The pseudo hallmarks, which include the initials of Carpenter, were misattributed by Peal to the pewterer's brother, John Carpenter.[2]

1. Jan Gadd, "The Spire Flagons of London," *Journal of the Pewter Society,* XVII (spring 2002), pp. 23–43.
2. Ronald F. Homer, "Thomas Carpenter," *Journal of the Pewter Society,* IX (spring 1993), pp. 18–19.

251 TANKARD

Maker unidentified
Scotland, 1720–1780

MARKS: None

INSCRIPTIONS: Owners' initials *I•B/A•D* scratched on underside of base

DIMENSIONS: OH. 6 3/16", Diam. (base) 3 3/4"

PROVENANCE: Purchased from A. H. Isher & Son, Cheltenham, Eng.; 1958-555

This tankard and no. 252 are of distinctive Scottish form with their tapered bodies simply banded and their perfectly flat covers fitted with archaic twin cusp thumb pieces and slender strap handles. In conformation and details, they recall standard Scottish church flagons of the eighteenth century (see no. 399). It is not known precisely how these modest lidded vessels were used. They probably served as drinking vessels and were not intended for storage or church use.

252 TANKARD

Maker unidentified
Scotland, 1720–1780

MARKS: None

INSCRIPTIONS: Owner's initials *KB* engraved on face of body below rim opposite handle

251–252

DIMENSIONS: OH. 8 1/8", Diam. (base) 4 11/16"

PROVENANCE: Purchased from A. H. Isher & Son, Cheltenham, Eng.; 1963-151

EXHIBITED: William Hogarth exhibition, Virginia Museum of Fine Arts, Richmond, Va., 1967

253 TANKARD

William Eddon or Eden
London, 1730–1745

MARKS: Touchmark of an hourglass with *W* to the left and *E* to the right within an outlined and beaded circle on interior center-bottom of base (Cotterell, *Old Pewter,* 1503); pseudo hallmarks (1) leopard's head within a conforming reserve, (2) buckle within a shaped rectangle, (3) lion passant within a shaped rectangle, and (4) indistinct on face of body to left of handle (Cotterell, *Old Pewter,* 1503); verification mark *WR* with crown above on face of body below pseudo hallmarks

INSCRIPTIONS: Owner's initials *W•R* engraved on face of handle; later owner's cipher *WR* with foliate embellishment engraved on face of body opposite handle

DIMENSIONS: OH. 7 1/16", Diam. (base) 4 15/16"

202   PEWTER AT COLONIAL WILLIAMSBURG

PROVENANCE: Purchased from A. V. Sutherland-Graeme, London; 1954-940

This tankard and nos. 254–255 are standard examples from the second quarter of the eighteenth century. Their scrolled handles are fitted with chair-back thumb pieces and ball terminals. They are the work of one of the principal London makers of those years, Eddon. A specialist in hollowware, he produced many fine tankards and other drinking vessels over a long and productive career. He was also a major maker of export wares for the American market.

254 TANKARD

William Eddon or Eden
London, 1730–1745

MARKS: Touchmark of an hourglass with *W* to the left and *E* to the right within an outlined and beaded circle on interior center-bottom of base (Cotterell, *Old Pewter,* 1503)

INSCRIPTIONS: None

DIMENSIONS: OH. 7 1/8", Diam. (base) 5 1/16"

PROVENANCE: Purchased from Dr. Percy E. Raymond, Lexington, Mass.; 1950-790

255 TANKARD

William Eddon or Eden
London, 1730–1745

MARKS: Touchmark of an hourglass with *W* to the left and *E* to the right within an outlined and beaded circle on interior center-bottom of base (Cotterell, *Old Pewter,* 1503); verification mark

253–255

WR with crown above on face of body below pseudo hallmarks; pseudo hallmarks (1) leopard's head with a conforming reserve, (2) buckle within a shaped rectangle, (3) lion passant within a shaped rectangle, and (4) indistinct on face of body to left of handle (Cotterell, *Old Pewter,* 1503)

INSCRIPTIONS: Owners' initials *H/AE* engraved on face of handle

DIMENSIONS: OH. 5 5/8", Diam. (base) 4 1/16"

PROVENANCE: Purchased from A. V. Sutherland-Graeme, London; 1954-942

256 Tankard

Maker unidentified
England, 1720–1740

MARKS: Indistinct touchmark incorporating, in part, the Prince of Wales feathers issuing from a crown with *S* to the right on interior center-bottom of base (Peal, *More Pewter Marks,* 5913a)

INSCRIPTIONS: None

DIMENSIONS: OH. 5 1/2", Diam. (base) 3 15/16"

PROVENANCE: Purchased from A. V. Sutherland-Graeme, London; 1954-941

This example, no. 255, and nos. 257–259 are all tankards of small size, approximately a half pint in capacity.

257 Tankard

George Grenfell or Granville
London, 1760–1775

MARKS: Touchmark of a griffin passant on a wreath bar with *GRENFELL* in semicircular arrangement below within a circle on interior center-bottom of base

INSCRIPTIONS: None

DIMENSIONS: OH. 5 3/16", Diam. (base) 4"

PROVENANCE: Purchased from Thomas D. and Constance R. Williams, Litchfield, Conn.; 1966-428

Grenfell led, in part, an enigmatic life. The son of a Cornish merchant from Penzance, he commenced his apprenticeship under Robert Hitchman of London in 1750 and appears to have opened a prosperous London business in 1757. It is not known why he moved to Exeter in 1763 or 1764 and established George Grenfell & Co., a business that appears to have had little to do with pewter and went bankrupt in 1767. During the 1770s, he was fined for declining positions in the Pewterers' Company, and he is not listed as an active pewterer in the fifteen years before his death in 1784. His will, however, contains large bequests to family members. In his last years, he preferred to be known as George Granville, acknowledging a tie to the Granville family, Earls of Bath, whose crest is featured in his touchmark.[1] With all this distraction, Grenfell was a substantial exporter of pewter to America.

1. Ronald F. Homer, "The Enigma of George Grenfell and the Westcountry Connection," *Journal of the Pewter Society,* XII (spring 1999), pp. 30–33.

258 Tankard

Maker unidentified
England, 1730–1750

MARKS: Touchmark *IB* with a mullet above and below within an oval with a fan in a contiguous oval above on interior center-bottom of base

INSCRIPTIONS: Owner's initials *EL* stamped on exterior of cover

DIMENSIONS: OH. 5 3/4", Diam. (base) 4 1/8"

PROVENANCE: Purchased from A. V. Sutherland-Graeme, London; 1961-151

259 Tankard

Richard Pitt & John Floyd
London, 1769–1789

MARKS: Touchmark of a hare courant with *PITT* in a curved reserve with foliate ornament above and *& FLOYD* in a curved reserve with foliate ornament below on interior center-bottom of

256–259

259.1 Engraved cipher

base (London Touch Plate IV, 1018; Cotterell, *Old Pewter*, 3695)

INSCRIPTIONS: Owner's initials *I*A* engraved on face of handle; later cipher *IA* engraved on face of body opposite handle

DIMENSIONS: OH. 4 9/16", Diam. (base) 3 3/8"

PROVENANCE: Purchased from A. V. Sutherland-Graeme, London; 1959-381

This tankard is particularly small. Its diminutive size is suggestive of a specialized use, such as for juveniles.

260 TANKARD

Edward Quick
London, 1741–1760

MARKS: Touchmark of the arms of Quick (a chevron checky between three griffins' heads erased) within a cartouche with a scrolled and foliate surround with *EDWARD* and *QUICK* within banners above and below, all within a vertical oval (London Touch Plate IV, 900; Cotterell, *Old Pewter*, 3805); secondary mark of a quality *X* stamped on face of body above pseudo hallmarks; pseudo hallmarks of a lion rampant within a shield stamped four times on face of body to left of handle; verification mark *WR* with crown above within a conforming reserve on face of body below pseudo hallmarks

INSCRIPTIONS: Owner's initials *IK* stamped on underside of base

DIMENSIONS: OH. 7 1/2", Diam. (base) 4 3/4"

PROVENANCE: Purchased from Avis and Rockwell Gardiner, Stamford, Conn.; 1957-9

Tankards of baluster or tulip shape became one of the basic hollowware forms in British pewter after their introduction about 1740. Several examples bear the mark of William Eddon, who worked until the mid- to late 1740s, and they are presumably among the earliest datable examples.[1]

1. Capt. A. Sutherland-Graeme, "William Eden, Master-Pewterer," *Connoisseur*, CI (April 1938), p. 197, fig. IX; Ian Robinson, "William Eddon: Master Pewterer Extraordinary," *Journal of the Pewter Society*, II (autumn 1979), pp. 9–13.

261 TANKARD

John Townsend
London, 1775–1802

MARKS: Touchmark of a paschal lamb with dove with olive branch in bill in flight above framed within a vertical oval by *IOHN* and *TOWNSEND* within curved reserves above and below and with *17* to the left and *48* to the right on interior center-bottom of base (Cotterell, *Old Pewter*, 4795)

INSCRIPTIONS: None

DIMENSIONS: OH. 7 1/4", Diam. (base) 4 3/8"

PROVENANCE: Purchased from Charlotte and Edgar Sittig, Shawnee-on-Delaware, Pa.; 1955-355

This tankard is decidedly later than no. 260. Its more slender double-scroll handle does not appear on English pewter tankards until the mid-1770s. The open, scrolled thumb piece is of comparable date. This tankard raises questions about the dating of pewter bearing Townsend's touchmark. Townsend obviously used his individual touchmark after he had entered into a series of partnerships beginning in 1766. Presumably, its use would have ceased with the death of Townsend in 1801 and the final appearance of Townsend and Compton in an 1802 trade directory.[1]

1. Hayward, "Townsend and Compton Businesses," pp. 2–12.

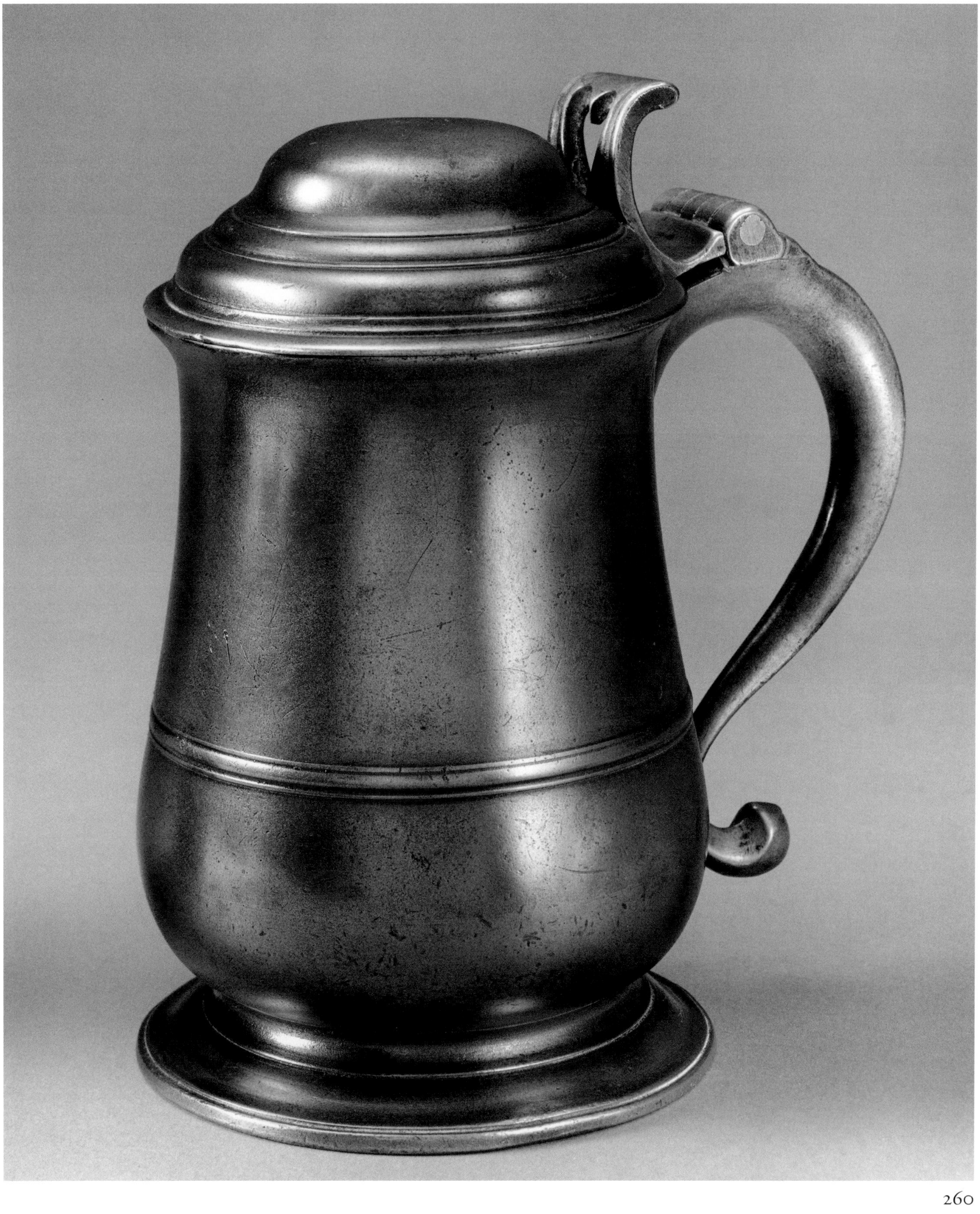

262 TANKARD

John Ingram II & Charles Hunt
Bewdley, Eng., 1778–1807

MARKS: Touchmark *I&H* within an oblong cartouche on interior center-bottom of base (Peal, *More Pewter Marks,* 2540a; Homer and Hall, *Provincial Pewterers,* 31); verification mark *WR* with crown above within a conforming reserve on face of body to right of handle

INSCRIPTIONS: None

DIMENSIONS: OH. 6 3/16", Diam. (base): 3 7/8"

PROVENANCE: Purchased from Thomas D. and Constance R. Williams, Litchfield, Conn.; 1956-78

The firm of Ingram & Hunt operated an extremely large and prosperous provincial business during the late eighteenth and early nineteenth centuries. The pewterers formed a partnership sometime before 1778. Records of the firm and its immediate antecedents between 1769 and 1790 include the names of seven hundred customers. The firm conducted a large-scale export trade to America.[1] A pair of tankards of this same design, also by Ingram & Hunt, are in the collections of the Museum of Fine Arts, Boston. They have the same unusual plumed thumb pieces with central shells.[2]

1. Homer and Hall, *Provincial Pewterers,* pp. 67–72.
2. Elizabeth Ely, "British Pewter at the Museum of Fine Arts (Boston, Mass.)," *Journal of the Pewter Society,* I (autumn 1978), ill. p. 27.

261–262

263 TANKARD

Edmund Harvey
Stockton-on-Tees, Eng., 1730–1750

MARKS: Touchmark of a bird with raised wings and an olive branch in its bill standing on a mound facing left with *E* to the left and *H* to the right within a beaded circle on interior center-bottom of base (Cotterell, *Old Pewter*, 2185)

INSCRIPTIONS: None

DIMENSIONS: OH. 6 3/8", Diam. (base) 4 11/16"

PROVENANCE: Purchased from A. V. Sutherland-Graeme, London; 1956-74

The maker of this tankard and no. 264 is probably Edmund Harvey who, according to the Stockton-on-Tees Parish Register, was born in 1698 and died in 1781. This small touchmark of a bird in a beaded circle appears primarily on his hollowware forms, including church flagons, tankards, mugs, and at least one porringer and salt. He is not to be confused with the pewterer of the same name who worked in the late seventeenth century in Wigan, Lancashire.[1]

1. Malcolm L. Toothill, "Edmund Harvey—Pewterer of Stockton-on-Tees," *Journal of the Pewter Society*, VII (spring 1989), pp. 3–6.

264 TANKARD

Edmund Harvey
Stockton-on-Tees, Eng., 1730–1750

265–267

MARKS: Touchmark of a bird with raised wings and an olive branch in its bill standing on a mound facing left with *E* to the left and *H* to the right within a beaded circle on interior center-bottom of base (Cotterell, *Old Pewter,* 2185)

INSCRIPTIONS: Owners' initials *I/CB* with crown above each stamped on upper face of rim opposite handle

DIMENSIONS: OH. 7 1/16", Diam. (base) 4 15/16"

PROVENANCE: Purchased from A. V. Sutherland-Graeme, London; 1958-431

265 TANKARD

Richard Going
Bristol, Eng., 1730–1750

MARKS: Touchmark of a paschal lamb with a mullet to either side with *RICHARD* above and *GOING* below within an outlined circle on interior center-bottom of base (Peal, *More Pewter Marks,* 1909)

INSCRIPTIONS: Owner's initials *GI* stamped on upper face of cover flange opposite handle

DIMENSIONS: OH. 6 3/16", Diam. (base) 4 7/16"

PROVENANCE: Purchased from Thomas D. and Constance R. Williams, Litchfield, Conn.; 1956-75

This tankard and nos. 266–267 are representative examples from the second quarter of the eighteenth century. Their bodies are broadly proportioned with a fairly low fillet banding. They have appropriately heavy and strongly curved handles fitted with scroll thumb pieces and fishtail terminals. Going was a prominent Bristol maker and exporter of pewter to America. His shop with pewter hollowware in the front windows appears in the foreground of Peter Monamy's painting of the Broad Quay in Bristol in the Bristol City Museum & Art Gallery.[1]

1. This painting is illustrated in Cotterell, *Old Pewter,* p. 21, pl. V.

210   PEWTER AT COLONIAL WILLIAMSBURG

266 TANKARD

Richard Going
Bristol, Eng., 1730–1750

MARKS: Indistinct touchmark incorporating an apparent paschal lamb with R^D above and *GOEING* below within a circle on interior center-bottom of base (Cotterell, *Old Pewter,* 1909)

INSCRIPTIONS: None

DIMENSIONS: OH. 7 1/4", Diam. (base) 5 5/16"

PROVENANCE: Purchased from A. V. Sutherland-Graeme, London; 1955-154

267 TANKARD

Richard Going
Bristol, Eng., 1730–1750

MARKS: Touchmark of a paschal lamb with a mullet to either side with *RICHARD* above and *GOING* below within an outlined circle on interior center-bottom of base (Peal, *More Pewter Marks,* 1909)

INSCRIPTIONS: None

DIMENSIONS: OH. 5 5/8", Diam. (base) 4 1/8"

PROVENANCE: Purchased from A. V. Sutherland-Graeme, London; 1955-418

268 TANKARD

Allen Bright
Bristol, Eng., and Colwell, Eng., 1742–1763

MARKS: Touchmark of a fleur-de-lis framed by *ALLEN•BRIGHT* within a circle on interior center-bottom of base (Cotterell, *Old Pewter,* 574)

268–269

DRINKING VESSELS 211

270–271

INSCRIPTIONS: None

DIMENSIONS: OH. 7 3/8", Diam. (base): 4 1/4"

PROVENANCE: Purchased from A. V. Sutherland-Graeme, London; 1960-739

EXHIBITED: William Hogarth exhibition, Virginia Museum of Fine Arts, Richmond, Va., 1967

269 TANKARD

Allen Bright
Bristol, Eng., and Colwell, Eng., 1745–1763

MARKS: Touchmark of a fleur-de-lis framed by *ALLEN•BRIGHT* within a circle on interior center-bottom of base (Cotterell, *Old Pewter,* 574)

INSCRIPTIONS: None

DIMENSIONS: OH. 7 3/8", Diam. (base) 4 5/16"

PROVENANCE: Purchased from A. V. Sutherland-Graeme, London; 1960-738

270 TANKARD

Robert Bush I & Richard Perkins
Bristol, Eng., and Bitton, Eng., 1771–1781

MARKS: Touchmark of the seated figure of Britannia framed by *BUSH & PERKINS* within a circle on interior center-bottom of base (Cotterell, *Old Pewter,* 740)

INSCRIPTIONS: None

212 PEWTER AT COLONIAL WILLIAMSBURG

DIMENSIONS: OH. 7 15/16", Diam. (base) 4 11/16"

PROVENANCE: Purchased from George C. Gebelein, Boston, Mass.; 1933-21

Robert Bush I & Richard Perkins, a former apprentice, were in partnership from 1771 to 1781.

271 TANKARD

Robert Bush I & Richard Perkins
Bristol, Eng., and Bitton, Eng., 1771–1781

MARKS: Touchmark of the seated figure of Britannia framed by *BUSH & PERKINS* within a circle on interior center-bottom of base (Cotterell, *Old Pewter,* 740)

INSCRIPTIONS: None

DIMENSIONS: OH. 7 3/4", Diam. (base) 4 7/16"

PROVENANCE: Purchased from A. V. Sutherland-Graeme, London; 1955-155

272 TANKARD

Robert Bush I & Richard Perkins
Bristol, Eng., and Bitton, Eng., 1771–1781

MARKS: Touchmark of the seated figure of Britannia framed by

272–273

DRINKING VESSELS 213

274

BUSH & PERKINS within a circle on interior center-bottom of base (Cotterell, *Old Pewter,* 740)

INSCRIPTIONS: None

DIMENSIONS: OH. 7 5/16", Diam. (base) 5 1/16"

PROVENANCE: Purchased from Thomas D. and Constance R. Williams, Litchfield, Conn.; 1956-76

within a circle on interior center-bottom of base (Cotterell, *Old Pewter,* 737)

INSCRIPTIONS: None

DIMENSIONS: OH. 7 1/4", Diam. (base) 5"

PROVENANCE: Purchased from George C. Gebelein, Boston, Mass.; 1933-22

273 TANKARD

Robert Bush I
Bristol, Eng., and Bitton, Eng., 1770–1785

MARKS: Touchmark of a harp framed by *ROBERT•BUSH*

274 TANKARD

John Will I
New York, N. Y., 1752–1774

MARKS: Touchmark *IW* with a mullet above and below within a beaded circle with a scalloped edge on interior center-bottom of base (Laughlin, *Pewter in America,* II, 481)

INSCRIPTIONS: None

DIMENSIONS: OH. 7 1/8", Diam. (base) 4 15/16"

PROVENANCE: Purchased from Thomas D. and Constance R. Williams, Litchfield, Conn.; 1959-1

PUBLISHED: "Accessions of Museums, 1959," p. 390

Will trained and worked as a pewterer in his native Germany before emigrating with his family to New York City in 1750. Although fifty-six years old in 1750, he had a creative and productive career in New York City that lasted into the early 1770s. His influence was extended through the work of three of his remarkable pewtering sons, Henry, Philip, and especially William.

His work shows obvious adjustment not only to dominant English taste but also to local preference. New York tankards in silver and pewter often tend to retain early features, such as the projecting cover flange with bold denticulations opposite the handle, details expected on early flat-lidded tankards. There is often a generosity to the proportions of New York tankards as well.

275 TANKARD

William Will
Philadelphia, Pa., 1764–1798

MARKS: Touchmark W^M *WILL* within a serrated rectangle on interior center-bottom of base (Laughlin, *Pewter in America,* II, 539)

INSCRIPTIONS: None

DIMENSIONS: OH. 7 7/8", Diam. (base) 4 7/16"

PROVENANCE: Purchased from Thomas D. and Constance R. Williams, Litchfield, Conn.; 1959-414

PUBLISHED: Hornsby, *Pewter of the Western World,* p. 276, fig. 936

Will, the fourth son of the pewterer John Will, was born in Germany in 1742. He learned his trade from his father and brother Henry in New York City before moving to Philadelphia with his brother Philip in the early 1760s. Will distinguished himself as an officer in the Revolution and served in the General Assembly of Pennsylvania. He produced a prodigious amount of important domestic and ecclesiastical pewter before his death in 1798. Tankards and mugs of baluster or tulip form were particular specialities of Philadelphia pewterers and especially of Will.[1]

1. One useful resource on the Will family and its work that should not be overlooked is Donald M. Herr's excellent study, *Pewter in Pennsylvania German Churches.*

276 TANKARD

Love touch
Philadelphia, Pa., 1790–1810

MARKS: Touchmark of two standing birds facing one another with *LO* to the left, *VE* to the right, and a crown above within a beaded circle on interior center-bottom of base (Laughlin, *Pewter in America,* III, 868); secondary mark of a quality *X* with crown above stamped within base adjacent to touchmark

INSCRIPTIONS: None

DIMENSIONS: OH. 7 1/2", Diam. (base) 4 3/4"

PROVENANCE: Gift of Mr. and Mrs. Foster McCarl, Jr., Beaver Falls, Pa.; G1983-433

It is now generally agreed that several Philadelphia makers used the Love touch on their wares between about 1760 and 1810. More specific attributions to John Andrew Brunstrom and his father-in-law, Abraham Hasselberg, both of Swedish background, have generally been broadened to include other makers. Tankards, such as this fine example, are of a distinctive Philadelphia type. They have flattened domed covers and the bold bands of multiple reeding encircling tapered bodies display that Swedish influence. The repetition of delicate beaded edges, also a favored Philadelphia treatment, lends a heightened sense of elegant refinement that one associates with neoclassic style.

A similar tankard, also with the same marks, was formerly owned by Zion Lutheran Church, Middle Smithfield Township, Monroe Co., Pa.[1]

1. Herr, *Pewter in Pennsylvania Churches,* p. 120, fig. 250.

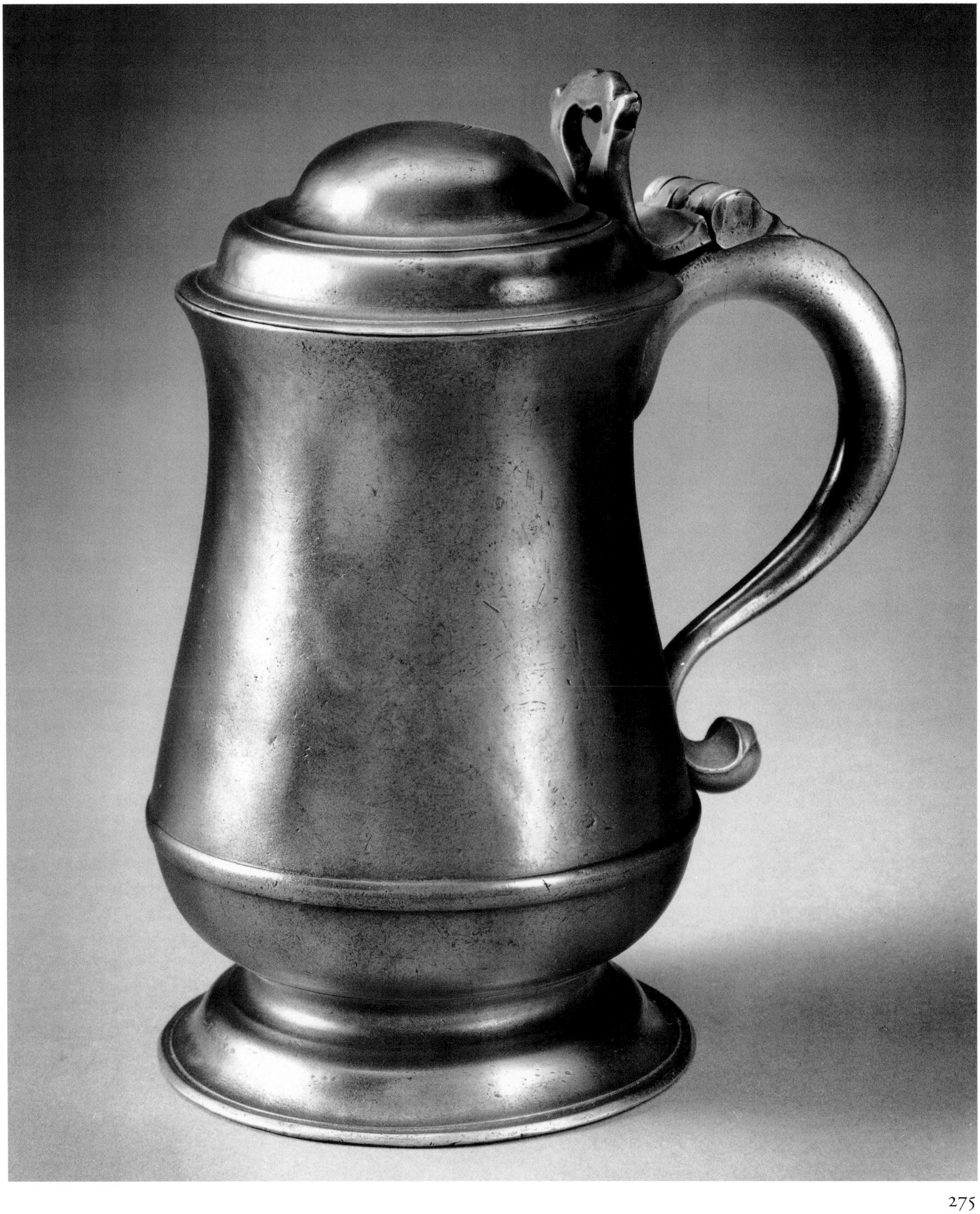

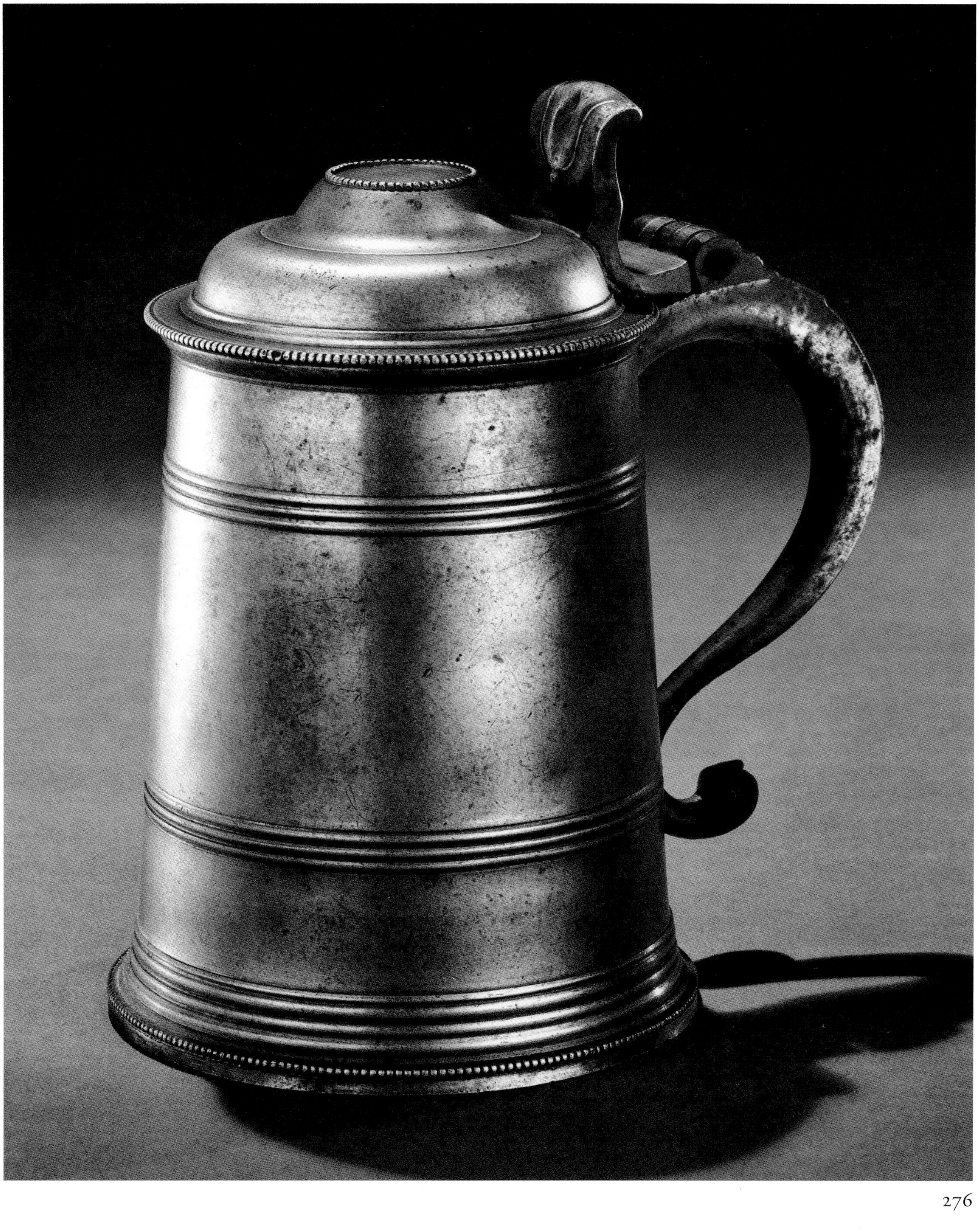

277 MUG

Possibly Edward Burren
Reading, Eng., 1685–1705

MARKS: Touchmark *EB* with a small device above and below within a beaded circle on interior center-bottom of base

INSCRIPTIONS: Owners' initials stamped on upper face of handle and on face of body to right of handle, possibly for John Little and his wife, who operated the Horse & Jockey, an inn in Reading, Eng.

DIMENSIONS: OH. 5 7/8", Diam. (base) 4"

PROVENANCE: Purchased at Sotheby's, 1980; 1980-53

PUBLISHED: Sales cat., Sotheby's, Mar. 28, 1980, p. 14, lot 49, ill.

This splendid mug is representative of the earliest major type that dates from the last decades of the seventeenth century and into the first decade of the eighteenth century. Such mugs have tall bodies with tapered straight sides that are usually bound by two broad bands and fitted with a slender strap handle. They are often inscribed with the name of a public house or its proprietors, and accordingly they are usually referred to as tavern pots.

277.1 Stamped owners' initials on face of body

This mug bears the same triad of owners' initials as the important one that was formerly in the Minchin Collection and is presently in the Neish Collection at the Museum of

British Pewter. That one has the advantage of being further engraved with John Little's name, place of business, and the date, 1699. It is the work of Henry Frewen II of Reading.[1] The *EB* touchmark on the CWF piece is unrecorded, yet, considering the shared owners' initials, it is tempting to attribute the mark of the CWF example to Edward Burren, who was the last apprentice of Henry Frewen II's father. Having completed his apprenticeship by 1659, Burren is recorded in the Pewterers' Company searches of Reading in 1669, 1677, 1683, 1692, and 1702. He died in 1711.[2] There are, at present, no marks associated with him.

1. This mug is illustrated and discussed, among other places, in A. Sutherland-Graeme, "Pewter Tavern-Pots," *Country Life,* CXVI (Oct. 28, 1954), pp. 1484–1485, fig. 3; Cyril C. Minchin, "Some Uncommon Examples of Old English Pewter," *Antique Collector,* XLII (February–March 1971), pp. 25–26, figs. 13–14; Hornsby, *Pewter of the Western World,* p. 279, fig. 943.
2. Val Watson, "Reading Pewterers and Braziers: Their History and Times," *Journal of the Pewter Society,* XII (autumn 1999), pp. 16–35.

278 MUG

Maker unidentified
England, 1700–1730

MARKS: No touchmark apparent

INSCRIPTIONS: None

DIMENSIONS: OH. 2 15/16", Diam. (base) 2 9/16"

PROVENANCE: Purchased from A. H. Isher & Son, Cheltenham, Eng.; 1963-152

279 MUG

Henry Hammerton
London, 1715–1730

MARKS: Touchmark of a tun surmounted by a royal crown with an *H* to either side and *1707* below within a beaded circle on interior center-bottom of base (London Touch Plate III, 642; Cotterell, *Old Pewter,* 2105); verification mark *W•R* with royal crown above within a conforming reserve on face of body to left of handle

INSCRIPTIONS: Owner's initials *M•D* engraved on upper face of handle

DIMENSIONS: OH. 3 11/16", Diam. (base) 3 1/8"

PROVENANCE: Found in the silt of the Thames River; purchased from Robin Bellamy Antiques, Witney, Eng.; 1985-160

This handsome mug of half-pint size is a stylish example. It is of early baluster form, and it replicates in size and design contemporary silver mugs that have survived in greater number. Illustrative of this form of silver prototype is one from 1719/20 by Paul de Lamerie of London at CWF.[1] Another pewter example of this early baluster form by Thomas Carpenter of London is in the collections of The Worshipful Company of Pewterers of London. Bearing an applied plaque with the portraits of Prince Charles

279.1 Skimming marks on face of body

279.2 Finishing and engraving of handle

and Queen Anne and the legend *Long Live Prince and Princess of Orange,* it was made by Carpenter about 1713.[2]

This mug has survived in a remarkable state of preservation because of its apparent early deposit in the silt of the Thames. All its features are extremely crisp, and they exhibit little, if any, wear from use. Clearly evident are the skimming lines on the face of the body and the somewhat rude grating marks on the handle.

The burr on the engraved owner's initials on the handle is still rough to the touch.

1. John D. Davis, *English Silver at Williamsburg* (Williamsburg, Va., 1976), p. 69, no. 58, ill.
2. *Supplementary Catalogue of Pewterware, 1979,* p. 40, no. S3/308, ill. p. 48.

280 MUG

John Townsend
London, 1748–1767

MARKS: Partially indistinct touchmark of a paschal lamb within a vertical oval with *IOHN* and *TOWNSEND* above and below within scrolled reserves with *17* to the left and presumably *48* to the right on interior center-bottom of base (Cotterell, *Old Pewter,* 4795); verification mark *W.R* with royal crown above within a conforming reserve on face of body to left of handle

INSCRIPTIONS: None

280–281

220 PEWTER AT COLONIAL WILLIAMSBURG

DIMENSIONS: OH. 6 1/4", Diam. (base) 4 11/16"

PROVENANCE: Purchased from Dr. Percy E. Raymond, Lexington, Mass.; 1950-859

281 MUG

Maker unidentified
England, 1750–1770

MARKS: Indistinct touchmark on interior center-bottom of base; verification mark *W•R* with royal crown above within a conforming reserve on face of body to left of handle

INSCRIPTIONS: None

DIMENSIONS: OH. 6 3/8", Diam. (base) 4 1/2"

PROVENANCE: Purchased from Avis and Rockwell Gardiner, Stamford, Conn.; 1950-234

282 MUG

John Townsend
London, 1748–1767

MARKS: Indistinct touchmark with paschal lamb within a vertical oval, probably framed by *IOHN* above and *TOWNSEND* below within scrolled reserves with *17* to the left and *48* to the right on interior center-bottom of base (Cotterell, *Old Pewter,* 4795); verification mark *W•R* with royal crown above within a conforming reserve below rim to left of handle

INSCRIPTIONS: None

DIMENSIONS: OH. 4 3/4", Diam. (base) 3 7/8"

PROVENANCE: Purchased from Thomas D. and Constance R. Williams, Litchfield, Conn.; 1956-79

282–283

DRINKING VESSELS 221

284–285

283 MUG

Maker unidentified
England, 1800–1820

MARKS: No touchmark apparent; pseudo hallmarks of a rosette or star within a circle stamped three times on face of body to left of handle; verification mark *W•R* with royal crown above within a conforming reserve on face of body below pseudo hallmarks; later verification marks *WIV* with royal crown above and *AH-SH* below and *GII* with royal crown above, both on face of body

INSCRIPTIONS: None

DIMENSIONS: OH. 4 3/4", Diam. (base) 3 7/8"

PROVENANCE: Purchased from Dr. Percy E. Raymond, Lexington, Mass.; 1950-791

The repeated motif in the pseudo hallmarks resembles that used by Gerardin & Watson of London. This firm did not enclose such secondary marks within circles, and its floral device has fourteen petals, as compared with the eight petals in the device used on this mug.[1]

1. Peal, *More Pewter Marks,* no. 1837; Peal, *Addenda,* no. 1837.

284 MUG

Edgar, Curtis & Co.
Bristol, Eng., ca. 1793–1801

MARKS: Small-size touchmark with standing figure of Neptune with trident in right hand and the tail of a dolphin in his left hand framed by *EDGAR CURTIS & C°* within an outlined circu-

222 PEWTER AT COLONIAL WILLIAMSBURG

lar band on interior of base in center (Peal, *More Pewter Marks,* 1508)

INSCRIPTIONS: None

DIMENSIONS: OH. (handle) 6 1/16", OH. (rim) 5 15/16", Diam. (rim) 4 1/16", Diam. (base) 4 7/8"

PROVENANCE: Purchased from Thomas C. Campbell, Hawleyville, Conn.; 2000-138

PUBLISHED: Sale ad, Thomas C. Campbell, *Maine Antique Digest,* XXVIII (December 2000), p. 33-A, ill.

This firm consisted of a partnership between Preston Edgar I and James Curtis, both of Bristol. They had previously been partners with Robert Bush I in the firm of Robert Bush & Co., dissolved in 1793. Edgar, Curtis & Co. began in that year, for, according to Cotterell, it is mentioned in the Matthew's First Bristol Directory of 1793/4, as well as in the directory of 1801.[1] The figure of Neptune appropriately appears in the mark of this firm that sent cargoes of its product by ship to America. Such imported mugs served as models for American artisans.

1. Cotterell, *Old Pewter,* pp. 201–202, nos. 1506, 1508, 1511.

285 MUG

Samuel Hamlin
Middletown, Conn., Hartford, Conn., and Providence, R. I., 1767–1801

MARKS: Touchmark of label form with *SAMUEL/HAMLIN* in curved reserves with central shells and foliated scrolls below on face of body to left of handle (Laughlin, *Pewter in America,* I, 330); pseudo hallmarks (1) *SH,* (2) seated figure of Britannia or Columbia, (3) dagger, and (4) golden fleece, each within a shaped rectangle on face of body below touchmark (Laughlin, *Pewter in America,* I, 331)

INSCRIPTIONS: None

DIMENSIONS: OH. 6", Diam. (base) 4 7/8"

PROVENANCE: Gift of Mr. and Mrs. Foster McCarl, Jr., Beaver Falls, Pa.; G1991-648

Hamlin's mugs are particularly successful examples of a prominent English and American type. His are nuanced in design and especially well made, setting them apart from most others.

286 MUG

Joseph Danforth I
Middletown, Conn., 1780–1788

MARKS: Touchmark *I•D* within a rectangle with a crown stamped separately above on face of body to left of handle (Laughlin, *Pewter in America,* I, 374)

INSCRIPTIONS: None

DIMENSIONS: OH. 6", Diam. (base) 4 11/16"

PROVENANCE: Purchased from Dr. Percy E. Raymond, Lexington, Mass.; 1950-920

This pattern of mug was particularly popular in Connecticut. Members of the Danforth family produced such mugs in a variety of sizes from at least the 1780s until well into the nineteenth century. Joseph Danforth I used these particular marks, especially on mugs.[1]

1. Thomas, *Connecticut Pewter and Pewterers,* p. 88.

287 MUG

Maker unidentified
New England, 1770–1810

MARKS: None

INSCRIPTIONS: None

DIMENSIONS: OH. 6 1/8", Diam. (base) 4 3/4"

PROVENANCE: Purchased from Dr. Percy E. Raymond, Lexington, Mass.; 1950-919

This form of mug is a distinctive and idiosyncratic New England type with its straight sides, highly placed fillet banding, and slender strap handle with incidental relief-cast decorative detail.

286–287

288 WINE CUP

Maker unidentified
England, 1616–1625

MARKS: Touchmark or ownership stamp of a royal crown with an apparent rose below within a conforming reserve on underside of foot near outer edge

INSCRIPTIONS: Prince of Wales feathers issuing from a simple crown with *C* to the left and *P* to the right within a roundel in upper band of relief-cast decoration for Charles I (1600–1649) as Prince of Wales

DIMENSIONS: OH. 7 1/4", Diam. (base) 3 11/16"

PROVENANCE: Purchased from Richard Mundey, London, who bought it within the trade as a result of an itinerant peddler's having sold it at the Bermondsey Market, London; 1983-57

PUBLISHED: *Pewterware with Royal Associations,* p. 6, no. 10, ill.; Mundey, "Worshipful Company 500th Anniversary," p. 271, fig. 4; Mundey, "Footed Cup with Bands," pp. 116–117, ill.; *Mundey's Pewter Snippets,* p. 9, ill.; Law, "Williamsburg, Virginia—1994," p. 159, ill.

EXHIBITED: Pewterware with Royal Associations, Pewterers Hall, London, 1974; A Toast to the Globe: Drinking Vessels of Shakespeare's Time, Steuben Galleries, New York, N. Y., 1990

This magnificent and rare wine cup was probably made for royal use. Its upper band of relief-cast floral decoration contains a roundel with the Prince of Wales feathers issuing from a simple crown. The initials *CP* flank the emblematic feathers for Charles, the second son of James I, as *Carolus Princeps,* or Prince of Wales. Charles received this title in 1616, succeeding his brother Henry,

288.1 Roundel with emblem of the Prince of Wales of three feathers issuing from a simple crown and the initials *CP* for *Carrolus Princeps* or, in this instance, Charles I as Prince of Wales

288

DRINKING VESSELS 225

who served for only two years as Prince of Wales from 1610 until his early death in 1612.

Fewer than twenty pieces of English pewter from the first four decades of the seventeenth century are embellished with this type of dense relief-cast decoration. A number of these decorated examples, such as this cup, have emblems of royal ownership that relate to James I and his children.[1] The use in this manner of dense bands of naturalistic decoration in low relief is rare in English metal wares and is more commonly found in German work. At the upper end of English work is a large London covered cup in silver gilt of 1611/2 in the collections of the Victoria and Albert Museum, London.[2] Its decorative bands do not involve casting, as in the CWF cup; rather, they involve application of wire filigree in relief against a matted ground. Its bowl has three bands of filigree ornament, and the shaping and decorating of its foot is similar to that of the CWF cup.

One of the advantages of relief-cast decoration is that it cannot be skimmed and cleaned up like a plain body, so one can see that the bowl of this cup was cast in a two-part mold.

1. *Pewterware with Royal Associations*, p. 1.
2. Philippa Glanville, *Silver in Tudor and Early Stuart England: A Social History and Catalogue of the National Collection, 1480–1660* (London, 1990), pp. 405–406, no. 18, ill.

289 TWO-HANDLED CUP

William Wood II
Birmingham, Eng., 1675–1695

MARKS: Touchmark not apparent; pseudo hallmarks (1 and 2) *W•W* with rose below and (3 and 4) griffin's head erased, each within a rectangle with canted corners on face of body below rim (Cotterell, *Old Pewter*, 6031; Peal, *More Pewter Marks*, 6032; Homer and Hall, *Provincial Pewterers*, 44)

INSCRIPTIONS: Owner's initials *AW* engraved on face of body

DIMENSIONS: OH. 5 3/4", OW. 9 3/16", Diam. (base) 5 1/8"

PROVENANCE: P. G. Kydd, Bristol, Eng.; purchased from Robin Bellamy Antiques, Witney, Eng., with funds provided by the Antique Collectors' Guild in memory of William Kayhoe, Richmond, Va.; past president of the Pewter Collectors Club of America; G1987-688

PUBLISHED: Hornsby, *Pewter of the Western World*, p. 292, fig. 997

290

This large cup is unusual because it is directly modeled on an earthenware prototype. Homer and Hall illustrate another cup of the same size and design by Wood, although it has a more developed foot of flagon or tankard type.[1]

1. Homer and Hall, *Provincial Pewterers*, fig. 12.

290 Two-Handled Cup

Maker unidentified
England, 1690–1705

MARKS: No touchmark apparent; pseudo hallmarks (1–3) *IL* within an outlined heart centered between handles on face of body

INSCRIPTIONS: Owner's initials *AS* stamped on face of body on side opposite from pseudo hallmarks

DIMENSIONS: OH. 5 3/4", OW. 9 1/2", Diam. (base) 4 1/2"

PROVENANCE: Acquired by Kenneth W. Bradshaw, Lincoln, Eng., from Sotheby's in 1971; sold by Bradshaw and purchased by CWF at Sotheby's in 1977; 1977-222

PUBLISHED: Sales cat., Sotheby's, Oct. 25, 1971, lot 192, ill.; *Art at Auction, 1971–72*, p. 336, ill.; sales cat., Sotheby's, June 13, 1977, p. 25, lot 85, ill.; *Art at Auction, 1976–77*, p. 302, ill.; Hornsby, *Pewter of the Western World*, p. 292, fig. 998; Law, "Williamsburg, Virginia—1994," p. 159, ill.

290.1 Stamped owner's initials

This splendid cup is as fine an exemplar of its type as survives. Its conformation and condition leave nothing to be desired. A similar cup in the possession of The Worshipful Company of Pewterers of London has *GOD SAVE QUEEN ANNE* relief cast in large letters on

DRINKING VESSELS 227

one side of its body and the arms of the Pewterers' Company on the other.[1] A cup of similar size and design by Adam Banks of Wigan was auctioned in 2000.[2] Cups of this size not only were intended for individual use but also could be passed by the handles for communal toasting and drinking.

The mold marks, visible among the alternate flutes and gadroons, indicate that the body was cast in a three-part mold.

1. Michaelis, *British Pewter*, ill. p. 54; *Short history of The Worshipful Company*, p. 67, no. 381, fig. 35.
2. This cup was sold by Phillips Auctioneers in Chester, Eng. It is illustrated in "Chester Sale—September 8th 2000," *Journal of the Pewter Society*, XIV (autumn 2000), p. 47, fig. 50.

291 Pair of Two-Handled Cups

William Eddon or Eden
London, 1730–1745

MARKS: Touchmark of an hourglass with *W* to the left and *E* to the right within a beaded circle on the interior center-bottom of each base (Cotterell, *Old Pewter*, 1503); secondary mark of a quality *X* stamped above pseudo hallmarks on face of each bowl; pseudo hallmarks (1) leopard's head, (2) buckle, (3) lion passant, and (4) *WE*, each within a shaped reserve on face of each bowl (Cotterell, *Old Pewter*, 1503)

INSCRIPTIONS: None

DIMENSIONS: OH. 6 3/8", OW. 7 3/4", Diam. (base) 3 7/8"

PROVENANCE: Purchased from A. V. Sutherland-Graeme, London; 1957-105, 1–2

PUBLISHED: Sutherland-Graeme, "William Eden, Master-Pewterer," p. 193, fig. IV

292 RACE CUP

Maker unidentified
England, 1760–1780

MARKS: Pseudo hallmarks (1 and 3) buckle, and (2 and 4) horse's or unicorn's head erased within indistinct reserves centered between handles on face of body; indistinct mark centered in pseudo hallmarks and placed slightly above

INSCRIPTIONS: *H:Davis/won By/Ball* engraved on face of body within a wriggle-engraved cartouche; a castle flanked by trees with ✽M✽I✽T*AYLOR*✽ above later engraved on opposite side of body below pseudo hallmarks

DIMENSIONS: OH. 4", OW. 6 9/16", Diam. (base) 2 5/8"

PROVENANCE: Purchased from Price Glover Inc., New York, N. Y.; 1978-245

PUBLISHED: Hornsby, *Pewter of the Western World*, p. 294, fig. 1006

Another cup by the same maker, although with broken scroll handles, is in the collections of The Worshipful Company of Pewterers of London. Both cups clearly bear the same pseudo hallmarks and other ambiguous marks.[1]

1. This other cup is illustrated in *Short history of The Worshipful Company*, pp. 66–67, no. 382, fig. 36. The marks on this cup are photographically reproduced in *Supplementary Catalogue of Pewterware, 1979*, p. 126, no. 382.

292.1 Engraved name and picture of a castle

DRINKING VESSELS 229

293

293 CUP

Maker unidentified
England, 1680–1700

MARKS: Touchmark *RK* within a heart or a diamond on interior center-bottom of body

INSCRIPTIONS: Owner's initials *MM* with touchmark between

DIMENSIONS: OH. 2 1/16", Diam. (rim) 2 7/8", Diam. (base) 2 1/8"

PROVENANCE: Purchased from A. H. Isher & Son, Cheltenham, Eng.; 1962-245

294 BEAKER

Samuel Danforth
Hartford, Conn., 1795–1816

MARKS: Touchmark of an American eagle displayed with rays and stars above, striped shield superimposed on body, and a cluster of arrows and olive branch in talons with *S* to the left and no visible letter to the right within vertical ovals on underside of base (Laughlin, *Pewter in America,* II, 402); secondary mark of a quality *X* above touchmark

INSCRIPTIONS: None

DIMENSIONS: OH. 5 1/4", Diam. (rim) 9 3/16", Diam. (base) 3"

PROVENANCE: Gift of Mr. and Mrs. Foster McCarl, Jr., Beaver Falls, Pa.; G1991-649

Beakers are among the most popular hollowware forms in American pewter. They were made in several sizes with considerable variation in proportions and details. Although a few stand taller than six inches, the standard tall beaker became fixed at about five-and-a-quarter inches in height. Thought to have been first fashioned in this size by Robert Bonynge or Jonathan Jackson of Boston, such as this handsome one, they soon became a customary production of several generations of the Danforth and Boardman families.[1]

1. Montgomery, *History of American Pewter,* p. 66. A useful discussion of this topic is Donald M. Herr's article, "Marked American Beakers," *Pewter Collectors Club of America Bulletin,* VIII (March 1982), pp. 193–212.

294

295 FLASK

Maker unidentified
Probably America, 1770–1800

MARKS: None

INSCRIPTIONS: Owner's initials *HS* cut into one side

DIMENSIONS: OH. 4 1/16", Diam. 3 7/8"

PROVENANCE: Purchased from Joe Kindig, Jr., York, Pa.; 1941-38

296 PUNCH STRAINER

Maker unidentified
England, 1710–1740

MARKS: None

INSCRIPTIONS: None

DIMENSIONS: OH. (rim) 11/16", Diam. 2 11/16"

PROVENANCE: Gift of John A. Hyman, Williamsburg, Va.; purchased by donor from Robin Bellamy Antiques, Witney, Eng., said by dealer to have come out of the Thames River; G1987-709

Surviving punch strainers in a variety of materials date from the last quarter of the seventeenth century onward. The design of the piercing of this rare pewter example is of a common type in the form of a stylized floral blossom that could easily be laid out with the arcs of a compass. There is no evidence of the presence of a handle, and no known comparable example in pewter with which to compare it.

297 PUNCH LADLE

Fruitwood handle
Possibly Simeon Stedman
Hartford, Conn., and Springfield, Mass., 1815–1840

MARKS: None

INSCRIPTIONS: None

DIMENSIONS: OL. 15 1/4", Diam. (rim) 3 11/16"

PROVENANCE: Purchased from Mrs. Miles White, Jr., Baltimore, Md.; 1933-235

DRINKING VESSELS 231

New England artisans produced a considerable number of pewter ladles with wooden handles during the first half of the nineteenth century. This ladle is particularly reminiscent of those marked by Simeon Stedman of Hartford, Conn. It shares with Stedman's ladles a bent wooden handle with a turned urn-shaped finial fitting a long, tapered socket. Stedman patented such ladles in 1818. A cabinetmaker by training and married to a member of the Boardman pewtering family, he may have fashioned handles for bowls that he acquired elsewhere. Stedman moved to Springfield, Mass., in 1825, where he is believed to have lived until his death in 1842.[1]

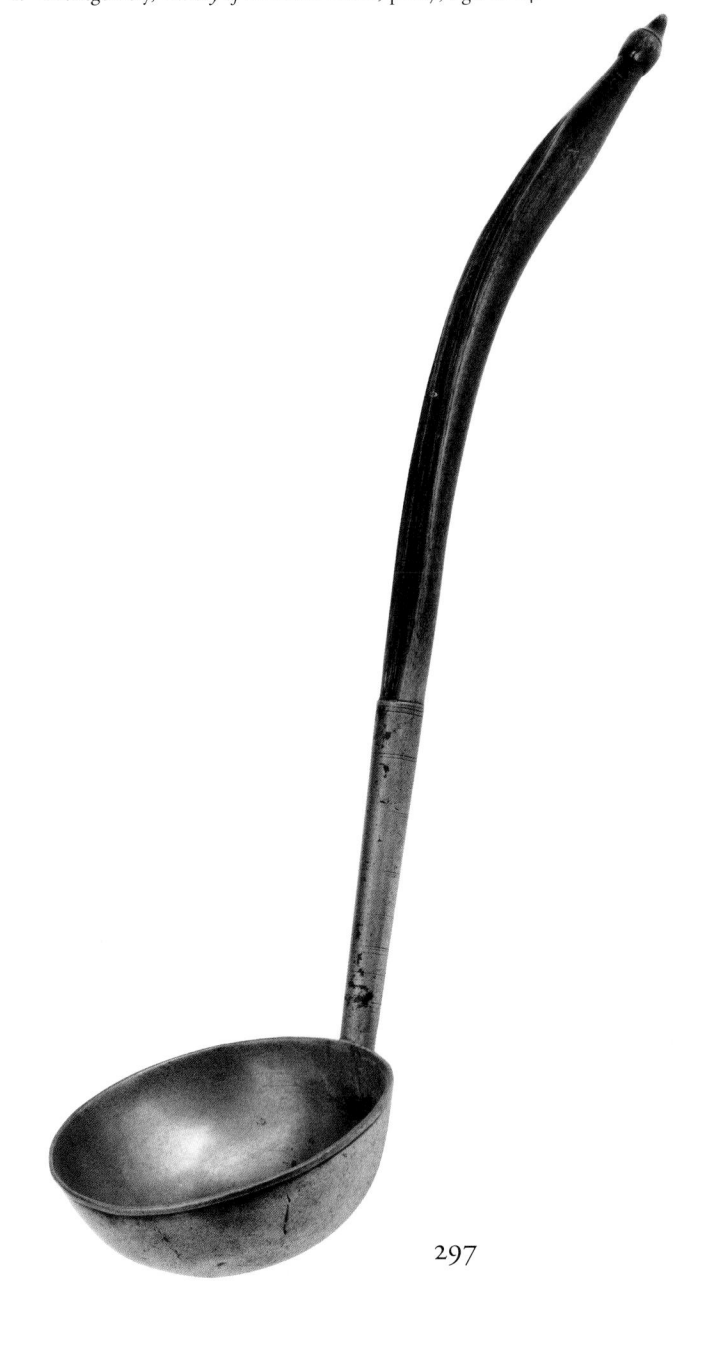

1. Montgomery, *History of American Pewter*, p. 167, figs. 10–14.

298 FUNNEL

Maker unidentified
England, 1780–1820

MARKS: None

INSCRIPTIONS: None

DIMENSIONS: OH. 6 1/16", Diam. (rim) 4 1/4"

PROVENANCE: Purchased from Dr. Percy E. Raymond, Lexington, Mass.; 1950-836

A considerable number of pewter funnels survive, yet few of them are marked.[1]

1. A useful discussion on pewter funnels is Jim Dunwell's article, "Poring over funnels," *Journal of the Pewter Society*, X (spring 1995), pp. 34–45.

299 JUG

James Vickers
Sheffield, Eng., 1790–1805

MARKS: Touchmark *I•VICKERS* on underside of base (Scott, *Pewter Wares from Sheffield*, 467)

INSCRIPTIONS: None

DIMENSIONS: OH. 7 5/16", Diam. (base) 3 1/4"

PROVENANCE: Purchased from Michael Allen Kashden, Edgware, Eng.; 1995-71

This handsome jug is in the early neoclassic style. Its body of slender barrel form reminds one of objects, especially in early silver plate from Sheffield, and small forms in sterling, such as coffee jugs, paired beakers, and the bodies of some nutmeg graters.

This jug was made in Sheffield by Vickers, who used some of the new technologies of the plating trade to make his Britannia wares. He strove to replicate in rolled sheet pewter the lightened neoclassic forms that were being turned out in that city in more costly metals. In this instance, Vickers used more traditional means, casting the body in upper and lower halves and joining them with a seam running around the middle at the point of the body's greatest diameter. The handle and pouring lip are also cast. The base plate was probably cut from a rolled sheet and then soldered.

299

300 MEASURE

Baluster type with hammerhead thumb piece
Half pint, Old English Wine Standard (OEWS)
Maker unidentified
England, 1695–1714

MARKS: Touchmark *R•W* with a mullet above and a pellet to either side and one below within a shaped reserve on face of body below rim to left of handle (Peal, *More Pewter Marks,* 6018b); verification mark *AR* with royal crown above within a conforming reserve on upper face of cover

INSCRIPTIONS: Housemark, or the emblematic mark of a business, of a standing angel with *GEORGE* above and [fleur-de-lis] *BV*[U]*SSEY* [fleur-de-lis] below within an outlined circle on upper face of cover in center; owner's initials *GB* with crowns above stamped on face of handle, presumably for George Bussey; owner's initials *EB* scratched on underside of base; collector's ink inscription *Minchin/415* on underside of base

DIMENSIONS: OH. 4 15/16", Diam. (base) 2 9/16"

PROVENANCE: Cyril C. Minchin, Bucklebury, Eng. (found near Reading).; Howard Herschel Cotterell, Croxley Green, Eng. (purchased from Minchin); Major John Richardson (purchased from Cotterell about 1931); F. Scott-Nicholson (purchased from Richardson); Royal Institution of Cornwall (given by Scott-Nicholson); Minchin (acquired by exchange for a piece of Cornish pewter from the Royal Institution of Cornwall in Truro); purchased by CWF from Minchin; 1981-178

PUBLISHED: Ullyett, *Guide for Collectors,* color pl. opposite p. 50

Pewter measures in standard sizes of verified capacities have been used in England in the commerce of alcoholic beverages since at least the fifteenth century. Inventories indicate their presence in taverns and households. Most surviving English measures dating before 1800 are of baluster form. Two of the earliest of this type display a squat baluster shape with a pronounced outward inclination to the upper part of their bodies. The earlier of these measures from the Thames River is thought to date from the mid- to late sixteenth century, while the other was aboard Henry VIII's warship *Mary Rose,* which sank off Portsmouth, Eng., in 1545.[1] Usually, baluster measures of sixteenth or early seventeenth century date are of slender outline with their covers raised with the aid of a hammerhead, ball, or wedge thumb piece.[2] Most baluster measures are lidded, and they are classified according to their form of thumb piece. This measure is a very late hammerhead example with most baluster measures of this date having the newer bud thumb piece (nos. 301–309).

This splendid measure has all the features one could want in a measure of its date, starting with its handsome conformation and condition, continuing with its marks of manufacture and ownership, and ending with its provenance of familiar and evocative names. It has the less common hammerhead thumb piece. It is clearly marked by the maker, which is not always the case with

234 PEWTER AT COLONIAL WILLIAMSBURG

300

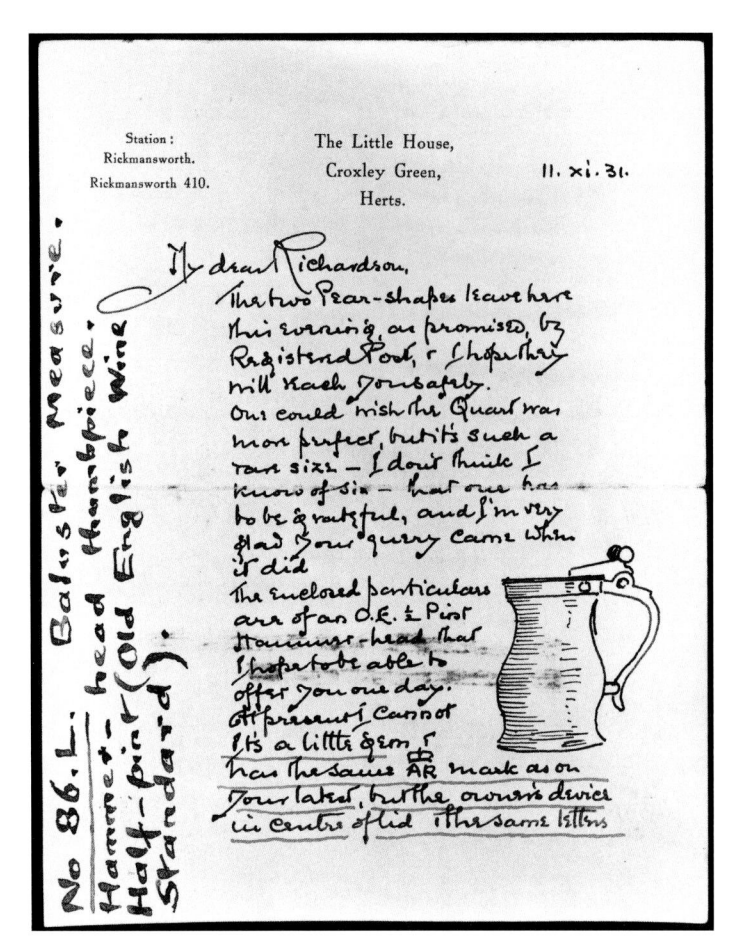

300.1 Letter from Howard Herschel Cotterell to Major John Richardson, Nov. 11, 1931 (object files, CWF)

measures. When Peal recorded this unidentified mark, he took it from a smaller hammerhead measure of gill size in his own collection.[3] He also drew attention to an unidentified *IW* touchmark of similar design and date.[4] Peal noted that this mark also appears on a hammerhead and bud measure, both about 1700. These touches might have belonged to members of a family that specialized in the production of measures.

The large pictorial mark in the center of the cover is a representative housemark, sometimes found on the covers of measures belonging to public houses or taverns. Of good size and distinctive design, these identifying marks usually contain the emblem of the house and the initials or name of the owner. Not only does George Bussey's name appear within the housemark, but also his initials are stamped on the handle.

The English have used marks to verify the capacity of measures from the reign of Henry VII (1485–1509). These verification marks usually involve the initials of a sovereign with royal crown above. Regarding the CWF Collection, certain marks, such as *WR* with royal crown above, are not particularly helpful in precise dating. It was used from the reign of William III (1688–1702) until the adoption of the imperial standard in 1826 and concurrently with *AR* and various *GR* marks. The *AR* with royal crown above, as on this measure, probably was used only during the reign of Queen Anne (1702–1714).

One of the pleasures of early pewter, especially with pieces of conspicuous quality, is often an association with notable collectors and dealers. The charming notes from Howard Herschel Cotterell to Major John Richardson, dated Nov. 11 and 25, 1931, came folded up inside this measure. They give a sense of immediacy and characterization to these individuals with familiar names. Cotterell writes of the virtues of this "little gem." Then he observes, "Its only blemish—this is rather quaint—some one, at some time, has pulled out the front of lip to form a small spout . . . . It could easily be hammered back, but to me these signs of former use do not detract from, but rather add to the interest of such a piece."

This measure was made in the same manner as that of most baluster measures. The body was cast in upper and lower sections

236 PEWTER AT COLONIAL WILLIAMSBURG

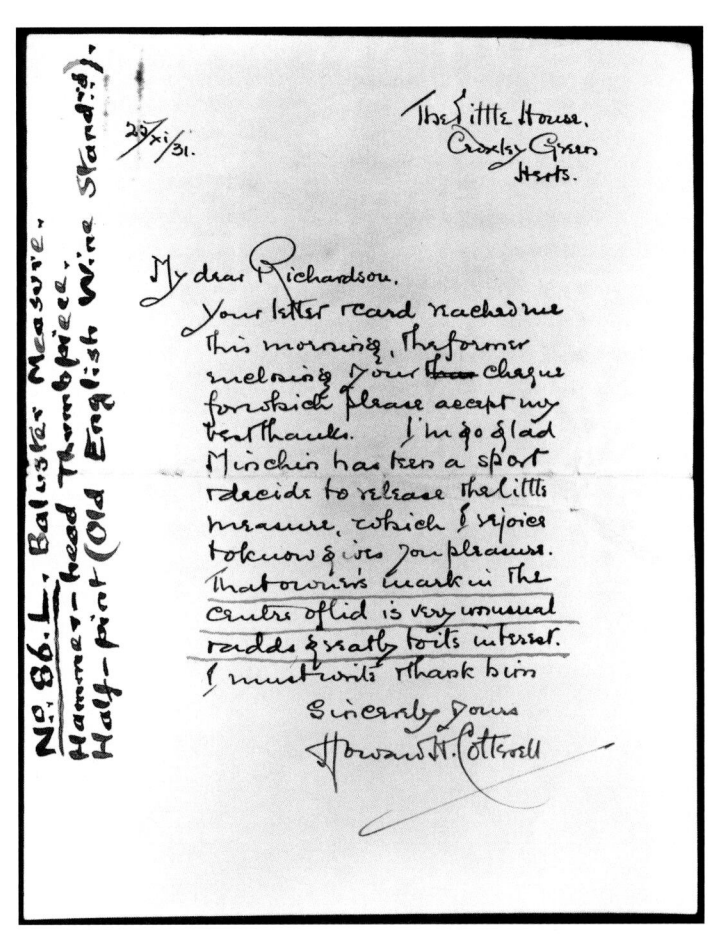

300.2 Letter from Howard Herschel Cotterell to Major John Richardson, Nov. 25, 1931 (object files, CWF)

with the break at the broadest swell of the body. The cover was cast in the form of a thick disk. These castings were skimmed, and circles were turned into the cover before assembly and before the body was soldered together. The thumb piece (including wedge and central knuckle of the hinge), and the handle (including outer hinge knuckles and lower handle strut) were each cast in a single mold. For greater strength, during casting these molds were clamped or held directly against the cover and body. Elements applied in this manner were described in the period as burned on, for the metal of the parts being cast against, in this instance, the cover and the body, actually melt when the new metal is cast. In this process, a pewterer placed a damp cloth between the underside of the cover and the clamp or tongs used to hold the mold and inside the body at both points of the attachment of the handle. Since metal is momentarily melted at the points of attachment, the fabric leaves an impression, known as a linen mark. Its presence is useful information about fabrication and authenticity. One is most used to seeing linen marks in the attachment of handles, or ears, on porringers.

1. Ronald F. Homer, "Pewter in Medieval England," *Journal of the Pewter Society,* XII (autumn 1999), p. 13, figs. 12–13.
2. For representative early examples, see Michaelis, *British Pewter,* pp. 78–79, ill.; Homer and Shemmell, *Pewter: Tudor and Stuart Pieces,* pp. 7–9; Hornsby, Weinstein, and Homer, *Celebration of the craft,* p. 88, no. 101, ill.; North and Spira, *Pewter at Victoria and Albert,* p. 145, figs. 222a and b.
3. Christopher A. Peal, *British Pewter and Britannia Metal: for pleasure and investment* (London, 1971), p. 67, fig. 15c; Peal et al., *Pewter of Great Britain,* p. 67, fig. 37; Christopher A. Peal, "18th Century British Pewter," *Antique Collector,* XLIV (June–July, 1973), p. 159, fig. 6. This measure has not only the same touchmark as the CWF measure, but also the same *AR* with royal crown verification mark stamped on its cover, as well as stamped owner's initials *IB,* possibly for another member of the Bussey family. This measure was in Peal's collection. It was sold by Price Glover Inc., New York, N. Y., to Peter Thompson, Easton, Md., in 1978.
4. Peal, *More Pewter Marks,* p. 92, no. 6003.

DRINKING VESSELS 237

301 MEASURE

Baluster type with bud thumb piece
Half gallon (OEWS)
Maker unidentified
England, 1690–1720

MARKS: Touchmark *IF* with a rosette between with crossed sprigs and a pellet above and below within an outlined circle on face of body below rim to right of handle (Laughlin, *Pewter in America,* II, 585; Peal, *More Pewter Marks,* 5595)

INSCRIPTIONS: None

DIMENSIONS: OH. 11 1/8", Diam. (base) 4 7/8"

PROVENANCE: Purchased from James L. Batey and Edward Lee Spence, Sullivan's Island, S. C., who found it in the Ashley River; 1969-34

PUBLISHED: Robinson, "British Pewter in New England," p. 192, fig. 156; Scarborough, *Carolina Metalworkers,* pp. 30–31, fig. 27

Baluster measures are among the most pleasing and personally satisfying objects in English pewter. The baluster has long been an essential element in western and eastern design. It is accepted as a complete and beautiful shape. These simple and graceful forms seem ideally suited to pewter and their basic utility. Baluster measures were made throughout the colonial period and impart a unity to measures over time.

Baluster measures are classified by their various thumb pieces. Hammerhead examples, such as no. 300, are rare in comparison with succeeding ones of this bud type. First appearing in the 1670s and coexisting with late hammerheads, bud thumb pieces consist of a bifurcated natural form with an opening bud or emerging young leaf to either side. The cover attachment to the hinge is further strengthened by the long wedge-shaped extension in front of the thumb piece.

301–303

This measure was found in the Ashley River below Doncaster, about thirty miles northwest of Charleston, S. C. When CWF acquired it in 1969, the hope still persisted that the touchmark might be that of John Fryers of Newport, R. I., although Laughlin had expressed caution in accepting the attribution by Louis G. Myers without further support.[1] When Laughlin issued his third volume in 1971, he placed this mark in the English column on the advice of Ronald Michaelis.[2]

1. Laughlin, *Pewter in America,* II, pl. LXIX, no. 585.
2. *Ibid.,* III, p. 162; "Marks," *Journal of the Pewter Society,* XI (autumn 1997), p. 52, no. J280.

302 MEASURE

Baluster type with bud thumb piece
Gallon (OEWS)
Maker unidentified
England, 1750–1780

MARKS: None

INSCRIPTIONS: Probable American verification mark *CM* for colony or commonwealth of Massachusetts and *Y* possibly for the town of Yarmouth stamped on face of body below rim to right of handle; larger *Y* also possibly for the town of Yarmouth stamped on upper face of cover opposite handle

DIMENSIONS: OH. 12 7/8", Diam. (base) 6 5/16"

PROVENANCE: Purchased from Mrs. Miles White, Jr., Baltimore, Md.; 1933-231

A considerable number of eighteenth-century baluster measures are stamped with raised-letter dies with what are probably the initials of various American colonies, commonwealths, and provinces, as well as towns within them. Most of these marks are associated with the New England region. They occur most frequently on baluster measures with double-volute thumb pieces. It is not surprising to find these marks on measure nos. 302 and 303, since these are late bud examples from the double-volute period.

303 MEASURE

Baluster type with bud thumb piece
Half gallon (OEWS)
Maker unidentified
England, 1750–1780

MARKS: None

INSCRIPTIONS: Probable American verification marks *CM* for colony or commonwealth of Massachusetts and *Y* possibly for the town of Yarmouth stamped on face of body below rim to right of handle; larger *Y* also possibly for the town of Yarmouth stamped on upper face of cover opposite handle

DIMENSIONS: OH. 10 3/4", Diam. (base) 5 1/16"

PROVENANCE: Purchased from Mrs. Miles White, Jr., Baltimore, Md.; 1933-230

304 MEASURE

Baluster type with bud thumb piece
Half gallon (OEWS)
Maker unidentified
England, 1680–1710

MARKS: Indistinct touchmark incorporating, in part, *A*[?] within an outlined lozenge on face of body below rim to right of handle; verification mark *H* [dagger]*R* with royal crown above within a conforming reserve on face of body below rim to left of handle

INSCRIPTIONS: None

DIMENSIONS: OH. 11 3/8", Diam. (base) 4 7/8"

PROVENANCE: Purchased from A. H. Isher & Son, Cheltenham, Eng.; 1958-587

There has been considerable discussion about the origin and meaning of the *hR* or *HR* initials with royal crown above in this verification mark. That these marks are believed "to indicate that the capacity conforms to that of the 1497 gallon of Henry VII" seems reasonable, in the same way that *WR* stamps relate to standards established by William III in 1700, or *AR* stamps, to the introduction of Queen Anne's wine gallon in 1707.[1]

1. Homer and Shemmell, *Pewter: Tudor and Stuart Pieces,* p. 23.

304–309

305 MEASURE

Baluster type with bud thumb piece
Quart (OEWS)
John Carr
London, 1697–1720

MARKS: Touchmark of a wheel with *I* to the left, *C* to the right, and *1697* below within a beaded circle on face of body below rim to right of handle (London Touch Plate II, 537; Cotterell, *Old Pewter,* 814); verification mark *GR* with royal crown above within a conforming reserve on upper face of cover opposite handle

INSCRIPTIONS: Owners' initials *TB* engraved on face of handle and *MI* stamped on upper face of cover in center

DIMENSIONS: OH. 7 15/16", Diam. (base) 4"

PROVENANCE: Purchased from Dr. Percy E. Raymond, Lexington, Mass.; 1950-851

305.1 Engraved owner's initials on face of handle

305.2 Stamped owner's initials on face of cover

306 MEASURE

Baluster type with bud thumb piece
Pint (OEWS)
Maker unidentified
England, 1671–1710

MARKS: Touchmark of a standing bird with *AB* above and *71* below within an outlined circle on face of body below rim to left of handle

INSCRIPTIONS: Owner's initials *R✲P* stamped on upper face of cover opposite handle

306.1 Stamped owner's initials on cover

307.1 Stamped owners' initials on body

DIMENSIONS: OH. 6 3/8", Diam. (base) 3 5/16"

PROVENANCE: Purchased from A. H. Isher & Son, Cheltenham, Eng.; 1958-586

307 MEASURE

Baluster type with bud thumb piece
Pint (OEWS)
Maker unidentified
England, 1690–1720

MARKS: Touchmark *FB* with three pellets above and a device below within an outlined circle on upper face of cover in center (Peal, *More Pewter Marks,* 5423a)

INSCRIPTIONS: Owners' initials *E/TA* stamped on face of body to left of handle

DIMENSIONS: OH. 6 7/16", Diam. (base) 3 1/16"

PROVENANCE: Purchased from A. V. Sutherland-Graeme, London; 1955-419

308 MEASURE

Baluster type with bud thumb piece
Half pint (OEWS)
Thomas Matthews
London, 1716–1740

MARKS: Touchmark *TM/1716* within a rectangle on face of body below rim to right of handle (Cotterell, *Old Pewter,* 5800; Peal, *More Pewter Marks,* 5800; Peal, *Addenda,* 5800)

DRINKING VESSELS 241

308.1 Stamped and engraved owners' initials on face of cover

INSCRIPTIONS: Owners' initials *CT* engraved on upper face of cover and on face of handle and *S/RA* stamped on upper face of cover

DIMENSIONS: OH. 4 11/16", Diam. (base) 2 5/8"

PROVENANCE: Purchased from Dr. Percy E. Raymond, Lexington, Mass.; 1950-853

309 MEASURE

Baluster type with bud thumb piece
Gill (OEWS)
Maker unidentified
England, 1740–1770

MARKS: None

INSCRIPTIONS: None

DIMENSIONS: OH. 4 3/16", Diam. (base) 2 3/32"

PROVENANCE: Purchased from A. H. Isher & Son, Cheltenham, Eng.; 1966-303

310 MEASURE

Baluster type with double-volute thumb piece
Gallon (OEWS)
Maker unidentified
England, 1750–1780

MARKS: None

INSCRIPTIONS: Probable American verification marks with *CM* possibly for colony or commonwealth of Massachusetts stamped on face of body below rim to left of handle and *CS* possibly for county of Suffolk stamped above on upper face of cover

DIMENSIONS: OH. 12 15/16", Diam. (base) 5 15/16"

PROVENANCE: Purchased from Carl Jacobs, Southwick, Mass.; 1950-302

Although some baluster measures with bud thumb pieces date from the second half of the eighteenth century, they were largely supplanted in that period by those with double-volute thumb pieces. The attachment of the double-volute thumb piece to the cover was reinforced with a fleur-de-lis extension in front of the thumb piece. Many measures were made by firms that specialized in their manufacture. It is not a mistake or mere coincidence that many of these baluster measures bear the touchmark of William Fasson, who was one of their principal producers.

311 MEASURE

Baluster type with double-volute thumb piece
Gallon (OEWS)
Maker unidentified
England, 1740–1780

MARKS: None

INSCRIPTIONS: Probable American verification marks *CM* possibly for colony or commonwealth of Massachusetts stamped on face of body below rim to left of handle and a larger *CO* possibly for county of Oxford (now Maine) stamped on face of handle

DIMENSIONS: OH. 12 13/16", Diam. (base) 6"

PROVENANCE: Purchased from Carl Jacobs, Southwick, Mass.; 1950-36

312 MEASURE

Baluster type with double-volute thumb piece
Half gallon (OEWS)
Maker unidentified
England, 1740–1780

MARKS: None

INSCRIPTIONS: Probable American verification marks *CM* possibly for colony or commonwealth of Massachusetts stamped on face of body below rim to left of handle and a larger *CO* possibly for county of Oxford (now Maine) stamped on upper face of cover

310–317

DIMENSIONS: OH. 10 9/16", Diam. (base) 4 3/4"

PROVENANCE: Purchased from Dr. Percy E. Raymond, Lexington, Mass.; 1950-855

313 MEASURE

Baluster type with double-volute thumb piece
Pint (OEWS)
William Fasson
London, 1758–1780

MARKS: Touchmark *WF* within a rectangle on face of body below rim to right of handle (Peal, *More Pewter Marks,* 1639); verification mark *WR* with royal crown above on upper face of cover in center

INSCRIPTIONS: None

DIMENSIONS: OH. 6 1/6", Diam. (base) 3 1/4"

PROVENANCE: Howard Herschell Cotterell, Croxley Green, Eng. (trade label *1028* glued to underside of cover); purchased by CWF from A. V. Sutherland-Graeme, London; 1957-50

313.1 Dealer's label on underside of cover

314 MEASURE

Baluster type with double-volute thumb piece
Half pint (OEWS)
William Fasson
London, 1758–1780

MARKS: Touchmark *WF* within a rectangle on face of body below rim to right of handle (Peal, *More Pewter Marks,* 1639)

INSCRIPTIONS: None

DIMENSIONS: OH. 5 1/8", Diam. (base) 2 5/8"

PROVENANCE: Purchased from Dr. Percy E. Raymond, Lexington, Mass.; 1950-797

315 MEASURE

Baluster type with double-volute thumb piece
Quart (OEWS)
Probably William Fasson
London, 1758–1780

MARKS: Touchmark *W+F* within a serrated rectangle on face of body below rim to right of handle (Peal, *More Pewter Marks,* 5604b); verification mark *WR* with a royal crown above on upper face of cover in center

INSCRIPTIONS: None

DIMENSIONS: OH. 7 15/16", Diam. (base) 3 3/8"

PROVENANCE: Howard Herschell Cotterell, Croxley Green, Eng. (trade label *1027* glued to underside of cover); purchased by CWF from A. V. Sutherland-Graeme, London; 1957-51

316 MEASURE

Baluster type with double-volute thumb piece
Gill (OEWS)
William Fasson
London, 1758–1780

MARKS: Touchmark *WF* within a rectangle on face of body below rim to right of handle (Peal, *More Pewter Marks,* 1639)

INSCRIPTIONS: None

DIMENSIONS: OH. 3 31/32", Diam. (base) 2 1/8"

PROVENANCE: Purchased from Dr. Percy E. Raymond, Lexington, Mass.; 1950-798

317 MEASURE

Baluster type with double-volute thumb piece
Half gill (OEWS)
Maker unidentified
England, 1740–1780

MARKS: None

INSCRIPTIONS: None

DIMENSIONS: OH. 3 5/16", Diam. (base) 1 9/16"

PROVENANCE: Purchased from A. V. Sutherland-Graeme, London; 1956-441

318 MEASURE

Baluster type
Quart (OEWS)
Maker unidentified
Probably north of England, 1770–1800

MARKS: No touchmark apparent; verification mark *GR* with royal crown above within a vertical rectangle with rounded top on face of body below rim to left of handle

INSCRIPTIONS: None

DIMENSIONS: OH. 7 1/4", Diam. (base) 3 13/16"

PROVENANCE: Purchased from A. V. Sutherland-Graeme, London; 1959-377

319 MEASURE

Haystack type
Pint (OEWS)
M. Fothergill & Sons
Bristol, Eng., 1780–1805

MARKS: Touchmark of two clasped hands with pendant ringlike device framed by *FOTHERGILLS BRISTOL* within inner and outer circles on underside of base (Peal, *More Pewter Marks,* 1740)

INSCRIPTIONS: Owners' or sealers' marks *CP* and *N.P* stamped on underside of lip

DIMENSIONS: OH. 6 1/8", Diam. (base) 3 1/2"

PROVENANCE: Purchased from A. V. Sutherland-Graeme, London; 1959-153

319.1 Stamped initials on underside of lip

DRINKING VESSELS 245

PUBLISHED: Sales brochure, Robin Bellamy Antiques, autumn 1989, no. 5, ill.

This measure, in size and design, reminds one of friendly society, or gild, flagons, such as the example of about 1760 by William Munden and Edmund Grave of London that is engraved with the coat of arms of the Norwich Worsted Weavers' Company.[1] A later Norwich friendly society flagon by Geradin & Watson of London, dated 1819, was formerly in the Peal Collection.[2] Such flagons have domed covers with tankard thumb pieces. Another unlidded measure, like this one, of about 1780 is engraved *Thomas Chitty/White Hart/Harting*.[3]

1. Richard Mundey, "A Friendly Society or Gild Flagon," *Pewter Collectors Club of America Bulletin,* VIII (August 1983), p. 279.
2. Sales cat., Sotheby's, Oct. 6, 1981, p. 9, lot 23, ill.
3. Sales cat., Sotheby's, Feb. 27, 1975, lot 136, ill.; Brett, *Phaidon Guide to Pewter,* ill. p. 58.

320

320 ALE MEASURE

Flagon form
Gallon (AS)
Maker unidentified
England, 1775–1790

MARKS: No touchmark apparent; verification mark *WR* with royal crown above within a conforming reserve on face of body to left of handle

INSCRIPTIONS: *Clarke/Fox/Twickenham* engraved in script within a shaped circular reserve wriggle engraved on lower face of body opposite handle

DIMENSIONS: OH. 11 1/2", Diam. (base) 7 15/16"

PROVENANCE: Purchased from Robin Bellamy Antiques, Witney, Eng.; 1989-366

320.1 Engraved inscription on body

246 PEWTER AT COLONIAL WILLIAMSBURG

321–324 (counterclockwise from top)

321 MEASURE

Uncrested tappit-hen type
Scots pint
Maker unidentified
Scotland, 1730–1826

MARKS: None

INSCRIPTIONS: Owner's initials *P*T* engraved on upper face of cover

DIMENSIONS: OH. 10 7/8", Diam. (base) 4 7/8"

PROVENANCE: Howard Herschel Cotterell, Croxley Green, Eng. (trade label *1097* glued to underside of cover); purchased by CWF from A. V. Sutherland-Graeme, London; 1957-47

Although the Scots pint and related capacities were supposedly replaced in 1707 by English standards, the Scots continued to use their traditional capacities. The most distinctive Scottish measures are of this tappit-hen type. Of mallet shape with turned lines at intervals, they are fitted with a domed cover with a flat top, either crested, that is, with a finial, or left plain. A prominent thumb piece stands atop a slender strap handle that is attached with a short strut to the lower section of the body. A small raised bead of metal (known as a plouk) is usually found inside the body below the rim, and it indicates the point at which the proper capacity is achieved. Although the earliest measures of this type date from the late seventeenth century, most examples are from the half century before the introduction of the imperial standard in 1826. Marked examples are rare.

322 MEASURE

Uncrested tappit-hen type
Chopin capacity
Maker unidentified
Scotland, 1730–1826

MARKS: None

INSCRIPTIONS: None

DIMENSIONS: OH. 8 3/4", Diam. (base) 3 7/8"

PROVENANCE: Howard Herschell Cotterell, Croxley Green, Eng. (trade label *1207* glued to underside of cover); purchased by CWF from A. V. Sutherland-Graeme, London; 1957-48

321.1 Engraved owner's initials on cover

321.2 Trade label on underside of cover

322.1 Trade label on underside of cover

248 PEWTER AT COLONIAL WILLIAMSBURG

323 MEASURE

Uncrested tappit-hen type
Mutchkin capacity
Maker unidentified
Scotland, 1730–1826

MARKS: None

INSCRIPTIONS: Owner's initials *AS* engraved on upper face of cover

DIMENSIONS: OH. 6 5/8", Diam. (base) 3"

PROVENANCE: Howard Herschel Cotterell, Croxley Green, Eng. (trade label *1221* glued to underside of cover); purchased by CWF from A. V. Sutherland-Graeme, London; 1957-49

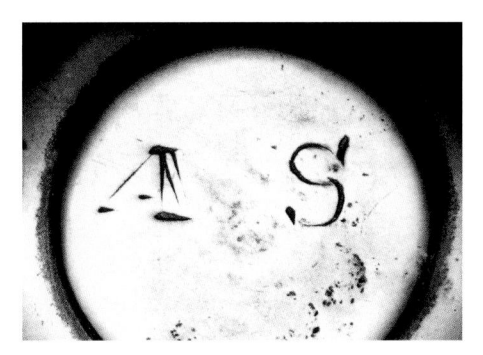

323.1 Owner's initials on cover

323.2 Trade label on underside of cover

324 MEASURE

Crested tappit-hen type
Scots pint
Maker unidentified
Scotland, 1750–1826

MARKS: None

INSCRIPTIONS: Owner's initials *WE* stamped on face of body to left of handle

DIMENSIONS: OH. 11 9/16", Diam. (base) 5 1/16"

PROVENANCE: Purchased from A. H. Isher & Son, Cheltenham, Eng.; 1960-793

324.1 Stamped owner's initials on body

DRINKING VESSELS 249

325–332 (on left and on right)

325 MEASURE

Jersey type
Pot size
John de St. Croix
Probably London, 1730–1765

MARKS: Touchmark *ISDX* with a star above and below within a circle on underside of cover (Cotterell, *Old Pewter,* 1360); verification mark *GR* with crown above stamped on face of body below rim to left of handle

INSCRIPTIONS: Owner's initials *ILG* engraved on face of handle

DIMENSIONS: OH. 10 9/16", Diam. (base) 5 1/16"

PROVENANCE: Purchased from A. V. Sutherland-Graeme, London; 1957-3, 1

Jean de Sainte Croix (anglicized John de St. Croix by him in his first touchmark of 1730) was the most important Jersey pewterer of the eighteenth century. He served his apprenticeship in London under Hellier Perchard, a fellow Jerseyman, beginning in 1722. He was admitted to The Worshipful Company of Pewterers of London in December 1729. Six months later, he struck his touchmark of armorial design on the touch plate at Pewterers' Hall. Although Stanley Woolmer and Charles Arkwright comment that the entry of one's mark was usually followed by the opening of one's shop, there is scant information about St. Croix's career, with the latest reference from 1765.[1] He is particularly known to students of pewter for his splendid measures of Jersey type. These vessels are characterized by graceful baluster forms with more relaxed contours than their English counterparts. French influence is apparent, as in Guernsey measures (see nos. 329–332), in their twin acorn thumb pieces with long wedge-shaped extensions onto the top of flat, pointed covers. It is customary for the handles on Jersey measures to be burned on or cast directly against the body. The hinge pins on many of St. Croix's measures, as in this one, are impressed on one side with the design of a floral blossom. Although other Jersey measures may have this treatment, none appears as decorative.

1. The information on John de St. Croix and Channel Islands pewter is mainly taken from the standard reference: Stanley C. Woolmer and Charles H. Arkwright, *Pewter of the Channel Islands* (Edinburgh, Scot., 1973), pp. 108–116.

325.1 Decorated hinge pin

325.2 Engraved owner's initials on handle

326 MEASURE

Jersey type
Quart size
John de St. Croix
Jersey, Channel Islands, or London, 1730–1765

MARKS: Touchmark *IDSX* with a star above and below within a circle on underside of cover (Cotterell, *Old Pewter,* 1360)

INSCRIPTIONS: Owner's initials *M.V.P.* engraved on face of handle

DIMENSIONS: OH. 8 3/16", Diam. (base) 4 1/4"

PROVENANCE: Purchased from A. V. Sutherland-Graeme, London; 1952-604

326.1 Engraved owner's initials on handle

327 MEASURE

Jersey type
Half-pint size
Maker unidentified
Jersey, Channel Islands, or London, 1754–1790

MARKS: No touchmark apparent; verification mark *GR* with crown above on face of body below rim to right of handle

INSCRIPTIONS: None

DIMENSIONS: OH. 5 1/2", Diam. (base) 2 5/8"

PROVENANCE: Purchased from A. V. Sutherland-Graeme, London; 1952-605

328 MEASURE

Jersey type
Noggin size
Maker unidentified
Jersey, Channel Islands, or London, 1754–1790

MARKS: No touchmark apparent; verification mark *GR* with crown above on face of body below rim to right of handle

INSCRIPTIONS: None

DIMENSIONS: OH. 4 1/4", Diam. (base) 2 1/16"

PROVENANCE: Gift of Dr. Percy E. Raymond, Lexington, Mass.; G1950-927

329 MEASURE

Guernsey type
Pot size
A. Carter
England, probably West Country, 1740–1770

MARKS: Partially indistinct touchmark with the arms of Carter (on a shield two lions combatant beneath a crescent) with the crest of a lion's head erased on a wreath bar with foliate tips to either side and the motto *A•POSSE•AD•ESSE* [From Possibility to Being] with palm frond at either end within a curved banner below, all within a conforming reserve stamped twice on face of cover (Cotterell, *Old Pewter,* 825; Peal, *More Pewter Marks,* 825); maker's label *A•C* within a rectangle on face of cover in center (Cotterell, *Old Pewter,* 825; Peal, *More Pewter Marks,* 825); label *LONDON* with *N*s reversed within an oblong rectangle on face of cover near point (Cotterell, *Old Pewter,* 825; Peal, *More Pewter Marks,* 825)

INSCRIPTIONS: Owner's initials *IGR* stamped on face of cover

DIMENSIONS: OH. 10 15/16", Diam. (base) 5 3/16"

PROVENANCE: Purchased from A. V. Sutherland-Graeme, London; 1954-944

The other major group of measures associated with the Channel Islands includes those of Guernsey type. They are also of baluster form, although their outlines are more fulsome, or voluptuous, than those of Jersey. Both have the same twin acorn thumb pieces with wedge-shaped attachments to flat, pointed covers. Both have slender strap handles that are burned on. Guernsey measures, however, are more resolutely banded around the neck and the widest part of the body, and they are supported on a taller splayed base.

The most noted maker of Guernsey measures marked his wares generally with a small *A•C* label and a much larger and more elaborate mark, usually stamped twice, with the Carter arms, crest, and motto. Like John de St. Croix, the shadowy Carter probably worked mainly in England, with Woolmer and Arkwright suggesting that he worked outside of London and perhaps in the West Country. *SM* and *CM* marks also appear on a number of measures with Carter's large mark, suggesting that they were probably partners of Carter.[1]

1. Woolmer and Arkwright, *Pewter of Channel Islands,* pp. 105–108.

330 MEASURE

Guernsey type
Pot size
Shop of A. Carter
England, probably West Country, 1740–1770

MARKS: Partially indistinct touchmark with the arms of Carter (on a shield two lions combatant beneath a crescent) with the crest of a lion's head erased on a wreath bar with foliate tips to either side and the motto *A•POSSE•AD•ESSE* [From Possibility to Being] with a palm frond to either side within a curved banner

252 PEWTER AT COLONIAL WILLIAMSBURG

below, all within a conforming reserve and stamped twice on face of cover (Cotterell, *Old Pewter,* 825; Peal, *More Pewter Marks,* 825); partner's or workman's mark *SM* within a peaked rectangle on face of cover near pointed end (Cotterell, *Old Pewter,* 825; Peal, *More Pewter Marks,* 825); label *LONDON* within an oblong rectangle on face of cover (Cotterell, *Old Pewter,* 825; Peal, *More Pewter Marks,* 825)

INSCRIPTIONS: Owner's initials *ER* stamped on face of cover

DIMENSIONS: OH. 10 3/4", Diam. (base) 5 1/4"

PROVENANCE: Gift of Mrs. Owen L. Coon, Wilmette, Ill.; G1954-944

331 MEASURE

Guernsey type
Quart size
Shop of A. Carter
England, probably West Country, 1740–1770

MARKS: Partially indistinct touchmark with the arms of Carter (on a shield two lions combatant beneath a crescent) with the crest of a lion's head erased on wreath bar with foliate tips to either side above and the motto *A•POSSE•AD•ESSE* [From Possibility to Being] with a palm frond to either side with a curved reserve below, all within a conforming reserve and stamped twice on face of cover (Cotterell, *Old Pewter,* 825; Peal, *More Pewter Marks,* 825); partner's or workman's mark *CM* within a horizontal beaded oval on face of cover (Peal, *More Pewter Marks,* 825); label *LONDON* within an oblong serrated rectangle on face of cover (Peal, *More Pewter Marks,* 825)

INSCRIPTIONS: Owner's initials *IRB* stamped on face of cover

DIMENSIONS: OH. 8 7/8", Diam. (base) 4 1/4"

PROVENANCE: Gift of Mrs. Owen L. Coon, Wilmette, Ill.; G1983-344

332 MEASURE

Guernsey type
Pint size
Shop of A. Carter
England, probably West Country, 1740–1770

MARKS: Partially indistinct touchmark with the arms of Carter (on a shield two lions combatant beneath a crescent) with the crest of a lion's head erased on a wreath bar with foliate tips to either side above and the motto *A•POSSE•AD•ESSE* [From Possibility to Being] with a palm frond to either end within a curved banner below, all within a conforming reserve stamped twice on face of cover (Cotterell, *Old Pewter,* 825; Peal, *More Pewter Marks,* 825); partner's or workman's mark *CM* within a horizontal beaded oval on face of cover (Peal, *More Pewter Marks,* 825); label *LONDON* within an oblong serrated rectangle on face of cover (Peal, *More Pewter Marks,* 825)

INSCRIPTIONS: Owner's initials *IRB* stamped on face of cover

DIMENSIONS: OH. 6 15/16", Diam. (base) 3 3/8"

PROVENANCE: Gift of Mrs. Owen L. Coon, Wilmette, Ill.; G1983-345

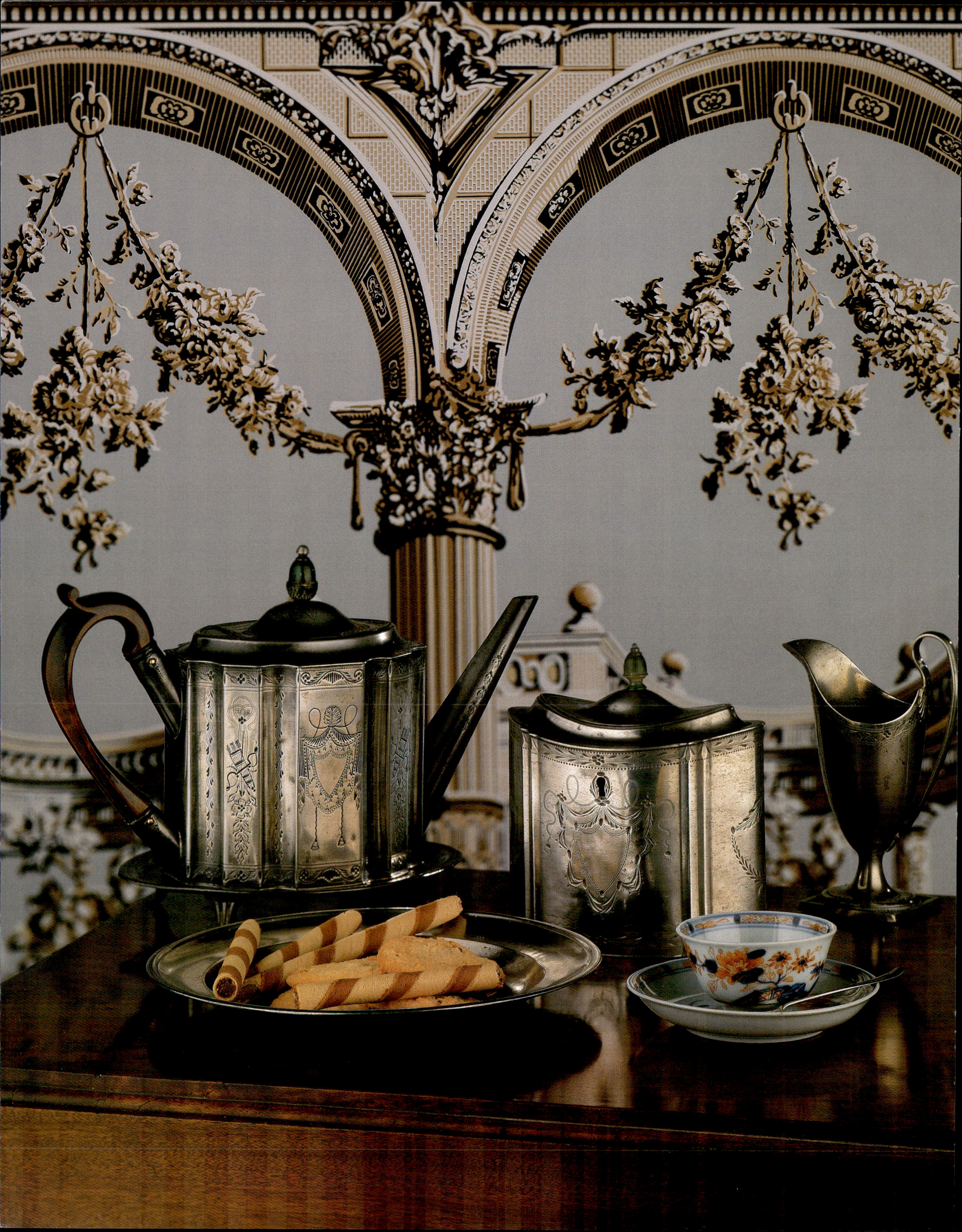

Tea and Coffee Equipage

The earliest English pewter teapots date from the first half of the eighteenth century, and surviving examples are extremely rare. More common pear-shaped ones were produced by English export makers for the American market, and they, in turn, prompted a fine group of American examples. Neoclassic teapots achieved considerable popularity in this country from the late eighteenth century through the first half of the nineteenth century. Tea caddies, cream jugs and ewers, and covered sugar bowls form part of the necessary equipage for tea and coffee drinking in the Colonial Williamsburg Collection.

333–334

333 TEAPOT

Edward Ubly
London, 1720–1735

MARKS: Touchmark of a standing deer with *E* to the left, *V* to the right, and *17* above within an outlined circle on underside of base; secondary mark of a quality *X* with crown above on underside of base

INSCRIPTIONS: None

DIMENSIONS: OH. 4 11/16", OL. 7 3/8", Diam. (base) 2 3/4"

PROVENANCE: Cyril C. Minchin, Bucklebury, Eng. (sold to David Walter Ellis, who sold it to Brand Inglis, London, from whom CWF purchased it); 1983-316

PUBLISHED: *Exhibition of British Pewterware,* p. 28, no. 194; Ullyett, *Guide for Collectors,* color pl. facing p. 51; *"Invitation to Tea,"* p. 16, pl. XIV

EXHIBITED: Exhibition of British Pewterware through the Ages from Romano-British Times to the Present Day, Reading Museum and Art Gallery, Reading, Eng., Sept. 20–Oct. 31, 1969

This teapot and no. 334 are certainly among the earliest of the few English pewter teapots that survive from the first half of the eighteenth century. This one, like other early examples, is of compact, globular design. The ranginess of the replaced handle violates the original intent. The design of the handle and its flatness on either side would indicate that a carpenter probably made it with the handle of his saw in mind.

334 TEAPOT

Maker unidentified
England, 1720–1740

MARKS: None

256 PEWTER AT COLONIAL WILLIAMSBURG

334.1 Engraved owner's cipher and coronet on body

INSCRIPTIONS: Owner's cipher *EB* doubled and reversed with a baron's coronet above engraved on face of body

DIMENSIONS: OH. 3 7/16", OL. 5 7/8", Diam. (base) 2 1/16"

PROVENANCE: Purchased from Brian Beet, London; 1999-53

PUBLISHED: Sale ad, Morland House, Fredericksburg, Va., *The Magazine Antiques,* CLII (December 1997), p. 777, ill.

This teapot is of unusually small size. It is even smaller than later teapots of bachelor size and much closer in capacity to contemporary cordial or saffron pots in silver. The specialized size and the ivory handle and finial inset may reflect the elevated baron's status of the teapot's original owner.

335 TEAPOT

Samuel Ellis I
London, 1740–1764

MARKS: Touchmark of a label with *S:ELLIS* within a rectangle on underside of body (Peal, *More Pewter Marks,* 1547); secondary mark of a quality *X* with crown above stamped on underside of body above touchmark

INSCRIPTIONS: None

DIMENSIONS: OH. 6 3/8", OL. 7 3/8"

PROVENANCE: Purchased from George C. Gebelein, Boston, Mass.; 1936-28

England is noted for its production of pottery and porcelain teapots. Ceramic ones obviously became the choice of most consumers, for relatively few pewter teapots were made in eighteenth-century England for domestic use. The many English pear-shaped examples in pewter, especially dating from the third quarter of the eighteenth century, were virtually all produced for the export trade and, not surprisingly, by principal makers, such as Ellis, Henry Joseph, and John Townsend, in particular. While few English silver teapots of pear form date from after the first quarter of the eighteenth century, American silversmiths in some centers continued to fashion silver teapots of this early form almost until the Revolution. Imported and domestically produced pewter examples played a significant role in extending the popularity of this form in American homes. The painted banner, carried on July 23, 1788, in the Federal Procession by the Society of Pewterers of New York City to celebrate the ratification of the Constitution, proudly displays a pear-shaped teapot as the crest to their arms and as one of the three emblematic forms shown above a shop scene.[1]

1. This banner, belonging to the New-York Historical Society, is illustrated on the back cover of Montgomery, *History of American Pewter,* and Brett, *Phaidon Guide to Pewter,* ill. pp. 172–173.

336 TEAPOT

John Townsend
London, 1748–1766

MARKS: Touchmark of a paschal lamb with a dove with olive branch in bill in flight above within a vertical oval frame bordered by *IOHN/TOWNSEND* on underside of base

INSCRIPTIONS: None

DIMENSIONS: OH. 7", OL. 9 1/2", Diam. (base) 3 1/2"

PROVENANCE: Purchased from Thomas D. and Constance R. Williams, Litchfield, Conn.; 1956-82

This example and others with marks of Townsend, both teapots and flatware, are dated before he entered into a series of partnerships in 1766. His baluster-shaped tankard, with an obviously later double-scroll handle and open, scroll thumb piece (no. 261), indicates that he used his own touchmark after 1766, and the tankard is dated accordingly.

TEA AND COFFEE EQUIPAGE 257

335–338

337 Teapot

Samuel Ellis I
London, 1740–1764

MARKS: Touchmark of a label with *S:ELLIS* within a rectangle on underside of base (Peal, *More Pewter Marks,* 1547); secondary mark of a quality *X* with crown above stamped on underside of base above touchmark

INSCRIPTIONS: None

DIMENSIONS: OH. 5 7/16", OL. 8 3/16", Diam. (base) 2 31/32"

PROVENANCE: Purchased from Dr. Percy E. Raymond, Lexington, Mass.; 1950-903

338 Teapot

John Townsend
London, 1748–1766

MARKS: Touchmark of a paschal lamb with a dove with olive branch in bill in flight above framed by *17 IOHN 48/TOWNSEND* within an outlined oval on

258 PEWTER AT COLONIAL WILLIAMSBURG

underside of base; quality *X* with crown above within a shaped rectangle above touchmark on underside of base

INSCRIPTIONS: None

DIMENSIONS: OH. 5 1/8", OL. 6 3/8", Diam. (base) 2 7/16"

PROVENANCE: Purchased from Needham's Antiques, New York, N. Y.; 1959-20

Townsend was a major maker of export pewter to this country. Daniel Wister, a Philadelphia merchant, was a regular customer. One of the three orders that he placed with Townsend in 1763 contained 12,916 pieces. Most of this order was sent in twenty-four identical barrels that could be individually wholesaled to stores in the Philadelphia area. Each barrel contained three teapots of this half-pint size and three of pint size, in both instances "without legs."[1] They were probably of similar shape to this example because those of pear form were the only kind of pewter teapot sold with or without legs at this time. No. 337 illustrates a conventional example with legs.

1. Montgomery, *History of American Pewter*, p. 8.

339 TEAPOT AND STAND

Richard Pitt
London, 1780–1800

MARKS: No touchmark apparent; pseudo hallmarks (1) lion passant, (2) leopard's head, (3) buckle, and (4) *R•P* within separate shaped rectangles on undersides of teapot, lid, and stand (Cotterell, *Old Pewter*, 3697)

INSCRIPTIONS: Owner's initials *EC* engraved on side of body in center

DIMENSIONS: OH. (with stand) 5 1/4", H. (teapot) 4 3/8", L. (teapot) 9 3/8", L. (stand) 5 1/2", W. (teapot) 3 1/4", W. (stand) 3 7/8"

PROVENANCE: Purchased from Richard Mundey, London; 1984-162, 1–2

Pitt was the principal London maker of tea wares in the early neoclassic style. Especially conspicuous among his surviving work is a group of remarkable oval teapots and tea caddies that were cast in apparently interchangeable molds, as in this teapot and nos.

339.1 Engraved owner's initials on side of body

340–341. A variation of this oval teapot and stand with reeded, rather than beaded, borders and a short, wide central foot to the stand was formerly in the Mundey Collection.[1] Pitt's work is cast, and is unlike that of James Vickers and other early Britannia metal makers, who tended to fashion bodies of geometric form, such as oval or cylindrical, out of rolled sheet metal (nos. 344–345).

1. "Photographs from the Mundey collection," *Journal of the Pewter Society*, VIII (autumn 1991), p. 68, fig. 2.

340 TEA CADDY

Richard Pitt
London, 1780–1800

MARKS: No touchmark apparent; pseudo hallmarks partially indistinct, incorporating, in part, a leopard's head and a buckle within separate shaped rectangles on underside of body (Cotterell, *Old Pewter*, 3697)

INSCRIPTIONS: Owners' initials *EWY* in script engraved within a shield on face of body below keyhole

DIMENSIONS: OH. 5 3/8", OL. 5", OW. 3 5/16"

PROVENANCE: Purchased from Richard Mundey, London; 1985-61

340.1 Engraved owners' initials on face of body below keyhole

The original contrast between panels of deep blue applied pigment and the light-gathering facets of the engraving must have been visually stunning. One is able to gain a sense of this form of decoration from the illustration in *Old Pewter* of another tea caddy with virtually identical engraving and most of its enameling in place from the de Navarro Collection at the Fitzwilliam Museum, Cambridge.[1] It is particularly clear from these illustrations of some panels and bands that the engraver cut through the applied pigment to create a precise contrast.

1. Cotterell, *Old Pewter*, p. 143, pl. LXXVa. This tea caddy is also shown in de Navarro, *Causeries on English Pewter*, p. 99, pl. I. De Navarro also illustrates a small two-handled cup, from the Carter Collection, that is decorated in this same shop style. *Ibid.*, pl. II.

TEA AND COFFEE EQUIPAGE 259

339–341

341 TEAPOT

Richard Pitt
London, 1780–1800

MARKS: No touchmark apparent; pseudo hallmarks (1) lion passant, (2) leopard's head, (3) buckle, and (4) R•P within separate shaped rectangles on underside of body and lid (Cotterell, *Old Pewter,* 3697)

341.1 Engraved owner's initials on side of body

INSCRIPTIONS: Owner's initials *RB* in script engraved within oval reserve on one side of body

DIMENSIONS: OH. 5", OL. 9 1/2", OW. 3 1/4"

PROVENANCE: Purchased from Price Glover Inc., New York, N. Y.; 1984-294

342 TEAPOT

John Ingram II & Charles Hunt
Wribbenhall, near Bewdley, Eng., 1778–1807

MARKS: Touchmark *I&H* within an oblong of ogival outline on underside of base (Cotterell, *Old Pewter,* 5708; Peal, *More Pewter Marks,* 2540a; Homer and Hall, *Provincial Pewterers,* 31); secondary mark of a quality *X* with crown above stamped on underside of base above touchmark

INSCRIPTIONS: None

DIMENSIONS: OH. 5 3/4", OL. 9 3/4", Diam. (base) 4 7/8"

PROVENANCE: Purchased from Thomas D. and Constance R. Williams, Litchfield, Conn.; 1956-81

Ingram (1731–1799) was closely related to the Woods and the Duncumbs, prominent pewtering families of the midlands.[1] He formed a partnership by 1778 with Hunt, his brother-in-law. This large firm exported considerable quantities of pewter to America. Its cast cylindrical teapots, such as this representative example, may have provided, in part, models for the handsome teapots of this general form made in Philadelphia during the 1780s and 1790s.

1. Homer and Hall, *Provincial Pewterers,* pp. 67–69.

343 TEAPOT

Robert Bush & Co. or Robert Bush II
Bristol, Eng., 1795–1805

MARKS: Touchmark *R•BUSH* on interior center-bottom of base (Peal, *More Pewter Marks,* 738); secondary mark of a quality *X* with crown above stamped above touchmark on interior of base

INSCRIPTIONS: None

DIMENSIONS: OH. 7", OL. 9 1/8", Diam. (base) 2 15/16"

TEA AND COFFEE EQUIPAGE

PROVENANCE: Purchased from Thomas C. Campbell, Hawleyville, Conn.; 1995-153

The mark on this piece is either a late mark of Robert Bush & Co. or a mark principally used by Robert Bush II, in either case for export wares. Its use appears limited to hollowware with an American background. This teapot is an early instance of a cast-metal handle that probably was originally painted, or japanned, black.

344 TEAPOT AND STAND

James Vickers
Sheffield, Eng., ca. 1787–1800

MARKS: Touchmark *I•VICKERS* on underside of teapot in center (Scott, *Pewter Wares from Sheffield,* 467); *I* above touchmark a possible workman's mark; stand unmarked

INSCRIPTIONS: Owner's name *James Cadkin*[?] scratched on underside of tray

DIMENSIONS: OH. (with stand) 8", H. (teapot) 7 1/8", L. (teapot) 11 3/8", L. (stand) 7 11/12", W. (teapot) 4 1/16", W. (stand) 5 23/32"

344.1 Stand for teapot with coffeepot stand (no. 351)

PROVENANCE: Purchased from Brian Beet, London; 1999-54, 1–2

This elegant teapot and stand in early neoclassic style are brilliant exemplars of Britannia metal wares by the developer of the medium. Vickers of Sheffield showed how a fine grade of pewter could be rolled out cold into a workable sheet and then fashioned into objects that possess the lightness of comparable examples in sterling or fused silver plate (Sheffield plate). Stylish engraved borders and panels with archery bows and quivers depending from bowknots are part of the appropriate classical dress. Elaborate cartouches with swagged drapery, ermine, and tassels frame shields for an owner's armorials or initials and are strong focal points in the center of both sides. These cartouches take their cue from those on silver plate. They were engraved at the factory, and most remain blank.

345 Tea Caddy

Maker unidentified
Probably Sheffield, Eng., 1785–1805
Retailed by Israel Trask, Beverly, Mass.

MARKS: Originally unmarked; subsequently marked *I•TRASK* within a rectangle on underside of body in center

INSCRIPTIONS: None

DIMENSIONS: OH. 6 1/8", OL. 5 1/2", OW. 3 15/16"

PROVENANCE: Purchased from Gordon and Genevieve Deming, Duxbury, Mass.; 1999-25

TEA AND COFFEE EQUIPAGE

345

Israel Trask worked as a silversmith and jeweler in Beverly, Mass., from about 1807 until he became a manufacturer of Britannia metal in 1813. Reverend William Bentley of Salem mentioned in his diary for Feb. 25, 1814, "Capt. Bowditch . . . informed me this day that he had begun the work of the Britannia Ware, which had been carried on for several months with success in Beverly . . . . I passed to Beverly & visited Mr. Trask who introduced the manufacture into that place. He was a goldsmith & jeweller & employs about a dozen hands, & sells his work in Boston."[1]

Trask is associated with wares of clean design with discrete engraved borders. Their shapes and their engraving schemes are much simpler than in this fully articulated example. Trask even adopted the Sheffield practice of supplying an empty engraved shield on some of his pots, although of a smaller and plainer sort.[2]

1. Laughlin, *Pewter in America,* III, p. 191–193.
2. Montgomery, *History of American Pewter,* p. 175, fig. 11–8.

346 TEAPOT

John Vickers
Sheffield, Eng., 1815–1825

MARKS: Touchmark *I•VICKERS* on underside of base (Scott, *Pewter Wares from Sheffield,* 467); *C* above touchmark a possible workman's mark

INSCRIPTIONS: None

DIMENSIONS: OH. 4 1/8", OL. 6 5/8", Diam. (base) 2 23/32"

PROVENANCE: Gift of Mrs. Owen L. Coon, Wilmette, Ill.; G1983-348

Teapots of this smallest of standard sizes from the first half of the nineteenth century are called bachelor size. They were a specialty of the Sheffield Britannia metal trade, in particular. Emphasized are squat, globular body shapes.[1]

1. For illustrations of the type, see Jack L. Scott, *Pewter Wares from Sheffield* (Baltimore, Md., 1980), and Robert E. Touzalin, "Bachelor Teapots," *Pewter Collectors Club of America Bulletin,* X (fall 1993), pp. 207–213.

347 TEAPOT

Thomas D. & Sherman Boardman
Hartford, Conn., 1815–1825

MARKS: Touchmark *TD&SB* within a rectangle on underside of base (Laughlin, *Pewter in America,* I, 428); secondary mark of a quality *X* stamped above touchmark on underside of base

INSCRIPTIONS: None

DIMENSIONS: OH. 7 15/16", OL. 8 7/8", Diam. (base) 3 9/16"

346

347

PROVENANCE: Gift of Mr. and Mrs. Foster McCarl, Jr., Beaver Falls, Pa.; G1991-646

Connecticut pewterers, in particular, produced large numbers of pear-shaped teapots, especially during the first half of the nineteenth century. The makers of this teapot had a large and thriving business. Thomas claimed at one point to have sold in a six-month period to one of their many customers three thousand teapots, many of which probably resembled this handsome example.[1] Its inward-drawn cover and black-japanned cast handle and finial inset are nineteenth-century features. The persistent popularity of the pear shape for teapots in certain parts of the United States and in selected media qualifies this example as an instance of baroque survival rather than revival.

1. Thomas, *Connecticut Pewter and Pewterers,* p. 119.

348 TEAPOT

George Richardson
Cranston, R. I., 1839–ca. 1841

MARKS: Touchmark of a label with *G.RICHARDSON* within a serrated rectangle on underside of base (Laughlin, *Pewter in America,* III, p. 111); secondary marks, also on underside of base, (1) *GLENNORE C°* within a curved and serrated rectangle, (2) *CRANSTON.R.I.* within a curved and serrated rectangle, (3) an American eagle displayed within a vertical oval, (4) *N°* within a serrated rectangle, and (5) *A* (Laughlin, *Pewter in America,* III, p. 111)

INSCRIPTIONS: None

DIMENSIONS: OH. 8 7/16", OL. 10 1/4", Diam. (base) 4 3/8"

PROVENANCE: Gift of Mr. and Mrs. Foster McCarl, Jr., Beaver Falls, Pa.; G1991-647

Richardson produced an ample quantity of handsomely designed and well-made teapots, in particular. He was born in London about 1782. He worked first for a decade in Boston after 1818 and then possibly as foreman of Burrage Yale's Britannia and pewter shop in South Reading, Mass., from 1829 to 1833. Richardson was in Cranston, R. I., by 1839, the year the Glennore Company was established. The teapots with the Cranston mark but lacking the Glennore mark were probably made between the dissolution of the Glennore Company in 1841 and Richardson's departure for Providence, R. I., in 1845. The handle and finial inset of this handsome example is cast and japanned black.[1]

1. For a full discussion of working dates and marks, as well as a study of Richardson's teapots, see Richard L. Bowen, Jr., "The G. Richardson Problem," *Pewter Collectors Club of America Bulletin,* VII (September 1978), pp. 321–333, and "The G. Richardson Problem II," *Pewter Collectors Club of America Bulletin,* VIII (March 1981), pp. 104–121.

348

349 COFFEEPOT

Maker unidentified
England, 1760–1780

MARKS: None

INSCRIPTIONS: Owners' cipher *WMS* engraved on face of body

DIMENSIONS: OH. 10 7/16", Diam. (base) 3 7/8"

PROVENANCE: Purchased from Michael Allen Kashden, Edgware, Eng.; 1995-48

Pewter baluster-shaped coffeepots from the eighteenth century are quite rare. More examples survive in silvered brass (known as French plating) and japanned copper. The English, though, had a decided preference for silver and ceramic coffeepots of this form, and, after about 1765, for ones of fused silver plate (Sheffield plate). Lamb illustrates an identical pewter coffeepot from the same molds, also unmarked, as well as another example with a

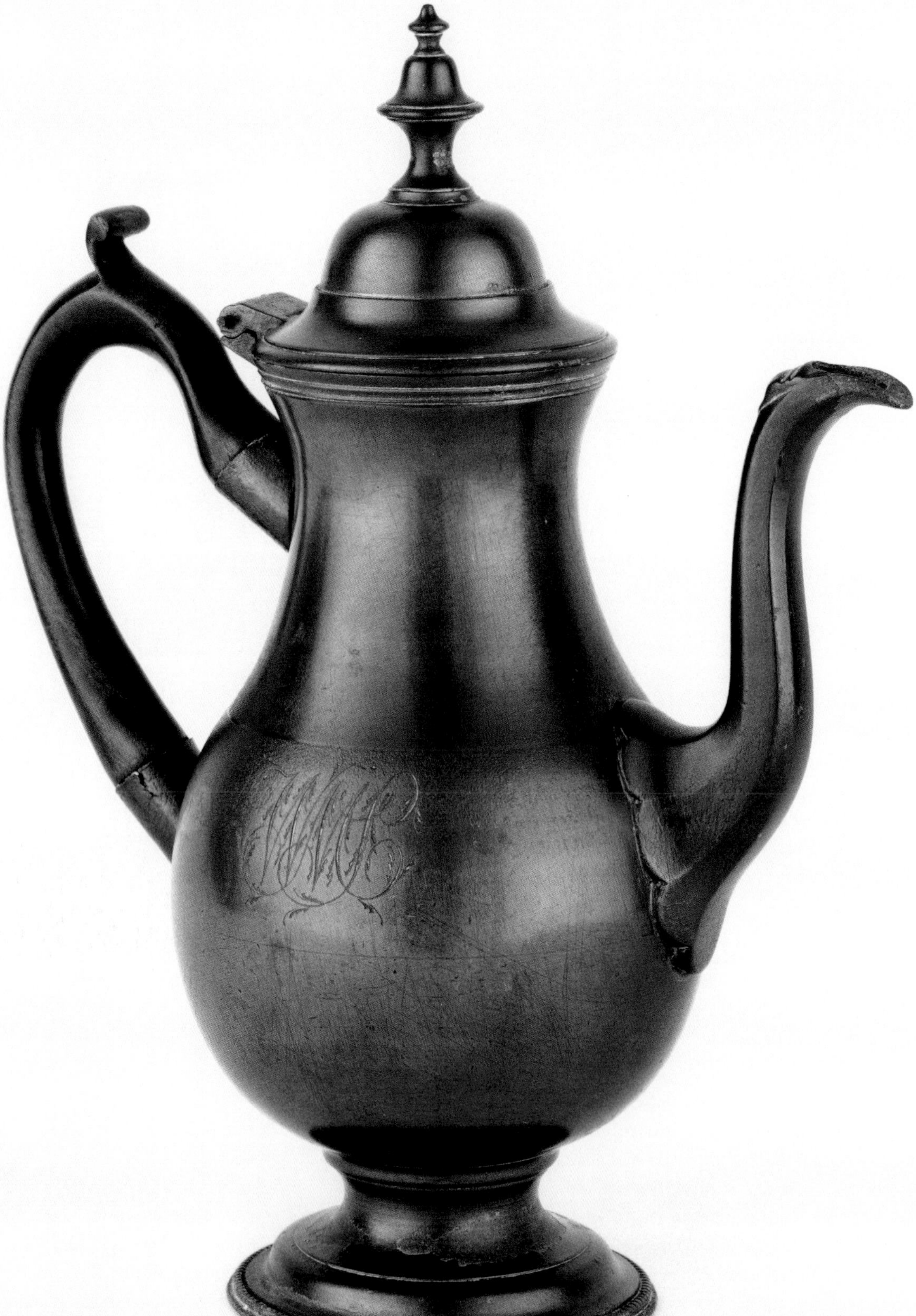

more fully articulated rococo spout.[1] A further coffeepot, identical with this one but with overall engraved decoration, is in the Swain Collection.[2]

1. David Lamb, "Four unusual 18th century items," *Journal of the Pewter Society,* IX (autumn 1993), pp. 69–70, figs. a–b.
2. Donald L. Fennimore, *Silver & Pewter* (New York, 1984), no. 275, ill.

350 COFFEEPOT

James Vickers
Sheffield, Eng., ca. 1787–1800

MARKS: Touchmark *I•VICKERS* on underside of base (Scott, *Pewter Wares from Sheffield,* 467)

INSCRIPTIONS: None

DIMENSIONS: OH. 10 1/8", OL. (base) 4 7/8", OW. (base) 3 1/2"

PROVENANCE: Purchased from Gordon and Genevieve Deming, Duxbury, Mass.; 1994-98

PUBLISHED: Sales ad, *Maine Antique Digest* (July 1994), p. 21–D, ill.

Surprisingly, the pewter trade was unknown in Sheffield, one of England's principal metalworking centers, when Vickers opened his shop on Hollis St. in 1769. According to the later reminiscence of Charles Dixon, Sheffield manufacturer, Vickers acquired in that same year for five shillings "the recipe for making white metal."[1] This event is the supposed beginning of the Britannia metal industry. Dixon placed emphasis on the recipe, but from tests of early Britannia metal wares, Britannia metal varied little from white and hard metals used particularly for flatware, such as plates and dishes. It contains more than 90 percent tin with the remainder predominantly antimony, sometimes with smaller amounts of copper and/or zinc. More innovative than the recipe is what Vickers and other early Britannia metal makers did with the metal. They learned how to reduce to workable sheet a silver-clad copper ingot by passing it repeatedly between the polished steel rollers of a flatting mill. Then, with the aid of die-stamping and related mechanical processes, identical copies could be produced in large quantities.

Sheffield and Birmingham were early centers of the industrial revolution and of the production of fused silver plate (Sheffield plate). By 1769, the fused silver plate industry was well on its way in both cities.

Vickers and other early makers of Britannia metal in Sheffield consciously emulated the appearance of early neoclassic wares in silver and silver plate, especially those for the service of tea and coffee. The new technologies of the silver plate industry were adopted, in particular the cold rolling of the metal into workable sheet and the use of steel-forming dies in shaping parts. Even so, some elements and entire objects were still, on occasion, made by traditional cast methods well into the nineteenth century. The body of this pot was made from sheet in two halves with a seam running behind the spout and the handle attachments. Part of this soldered seam is visible just below the opened cover in 350.1. The raised fillet on the upper and lower sides of the spout masks and strengthens the seams.

Britannia metal manufacturers borrowed another feature from silver platers. Vertical collars with turned-in lower edges are often attached within the rims of fused silver-plated coffeepots and coffee biggins made after the mid-1780s. They not only reinforce the insubstantial plated bodies, but also support the frame for a filter bag. This coffeepot retains this feature with the rare survival of its original linen bag stitched to a metal frame.[2]

Characteristic of the fashionable appearance of early Britannia metal is the prevalence of engraved friezes and incidental decoration in neoclassic style. The running borders and dense cartouche for the owner's initials are taken from the engraved let-in borders and soldered-in shields of thicker metal used for this type of engraving on fused silver plate, especially of the 1790–1805 period. Some of the edges are finely faceted to simulate the appearance and effect of narrow bright-cut borders.

1. Scott, *Pewter Wares from Sheffield*, p. 25. Bradbury, *History of Old Sheffield Plate*, pp. 494–495. For the most useful discussion on defining Britannia metal and its early development, see David Lamb, "Britannia metal—Cinderella of antiques," *Journal of the Pewter Society*, V (spring 1985), pp. 1–12.
2. Bradbury reproduces a page from an engraved trade catalog of about 1798 that illustrates a silver-plated coffee biggin with a removable finial for easy conversion into a vessel for chocolate. The period notation reads: "This Knob screws off, the Mill may be put thro the Cover, when used for Chocolate—the bag for Coffee being previously taken out." Bradbury, *History of Old Sheffield Plate*, p. 413.

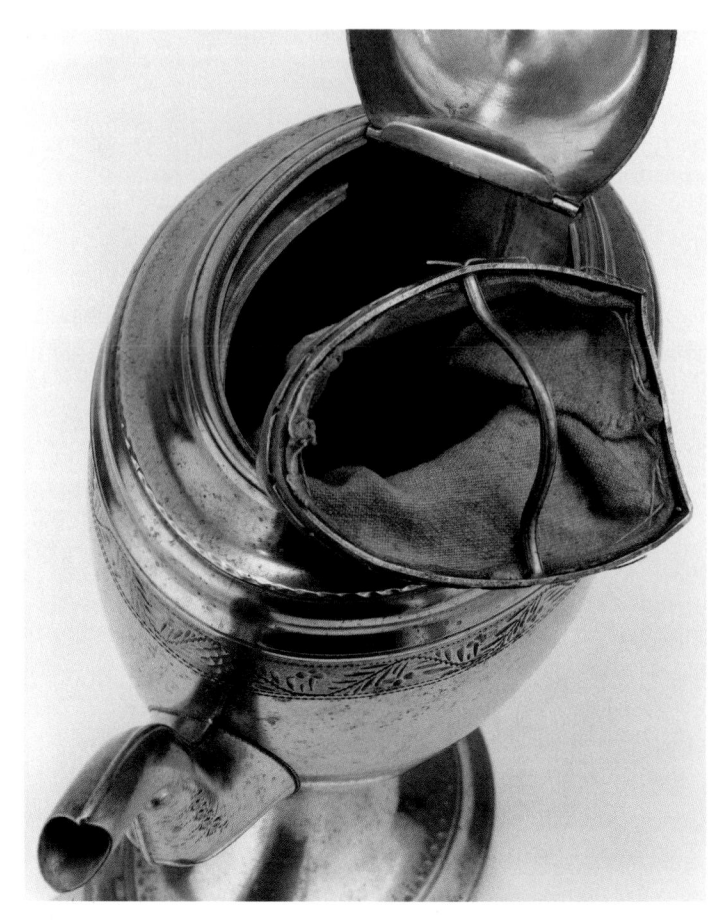

350.1 Detail showing interior construction and filter bag

351

351 COFFEEPOT STAND

Maker unidentified
Probably Sheffield, Eng., 1785–1800

MARKS: None

INSCRIPTIONS: None

DIMENSIONS: OH. 7/8", OL. 5 7/8", OW. 4 5/8"

PROVENANCE: Gift of Mrs. Owen L. Coon, Wilmette, Ill., who purchased it from Marshall Field's, Chicago, Ill.; Richard Mundey, London, supplied it to Marshall Field's; when it was given, his typed label was applied to the underside; G1983-347

The size of this stand suggests that it served as a coffeepot stand. It is too small to accommodate contemporary Britannia metal teapots from Sheffield.

352 COFFEEPOT

James Dixon & Son
Sheffield, Eng., 1823–1829

MARKS: Touchmark *Dixon & Son* with probable pattern numbers *8* above and *35* below on underside of base (Scott, *Pewter Wares from Sheffield*, 147)

INSCRIPTIONS: None

DIMENSIONS: OH. 11 5/16", Diam. (base) 5"

PROVENANCE: Gift of the John D. Rockefeller III Fund, Inc., through the generosity and interest of Mr. John D. Rockefeller III and other members of the family; G1979-151

Unless viewed as part of a service, it is sometimes difficult to distinguish between pewter tea- and coffeepots from the first half of the nineteenth century. The James Dixon firm of Sheffield, England's largest producer of Britannia metal in the nineteenth century, made this attractive example. Like many other hollow-ware forms of this date, it consists of a vertical stack of broad horizontal layers with a bold sequence of moldings or a flanged projection separating them. There is considerable curvilinear sweep to its outline. This pot is part of the Rockefeller furnishings of Bassett Hall in Williamsburg, Va.

352

353 CREAM JUG

Edward Quick
London 1725–1750

MARKS: Touchmark *EQ* with a pellet above and below within an outlined circle on underside of body (Peal, *More Pewter Marks*, 3802a); secondary mark of a quality *X* with crown above on underside of body

INSCRIPTIONS: None

TEA AND COFFEE EQUIPAGE 271

353–355

DIMENSIONS: OH. 3 7/8"

PROVENANCE: Purchased from Carl Jacobs, Southwick, Mass.; 1950-393

The earliest pewter cream jugs are of this baluster, or pear, form. Like their silver prototypes, most English examples supported on short cabriole legs date after 1725 with American ones making their appearance after midcentury.

354 CREAM JUG

Maker unidentified
Probably Philadelphia, Pa., 1760–1780

MARKS: None

INSCRIPTIONS: None

DIMENSIONS: OH. 4", Diam. (base) 2 3/8"

PROVENANCE: Purchased from Carl Jacobs, Southwick, Mass.; 1950-81

Cream jugs of this form and with this shaping to the rim probably were made in Philadelphia.

355 CREAM JUG

Probably John Will I
New York, N. Y., 1752–1766

MARKS: None

INSCRIPTIONS: None

DIMENSIONS: OH. 4 3/4"

PROVENANCE: Purchased from Thomas D. and Constance R. Williams, Litchfield, Conn.; 1971-90

Laughlin attributed to Will a similar cream jug with differences in the scalloping of the rim that was at that time in the Quigley Collection.[1]

1. Laughlin, *Pewter in America,* I, pl. XXX, fig. 201.

356 CREAM EWER

James Vickers
Sheffield, Eng., ca. 1787–1800

MARKS: Touchmark *I•VICKERS* on underside of base (Scott, *Pewter Wares from Sheffield,* 467); probable pattern number *3* stamped on underside of base

INSCRIPTIONS: None

DIMENSIONS: OH. 6 1/16", OW. (base) 2 5/16"

PROVENANCE: Purchased from George Broadbent, Scranton, Pa.; 1985-200

Pewter cream ewers of this fashionable silver pattern and engraved with running borders and a large central cartouche are a function of the Britannia metal trade in Sheffield. Its elegant body is made of rolled sheet metal with a seam running vertically behind the handle. This cream ewer and the sugar basket or basin (see no. 357) share the same stamped *3* pattern number, which indicates that they were intended to be used together.

356

357 SUGAR BASKET OR BASIN

James Vickers
Sheffield, Eng., 1769–ca. 1787

MARKS: Touchmark *I✻VICKERS* within a scalloped rectangle on underside of base (Scott, *Pewter Wares from Sheffield,* 466); pattern number *3* stamped on underside of base

INSCRIPTIONS: None

DIMENSIONS: OH. (handle extended) 6 5/8", OL. 4 7/8", L. (base) 3 11/16", OW. 4 7/16", W. (base) 2 11/16"

PROVENANCE: Purchased from David S. Moulson, Alcester, Eng.; 1998-152

357–358

The body and the foot are made from seamed sheet. The narrow milled border is applied at the rim. The dating of this piece is influenced by Scott's dating of this mark between 1769 and about 1787. The fact that this basket and the cream ewer (no. 356) share the same stamped *3* pattern number indicates that they were intended to be used together.

358 Cream Jug

Maker unidentified
England, 1810–1820

MARKS: None

INSCRIPTIONS: None

DIMENSIONS: OH. 3 3/4", OL. 4 3/4"

PROVENANCE: Purchased from David S. Moulson, Alcester, Eng.; 1993-3

This cream jug is a representative piece of early nineteenth-century Britannia metal. Its body is constructed from three pieces of sheet metal, a pair of side panels, and a base plate. The body is fitted with a U-shaped wire at the rim and a handle with squared shoulders and a molded face. The body is supported on four ball feet. The center of each side is engraved with foliate sprigs that stop before the vertical seams below the spout and behind the handle and indicate that the decoration was executed before the assembly of the object.

274　PEWTER AT COLONIAL WILLIAMSBURG

359 COVERED SUGAR BOWL OR BASIN

Maker unidentified
Probably United States, 1785–1810

MARKS: None

INSCRIPTIONS: None

DIMENSIONS: OH. 4 7/16", Diam. (cover) 5 1/4", Diam. (base) 3 1/8"

PROVENANCE: Purchased from Thomas D. and Constance R. Williams, Litchfield, Conn.; 1956-84

Surviving sugar bowls or basins are much more scarce than cream jugs and ewers.

360 COVERED SUGAR BOWL OR BASIN

George Richardson
Cranston, R. I., 1841–1845

MARKS: Touchmark of a label with *G.RICHARDSON* within a serrated rectangle on underside of base (Laughlin, *Pewter in America,* II, p. 111); secondary marks, also on underside of base (1) an American eagle displayed within a vertical oval (Laughlin, *Pewter in America,* II, p. 111), (2) *WARRANTED* within a serrated rectangle, (3) N^O within a serrated rectangle followed by the numeral *2,* and (4) *CRANSTON.R.I.* within a curved serrated rectangle (Laughlin, *Pewter in America,* II, p. 111)

INSCRIPTIONS: None

DIMENSIONS: OH. 5 5/16", OW. 6 9/16", Diam. (base) 3 7/8"

PROVENANCE: Gift of Mr. and Mrs. Foster McCarl, Jr., Beaver Falls, Pa.; G1977-314

Richardson specialized in the production of tea wares, and he created the most remarkable group of sugar bowls or basins in American pewter. They have always been well regarded by collectors. J. B. Kerfoot not only illustrated one as the frontispiece to his *American Pewter,* but also personified them as the Miss America of nineteenth-century American pewter.[1] This particular example probably dates between the dissolution in 1841 of the Glennore Company, whose mark does not appear on this piece, and Richardson's departure in 1845 from Cranston, R. I. (see no. 348).

1. J. B. Kerfoot, *American Pewter* (Boston, Mass., 1924), p. 173.

TEA AND COFFEE EQUIPAGE

best Tobacco
BRISTOL
JOHN DAVIES'S
Fine Ragg
AXFORD'S Best
Virginia Tobacco
Sweet Powder

Household and Personal Accessories

This section encompasses a wide range of goods. They are generally of a useful sort and were once part of the mix of objects used in activities that comprised much of daily life. Whether shaving basins or tobacco boxes, buttons or buckles, funnels or flasks, candle molds or bullets, organ pipes or chamber pots, pewter articles often had a natural and incidental presence that people took for granted. Now in the Colonial Williamsburg Collection, these miscellaneous accessories, in their re-created settings, become evocative of that past.

361 SHAVING BASIN

John Trapp II
Worcester, Eng., 1680–1700

MARKS: Touchmark within a beaded vertical oval practically indistinct and secondary mark of rose and crown type within a beaded vertical oval practically indistinct, both on underside of rim (Cotterell, *Old Pewter,* 5977; Homer and Hall, *Provincial Pewterers,* 39); quality *X* with crown above stamped between the other two marks

INSCRIPTIONS: None

DIMENSIONS: OH. 1 7/8", Diam. 11 3/4", OW. (rim) 1 7/8"

PROVENANCE: Purchased from Jellinek & Sampson, London; 1976-363

Pewter shaving basins are uncommon, and those dating from the seventeenth century are particularly so. This fine example shares with contemporary plates and dishes a rim of moderate width with a bold edging of multiple reeds. As with other pewter examples of similar date, it has an elliptical indentation to engage the neck, a small circular well for soap, and a rounded and unfooted base. A similar shaving basin, enhanced with wriggle-engraved floral decoration on its rim, is in the de Navarro Collection at the Fitzwilliam Museum, Cambridge, Eng.[1] On close examination of the marks on the CWF one, both appear to be the work of the same maker. That this touchmark was found on pewter partially marked by Sampson Bourne II of Worcester aided in the identification of the maker. Trapp was a member of a prominent Worcester pewtering family and Bourne's brother-in-law. Trapp died in 1713.[2]

1. Cotterell, *Old Pewter,* p. 86, pl. XVIIIa.
2. Homer and Hall, *Provincial Pewterers,* pp. 48–49, 138.

362 SHAVING BASIN

Thomas Munday
London, 1758–1774

MARKS: Touchmark of the bust-length portrait of a man with *THOMAS* and *MUNDAY* in curved reserves above and below within a vertical oval on underside of base (London Touch Plate IV, 978; Cotterell, *Old Pewter,* 3329); secondary mark of a label *MADE IN/LONDON* within a curved and outlined reserve with a scrolled lower edge below touchmark on underside of base (Cotterell, *Old Pewter,* 3329); pseudo hallmarks (1) *T•M* with two annulets both above and below within a two-lobed reserve,

362

(2) portrait of a man within a circle with four indentations, (3) leopard's head within an octagon, and (4) seated figure of Britannia within a rounded rectangle, all on underside of base opposite the other marks (Cotterell, *Old Pewter,* 3329)

INSCRIPTIONS: None

DIMENSIONS: OH. 2 1/4", OL. 15 7/16", OW. 12 1/4"

PROVENANCE: Purchased from A. V. Sutherland-Graeme, London; 1961-59

An earlier example of about 1710 by Hellier Perchard is part of the Yeates Collection at the Victoria and Albert Museum, London. North and Spira have commented that it derives from similar French and Spanish examples, sometimes of brass.[1]

1. North and Spira, *Pewter at Victoria and Albert,* p. 76, no. 58, ill. p. 75. Also illustrated in Cotterell, *Old Pewter,* p. 86, pl. XVIIIb.

363 CHAMBER POT

Maker unidentified
England, 1760–1790

MARKS: No touchmark apparent; secondary mark of a quality *X* with crown above on interior center-bottom of body

INSCRIPTIONS: None

DIMENSIONS: OH. 5 13/16", Diam. (rim) 8 1/8", Diam. (base) 6 9/16"

PROVENANCE: Purchased from H. W. Keil, Broadway, Eng.; 1960-489

The evolution of the chamber pot over time is most noticeable in the details, such as the subtle changes in handles and their terminals relative to those on other hollowware vessels.

364 CHAMBER POT

John Carruthers Crane
Bewdley, Eng., 1821–1838

MARKS: Touchmark *ICC* within a serrated rectangle on interior center-bottom of body (Cotterell, *Old Pewter,* 1197; Homer and Hall, *Provincial Pewterers,* 16); secondary mark of a quality *X* with crown above over touchmark on interior center-bottom of body

INSCRIPTIONS: None

DIMENSIONS: OH. 5 7/16", Diam. (rim) 6 5/8", Diam. (base) 5 13/16"

PROVENANCE: Purchased from The Old Pewter Shop, London; 1966-236

Crane went into business on his own in 1821. A surviving handbill indicates that the range of goods he made and/or retailed was extensive. It lists "Hard Chamber Pots" and "Common ditto."[1] Crane's retirement in 1838 marked an end to Bewdley as a pewtering center. That his molds passed into the possession of the Birmingham firm of Yates, Birch & Spooner is indicative of the centralization of England's failing pewter industry at that time.

1. Ronald F. Homer, "John Carruthers Crane," *Journal of the Pewter Society,* VII (autumn 1989), pp. 45–46.

365 COMMODE POT

William Wood II
Birmingham, Eng., 1680–1710

MARKS: Touchmark *W•W* with a rose below within a rounded rectangle on face of rim (Cotterell, *Old Pewter,* 6028; Peal, *More Pewter Marks,* 6028; Homer and Hall, *Provincial Pewterers,* 44)

INSCRIPTIONS: Owner's initials *IC* stamped on upper face of rim

DIMENSIONS: OH. 7 15/16", Diam. (rim) 13 1/16", Diam. (base) 6"

PROVENANCE: Purchased from The Old Pewter Shop, London; 1936-116

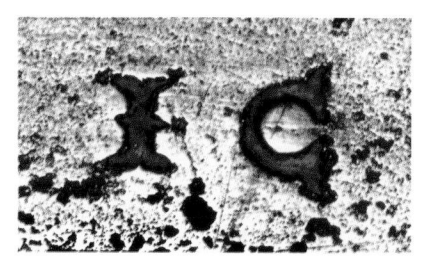

365.1 Stamped owner's initials on rim

Tapered pots with flaring rims were intended to fit frames with large circular openings in commode chairs and stools. The small *W•W* mark on this commode pot was long hoped by American collectors to be a mark of the noted Philadelphia pewterer William Will. When Swain wrote his informative article on commode pots in 1970, he illustrated a similar example with this mark, and he commented that he had never seen this mark "on a recognizable form of Will's."[1] Research by Homer and Hall identify Wood (1645–1726) of Birmingham as owner of the mark and place him in context as an important maker and regional figure. They also illustrate distinctive types of tankards, flagons, and cups that relate to examples of his making in the CWF Collection.[2]

1. Charles V. Swain, "Commode Forms," *Pewter Collectors Club of America Bulletin,* VI (August 1970), p. 82, fig. 5, p. 83.
2. Homer and Hall, *Provincial Pewterers,* pp. 62–63, figs. 9–12.

363

364

365–367

366 COMMODE POT

John Birch & William Villers
Birmingham, Eng., 1772–1786

MARKS: No touchmark apparent; pseudo hallmarks (1) apparent arms with chevron and three griffins' heads erased, (2) crest of a griffin's head erased on a wreath bar, (3) radiant sun or star, and (4) *B&V* with device below, each within an outlined shield, on upper face below rim (Cotterell, *Old Pewter,* 430; Homer and Hall, *Provincial Pewterers,* 6)

INSCRIPTIONS: None

DIMENSIONS: OH. 8 15/16", Diam. (rim) 12 1/16", Diam. (base) 5 1/4"

PROVENANCE: Purchased from The Quarters Antiques, Fredericksburg, Va.; 1941-84

367 COMMODE POT

Maker unidentified
England, 1770–1800

MARKS: No touchmark apparent; pseudo hallmarks (1) *GB* with two pellets above and one below, (2) lion passant with a pellet below, (3) leopard's head with pellet below, and (4) fleur-de-lis with a pellet below, each within a separate plain shield on upper face of body below rim (Peal, *More Pewter Marks,* 5423b)

INSCRIPTIONS: None

DIMENSIONS: OH. 7 1/8", Diam. (rim) 11", Diam. (base) 4 15/16"

PROVENANCE: Purchased from Scotney & Son, Stamford, Eng.; 1947-343

These marks resemble pseudo hallmarks shown with the touchmark of James Banks II of Bewdley and attributed to Christopher Banks II in Homer and Hall and with less precise attributions in Cotterell.[1]

1. Homer and Hall, *Provincial Pewterers,* p. 138, no. 3; Cotterell, *Old Pewter,* p. 154, no. 227.

368 Papboat

Maker unidentified
England, 1780–1810

MARKS: Indistinct touchmark incorporating, in part, $T[?]C^O$ within a shaped oblong reserve within body in center; secondary mark of a quality X with crown above touchmark

INSCRIPTIONS: None

DIMENSIONS: OL. 5 3/8", OW. 2 3/8"

PROVENANCE: Purchased from Price Glover Inc., New York, N. Y.; 1984-277

Papboats were useful vessels for feeding and administering medicine to the very young and the infirm. Early examples are vastly more common in silver than in pewter. Most pewter ones were made during the first half of the twentieth century.

369 Inkstand

William Hitchins III
London, 1759–1780

MARKS: Touchmark of a pair of clasped hands with a royal crown between with *W* and *H* above and *1709* below within a beaded circle on interior center-bottom of the first on the left of the smaller compartments (London Touch Plate IV, 984; Cotterell, *Old Pewter*, 2339); secondary mark of a label *LONDON* within a curved reserve with a foliated lower edge on face of central upright within middle compartment

371

INSCRIPTIONS: Owners' initials *S/RM* stamped below secondary mark

DIMENSIONS: OH. 2 1/8", OL. 8 9/16", OW. 5 5/8"

PROVENANCE: Purchased from Roger Warner, Burford, Eng.; 1960-516

Hitchins entered his touch in 1759. He adopted his grandfather's dated touch of 1709, the apparent date of the beginning of the family business.

 This inkstand and no. 370 are representative of this basic large type. Their bodies are in the form of a rectangular box, supported on bun feet. A piano-type hinge divides the body in half lengthwise. One side is further divided into three compartments for an ink bottle; a pounce pot, or sander; and a storage space between. The other side is left undivided for quill pens, styli, scrivener knives and quill cutters, sealing wax, and the like. The larger of these inkstands is missing the loose plate with a broad circular opening in the center that is placed over the ink bottle. The smaller inkstand has the customary narrow vertical strips that are soldered across the corners of one of the end compartments that presently supports a reproduction loose plate. Inkstands of this type, whether of pewter or silver, are said to be of treasury type after the silver ones issued to the Treasury in 1686, although the type was established much earlier.[1] Pewter inkstands of this type were used for public and personal purposes. They appear not infrequently in portraits of gentlemen at their desks or writing tables, such as John Singleton Copley's portraits of John Scollay (1763–1764), Timothy Folger (1764), John Hancock (1765), Benjamin Hallowell (1765–1768), Thomas Lewis (1766–1767), Robert Hooper (1767), John Greene (ca. 1769), and Samuel Winthrop (ca. 1773).[2]

1. Michael Clayton, *The Collector's Dictionary of the Silver and Gold of Great Britain and North America,* reprint (Woodbridge, Eng., 1985), p. 162.
2. Jules David Prown, *John Singleton Copley* (Cambridge, Mass., 1966), figs. 105, 132, 153, 191, 194, 201, 262, 329.

370 INKSTAND

Joseph Spackman
London, 1749–1764

MARKS: Touchmark with central elements indistinct with *IOSEPH* and *SPACKMAN* within curved reserves above and below on underside of body (London Touch Plate IV, 982; Cotterell, *Old Pewter,* 4440)

INSCRIPTIONS: None

DIMENSIONS: OH. 2 3/32", OL. 6 1/4", OW. 4 1/2"

PROVENANCE: Purchased from A. V. Sutherland-Graeme, London; 1951-50

371 PIPE

Maker unidentified
England or Low Countries, 1770–1800

MARKS: None

INSCRIPTIONS: None

DIMENSIONS: OL. 7 5/8"

PROVENANCE: Purchased from The Old Pewter Shop, London; 1952-523

372 TOBACCO BOX OR JAR

Maker unidentified
England, possibly Yorkshire, 1780–1810

MARKS: None

INSCRIPTIONS: Cast-relief arms of the City of Leeds, Yorkshire, and medallions of Bishop Blaise and a ship under sail on face of body

DIMENSIONS: OH. 4 5/16", Diam. (cover) 4 3/8", Diam. (base) 4 1/8", Diam. (tamping plate) 3 11/16"

PROVENANCE: Purchased from Avis and Rockwell Gardiner, Stamford, Conn.; 1950-156

This attractive tobacco jar is representative of a large group cast in a soft metal with a substantial lead content. Its exterior retains traces of early red and ochre paint. The interior is fitted with a loose tamping plate with a small central knob. Bishop Blaise, the patron saint of wool combers, appears in one of the medallions, while others feature a sailing ship and the arms of the City of Leeds, in recognition of that city's prominence in the wool trade. The Leeds Pottery made creamware boxes with virtually identical decoration based on metal boxes that were locally produced in the 1780s and 1790s.[1]

1. Peter Walton, *Creamware and other English Pottery at Temple Newsam House, Leeds: A Catalogue of the Leeds Collection* (Bradford, Eng., 1976), p. 164, no. 683.

373 SNUFF BOX

W. Coldwell
Sheffield, Eng., 1792–1805

MARKS: Touchmark *COLDWELL* within an oblong rectangle with scalloped edges (Laughlin, *Pewter in America,* II, 508)

INSCRIPTIONS: None

DIMENSIONS: OH. 5/8", OL. 1 5/8", OW. 1 1/16"

PROVENANCE: Purchased from Christopher Bangs, London; 1994-139

Early Britannia metal makers in Sheffield produced large quantities of small snuff boxes from rolled sheet metal and decorated them in much the same way they did their early tea wares. Most are handsomely engraved in early neoclassic style with decorative borders and shields for an owner's initials. This maker has, on occasion, been confused with George Coldwell of New York, N. Y.[1]

1. Laughlin illustrated a small nutmeg grater with an engraved oval case that bears the same mark as this box. *Pewter in America,* I, pl. XL, fig. 260; II, pl. LXIII,

fig. 508, pp. 23–26. He attributed this piece to George Coldwell of New York, N. Y. His third volume, published in 1969, raised more questions than it solved in regard to this maker. Credit goes to Stevie Young for establishing in print that these engraved wares were from Sheffield and the work of another artisan with the same surname who happened to be the partner in the firm of Froggatt, Coldwell & Lean, among others. "Products by 'Coldwell,'" *Pewter Collectors Club of America Bulletin,* VIII (March 1981), pp. 95–98.

374 PAIR OF SHOE BUCKLES

William Tutin
Birmingham, Eng., 1785–1800

MARKS: Touchmark *W•T* within a rectangle on undersides of both frames; *W•TUTIN* stamped on both sets of chapes

INSCRIPTIONS: None

DIMENSIONS: OL. 3 1/4", OW. 2 5/8"

PROVENANCE: Purchased from Thomas C. Campbell, Hawleysville, Conn.; 1995-154, 1–2

If there is one product that is associated with Birmingham, it is a seemingly infinite variety of shoe buckles. Tutin was one of Birmingham's specialist makers of base-metal buckles and spoons.

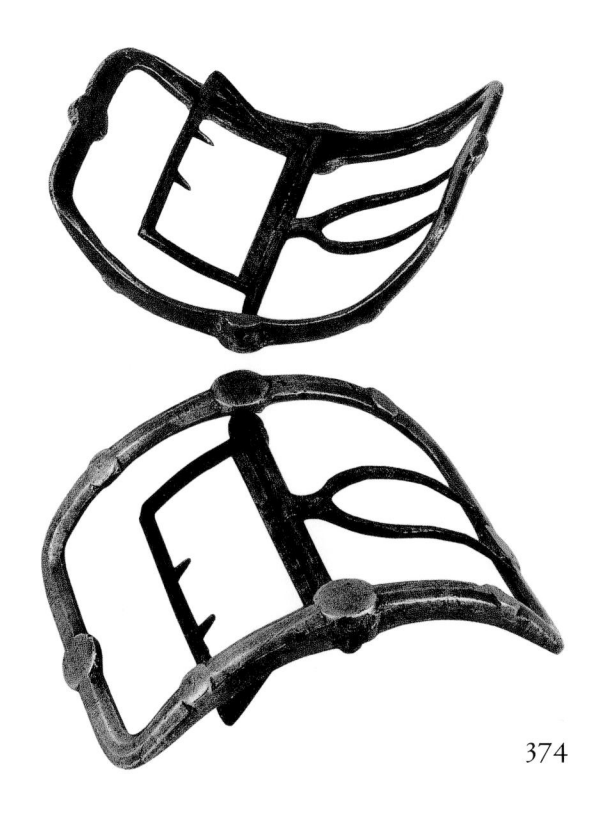

He was also the inventor of Tutania, apparently an antimony-rich alloy with similar properties to Britannia metal. His name appears in the Birmingham directories from 1767 to 1823. Records indicate that he was purchasing pewter from Ingram & Hunt in 1785.

Fennimore has published a pewter sugar bowl from the first years of the nineteenth century that is stamped with an American eagle with spread wings, striped shield, and banner framed within an oval of stars, indicating that Tutin may have produced not only pewter sugar bowls for the American market, but also stamped furniture brasses with this same patriotic decoration.[1]

1. Donald L. Fennimore, "William Tutin: Tutania Maker," *Pewter Collectors Club of America Bulletin,* VIII (March 1980), pp. 22–23; Homer and Hall, *Provincial Pewterers,* p. 79.

375 SUNDIAL

Possibly the Miller family
New York or New England, 1740–1780

MARKS: *NM* cast in relief on face of dial in front of angled end of gnomon

INSCRIPTIONS: None

DIMENSIONS: OH. 1 1/2", Diam. 3 1/16"

PROVENANCE: Purchased from Lotta F. Blount, West Brookfield, Mass.; 1932-60

Pewter sundials are uncommon. Those of brass survive in much larger numbers from many more regions and countries. A considerable group of pewter ones exists that either have the relief-cast name or initials of a member of the Miller family or are of similar character and have a gnomon of the same inclination. Josiah Miller's name most frequently appears, along with the initials *NM,* not only on sundials, but also on molds for spoons, buttons, and bullets. One can only presume the latter possibly to be a relative. Some of Josiah Miller's molds are marked *42* for the forty-second parallel that runs from near Plymouth, Mass., through Kingston, N. Y.[1] This example and nos. 376–378 all have gnomons of the same angle. They also were all acquired in Massachusetts or Connecticut.

Many of these rather small pewter sundials may have been mounted on windowsills. The damage in the area of mounting holes perhaps resulted from prying sundials free.

1. Montgomery, *History of American Pewter,* pp. 203–204.

375–378

376 SUNDIAL

Maker unidentified
Probably New York or New England, ca. 1770

MARKS: None

INSCRIPTIONS: None

DIMENSIONS: OH. 2", Diam. 4 9/16"

PROVENANCE: Purchased from Dr. Percy E. Raymond, Lexington, Mass.; 1950-842

377 SUNDIAL

Possibly the Miller family
New York or New England, 1740–1780

MARKS: *NM* cast in relief on face of dial in front of angled end of gnomon

INSCRIPTIONS: None

DIMENSIONS: OH. 1 1/2", Diam. 3 1/16"

PROVENANCE: Purchased from Dr. Percy E. Raymond, Lexington, Mass.; 1950-911

378 SUNDIAL

Maker unidentified
Probably New York or New England, dated 1762

MARKS: None

INSCRIPTIONS: *1762 price 3/0* cast in relief on face of dial near angled end of gnomon

DIMENSIONS: OH. 2", Diam. 4 1/2"

PROVENANCE: Purchased from Avis and Rockwell Gardiner, Stamford, Conn.; 1956-22

379 SUNDIAL

Goldsmith Chandlee
Winchester, Va., 1785–1821

MARKS: *CHANDLEE WINCHESTER* cast in relief on face

INSCRIPTIONS: None

DIMENSIONS: OW. 5 1/8"

PROVENANCE: Dr. and Mrs. Henry P. Deyerle, Harrisonburg, Va.; purchased at his estate auction conducted by Sotheby's in Charlottesville, Va., on May 26, 1995; 1995-91

PUBLISHED: Sales cat., Sotheby's, Charlottesville, Va., May 26, 1995, lot 709, ill.

This handsome sundial is remarkable both as a Virginia-made piece of pewter and as a scientific instrument. Chandlee, its maker, was a truly talented and versatile artisan who worked in a variety of related trades prior to his death in 1821. He is especially noted for his tall-case clocks and surveying compasses. Two parts of a three-part Chandlee mold for casting sundials of this pattern are in the collections of the Museum of Early Southern Decorative Arts in Winston-Salem, N. C.[1] This mold is for the upper face of the dial, and it shows that the gnomon was cast as an integral part with the base plate.

1. Paula Locklair, "New in the MESDA Collection," *Luminary,* XIX (spring 1998), p. 6, ill.

379

HOUSEHOLD AND PERSONAL ACCESSORIES 287

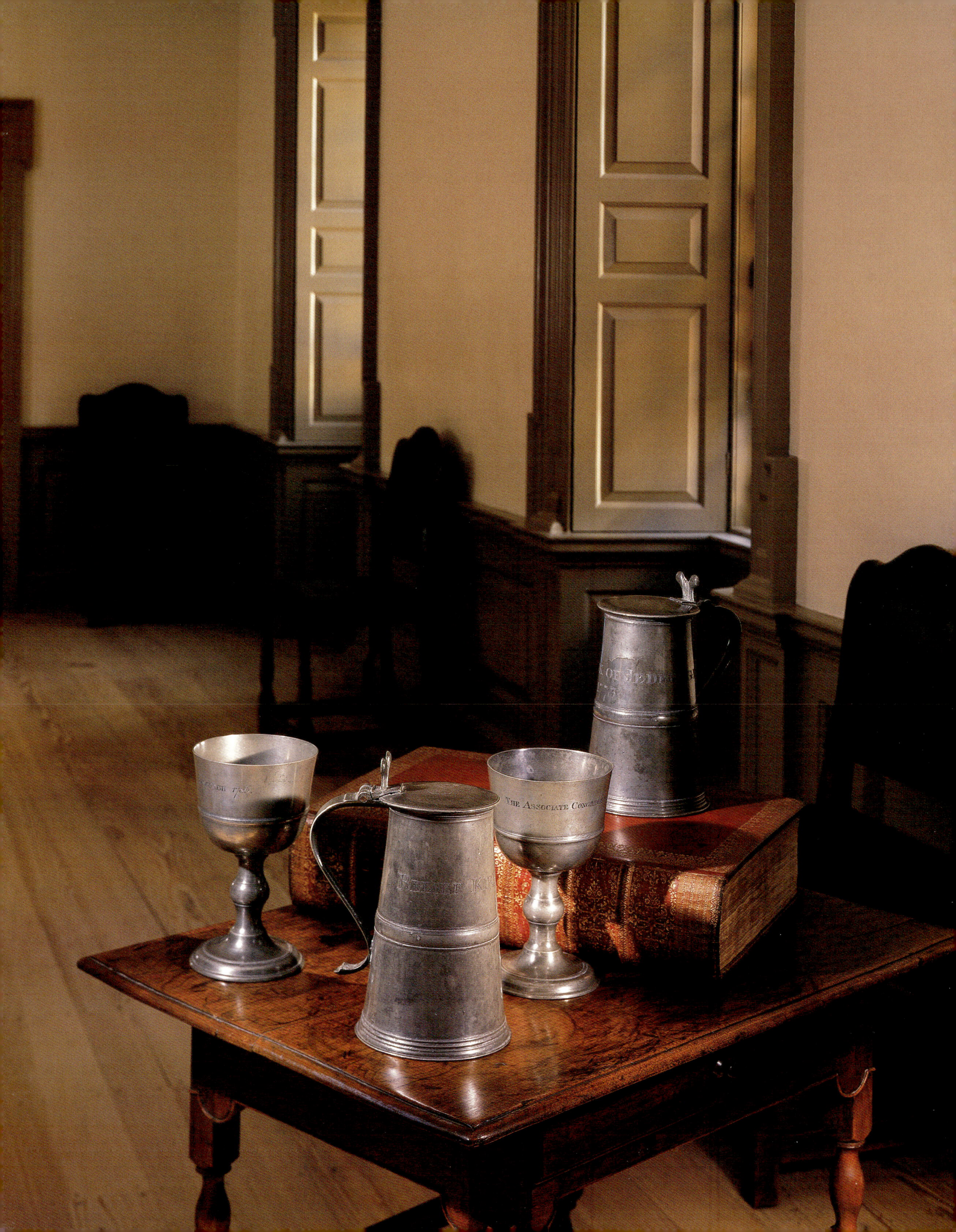
The Associate

Religious Objects

Long before the period of the Colonial Williamsburg Collection, pewter chalices, flagons, patens, and dishes had for centuries been made in England for religious use. Notable among these are the large number of surviving flagons, many of which possess considerable dignity and beauty. Flagons were also used in domestic circumstances, for they occasionally appear in household inventories, especially before 1720. Chalices and flagons of a later date represent some of the finest and most distinctive attainments in American pewter.

380–382

380 Flagon

Maker unidentified
England, probably West Country, 1620–1650

MARKS: Touchmark *MB* with four tear-shaped elements above and a mullet with a pellet to either side below within a beaded circle on underside of base

INSCRIPTIONS: Crest with banner bearing the motto of the Gwynne family of Wales engraved on face of body opposite handle; owner's initials *MH* in script engraved between crest and banner; owners' initials *MT* stamped and *M/T•I* engraved on face of handle

DIMENSIONS: OH. 9 3/16", Diam. (base) 4 5/8"

PROVENANCE: Purchased from A. H. Isher & Son, Cheltenham, Eng.; 1958-556

Although flagons are first thought of as church vessels for the communion of the faithful, many were used in other public and domestic circumstances. They appear with some regularity in Virginia household inventories, especially before 1720. This example, with its engraved crest and motto and a variety of owners' initials, both stamped and engraved, probably served most, if not all, of its life in family hands.[1]

1. For a helpful pictorial survey and discussion of flagons of this type and date, see Malcolm Toothill, "Charles I flagons," *Journal of the Pewter Society,* VIII (autumn 1991), pp. 41–51.

380.1 Engraved owner's crest and motto on body

381 FLAGON

Maker unidentified
England, 1620–1650

MARKS: Indistinct touchmark incorporating, in part, a full-length figure with an apparent *A* to the left and *P* to the right within a circle on face of handle

INSCRIPTIONS: Owner's initials *IB* stamped on face of handle

DIMENSIONS: OH. 10 3/8", Diam. (base) 4 3/4"

PROVENANCE: Purchased from A. H. Isher & Son, Cheltenham, Eng.; 1958-591

382 FLAGON

Maker unidentified
England, 1620–1650

MARKS: Indistinct maker's touch incorporating, in part, a full-length figure with an apparent *A* to the left and *P* to the right within a circle on face of handle

INSCRIPTIONS: None

DIMENSIONS: OH. 10 12/16", Diam. (base) 5 5/16"

PROVENANCE: Mason Collection; purchased from A. H. Isher & Son, Cheltenham, Eng.; 1960-795

383 FLAGON

Maker unidentified
England, 1630–1660

MARKS: Touchmark *IC* with a mullet above and to the left and right within an outlined lozenge on interior center-bottom of base; lower part of mark indistinct (Peal, *More Pewter Marks,* 5507b)

INSCRIPTIONS: None

DIMENSIONS: OH. 10 1/4", Diam. (base) 5 1/2"

PROVENANCE: Purchased from A. H. Isher & Son, Cheltenham, Eng.; 1966-293

Peal mistakenly dates this mark ca. 1730.[1]

1. Peal, *More Pewter Marks,* no. 5507b.

384 FLAGON

Francis Seegood
Norwich, Eng., or King's Lynn, Eng., 1660–1680

MARKS: Touchmark *F•S* with a mullet flanked by pellets above within an outlined circle on interior center-bottom of base (Peal, *More Pewter Marks,* 4168, 5921); pseudo hallmarks (1) indistinct, (2) lion passant within a rectangle with serrated upper and lower edges, (3) buckle within a lozenge, and (4) indistinct, on top of cover (Peal, *More Pewter Marks,* 5921)

INSCRIPTIONS: None

DIMENSIONS: OH. 9 5/32", Diam. (base) 5 9/16"

PROVENANCE: Purchased from A. H. Isher & Son, Cheltenham, Eng.; 1966-304

385 Flagon

Robert Marten
London, 1655–1674

MARKS: Touchmark of a standing bird facing left with *RM* above within an outlined circle on face of handle; pseudo hallmarks (1) leopard's head within a shaped shield or rectangle, (2) lion passant within a serrated rectangle, (3) obscure device, and (4) *RM* with a bird below within a heart on top of cover (Cotterell, *Old Pewter,* 3092)

INSCRIPTIONS: None

DIMENSIONS: OH. 10 1/8", Diam. (base) 6 3/8"

PROVENANCE: Purchased from A. H. Isher & Son, Cheltenham, Eng.; 1963-149

This flagon is of representative beefeater type, having a flat-topped cover with waisted sides that resemble the hats worn by beefeater guards at the Tower of London. Its general proportions are broad with an exaggerated spreading base, often, as in this instance, hollow with the base flush with the bottom. The thin strap handle has an inward-curved return below its upper attachment, and it ends in a spade terminal. Covers are raised with the assistance of a twin-cusp thumb piece. This type of flagon was probably introduced in the 1650s. Its influence is clear in Irish eighteenth-century flagons.

386 FLAGON

William Wood II
Birmingham, Eng., 1690–1710

MARKS: Touchmark *W•W* with rose below within a rounded rectangle on interior center bottom of base (Cotterell, *Old Pewter,* 6028; Peal, *More Pewter Marks,* 6028; Homer and Hall, *Provincial Pewterers,* 44); pseudo hallmarks (1 and 2) same as touchmark, (3) lion passant, and (4) lion's head erased, each within separate rounded rectangles on top of cover (Homer and Hall, *Provincial Pewterers,* 44)

INSCRIPTIONS: None

DIMENSIONS: OH. 9 5/8", Diam. (base) 5 1/8"

PROVENANCE: Purchased from A. H. Isher & Son, Cheltenham, Eng.; 1958-589

Wood (1645–1726) of Birmingham was the principal maker of this type of flagon. They are characterized by tall, vertical bodies that are fitted with flat-topped covers with projecting flanges with elaborate denticulation opposite twin-lobed thumb pieces. Their thin strap handles have twin-lobed terminals. This example has

386–387

RELIGIOUS OBJECTS 293

sustained damage to its cover denticulations and its handle. Wood cast this cover in the same mold as the cover of tankard no. 241. The tankard's cover gives a precise idea of the openwork denticulation that this cover originally had.

387 FLAGON

Possibly Leonard Terry
York, Eng., 1715–1735

MARKS: Indistinct touchmark with a *T* surname initial within a probable heart-shaped reserve on interior center-bottom of base (Peal, *More Pewter Marks,* 5977a)

INSCRIPTIONS: Owner's initials *SS* stamped on upper face of cover denticulation

DIMENSIONS: OH. 11 5/8", Diam. (base) 5 3/4"

PROVENANCE: Purchased from Dr. John F. Richardson, Sevenoaks, Eng.; 1994-128

This flagon and no. 388 represent the two basic types of flagons that are associated with Yorkshire makers. This one is of the earlier type with its tall body having inclined straight sides and a wide band of broad reeds immediately above the base. The body is fitted with a domed cover with a projecting flange and a slender strap handle.

294 PEWTER AT COLONIAL WILLIAMSBURG

388 Flagon

John Harrison
York, Eng., dated 1750

MARKS: Touchmark *I•H* within a rectangle on interior center-bottom of base (Peal, *More Pewter Marks*, 5668b)

INSCRIPTIONS: *Bought at the Expense of the Parish of St. Saviours and St. Andrews/Richd. Cussons & Robt. Cundell Church Wardens 1750* engraved in script on lower section of body above midband

DIMENSIONS: OH. 12 1/4", Diam. (base) 5 7/8"

PROVENANCE: Church of Saint Saviour's, York, until 1912; purchased from William Lee by Howard Herschel Cotterell, Croxley Green, Eng. (Cotterell's trade label *1191* glued to underside of cover); sold to F. Scott-Nicholson, Carlisle, Eng.; acquired after his death about 1949 by Bertram Isher, Cheltenham, Eng.; sold to Christopher A. Peal, Norwich, Eng.; after Peal's death in 1980 acquired by J. R. Franklin, Shamley Green, Eng.; purchased by CWF from Robin Bellamy Antiques, Witney, Eng.; 1986-86

PUBLISHED: Fallow and McCall, *Yorkshire Church Plate*, I, p. 28; Cotterell, "Pewter: Work of York Craftsmen," p. 13; Cotterell, "Great Pewter Collections," pp. 97–98, figs. IX, X; Peal, "Notes on Pewter Flagons," p. 143. fig. IV; Michaelis, "Pear-Shaped Pewter Flagons," p. 191, fig. 9; *Exhibition of British Pewterware*, p. 27, no. 176; Peal, *British Pewter and Britannia Metal*, p. 131, fig. 55; Peal, "18th Century British Pewter," *Antique Collector*, XLIV (June–July, 1973), p. 160, fig. 8; sales cat., Sotheby's, July 25, 1974, p. 29, lot 139, frontis.; sales cat., Sotheby's, Nov. 13, 1980, pp. 10–11, lot 27, ill.; Peal et al., *Pewter of Great Britain*, p. 107, fig. 75; Hornsby, *Pewter of the Western World*, p. 80, fig. 137; *Pewter Collectors Club of America Bulletin*, XI (fall 1994), p. 47, ill. p. 45 (front cover)

EXHIBITED: Exhibition of British Pewterware through the Ages from Romano-British Times to the Present Day, Reading Museum and Art Gallery, Reading, Eng., Sept. 20–Oct. 31, 1969

388.1 Trade sticker of Howard Herschel Cotterell with inked number *1191* glued on inside of cover

For every significant type of object, curators and collectors have their own favorites against which they judge other examples. This acorn flagon from Yorkshire is one of the quirkiest regional types in English pewter. Its body gives the appearance of the upper part of a spire flagon issuing from an impossibly large trencher salt. Their finials are invariably insubstantial and lack the architectural character and presence of finials on other English flagons of similar date. This flagon and its mate in the Shemmel Collection merit the distinction of being the specimen examples of this distinctive type. They are the most fully articulated of their type and the most fully documented as to maker, church, donors, and subsequent owners.

389 Flagon

Maker unidentified
London, 1691–1715

MARKS: Touchmark of the apparent cipher *TAOB* within a beaded circle struck twice on face of handle (London Touch Plate II, 471; Cotterell, *Old Pewter*, 5474)

INSCRIPTIONS: *Ex Dono Samuel Symonds Gent:* engraved in script on face of body opposite handle

DIMENSIONS: OH. 12 1/2", Diam. (base) 5 1/2"

PROVENANCE: Saint Nicholas Church, Oxfordshire; F. Scott-Nicholson, Carlisle, Eng.; Cyril C. Minchin, Bucklebury, Eng., from whom CWF purchased it; 1981-175

PUBLISHED: Evans, *Church plate of Oxfordshire*, pp. 69–70; Minchin, "Some Uncommon Examples," p. 30, fig. 2; Michaelis, *Antique Pewter of British Isles*, pl. XXVI, fig. 65; Lobel, ed., *Victoria history of Oxford*, V, p. 133; *Exhibition of Pewter*, no. 59; cover ill.; Michaelis, *British Pewter*, p. 44, ill.; *Exhibition of British Pewterware*, p. 26, no. 167, ill.; Hatcher and Barker, *History of British Pewter*, pl. 13; "More Rare Pieces from Minchin Collection," p. 17, ill.

EXHIBITED: Exhibition of Pewter, City of Lincoln Usher Gallery, Lincoln, Eng., Sept. 29–Oct. 27, 1962; Exhibition of British Pewterware through the Ages from Romano-British Times to the Present Day, Reading Museum and Art Gallery, Reading, Eng., Sept. 20–Oct. 31, 1969

This splendid flagon is particularly handsome in its general stance and various details. Its strap handle and expressive thumb piece appear as holdovers from the late seventeenth century, while its elegantly slender and tailored body are consonant with the late baroque principles of the first years of the eighteenth century.

390 PATEN

James Spackman and Edward Grant
London, 1709–1720

MARKS: Indistinct touchmark on underside of rim (London Touch Plate III, 662; Cotterell, *Old Pewter,* 4435); secondary marks (1) indistinct label below touchmark, and (2) quality *X* above pseudo hallmarks on underside of rim opposite touchmark; pseudo-hallmarks (1) lion passant within a serrated rectangle, (2) leopard's head crowned within a shaped shield, (3) buckle within a shaped shield, and (4) indistinct on underside of rim opposite touchmark

INSCRIPTIONS: *Ex Dono Samuel Symonds Gent:* engraved in script on face of rim

DIMENSIONS: OW. (rim) 2", Diam. 9 3/8"

PROVENANCE: Saint Nicholas Church, Oxfordshire, Eng.; F. Scott-Nicholson, Carlisle, Eng.; Cyril C. Minchin, Bucklebury, Eng., from whom CWF purchased it; 1981-176

PUBLISHED: Minchin, "Some Uncommon Examples," p. 30, fig. 3; Michaelis, *Antique Pewter of British Isles,* p. 73, pl. III, fig. 20; *Exhibition of British Pewterware,* p. 26, no. 166; "More Rare Pieces from Minchin Collection," p. 17, ill.

EXHIBITED: Exhibition of British Pewterware through the Ages

This flagon shares some of the same aspects as the spire flagon that was evolving at this same time (see nos. 391–394 for developed examples of a later date). Its maker, although unidentified, struck this touchmark on London Touch Plate II in 1691. This piece and the following paten (no. 390) were originally the gift of Samuel Symonds to Saint Nicholas Church, near Oxford.

from Romano-British Times to the Present Day, Reading Museum and Art Gallery, Reading, Eng., Sept. 20–Oct. 31, 1969

Although the touchmark and pseudo hallmarks on this piece are illustrated in Cotterell, the compromised condition of the touchmark and the commonness of the pseudo hallmark devices and their sequence made it necessary to compare these marks directly with images of marks on another piece. Close comparison with a photograph of the marks on a salver with a central foot in the collections of The Worshipful Company of Pewterers of London confirms the attribution.[1] This piece and no. 389 were originally the gift of Samuel Symonds to Saint Nicholas Church, near Oxford.

1. *Supplementary Catalogue of Pewterware, 1979,* p. 127, figs 438A and B.

391 FLAGON

Henry Joseph
London, 1750–1780

MARKS: Touchmark *H•I* within a shaped rectangle with pseudo hallmarks on face of body to left of upper handle attachment (Peal, *More Pewter Marks,* 2687); pseudo hallmarks include a lion passant within a shaped rectangle struck three times in conjunction with touchmark; secondary mark of a quality *X* with crown above over hallmarks

INSCRIPTIONS: None

DIMENSIONS: OH. 11 3/8", Diam. (base) 5 7/16"

PROVENANCE: Kenneth G. Gordon, Congleton, Eng.; purchased by CWF from Robin Bellamy Antiques, Witney, Eng.; 1986-87

392 FLAGON

Henry Joseph
London, 1750–1780

MARKS: No touchmark apparent; pseudo hallmarks (1) indistinct device within a shaped shield, (2) an apparent leopard's head within an indistinct surround, (3) a possible lion passant within an indistinct surround, and (4) *H•J* within a rectangle on face of body to left of upper handle attachment

INSCRIPTIONS: None

DIMENSIONS: OH. 16 1/2", Diam. (base) 6 1/2"

PROVENANCE: Purchased from Richard Mundey, London; 1985-70

391–392

393 FLAGON

Maker unidentified
England, 1760–1780

MARKS: None

INSCRIPTIONS: None

DIMENSIONS: OH. 12 3/4", Diam. (base) 6 9/16"

PROVENANCE: Purchased from Dr. Percy E. Raymond, Lexington, Mass.; 1950-857

PUBLISHED: Raymond, "Ancestral Pewter," p. 8, fig. 2

393–394

394 Flagon

Maker unidentified
England, 1770–1800

MARKS: None

INSCRIPTIONS: None

DIMENSIONS: OH. 13 5/8", Diam. (base) 7 7/16"

PROVENANCE: Purchased from A. V. Sutherland-Graeme, London; 1957-149

The presence of a strainer with large circular perforations behind the pouring lip indicates that this flagon was most likely made for tavern use and that a strainer of this type was intended to retain hops.

395 Flagon

John Heaney
Dublin, Ireland, 1767–1798

MARKS: Touchmark of an embowed arm upholding a dagger with *IOHN* and *HEANEY* within curved reserves above and below and fronds to either side on interior center-bottom of base (Cotterell, *Old Pewter*, 2242; Hall, *Irish Pewter*, 215)

INSCRIPTIONS: None

DIMENSIONS: OH. 11 7/16", Diam. (cover) 4 13/16", Diam. (base) 7 1/8"

PROVENANCE: Purchased from David S. Moulson, Alcester, Eng.; 2000-78

395

Relatively few hollowware forms in Irish pewter survive in significant numbers. Flagons are the most distinctive of these Irish forms. This example is thoroughly representative of the standard eighteenth-century model. Its body of these proportions with its domed and spreading base clearly derives from English flagons of the mid-seventeenth century of beefeater type (see nos. 384–385). The Irish also spouted most of their flagons with pronounced articulation to the pointed bottom ends of the spouts. Covers on early examples are sometimes reminiscent of beefeater shapes, yet most eighteenth-century examples are of this double-domed form. Most distinctive are the expressively curved handles in the form of a question mark, often described as being of spring type. The continuation of the handle beyond its upper join with the body is again borrowed from early flagons, yet it is consistently done in this later Irish context with a sense of exaggeration and panache all its own.

Marked Irish flagons are uncommon. Even with all the appropriate details, if they are unmarked, one cannot be certain of their origin, for Bristol makers probably produced flagons of this type for export to Ireland.[1] Hall illustrates a virtually identical flagon from the O'Connor Collection. Since it has an unidentified *P* mark, it can only be said to be of Irish type.[2] Trish and Peter Hayward illustrate a similar unmarked flagon with a different thumb piece and comment that two flagons marked by Heaney appear in the papers of H. H. Cotterell.[3]

1. Hall, *Irish Pewter*, p. 11.
2. *Ibid.*, p. 28, pl. 27. Hall illustrates the mark on p. 70.
3. Trish Hayward and Peter Hayward, "Church pewter on the Isle of Man," *Journal of the Pewter Society*, XII (spring 1999), p. 24, fig. 28.

396 PLATE

Alexander Cleeve I
London, dated 1700

MARKS: Touchmark of a stemmed and leafed rose upheld in a hand flanked by a palm frond to either side with *ALEX* and *CLEEVE* within curves reserves above and below on underside of rim; secondary mark of a rose with a royal crown and apparently *LONDON* above within a vertical beaded oval below touchmark (Cotterell, *Old Pewter*, 961); pseudo hallmarks (1) a lion passant within a shaped rectangle, (2) a leopard's head within a shaped shield, (3) a buckle within a shaped shield, and (4) *NK* with a rosette above within a shaped shield on underside of rim opposite touchmark (Cotterell, *Old Pewter*, 2704)

INSCRIPTIONS: Engraved *1700* within a baroque cartouche surmounted by a coronet on face of rim; name and position of probable donor *William Knight Church Warden* engraved in script on face of rim opposite cartouche with date

DIMENSIONS: OW. (rim) 1 7/16", Diam. 9 7/16"

PROVENANCE: Purchased from Robin Bellamy Antiques, Witney, Eng.; 1984-156

396.1 Engraved donor's name on rim

397 Pair of Communion Cups

Maker unidentified
England, 1740–1770

MARKS: No touchmark apparent; four indistinct pseudo hallmarks on face of each bowl below rim

INSCRIPTIONS: None

DIMENSIONS: OH. 8 1/2", Diam. (rim) 4 3/16", Diam. (base) 4"

PROVENANCE: Purchased from David S. Moulson, Alcester, Eng.; 1995-6, 1–2

PUBLISHED: Sales brochure, David Moulson (autumn 1994), no. 7, ill.

398 Pair of Dishes

Thomas Simpson
Edinburgh, Scot., dated 1748

MARKS: Touchmark of a waist-length figure of a man with *SIMPSON* and *SUPER FINE* within curved reserves above and below on underside of well; secondary marks (1) oblong rectangular label containing *HARD•METAL* with scalloped upper and lower edges, and (2) quality *X* with crown above, both on underside of well; pseudo hallmarks (1) thistle, (2) *TS* in script, (3) rose, and (4) fleur-de-lis, each within a separate shield on underside of well

INSCRIPTIONS: The face of each rim engraved *ASSOCIATE CONGREGATION OF JEDBURGH 1748*

DIMENSIONS: OL. 18 1/8", OW. (rim) 2 3/8"

PROVENANCE: Purchased from Richard Mundey, London; 1973-244, 1–2

399 Pair of Flagons

Maker unidentified
Scotland, dated 1773

MARKS: None

INSCRIPTIONS: *RELIEF KIRK OF JEDBURGH/1773* engraved on the face of each body opposite handle

DIMENSIONS: OH. 10 11/16", Diam. (base) 6 1/8"

PROVENANCE: Purchased from Richard Mundey, London; 1973-243, 1–2

As with Irish pewter flagons, there is an equally distinctive appearance to Scottish ones. Clearly conveyed in their straight, inclined sides with broad midbands is their derivation from early bound wooden water-carrying vessels. This same source of design is also quite evident in a number of other drinking vessels. The solid strap handles and flat lids with twin-lobed thumb pieces are older features that have been repeated numerous times and reinforce a desired sense of lineage and tradition.

Another flagon of 1773 from Jedburgh was advertised for sale in 1973. Other pieces from this communion service, including a matching flagon of 1773 and two other dishes of 1748 (see no.

398–400

398), as well as five nineteenth-century communion tokens from the church (see nos. 401–402), were sold at auction in 1985.[1]

1. Sales cat., Sotheby's, Oct. 31, 1985, lot 26, pl. II.

400 PAIR OF COMMUNION CUPS

Maker unidentified
Scotland, ca. 1786

MARKS: None

INSCRIPTIONS: *THE ASSOCIATE CONGREGATION OF JEDBURGH 1786* engraved on face of each bowl

DIMENSIONS: OH. 9 3/16", Diam. (rim) 5 5/16", Diam. (base) 4 15/16"

PROVENANCE: Purchased from Richard Mundey, London; 1973-242, 1–2

During the middle decades of the eighteenth century, most Scottish pewter communion cups were of this commodious form. Their particularly large bowls feature a fillet midband and are supported on a stem of turned design with a central knop above a splayed circular foot.

401 COMMUNION TOKEN

Maker unidentified
Scotland, dated 1825

MARKS: None

INSCRIPTIONS: *I/U.A.C/JEDB* in relief on one side and *W.N/1825* in relief on the other

DIMENSIONS: OL. 3/4", OW. 5/8"

PROVENANCE: Gift of Peter R. G. Hornsby, Witney, Eng.; G1974-181

Communion tokens have been used in the Presbyterian church in Scotland from the late sixteenth century to ensure that those partaking of the sacrament of the Last Supper were considered spiritually fit. The earliest were in the form of paper tickets. Metallic ones soon replaced these less desirable paper ones, with pewter being the most common material. They continued to be used in Scotland into the first half of the twentieth century. The initials on one side of this token stand for the United Associate Congregation of Jedburgh, and those on the other with the date are the initials of the minister.[1]

1. John H. Carter, Sr., "Four Centuries of Scottish Communion Tokens—Mostly Pewter," *Pewter Collectors Club of America Bulletin*, VI (December 1972), pp. 252–254.

401

401

402

402 COMMUNION TOKEN

Maker unidentified
Scotland, dated 1841

MARKS: None

INSCRIPTIONS: *JEDBURGH./RELIEF CHURCH/1841.* stamped in relief on one side

DIMENSIONS: OL. 1 1/16", OW. 3/4"

PROVENANCE: Gift of Peter R. G. Hornsby, Witney, Eng.; G1974-180

403 CHALICE

Johann Christoph Heyne
Lancaster, Pa., 1752–1781

MARKS: None

INSCRIPTIONS: None

DIMENSIONS: OH. 8 7/8", Diam. (rim) 4 1/16", Diam. (base) 4 1/2"

PROVENANCE: Gift of Mr. and Mrs. Foster McCarl, Jr., Beaver Falls, Pa.; G1982-167

Heyne (1715–1781), who was trained in his native Saxony and worked in Stockholm before migrating from London to Philadelphia in 1742, had established himself by 1752 as a pewterer in Lancaster, Pa. A deeply and actively religious man, he produced an extraordinary body of church pewter, notable among which is a large number of chalices and flagons, many still owned by German congregations in southeastern Pennsylvania. In their amalgam of Continental and Anglo-American elements, the chalices and flagons constitute an important and highly personal attainment and one of the great monuments in American pewter of the colonial period. This assimilation of influences contributes to the strength and distinction not only of Heyne's work but also of much American pewter. This splendid chalice was given with flagon no. 404. There is every indication that they have been together since they were made. Like the flagon, this chalice has been subsequently silvered.

404 FLAGON

Johann Christoph Heyne
Lancaster, Pa., 1752–1781

MARKS: Touchmark *I•C•H* with crown above within a conforming reserve on underside of base (Laughlin, *Pewter in America,* II, 530); secondary mark of a label with *LANCASTER* within a rectangle below touchmark on underside of base (Laughlin, *Pewter in America,* II, 532)

INSCRIPTIONS: None

DIMENSIONS: OH. 11 1/4", Diam. (base exclusive of feet) 5 7/8"

PROVENANCE: Gift of Mr. and Mrs. Foster McCarl, Jr., Beaver Falls, Pa.; G1982-166

This flagon and the preceding chalice (no. 403) have been subsequently silvered.

403–404

Detail from *Beer Street*, William Hogarth, designer and engraver, London, February 1, 1751, black-and-white line engraving, 1972-409, 93

Pewter Marks

Frontis

1

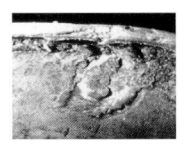

2

4

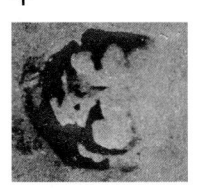

11

12

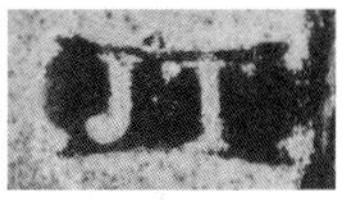

13

14

15

16

17

18

19

20

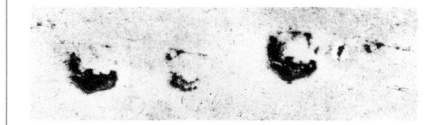

21

22

23

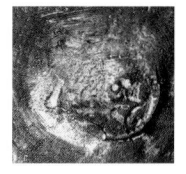

308 PEWTER AT COLONIAL WILLIAMSBURG

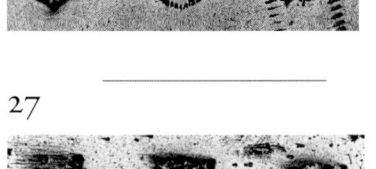

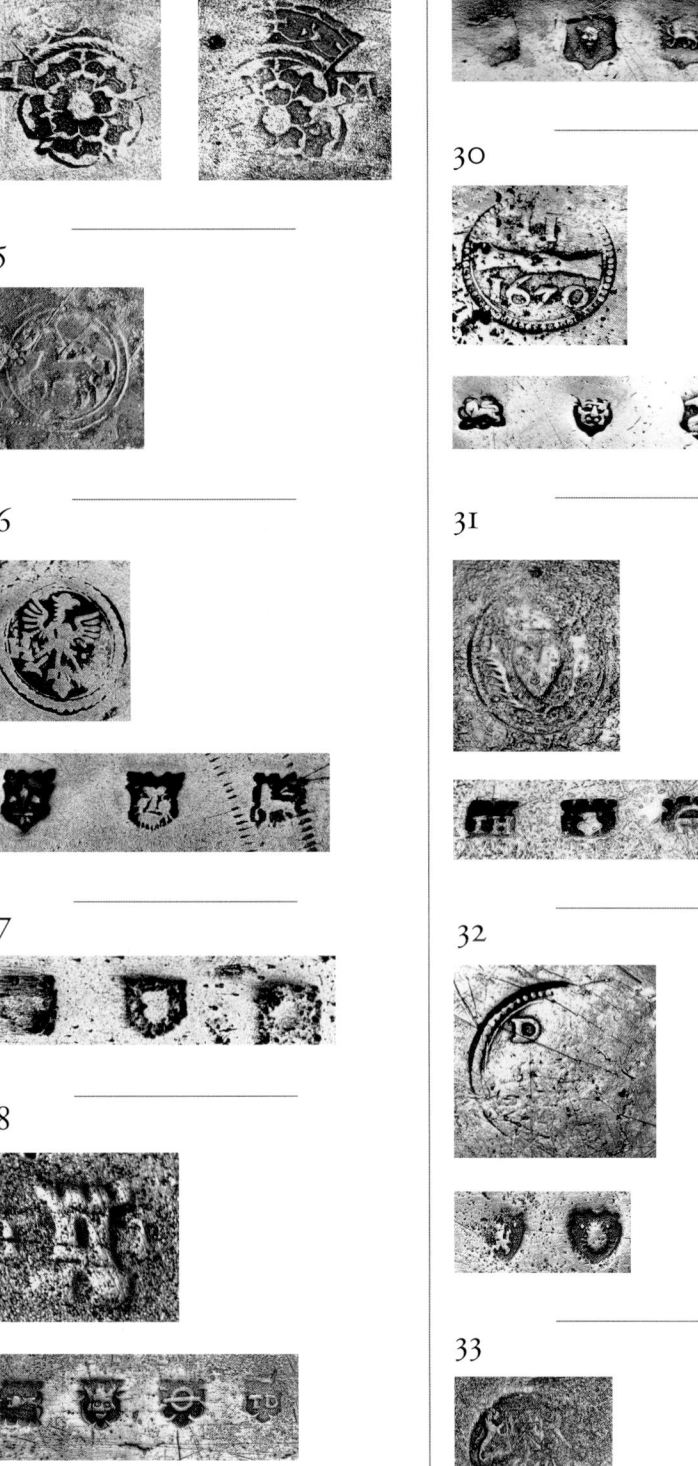

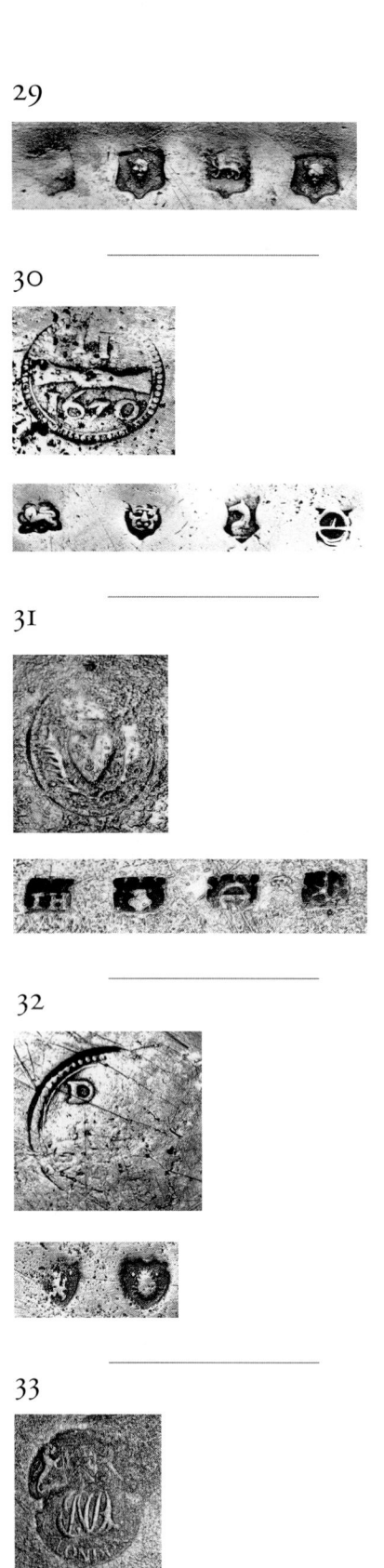

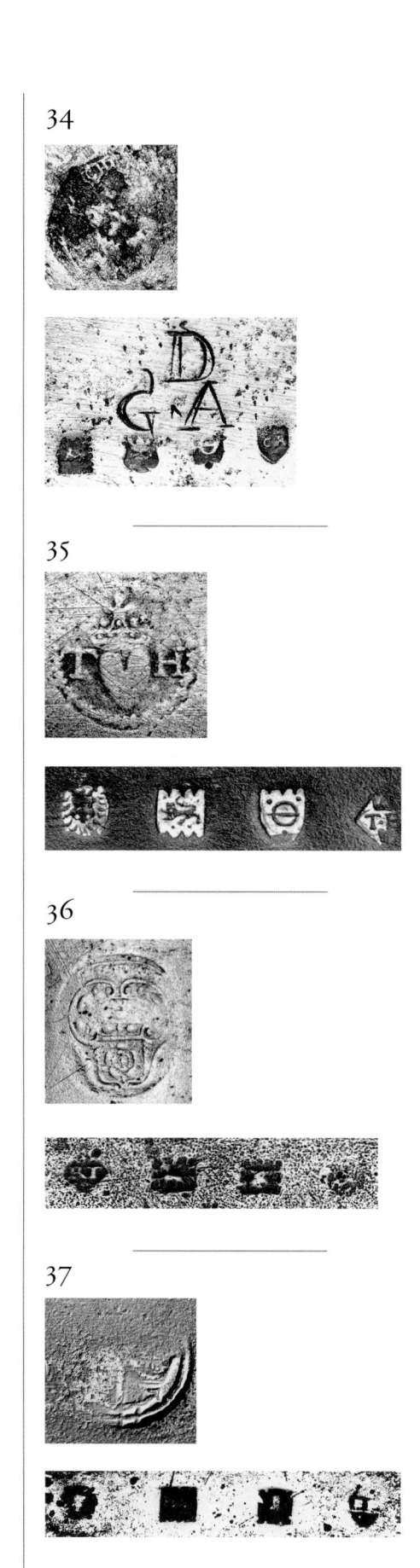

38

39

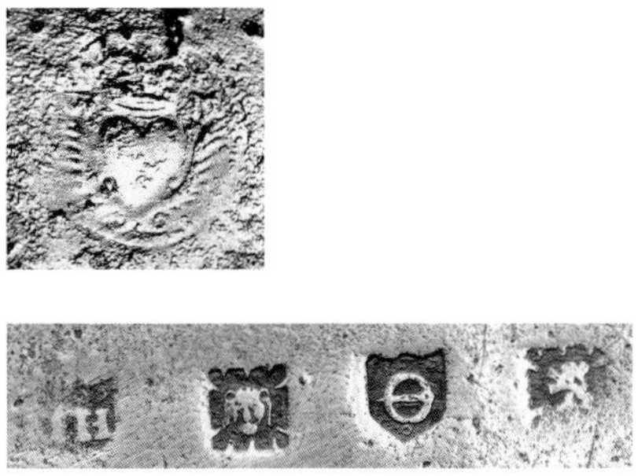

40

41

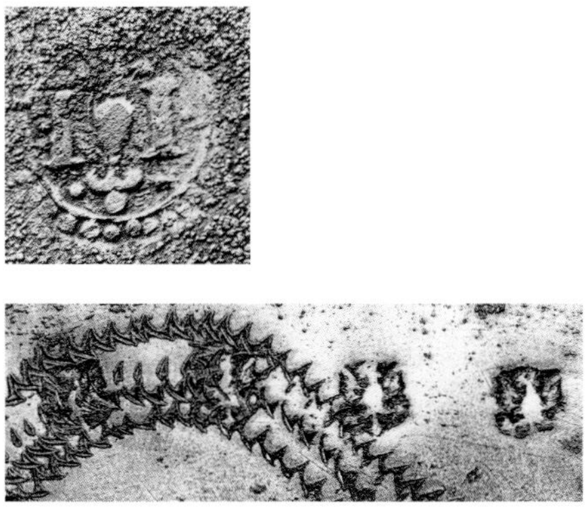

42

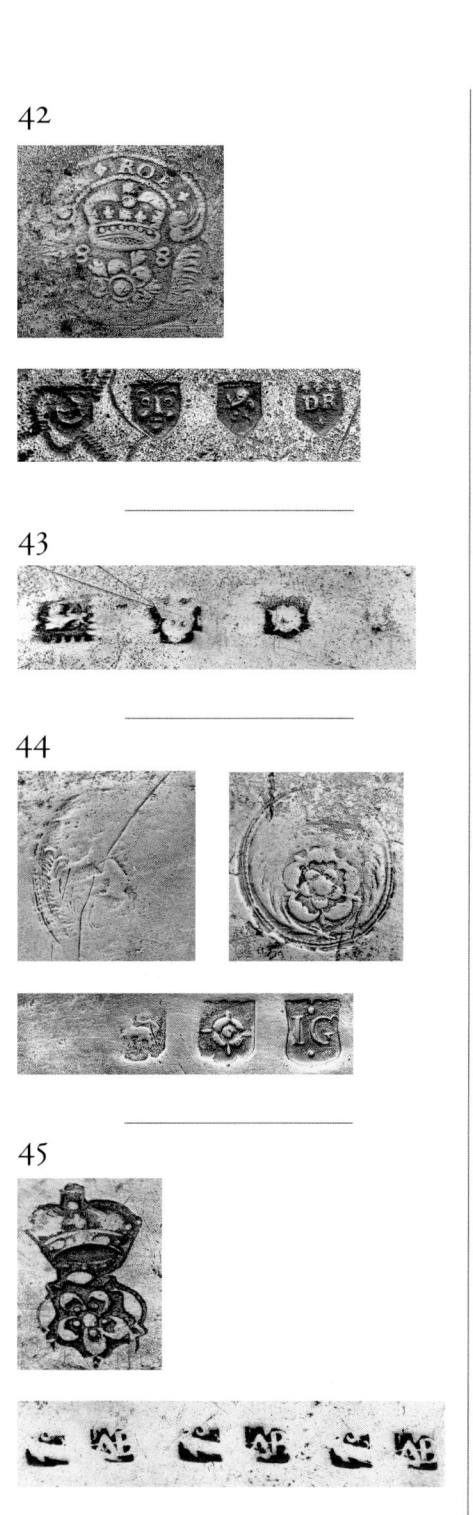

43

44

45

46

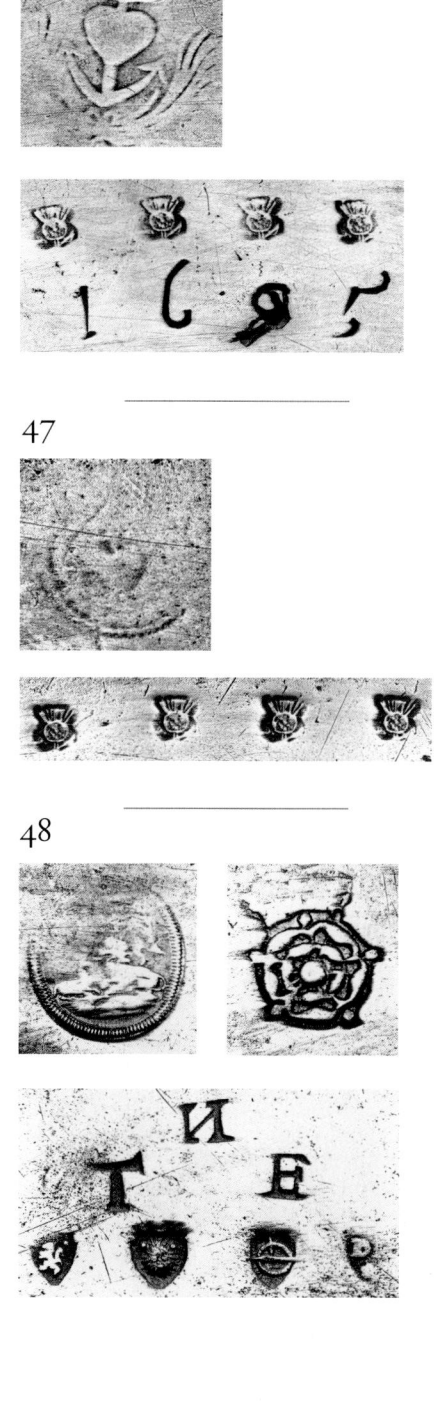

47

48

PEWTER MARKS 309

310 PEWTER AT COLONIAL WILLIAMSBURG

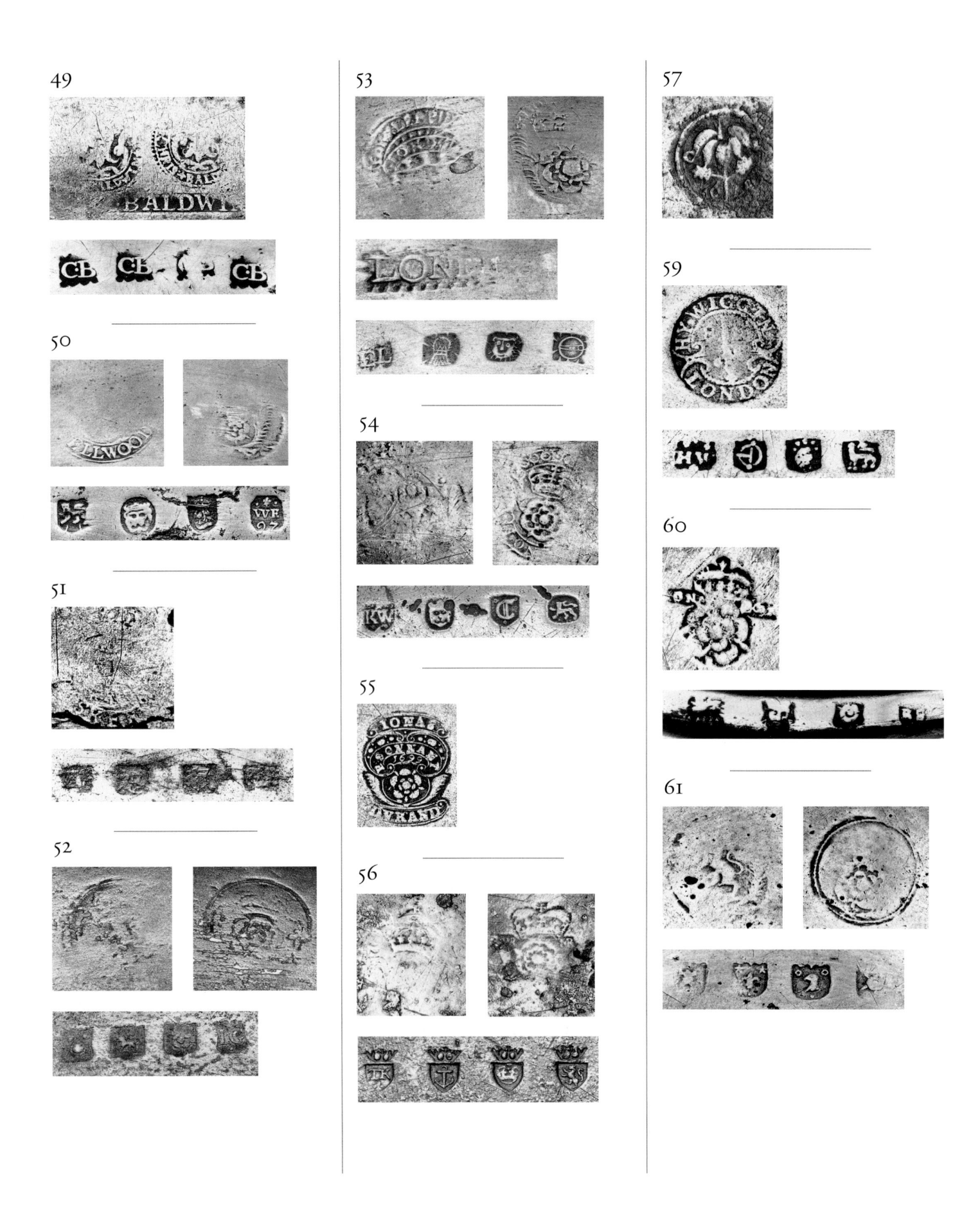

62

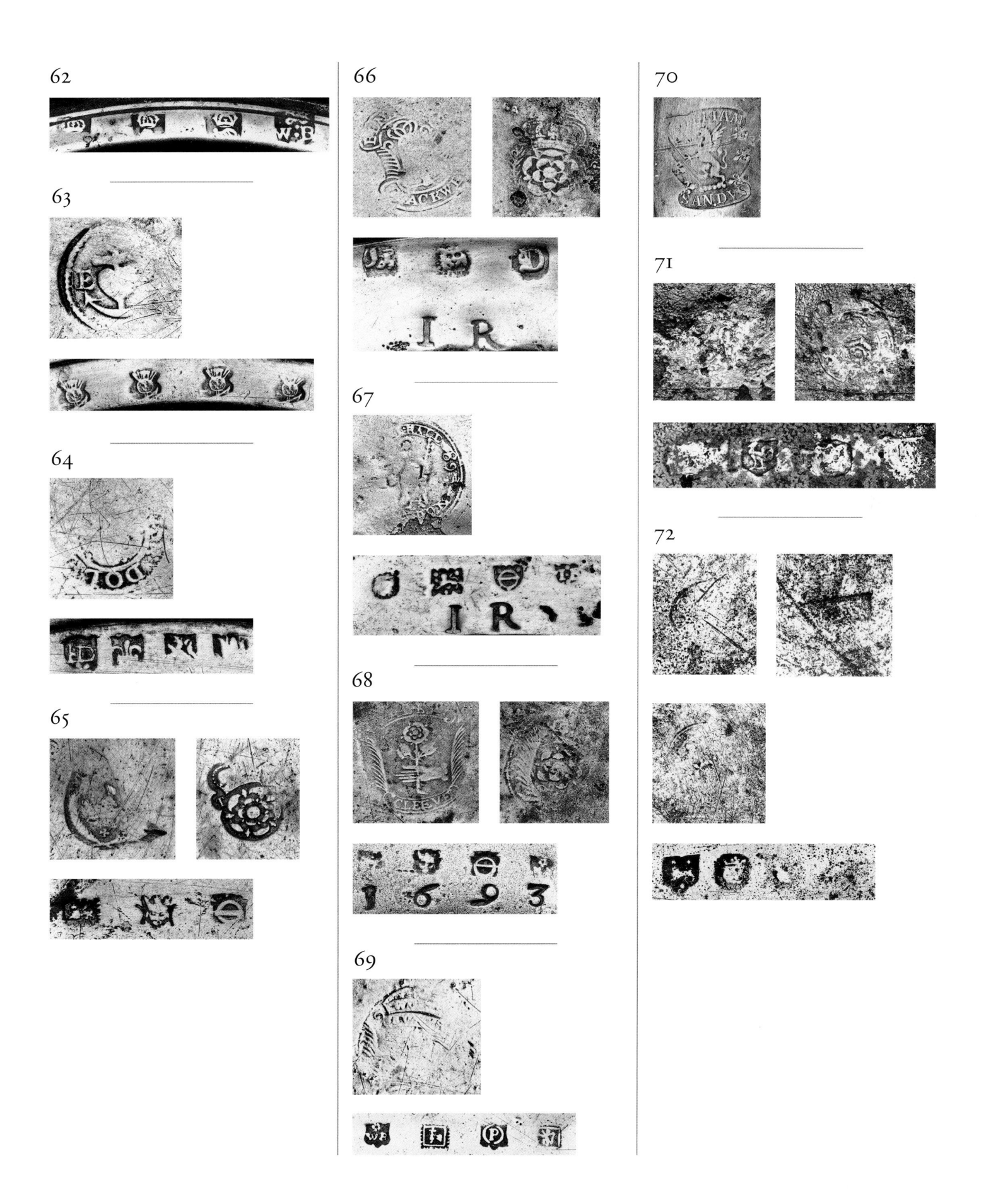

63

64

65

66

67

68

69

70

71

72

PEWTER MARKS

312 PEWTER AT COLONIAL WILLIAMSBURG

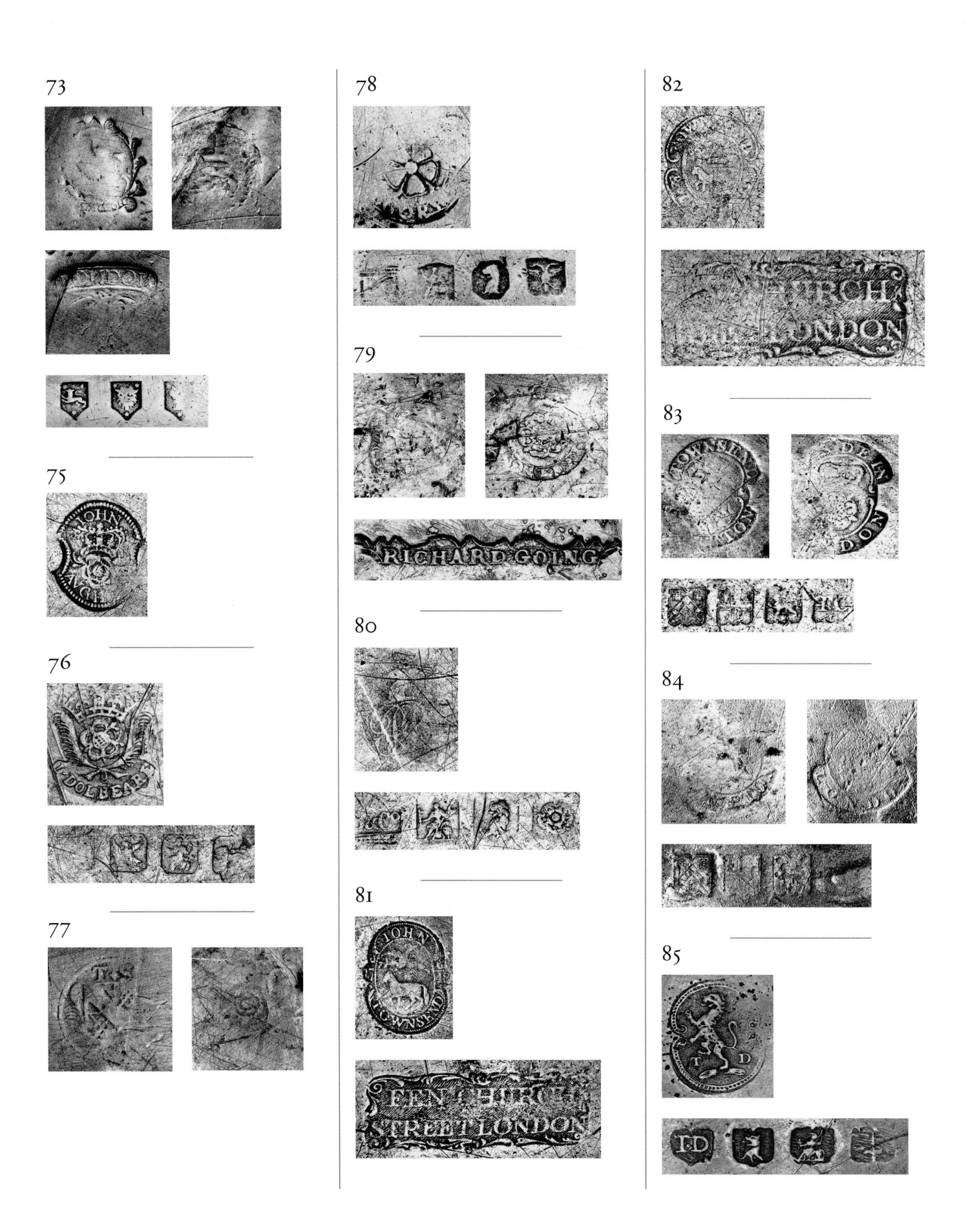

86

B. BARNS
PHILA

87

88

89

NICHOLSON

90

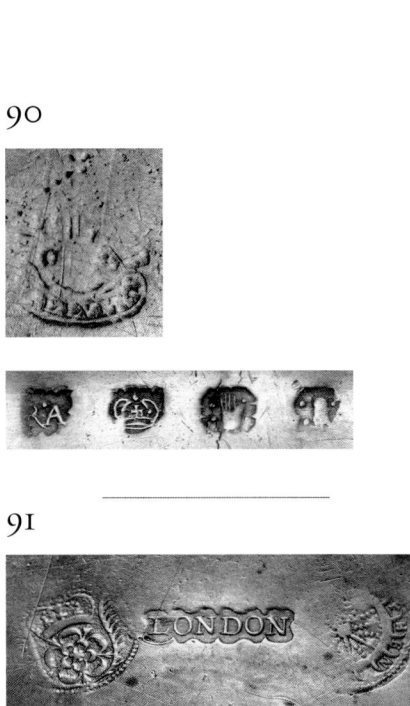

91

92

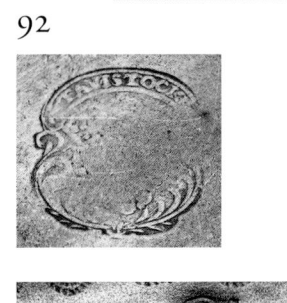

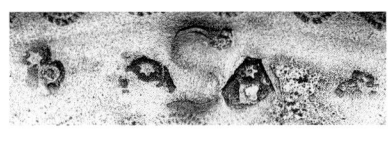

93

94

LONDON

95

96

97

98

PEWTER MARKS 313

314 PEWTER AT COLONIAL WILLIAMSBURG

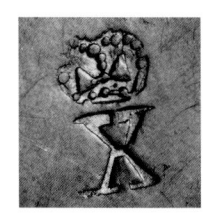

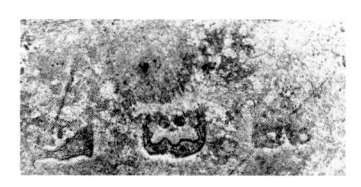

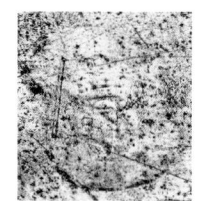

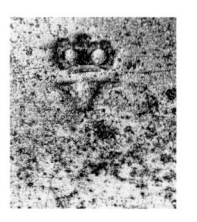

113

114

115

116

117

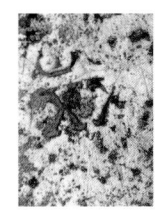

118

119

120

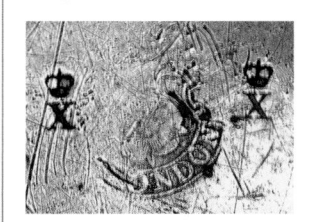

121

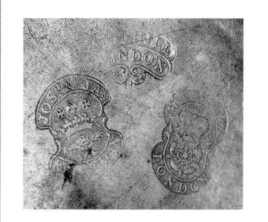

122

124

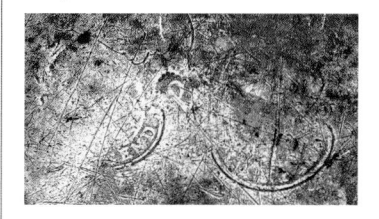

125

126

PEWTER MARKS 315

316 PEWTER AT COLONIAL WILLIAMSBURG

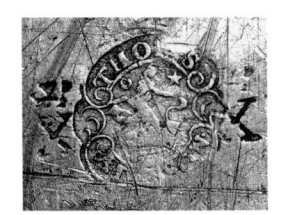

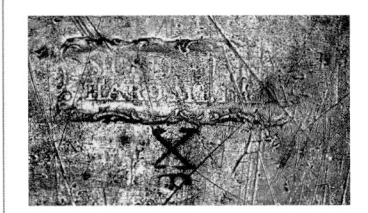

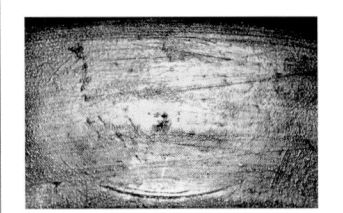

136

137

138

139

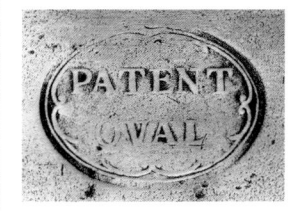

141

142

144

146

148

149

PEWTER MARKS

150

151

152

153

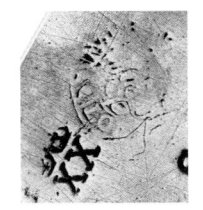

154

155

156

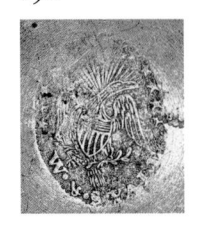

157

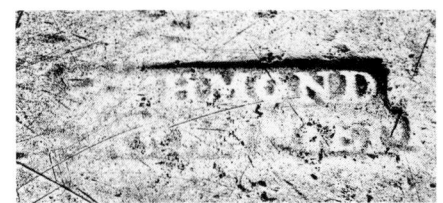

158

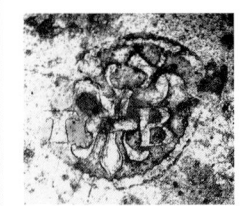

159

160

161

162

318   PEWTER AT COLONIAL WILLIAMSBURG

164

166

167

170

171

172

174

175

179

180

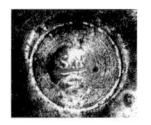

181

182

183

184

185

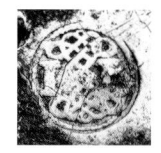

186

188

189

190

PEWTER MARKS 319

191

192

193

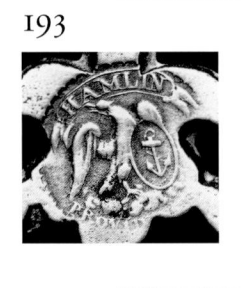

194

195

196

197

199

202

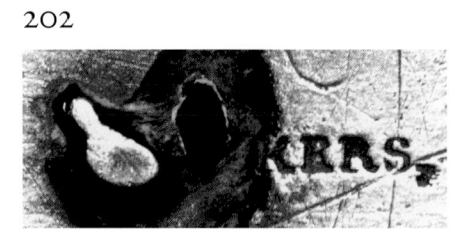

203

204

205

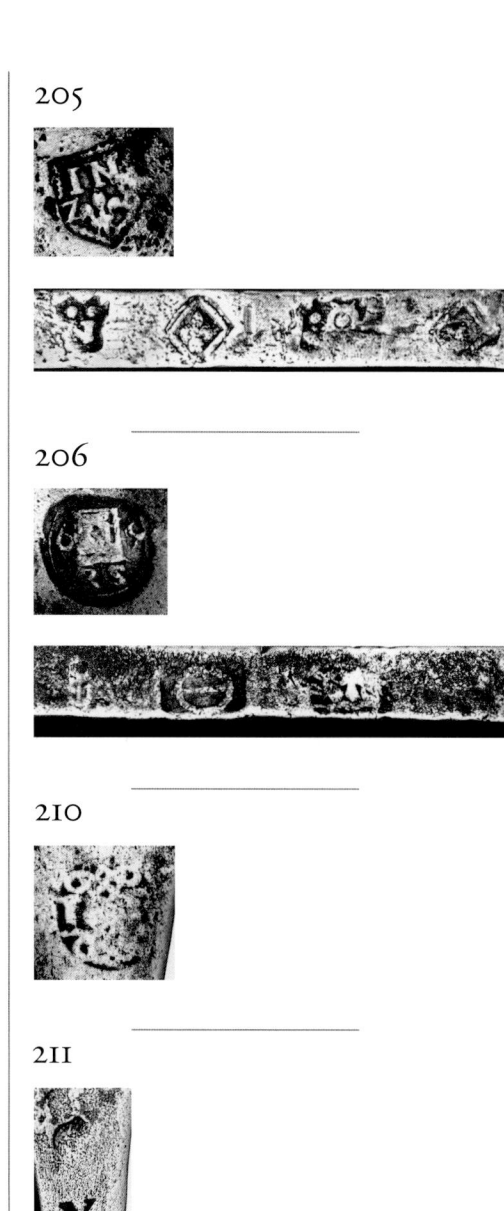

206

210

211

320 PEWTER AT COLONIAL WILLIAMSBURG

212

216

217

218

219

220

221

222

223

224

225

227

PEWTER MARKS 321

229

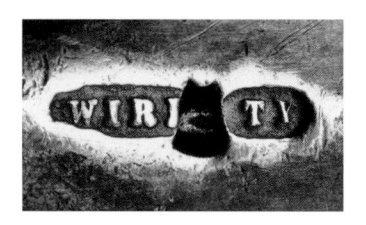

231

232

233

234

235

236

237

238

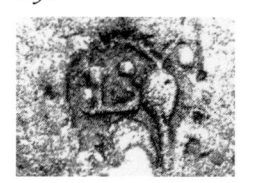

239

240

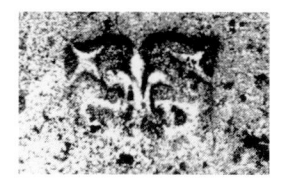

241

243

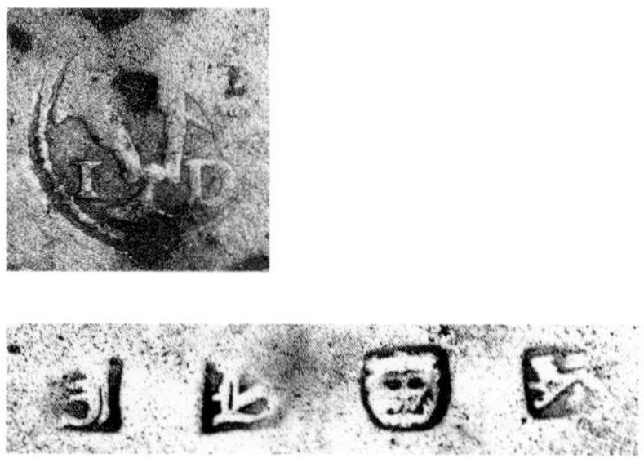

244

245

322 PEWTER AT COLONIAL WILLIAMSBURG

246

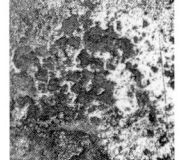

248

249

250

253

254

255

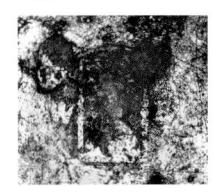

256

257

258

259

260

261

262

PEWTER MARKS 323

263

264

265

267

268

269

270

271

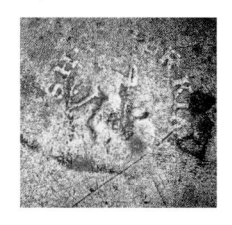

272

273

274

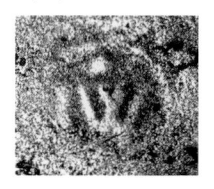

275

276

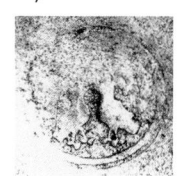

277

279

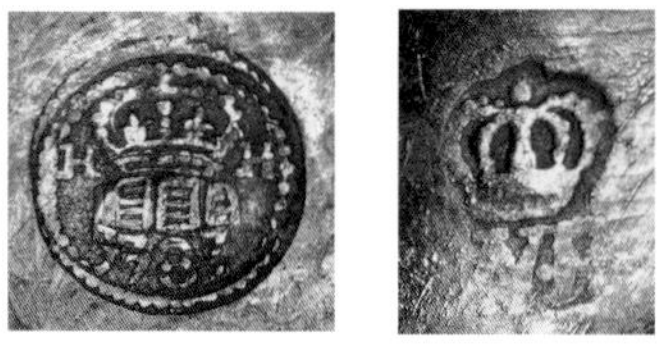

280

281

282

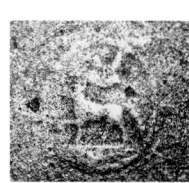

324 Pewter at Colonial Williamsburg

283

284

285

286

288

289

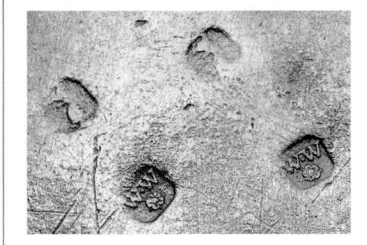

290

291

292

293

294

299

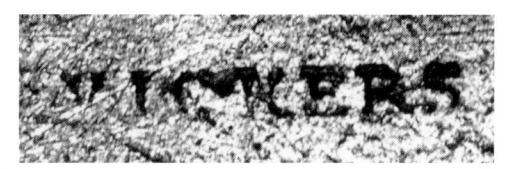

300

301

302

303

304

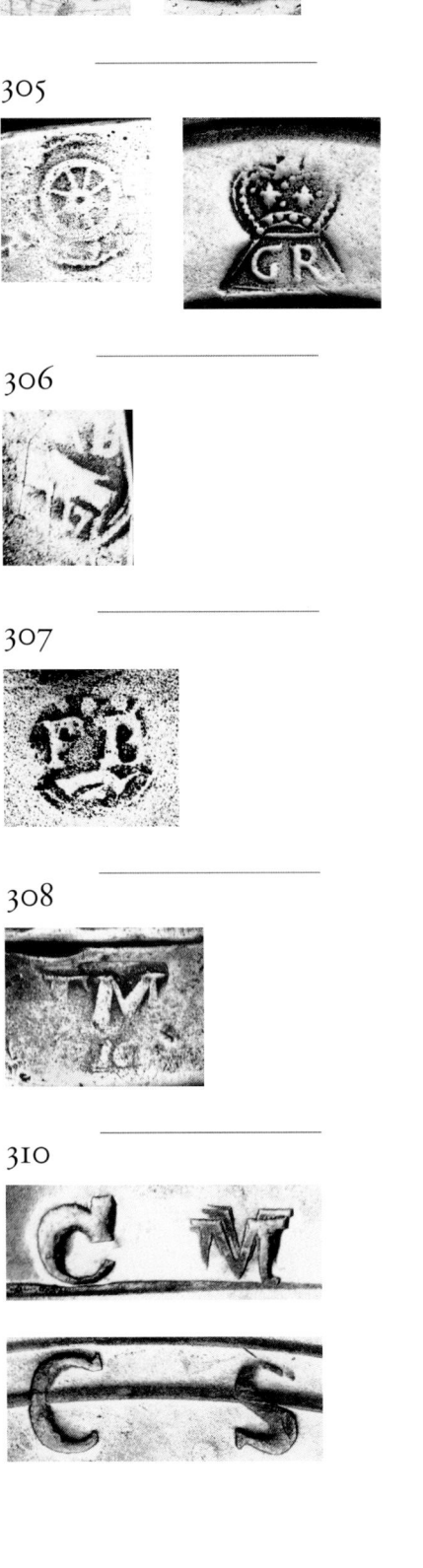

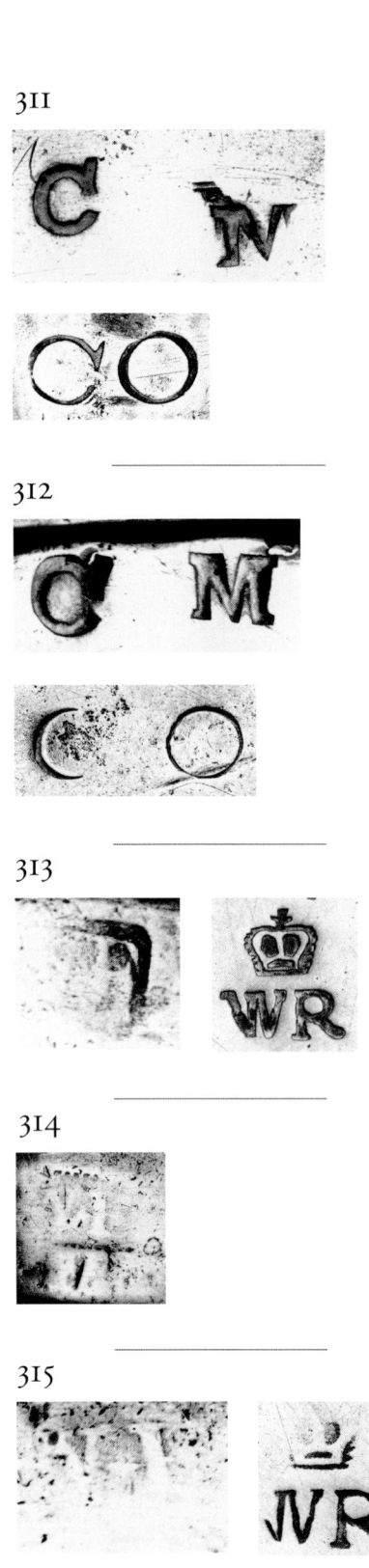

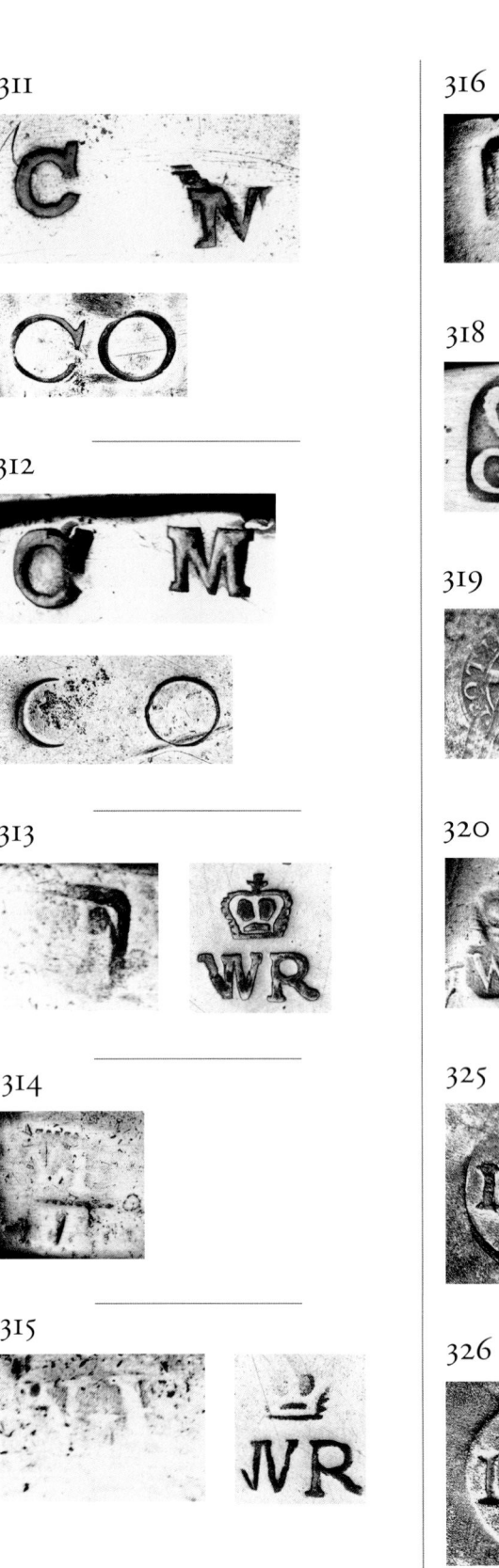

305

306

307

308

310

311

312

313

314

315

316

318

319

320

325

326

326 PEWTER AT COLONIAL WILLIAMSBURG

327

328

329

330

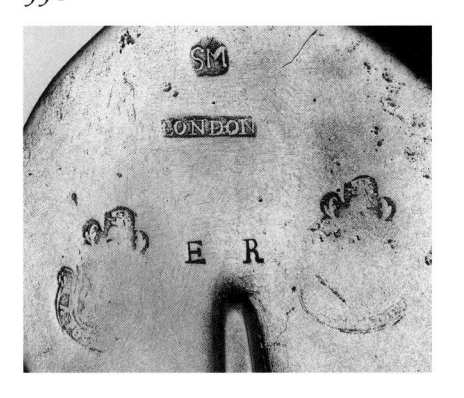

331

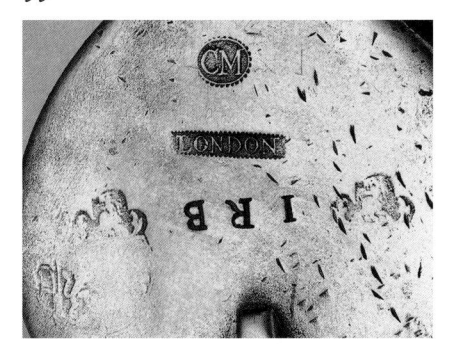

332

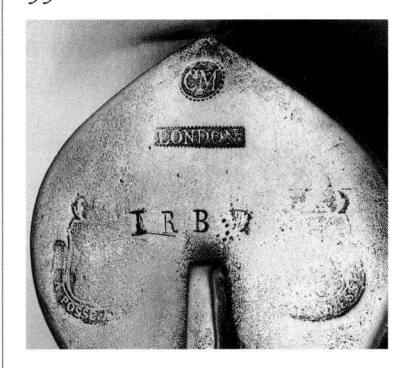

333

335

336

337

338

339

341

342

343

344

PEWTER MARKS 327

345

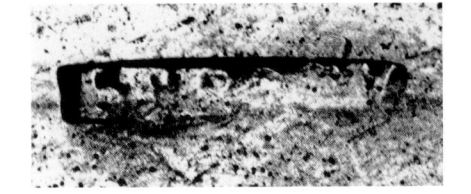

346
C
I·VICKERS

347
X
D&SB

348
GLENNORE Co
G.RICHARDSON
A
CRANSTON R.I

350
I·VICKERS

352
3
D.FURNIVAL[?]
3b

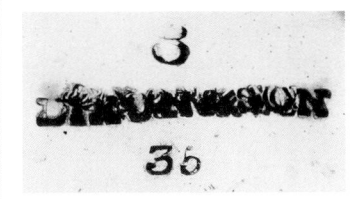

353

356
I·VICKERS

357

360
G.RICHARDSON
WARRANTED
CRANSTON R.I

361

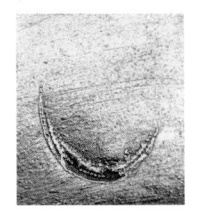

362
LONDON
MADE IN LONDON

T·M

363

364
X
IC Co

365

328 PEWTER AT COLONIAL WILLIAMSBURG

366

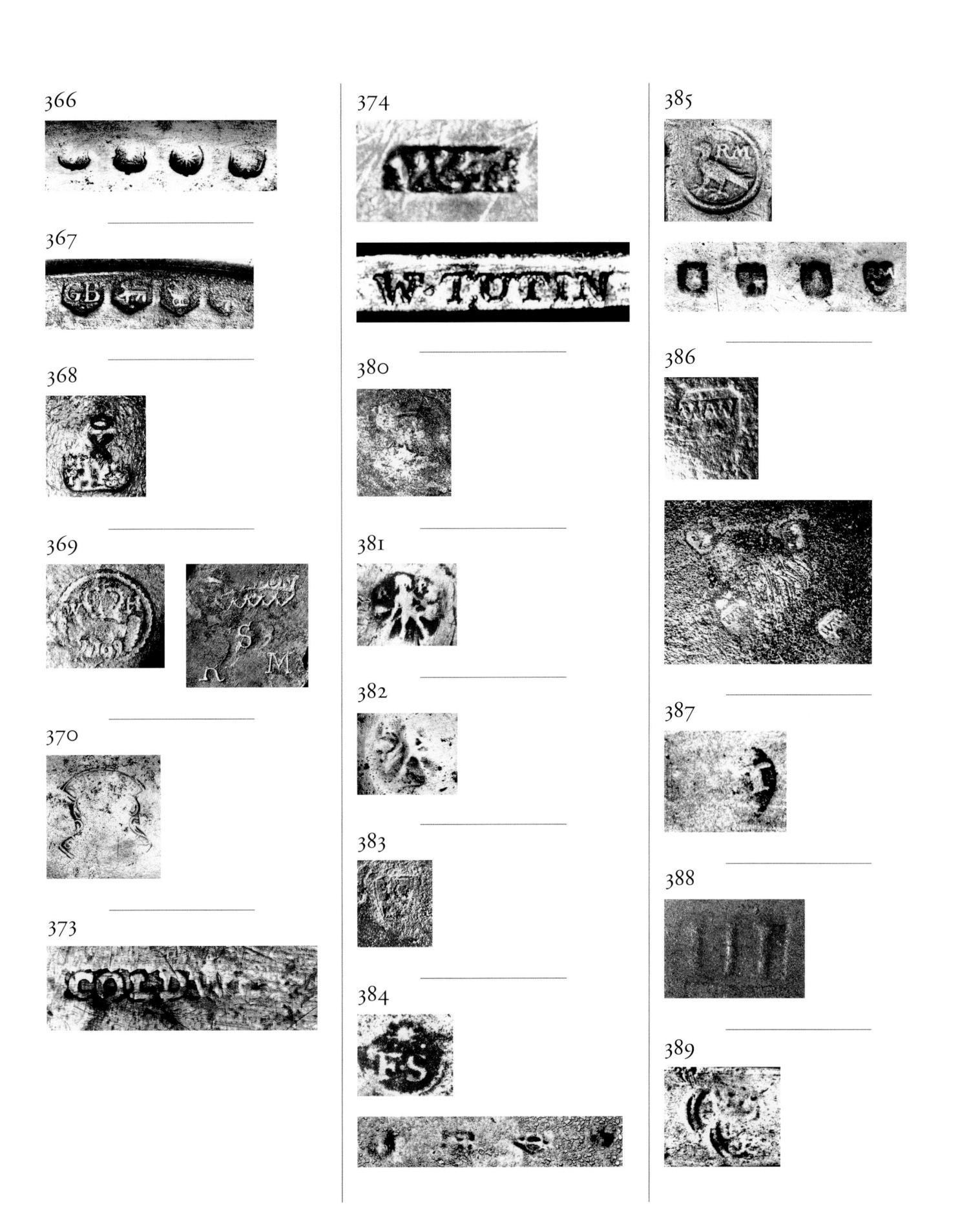

367

368

369

370

373

374

W? TUTIN

380

381

382

383

384

385

386

387

388

389

PEWTER MARKS

390

391

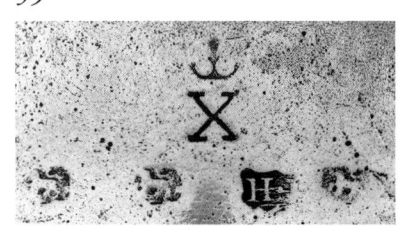

392

395

396

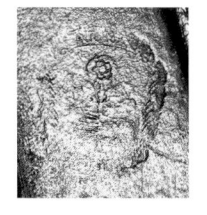

397

398

404

Glossary

ACCOLLÉ heraldry: Joined or touching at the neck, such as shields of related arms, often of oval shape, tilted toward and touching the other.

ADDORSED heraldry: Placed back to back.

ARMS AND CRESTS heraldry: Coats of arms derive from the emblems and designs borne on shields and banners in the Middle Ages. They identify individuals, families, institutions, or places. Elements are depicted and arranged in a conventional and understood manner. They are described and replicated through a brief blazon or written description in heraldic terms. Coats of arms are specific to an individual, family, institution, or place, whereas a crest is a heraldic device often shared more widely. Crests began as emblematic devices worn atop helmets in the Middle Ages. They are usually depicted at a later date as supported on a wreath bar of twisted form atop a helmet above the coat of arms or simply on a wreath bar above the arms or by themselves.

BOOGE The short, curved sides of the well of a plate, dish, or porringer of common configuration.

BRITANNIA METAL A product that involves considerations of both alloy and technology in its understanding. First developed by James Vickers of Sheffield in the second half of the eighteenth century, it used a lead-free pewter with a prominent admixture of antimony that could be cold rolled into workable sheet. Vickers adapted, in part, the methods of the fused silver plate (Sheffield plate) industry in creating lightened neoclassic forms from rolled sheet. Bright-cut engraving was the principal means of decoration, with simplified borders and cartouches appearing on American examples.

BURNED ON The casting of a secondary element, such as a handle or a finial, directly against a major component, such as the body or the cover, which is done for added strength.

CADENCY MARK heraldry: A small device included in the shield of arms to indicate numerically the son using the arms.

CHECKY heraldry: Composed of a grid of squares of contrasting colors.

CHEVRON heraldry: An inverted V-shaped division of a coat of arms or of a principal part.

COUCHANT heraldry: An animal in a crouching posture.

COUPED heraldry: A principal element of an animal, such as a head or a limb, separated from the body, leaving a straight line.

COURANT heraldry: An animal in a running posture.

DISH Most follow the shape of smaller plates of the same pattern, yet are distinguished from them by their greater size, usually measuring in excess of eleven or twelve inches.

ERASED heraldry: A principal element of an animal, such as a head or a limb, separated from the body, leaving a jagged line.

FLAGON A large vessel for transporting and serving liquids, usually lidded and taller than a tankard. Used for church and domestic purposes, especially before 1720.

GOLDEN FLEECE	heraldry: The limp form of a sheep with circlet for hanging.
GUARDANT	heraldry: Looking out with head turned toward spectator. Termed reguardant when looking back over the shoulder.
IMPALED	heraldry: The vertical division of a coat of arms with the arms on the left belonging to the husband and those on the right belonging to the wife.
LINEN MARK	The textured impression left by the cloth used when a handle or another part of the object is cast directly against or burned onto the body or cover. Considered an important indicator of authenticity on the inside of a porringer bowl in front of the handle attachment.
MULLET	heraldry: A star form.
PASSANT	heraldry: An animal in a walking posture with right forepaw raised.
PLATE	Most are distinguished from dishes by their lesser size, usually measuring less than eleven inches.
PSEUDO HALLMARKS	A group of relatively small marks, usually four in number, that emulate those on assayed silver items. They are relatively common between 1630 and 1770.
RAMPANT	heraldry: An animal in a standing posture with its left hind paw on the ground and its other legs raised.
SALIENT	heraldry: An animal in the act of leaping.
SEGREANT	heraldry: Descriptive of a griffin in a rampant position.
SEJANT	heraldry: An animal in a seated posture with all four paws on the ground.
SKIMMING	To smooth rough-cast surfaces on a lathe with a scraping tool. This technique is a customary means of finishing a plate, dish, and a basin or major components, such as the bodies and covers of porringers, teapots, measures, tankards, mugs, and the like. The pronounced skimming lines on the undersides of many porringers and basins are one of the visual pleasures of American pewter.
STATANT	heraldry: An animal in a standing posture with all four paws on the ground.
TOUCHMARK	These distinctive marks of makers were registered in London at the guildhall by stamping or entering the mark on a touch plate. There is a stylistic chronology to such marks that is helpful in dating objects.
TRIPPANT	heraldry: For deer and other animals of chase, in a trotting posture with one foot up.
WRIGGLED ENGRAVING	A form of decorative engraving that was particularly popular from 1680 to 1740. It was accomplished with a broad rocker tool that was walked back and forth to create a characteristic zigzag line. Used mainly for naturalistic motifs.

Short-Title List

"Accessions of Museums, 1959"
: "Accessions of American and Canadian Museums, July–September 1959." *Art Quarterly,* XXII (winter 1959).

"Accessions of Museums, 1960"
: "Accessions of American and Canadian Museums, July–September 1960." *Art Quarterly,* XXIII (winter 1960).

Art at Auction, 1971–72
: *Art at Auction, 1971–72.* New York: Sotheby's, 1972.

Art at Auction, 1976–77
: *Art at Auction, 1976–77.* New York: Sotheby's, 1977.

Art Treasures Exhibition
: *Art Treasures Exhibition.* New York: National Antique & Art Dealers Association of America, 1967.

Bradbury, *History of Old Sheffield Plate*
: Bradbury, Frederick. *History of Old Sheffield Plate; Being an Account of the Origin, Growth, and Decay of the Industry, and of the Antique Silver and White or Britannia Metal Trade, with Chronological Lists of Makers' Marks and Numerous Illustrations of Specimens.* 1912. Reprint. Sheffield, Eng.: J. W. Northend, 1983.

Brett, *Phaidon Guide to Pewter*
: Brett, Vanessa. *Phaidon Guide to Pewter.* Oxford, Eng.: Phaidon Press, 1981.

Butler, *Candleholders in America*
: Butler, Joseph T. *Candleholders in America, 1650–1900; A Comprehensive Collection of American and European Candle Fixtures Used in America.* New York: Crown Publishers, 1967.

Cotterell, "Great Pewter Collections"
: Cotterell, Howard Herschel. "Great Pewter Collections: Treasures in the Scott-Nicholson Collection." *Apollo,* XIX (February 1934).

———, *Old Pewter*
: Cotterell, Howard Herschel. *Old Pewter, Its Makers and Marks in England, Scotland and Ireland; An Account of the Old Pewterer & His Craft.* 1929. Reprint. Rutland, Vt.: Charles E. Tuttle, 1963.

———, *Pewter down the Ages*
: Cotterell, Howard Herschel. *Pewter down the Ages from Mediæval Times to the Present Day with Notes on Evolution.* Foreword by Antonio de Navarro. London: Hutchinson, 1932.

———, "Pewter: Work of York Craftsmen"
: Cotterell, Howard Herschel. "Pewter: Fine work of the York Craftsmen." *Apollo,* XVIII (July 1933).

Davis, "Metals for fashion-conscious consumer"
: Davis, John D. "Metals for the fashion-conscious consumer." *The Magazine Antiques,* CLIX (January 2001).

de Navarro, *Causeries on English Pewter*
: de Navarro, Antonio. *Causeries on English Pewter.* London: Offices of "Country Life," [1911].

Douglas, "English Strawberry Dish"
: Douglas, John. "An English Strawberry Dish." *Journal of the Pewter Society,* XVIII (autumn 2002).

Edinburgh Touch Plates I–II
: Edinburgh Touch Plates I–II. Collections of the National Museums of Scotland, Edinburgh, Scot., reg. nos. H.MET 46 & 47.

Evans, *Church plate of Oxfordshire*
: Evans, John Thomas. *The church plate of Oxfordshire.* Oxford, Eng.: Alden Press, 1928.

Exhibition of British Pewterware
: *Exhibition of British Pewterware through the Ages from Romano-British Times to the Present Day Held at Reading Museum and Art Gallery 20th September to 31st October 1969.* Reading, Eng.: Pewter Society, 1969.

Exhibition of Pewter
: *Exhibition of Pewter.* Lincoln, Eng.: City of Lincoln Usher Gallery, 1962.

Fairbanks and Trent, eds., *New England Begins*
: Fairbanks, Jonathan L., and Robert F. Trent, eds. *New England Begins: The Seventeenth Century.* 3 vols. Boston, Mass.: Museum of Fine Arts, Boston, 1982.

Fallow and McCall, *Yorkshire Church Plate*
: Fallow, Thomas M., and Hardy B. McCall. *Yorkshire Church Plate.* 2 vols. Leeds, Eng.: Yorkshire Archaeological Society, 1912–1915.

"Fashionable, Neat, and Good"
: ". . . let them be fashionable, neat, and good in their several kinds . . .": *The Williamsburg Collection of Antique Furnishings.* Williamsburg, Va.: Colonial Williamsburg Foundation, 1973.

Gadd, "Candlesticks of the Baroque Period"
: Gadd, Jan. "English Pewter Candlesticks of the Baroque Period." *Journal of the Pewter Society,* XIV (autumn 2000).

———, "Disc-base Candlesticks"
: Gadd, Jan. "Disc-base Candlesticks with Pillar Stems in Brass." *Journal of the Antique Metalware Society,* X (June 2002).

———, "Famous Old Candlesticks"
: Gadd, Jan. "Famous Old Candlesticks." *Journal of the Pewter Society,* XI (spring 1998).

Glen-Sanders Collection
> *The Glen-Sanders Collection from Scotia, New York.* Colonial Williamsburg Department of Collections, and the Abby Aldrich Rockefeller Folk Art Collection. Williamsburg, Va.: Colonial Williamsburg, 1966.

Gordon, *Candlestick Maker's Bawle*
> Gordon, Kenneth G. *Pewter: The Candlestick Maker's Bawle, 'A Family Portrait.'* Congleton, Eng.: Kenneth G. Gordon, 1994.

Hall, "Four saucers"
> Hall, David. "Four saucers." *Journal of the Pewter Society*, VII (autumn 1989).

———, *Irish Pewter*
> Hall, David W. *Irish Pewter: A History.* [Great Britain]: Pewter Society, 1995.

Hatcher and Barker, *History of British Pewter*
> Hatcher, John, and T. C. Barker. *A History of British Pewter.* London: Longman, 1974.

Hayward, "Townsend and Compton Businesses"
> Hayward, Peter. "The Townsend and Compton Sequence of Businesses." *Journal of the Pewter Society*, XI (autumn 1997).

Herr, *Pewter in Pennsylvania German Churches*
> Herr, Donald M. *Pewter in Pennsylvania German Churches.* Birdsboro, Pa.: Pennsylvania German Society, 1995.

Hilt, "Henry Joseph"
> Hilt, Wayne A. "Henry Joseph—Master Pewterer." *Pewter Collectors Club of America Bulletin*, VII (September 1978).

Homer, "John Shorey senior and junior"
> Homer, Ronald F. "John Shorey senior and junior." *Journal of the Pewter Society*, VIII (autumn 1991).

Homer and Hall, *Provincial Pewterers*
> Homer, Ronald F., and David W. Hall. *Provincial Pewterers: A Study of the craft in the West Midlands and Wales.* London: Phillimore, 1985.

Homer and Shemmell, *Pewter: Tudor and Stuart Pieces*
> Homer, Ronald F., and Stanley Shemmell. *Pewter: A Handbook of selected Tudor and Stuart pieces.* London: Pewter Society, 1983.

Hood, "American Pewter, Garvan"
> Hood, Graham. "American Pewter: Garvan and Other Collections at Yale." *Yale University Art Gallery Bulletin*, XXX (fall 1965).

———, *Governor's Palace in Williamsburg*
> Hood, Graham. *The Governor's Palace in Williamsburg: A Cultural Study.* Williamsburg, Va.: Colonial Williamsburg Foundation, 1991.

Hornsby, *Pewter of the Western World*
> Hornsby, Peter R. G. *Pewter of the Western World, 1600–1850.* Exton, Pa.: Schiffer Publishing, 1983.

Hornsby, Weinstein, and Homer, *Celebration of the craft*
> Hornsby, Peter R. G., Rosemary Weinstein, and Ronald F. Homer. *Pewter: A celebration of the craft 1200–1700.* London: Museum of London, 1989.

Invitation to Tea
> "An Invitation to Tea." Witney, Eng.: Witney Antiques, 1991.

Lamb, "Newcastle pewter and pewterers"
> Lamb, David. "Newcastle pewter and pewterers, Part 1 Pewterers—Lowes, Saddler and Hogg." *Journal of the Pewter Society*, VIII (autumn 1992).

Laughlin, *Pewter in America*, I–II
> Laughlin, Ledlie Irwin. *Pewter in America, Its Makers and Their Marks.* 2 vols. 1940. Reprint. 1969. Barre, Mass.: Barre Publishers, 1969.

———, *Pewter in America*, III
> Laughlin, Ledlie Irwin. *Pewter in America, Its Makers and Their Marks.* III. Barre, Mass.: Barre Publishers, 1971.

Law, "Williamsburg, Virginia—1994"
> Law, A. S. "Williamsburg, Virginia—1994." *Journal of the Pewter Society*, IX (autumn 1994).

Lobel, ed., *Victoria history of Oxford*
> Lobel, Mary D., ed. *The Victoria history of the county of Oxford.* V. London: Oxford University Press, 1957.

London Touch Plates I–V
> London Touch Plates I–V. Collections of The Worshipful Company of Pewterers of London, cat. nos. T1/1–5.

"Marks"
> "Marks." *Journal of the Pewter Society*, XVIII (autumn 2002).

Marx, *Silver and Pewter Recovered*
> Marx, Robert F. *Silver and Pewter Recovered from the Sunken City of Port Royal, Jamaica, May 1, 1966–March 31, 1968.* Kingston, Jamaica: Jamaica National Trust Commission, 1971.

Michaelis, *Antique Pewter of British Isles*
> Michaelis, Ronald F. *Antique Pewter of the British Isles; a brief survey of what has been made in pewter in England and the British Isles, from the time of Queen Elizabeth I to the reign of Queen Victoria.* London: G. Bell, 1955.

———, *British Pewter*
> Michaelis, Ronald F. *British Pewter.* London: Ward Lock, 1969.

———, "Decoration on English Pewterware Part II"
> Michaelis, Ronald F. "Decoration on English Pewterware, Part II: 'Punched' Ornamentation." *Antique Collector*, XXXV (February–March 1964).

———, "Decoration on English Pewterware Part III"

Michaelis, Ronald F. "Decoration on English Pewterware, Part III: 'Punched' and 'Hammered' Ornamentation." *Antique Collector,* XXXV (August–September 1964).

———, "Early Stuart Pewter"
Michaelis, Ronald F. "Early Stuart Pewter from Cotehele, Co. Cornwall." *Antique Collector,* XXX (February 1959).

———, "English Pewter Porringers—Part II"
Michaelis, Ronald F. "English Pewter Porringers: Their evolution over three hundred years. Part II." *Apollo,* L (August 1949); reprint, *Pewter Collectors Club of America Bulletin,* VII (February 1976).

———, "English Pewter Porringers—Part IV"
Michaelis, Ronald F. "English Pewter Porringers: Their evolution over three hundred years. Part IV." *Apollo,* L (October 1949); reprint, *Pewter Collectors Club of America Bulletin,* VII (August 1976).

———, "More English commemorative pewter porringers"
Michaelis, Ronald F. "More English commemorative pewter porringers." *The Magazine Antiques,* LXXVIII (July 1960).

———, *Old Domestic Base-Metal Candlesticks*
Michaelis, Ronald F. *Old Domestic Base-Metal Candlesticks from the 13th to 19th Century: Produced in Bronze, Brass, Paktong and Pewter.* Woodbridge, Eng.: Antique Collectors' Club, 1978.

———, "Pear-Shaped Pewter Flagons"
Michaelis, Ronald F. "Pear-Shaped Pewter Flagons of the 16th and 17th Centuries." *Antique Collector,* XXXII (October 1961).

———, "Royal Occasions Commemorated"
Michaelis, Ronald F. "Royal Occasions Commemorated in English Pewterware." *Antique Collector,* XXXVII (August–September 1966).

———, "Royal Portrait Spoons in Pewter"
Michaelis, R. F. "Royal Portrait Spoons in Pewter: A Mystery Unexplained." *Apollo,* LI (June 1950).

———, "'Wriggled' Decoration on Pewter"
Michaelis, Ronald F. "'Wriggled' Decoration on Pewter." *Antique Collector,* XXXIV (October 1963).

Minchin, "Pewter Flagons and Tankards"
Minchin, Cyril C. "Pewter Flagons and Tankards: Some Uncommon English Examples." *Antique Collector,* XXIII (February 1952).

———, "Some Uncommon Examples"
Minchin, Cyril C. "Some Uncommon Examples of Old English Pewter." *Antique Collector,* XLII (February–March 1971).

Montgomery, *History of American Pewter*
Montgomery, Charles F. *A History of American Pewter.* New York: Praeger Publishers, 1973.

———, "John Townsend, English Quaker"
Montgomery, Charles F. "John Townsend, English Quaker with American Connections." *Pewter Collectors Club of America Bulletin,* V (December 1964).

"More Rare Pieces from Minchin Collection"
"More Rare Pieces from the Minchin Collection." *Journal of the Pewter Society,* II (autumn 1980).

Moulson, "Development of Modern Spoon Shape"
Moulson, David. "The Development of the Modern Spoon Shape." *Journal of the Pewter Society,* XI (autumn 1998).

Mundey, "Footed Cup with Bands"
Mundey, Richard. "A Footed Cup with Bands of Cast Relief Decoration." *Journal of the Pewter Society,* III (autumn 1982).

———, "Great Dish"
Mundey, Richard. "The Great Dish." *Pewter Collectors Club of America,* VII (September 1977).

———, "Sale of Michaelis Collection"
Mundey, Richard. "The Sale of the Michaelis Collection." *Pewter Collectors Club of America,* VII (December 1974).

———, "Worshipful Company 500th Anniversary"
Mundey, Richard. "The Worshipful Company of Pewterers 500th Anniversary, 1474–1974." *Pewter Collectors Club of America,* VII (March 1978).

Mundey's Pewter Snippets
Mundey's Pewter Snippets: 600 years of Romance and Life with the Pewterers Company. [Caterham, Eng.: Peter Johnson, n.d.]

Neish, "Supreme Candlesticks"
Neish, Alex. "The Supreme Candlesticks." *Pewter Collectors Club of America Bulletin,* XI (spring 1997).

North and Spira, *Pewter at Victoria and Albert*
North, Anthony, and Andrew Spira. *Pewter at the Victoria and Albert Museum.* London: V&A Publications, 1999.

Page and Ditchfield, *Victoria History of Berkshire*
Page, William, and P. H. Ditchfield, eds. *The Victoria History of the County of Berkshire.* III. London: St. Catherine Press, 1923.

Peal, *Addenda*
Peal, Christopher A. *Addenda to More Pewter Marks.* Norwich, Eng.: Norwich Print Brokers, 1977.

———, *British Pewter and Britannia Metal*
Peal, Christopher A. *British Pewter and Britannia Metal: for pleasure and investment.* London: John Gifford, 1971.

SHORT-TITLE LIST 335

———, "18th Century British Pewter"
    Peal, Christopher A. "18th Century British Pewter." *Antique Collector,* XLIV (June–July 1973).

———, "Great collection dispersed"
    Peal, Christopher. "A great collection dispersed: Pewter assembled by R. F. Michaelis." *Antique Collector,* XLV (March 1974).

———, *More Pewter Marks*
    Peal, Christopher A. *More Pewter Marks.* Norwich, Eng.: Christopher A. Peal, 1976.

———, "Notes on Pewter Flagons"
    Peal, Christopher A. "Notes on Pewter Flagons." *Apollo,* LI (May 1959).

Peal et al., *Pewter of Great Britain*
    Peal, Christopher A. et al. *Pewter of Great Britain.* London: John Gifford, 1983.

Pewterware with Royal Associations
    Pewterware with Royal Associations: An Exhibition at Pewterers Hall from 1st to 13th July 1974. [London: The Worshipful Company of Pewterers], 1974.

Ramsey, "Notable Private Collection"
    Ramsey, L. G. G. "A Notable Private Collection—III. Fine Examples of British Pewter: The Property of Captain A. V. Sutherland-Graeme." *Connoisseur,* CXXX (September 1952).

Raymond, "American Pewter Porringers"
    Raymond, Percy E. "American Pewter Porringers with Flowered Handles." *American Collector,* XVI (November 1947).

———, "Ancestral Pewter"
    Raymond, Percy E. "Ancestral Pewter." *American Collector,* XVI (August 1947).

Ricketts, *Pewterers of London*
    Ricketts, Carl. *Pewterers of London, 1600–1900.* London: Pewter Society, 2001.

Robinson, "Big Chargers"
    Robinson, Ian. "Where Have All the Big Chargers Gone?" *Journal of the Pewter Society,* I (spring 1977).

———, "Big Chargers (Followup)"
    Robinson, Ian. "Where Have All the Big Chargers Gone? (A Followup)." *Journal of the Pewter Society,* II (autumn 1980).

———, "British Pewter in New England"
    Robinson, Ian D. "British Pewter in New England." In *Pewter of Great Britain.* Edited by Christopher A. Peal, et al. London: John Gifford, 1983.

———, "English Pewter Coronet Ear Porringers"
    Robinson, Ian D. "English Pewter Coronet Ear Porringers and Related Matters—(Who Was T.B.?)" *Journal of the Pewter Society,* XI (autumn 1998).

Scarborough, *Carolina Metalworkers*
    Scarborough, Quincy. *Carolina Metalworkers: Coppersmiths, Pewterers, Tinsmiths of North Carolina and South Carolina.* Fayetteville, N. C.: Quincy Scarborough, 1995.

Scott, *Pewter Wares from Sheffield*
    Scott, Jack L. *Pewter Wares from Sheffield.* Baltimore, Md.: Antiquary Press, 1980.

Short history of The Worshipful Company
    A short history of The Worshipful Company of Pewterers of London and a catalogue of pewterware in its possession. London: published by authority of the Court of Assistants, Pewterers Hall, 1968.

Supplementary Catalogue of Pewterware, 1979
    The Worshipful Company of Pewterers of London: Supplementary Catalogue of Pewterware, 1979. London: published by authority of the Court of Assistants, Pewterers Hall, 1978.

Sutherland-Graeme, "British Pewter in American Collections"
    Sutherland-Graeme, A. "Fine British Pewter in American Collections." *Apollo,* LXXI (January 1960).

———, "Pewter Church Flagons"
    Sutherland-Graeme, Capt. A. "Pewter Church Flagons." *Connoisseur,* CXVII (June 1946).

———, "Pewter Rose-water Dishes"
    Sutherland-Graeme, Capt. A. "Pewter Rose-water Dishes." *Connoisseur,* VC (June 1935).

———, "Some British Pewter"
    Sutherland-Graeme, A. "Some British Pewter." *The Magazine Antiques,* XLIX (June 1946).

———, "William Eden, Master-Pewterer"
    Sutherland-Graeme, Capt. A. "William Eden, Master-Pewterer." *Connoisseur,* CI (April 1938).

Thomas, *Connecticut Pewter and Pewterers*
    Thomas, John Carl. *Connecticut Pewter and Pewterers.* Hartford, Conn.: Connecticut Historical Society, 1976.

Thomas, ed. *American and British Pewter*
    Thomas, John Carl, ed. *American and British Pewter: An Historical Survey.* New York: Main Street/Universe Press, 1976.

Ullyett, *Guide for Collectors*
    Ullyett, Kenneth. *Pewter: A Guide for Collectors.* London: Frederick Muller, 1973.

Woolmer and Arkwright, *Pewter of Channel Islands*
    Woolmer, Stanley C., and Charles H. Arkwright. *Pewter of the Channel Islands.* Edinburgh, Scot.: John Bartholomew, 1973.

INDEX

Boldface page numbers refer to illustrations.

Alderson, George: maker, 114
Alderson, Thomas: maker, 110–111, 142
Ale measures, 246, **246**; inscription on, **246**. *See also* measures
Alekian, Mrs. A. E.: donor, 181
Allen, William: maker, 19
Allum, Richard: maker, 84
Antique Collectors' Guild, Richmond, Va., 28, 132–133, 226
Arlington Court, Barnstaple, Eng., 135
Ashbaugh, Mr. and Mrs. Robert L.: donors, 146
Ashberry, Philip: maker, 182
Ashburton, Eng., 74–75
Ashley River, 238–239
Asner, Norton: collector, 45, 79
Atkins, Gary: collector, 165
Atwood, Mrs. L. A.: collector, 196
Aughton, John: maker, 74
Augusta, Ga., 133
Australia, 181

Bacon, Thomas: maker, 103
Bailey family, 181
Baines, Dr. H.: collector, 72
Baldwin, Christopher: maker, 57
Baltimore, Md., 82, 93, 133
Banbury, Eng., 34
Bangs, Christopher: collector, 32, 284
Banks family, 55
Banks, Adam: maker, 55, 228
Banks, Christopher, I: maker, 55
Banks, Christopher, II: maker, 281
Banks, James, II: maker, 281
Banks, Robert: maker, 136
Banks, Thomas: maker, 136
Banks, Thomas, III: maker, 198–199
Bar fittings, 181
Barns, Blakslee: maker, 80
Baron, W.: maker, 65
Basins, 3, 5, 8, 35, 95, 132, **132**, 133, **133–134**, 196, 275. *See also* shaving basins; sugar basins; wash basins
Baskerville, John: maker, 58
Baskets, 164, **164**. *See also* sugar baskets
Bass, Daniel: maker, 82
Bassett Hall, Williamsburg, Va., 271
Basting spoons, **174–175**, 176. *See also* spoons
Batcheler, John: maker, 135
Batey, James L., and Edward Lee Spence: collectors, 238
Bayley, Edmund, 103
Bayou Bend Collection, Houston, Tex., 19
Beakers, 230, **230**, 233
Bedpans, 5, 95
Beer machines, 181
Beet, Brian: collector, 263
Bentley, William, 265
Berkeley, John Symes, 61

Berlin, Conn., 80, 82
Bermondsey Market, London, 225
Beverly, Mass., 263
Bewdley, Eng., 55, 98, 120, 136, 208, 261, 279
Biggar, Scot., 32
Billings, Samuel: maker, 188
Birch, John, & William Villers: makers, 113, 161, 281
Birmingham, Eng., 98, 113–114, 161, 164, 181, 183, 187, 194, 226, 270, 280–281, 285, 293
Bishop Blaise, 284
Bishop-Vellacott Collection, 173
Bitton, Eng., 212–214
Bivins, John, Jr., 3, 82
Blackwell, Benjamin: maker, 67
Blout, Lotta F.: collector, 285
Blout, Thomas, 135
Boardman family, 230, 232
Boardman, Thomas D. & Sherman: makers, 265, 267
Bodendick, Jacob, 15
Bonynge, Robert: maker, 132, 230
Booth, Richard: maker, 14
Boston, Mass., 91, 132, 154, 230, 267
Bottles, 79
Bourne, Sampson, II: maker, 278
Bowling Green, Ky., 3
Bowls, 8, 160, **160**, 161, 275, **275**. *See also* broth bowls; slop bowls; sugar bowls; waste bowls
Bozarth, William: collector, 58, 74
Bradshaw Collection, 48, 50, 146, 188
Bradshaw, Kenneth W.: collector, 70, 95, 151, 163, 227
Bridges, Stephen: maker, 84, 168
Bright, Allen: maker, 156, 211–212
Bristol City Museum & Art Gallery, Eng., 210
Bristol, Eng., 5, 66, 76, 87, 119, 135, 154, 156–157, 160, 210–214, 222–223, 245, 261
Britannia metal, 8, 164, 233, 259, 263, 265, 270–271, 273–274, 284–285
British Museum, London, 35–36
Broad Quay, Bristol, Eng., 76, 210
Broadbent, George: collector, 273
Brook Farm, 28–29
Brooklyn Museum, Brooklyn, N. Y., 8
Broth bowls, 161. *See also* bowls
Brown, Samuel, 154
Brunston, John Andrew: maker, 91, 215
Buckles, 8, 277, 285, **285**
Bucks Co., Pa., 154
Buell family, 19
Bullets, 277, 285
Burford, Thomas, & James Green: makers, 87, 116
Burgum & Calcott: makers, 156
Burren, Edward: maker, 218–219
Burton, William: maker, 68
Bush, Robert, & Co.: makers, 76, 223, 261–262
Bush, Robert, I: maker, 76, 119, 156, 214, 223

INDEX 337

Bush, Robert, I, & Richard Perkins: makers, 212–213
Bush, Robert, II: maker, 261–262
Bussey family, 237
Bussey, George, 236
Buttons, 8, 277, 285
Byrd, Mary Willing, 176
Byrd, William, III, 176

Cake plates, 60. *See also* plates
Campbell, Thomas C.: collector, 106, 223, 262, 285
Campkin, R. S.: collector, 124
Candlesticks, 5, **6**, 7, **10**, **11**, 145; American, 28, **28**; ball-knop type, 20, **20**–**21**, 22, **22**, 23, **23**; baroque style, **12**, 13–14, **15**, 16, **17**–**18**, 19; brass and pewter, compared, **21**; for religious use, 28; inverted baluster stem type, 26, **27**; original removable nozzles of, **14**; owners' initials on, **25**; pillar type, 19, **19**, 20; polygonal type, 25–26, **26**; relief-cast decoration on, **16**; threaded female fittings of, **14**; unimpaled arms on, **13**; with baluster stems, 7, **24**, 25
Cane-back chairs, 172
Capen, Ephraim: maker, 28–29
Carpenter, John: maker, 99, 118, 201
Carpenter, Thomas: maker, 201, 219
Carr, John: maker, 241
Carter Collection, 259
Carter's Grove, James City Co., Va., 6
Carter, A.: maker, 252–253
Carvick-Webster Collection, 136
Catherine of Bragnza, 40
Cave, John, I: maker, 34
Cave, John, II: maker, 34
Centennial exhibition, 154
Chalices, **288**, 289, 304, **305**
Chamber pots, 5, 8, 95, 277, 279–280, **280**
Chamberlain, Thomas: maker, 125–127, 131, 138–140, 142
Chandlee, Goldsmith: maker, 287
Chandler, Edward, 104
Chargers, 38. *See also* dishes
Charleston, S. C., 108, 239
Charlestown, R. I., 151
Cheltenham Art Gallery and Museum, Cheltenham, Eng., 50
Chester, Eng., 55, 57
Chopin capacity, 248
Church of Saint Mark, Englefield, Eng., 187
Church of Saint Nicholas, Stockholm, Sweden, 13
Church of Saint Saviour's, York, Eng., 295
Churchill, John, 154
Circular dishes, 142. *See also* dishes
Cleeve, Alexander, I: maker, 68, 300
Cleeve, Alexander, II: maker, 95, 97
Cleeve, Richard: maker, 95
Coffee biggins, 270
Coffeepot stands, **263**, 271, **271**
Coffeepots, 8, 159, 267, **268**, 269, **269**, 270–271, **271**; interior construction of, **270**; linen bag of, 270
Cogan, Lillian Blankley: collector, 176
Colanders, 161, **161**
Coldwell, George: maker, 180, 284–285
Coldwell, W.: maker, 284–285
Collections. *See* individual listings

Collectors. *See* individual names
Collier, Joseph, and Timothy Blackwell: makers, 151
Colwell, Eng., 211–212
Commode pots, 8, 280–281, **281**; owner's initials on, **280**
Communion cups, 301, **301**–302, 303. *See also* cups
Communion tokens, 303, **303**, 304, **304**
Company of Plumbers, Pewterers, Glaziers, and Painters, 26, 176
Compton, Thomas: maker, 112, 143
Compton, Thomas & Townsend: makers, 178
Condiment dishes, **162**, 163; Hebrew letters on, **163**. *See also* dishes
Connecticut Courant, 159
Connecticut Historical Society, 160
Connecticut River Valley, 43, 191
Coon, Mrs. Owen L.: donor, 253, 265, 271
Cooper Collection, 25
Cooper, Benjamin: maker, 13, 25–26
Cooper, R. W.: collector, 38
Copley, John Singleton, 283
Cordial pots, 257
Corporation of Trinity House, Tower Hill, Eng., 143
Cotehele House, Ashburton, Eng., 75
Cotterell, Howard Herschel: collector, 3, 50, 234, 236–237, 244, 248–249, 295
Coventry, Eng., 188
Cox, Stephen: maker, 156
Crane, John Carruthers: maker, 279–280
Cranston, R. I., 267, 275
Cream ewers, **254**, 255, 273, **273**, 275. *See also* ewers
Cream jugs, 255, 271–272, **272**, 273–274, **274**, 275
Cromwell, 46
Croshaw, Major Joseph, 5
Cups, 196, 230, **230**. *See also* communion cups; race cups; two-handled cups; wine cups
Curtis, George W., 28
Curtis, James: maker, 76, 223

Daily Journal, 196
Dana, Charles A., 28
Dandridge family, 114
Danforth family, 91, 223, 230
Danforth, John: maker, 159
Danforth, Joseph, I: maker, 159, 223
Danforth, Joseph, II: maker, 133
Danforth, Samuel: maker, 230
Danforth, Thomas, II: maker, 159
Danforth, Thomas, III: maker, 80, 82, 91
Danforth, Thomas, IV: maker, 133
de Lamerie, Paul, 219
de Navarro Collection, 259, 278
de Navarro, Antonio: collector, 50
de Sainte Croix, Jean. *See* John de St. Croix
de St. Croix, John: maker, 251–252
Dean, M. B.: collector, 103
Decorative Arts & History Museum of the National Museum of Ireland, Dublin, Ireland, 32
Deep plates, 89. *See also* plates
Deming, Gordon and Genevieve: collectors, 263, 270
Deming, Oliver and Marion: collectors, 102
Deptford, Eng., 144

338 PEWTER AT COLONIAL WILLIAMSBURG

Derby, Thomas S.: maker, 133
Dessert dishes, 162, **162**, 163; coat of arms on, **163**; Hebrew letters on, **163**. *See also* dishes
Dessert spoons, 173. *See also* spoons
Devereux, Edward, 61
Deyerle, Dr. and Mrs. Henry P.: collectors, 106
Deyerle, Henry P.: collector, 287
Dinner plates, 95, 98, 101, 111, 139, 142. *See also* plates
Dinner services, 95, **96**, 116
Dishes, 3, 5–8, 30, 31, 48, 75, 95–96, 98–99, 101, 132, 194, 196, **xii**; border and owner's initials on, **72**; broad-rim type, 37, **37**, 38, **39**, 40, **41**, 42–43, 48; coat of arms and crest on, **131**; coat of arms on, **38**, **61**, **132**; crest on, **96–97**, **99**, **117**; fancy-rim type, 71, 116, **117**, 124, **124**, 127, **127**, **130**, 131–132; for religious use, 32, 72, 289, 301, **302**; inscription on, **42**; inset boss with enamels on, **32**; later owner's initials on, **56**; lion supporter on, **40**; multiple-reed type, 51, **51–52**, 53, **53**, 54, **54**, 55, **55**, 56–57, **57**, 58, **58**, 59, **59**, 60, **60**, 61, **61**, 62, **62**, 71; narrow-rim type, 62; owner's initials and date on, **56**, **76**; owner's initials and decoration on, **36**; owner's initials on, **40**, **42**, **56**, **59**, **72**, **76**; plain-rim type, 35, 71, 94–96, **96**, 97, **97**, 98, **98**, 99, 106, **107**, 116; single-bead type, 71, **71**, 72, 73, 74, **74**, 75, **75**, 76–77, **77–78**, 79–80, **81**, 82, **83**, 116; sunburst and owner's initials on, **38**; underside of, **73**; with central bosses, 32, **32–33**, 34, 36, **36**; with royal portraits, 191. *See also* chargers; circular dishes; condiment dishes; dessert dishes; fish strainer and dishes; great dishes; hot-water dishes; oval dishes; rosewater dishes; strawberry dishes
Dixon, Charles: maker, 270
Dixon, James: maker, 271
Dixon, James, & Son: makers, 271
Dolbeare family, 75
Dolbeare, Edmund: maker, 75
Dolbeare, John: maker, 74–75
Dole, Erasmus: maker, 66
Doncaster, S. C., 239
Donne, John: maker, 190–191, 195–196
Donors. *See* individual names
Dougal, Prof. D.: collector, 32
Drake family, 45
Drake, Sir Francis, 45
Drinkwater, Thomas: maker, 40
Dublin, Ireland, 298
Duffield, Peter: maker, 187
Duncan, Eleanor L., 103
Duncumb family, 261
Duncumb, John: maker, 98, 194
Duncumb, Stynt: maker, 120
Dunham, Rufus: maker, 28
Dunn, I. Malcolm: collector, 193
Durand, James: maker, 46
Durand, Jonas, I: maker, 61, 113
Durand, Jonas, II: maker, 113, 129
Durham Co., Eng., 16
Dustin, Hannah, 191–192

Eddon, William: maker, 191, 196, 202–203, 206, 228
Eden, William. *See* William Eddon
Edgar, Curtis, & Co.: makers, 157–158, 222–223
Edgar, Preston, I: maker, 76, 223
Edgcumbe family, 13–14, 75

Edgcumbe, Piers, 14
Edinburgh, Scot., 32, 111, 301
Eggleston, Jacob: maker, 80, 82, 133
Ekama, Mrs. Catherine Aafje, 177
Ellis, David Walter: collector, 256
Ellis, Samuel, I: maker, 87, 103, 108, 161, 257–258
Ellis, Samuel, II: maker, 87, 108, 129
Ellwood, William, I: maker, 58
Englefield, Eng., 187
Everett, Edward: maker, 47
Ewers, 32. *See also* cream ewers
Exeter, Eng., 204

Farmington, Conn., 133
Fasson & Son: makers, 87
Fasson & Sons: makers, 87
Fasson, John, II: maker, 87
Fasson, Thomas: maker, 87
Fasson, William: maker, 242, 244
Fayetteville, N. C., 80, 82, 133
Federal Procession, 257
Feeshel, Hanna, 106
Felix Farley's Bristol Journal, 119
Fish strainer and dishes, 106, 108, **108**, 109, **109**; cipher on, **109**. *See also* dishes
Fitzwilliam Museum, Cambridge, Eng., 50, 259, 278
Flagons, 5, 8, 196, 201, **288**, 289, **291–292**, 296; acorn type, **294**, 295; American, 8, 289, 304, **305**; beefeater type, 292, **292**, 293; Birmingham type, **293**; Charles I type, **291**; for religious use, 201, 209; gild type, 246; Irish, 8, 298, **299**, 300; owner's crest and motto on, **291**; owner's trade sticker on, **295**; public and domestic use of, 289–290, **290**, 291; Scottish, 8, 301, **302**, 303; spire type, 295–297, **297**, 298, **298**; tavern use of, 298, **298**; Yorkshire makers of, 294; Yorkshire type, **293**
Flasks, 231, **231**, 277
Fletcher, Richard: maker, 94–95
Folger, Timothy, 283
Ford, Thomas: maker, 34
Fort Crailo, Greenbush, N. Y., 103
Fothergill, M., & Sons: makers, 245
Foxall, F. H.: collector, 60, 114
Franklin, J. R.: collector, 165, 180, 295
French plating, 267
Frewen, Henry: maker, 219
Froggart, Coldwell & Lean: makers, 285
Fryers, John: maker, 239
Fuller, Margaret, 28
Funnels, 232, **232**, 277

Gadd Collection, 13
Gallon (OEWS), 239, 242, 246
Gardiner, Avis and Rockwell, 287; collectors, 161, 206, 221, 284
Gebelein, George C.: collector, 213–214, 257
General Assembly of Pennsylvania, 215
Geradin & Watson: makers, 222, 246
Germany, 215
Gill (OEWS), 242, 244
Gill size, 236
Glanville family, 13–14

INDEX 339

Glanville, Mary, 14
Glanville, Sir John, 14
Glen-Sanders Collection, 76
Glen-Sanders families, 76
Glennore Company, 267, 275
Glover, Mr. and Mrs. Price, III: donors, 160
Going, Richard: maker, 76, 154, 156, 160, 210–211
Golden Hind, 45
Gordon Collection, 25
Gordon, Kenneth G.: collector, 297
Governor's Palace, Williamsburg, Va., 61, 79, 108, 114
Graham, John M., III: collector, 8, 14
Grant, Edward: maker, 66
Grant, John L.: collector, 26, 72
Granville family, 204
Granville, George. *See* George Grenfell
Gray, Thomas A.: donor, 82
Great dishes, 38. *See also* dishes
Great Fire of London, 3, 38
Green, Thomas: maker, 132
Green, William Sandys: maker, 138
Greenbank family, 54–55, 59
Greenbank, John, II: maker, 54–55, 59, 65
Greenbank, William, II: maker, 65, 95
Greene, John, 283
Greenwich Hospital, Greenwich, Eng., 173
Gregory, Edward: maker, 76
Grenfell, George: maker, 204
Grenfell, George, & Co.: makers, 204
Griffith, John: maker, 87
Grigsby, Lindsay C.: collector, 165
Griswold, Giles: maker, 133
Griswold, Sylvester: maker, 133
Grossographia, 135
Grunwin, Richard: maker, 108
Gwynne family, 290

Half gallon (OEWS), 238–239, 242
Half gill (OEWS), 244
Half pint (OEWS), 234, 241, 244
Half-pint size, 252
Hall, William: maker, 68
Hallowell, Benjamin, 283
Hamlin, Samuel: maker, 159, 223
Hamlin, Samuel E.: maker, 159
Hammerton, Henry: maker, 156, 219
Hampton Court Palace, 35, 150
Hancock, John, 283
Harrison, John: maker, 295
Harrold family, 154
Hartford, Conn., 133, 223, 230–232, 265
Harthill Church, Yorkshire, Eng., 15
Harvey, Edmund: maker, 209
Hasselberg, Abraham: maker, 91, 215
Haverhill, Mass., 191
Haward, Thomas: maker, 42–43, 48
Hawthorne, Nathaniel, 28
Healey, Frances M.: collector, 59
Heaney, John: maker, 298, 300

Henrietta Maria, 168
Henry Francis du Pont Winterthur Museum, Winterthur, Del., 28
Herrick family, 154
Heyne, Johann Christoph: maker, 8, 28, 304
Heyrich, David: maker, 169
Hitchins, William, III: maker, 282–283
Hitchman, James: maker, 86
Hitchman, Robert: maker, 204
Hoffman, Mrs. Henry A.: collector, 159
Hogarth, William, 9
Hole, Gilbert L. D.: collector, 25
Holyoke, John: maker, 132
Homer Collection, 36
Hooper, Robert, 283
Hornsby, Peter R. G.: donor, 303–304
Hot-water dishes, 114, **115**, 161. *See also* dishes
Hot-water plates, 113, **113**, 114; coat of arms on, **113**. *See also* plates
Housemarks, 236
Hudson's Bay Company, 95
Hurstwaight, William: maker, 46
Hyman, John A.: donor, 82, 231

Independence National Historical Park, Philadelphia, Pa., 108
Inglis, Jonathan: maker, 42
Ingole, Daniel: maker, 43, 56
Ingraham, Mrs. James E.: collector, 180
Ingram & Hunt. *See* Ingram, John, II, & Charles Hunt
Ingram, John, II, & Charles Hunt: makers, 156, 208, 261, 285
Inkstands, 8, 95, 282, **282**, 283
Irvin, Mary Kayhoe: donor, 3
Isher Collection, 50
Isher, A. T.: collector, 38, 45, 48
Isher, Bertram: collector, 62, 295

Jackson, Jonathan: maker, 230
Jackson, Samuel: maker, 38
Jacobs, Carl: collector, 91, 242, 272
Jacobs, Carl and Celia: collectors, 8, 20, 99, 101, 129
Jaeger Collection, 36
Jaeger, Frederick: collector, 160
Janney, John Jay, 5
Jedburgh, Scot., 301
Jersey, Channel Islands, 251–252
Jewish Museum of London, 163
Johnson, Charles: maker, 101
Johnson, Dr. and Mrs. S. Harris, III: collectors, 133
Johnson, Jehiel: maker, 133
Jones, Gershom: maker, 158–159
Joseph, Henry: maker, 87, 144–145, 149, 160, 257, 297
Jugs, 232–233, **233**
Jupe, John: maker, 99

Kashden, Michael Allen: collector, 145, 233, 267
Kauffman, Henry J.: collector, 3, 153
Kayhoe Collection, 3
Kayhoe, William F., 28, 132; collector, 226
Keil, H. W.: collector, 65, 279
Kelk, Nicholas: maker, 68
Kilbourn, Samuel: maker, 82, 133

Kindig, Joe, Jr.: collector, 231
King Charles I, 8, 32, 225
King Charles II, 40, 45–46
King George, 196
King George III, 177, 180
King George IV, 110, 142
King Henry VII, 236, 239
King Henry VIII, 234
King James I, 32, 225–226
King James II, 190
King James VI of Scotland, 32
King William and Queen Mary, 62
King William III, 62, 154, 168, 191, 236, 239; 168
King's Lynn, Eng., 291
King, Richard: maker, 87, 120
King, Richard, II: maker, 131
King, Thomas: maker, 62
Kingston Museum and Heritage Service, Kingston, Eng., 111
Kingston, N. Y., 285
Kydd, P. G.: collector, 226

Lamps, 11, 28–29, **29**
Lancaster, Pa., 8, 28, 304
Lane, I. O.: collector, 161
Langford, John, I: maker, 153, 160
Langford, John, II: maker, 160
Lansing, Maria, 76
Lea, Francis: maker, 13
Leach, Thomas: maker, 176
Leapage, Edward, I: maker, 60, 137
Leapage, Edward, II: maker, 137
Lear Collection, 21
Lee, Phillip Ludwell, 103
Lee, William: collector, 295
Leeds Pottery, Leeds, Eng., 284
Lewis, Thomas, 283
Lightner, George: maker, 93
Lillehammer, Norway, 25
Linen marks, 237
Litchfield, Conn., 19, 133, 159
Little Collection, 45
Little, John, 219
Loudoun Co., Va., 5
Love touch: maker, 91, 215
Lowes, George: maker, 26, 175–176
Lucas, Francis, I: maker, 14
Ludlow Castle, Ludlow, Eng., 32

Mailhaugen Open Air Museum, Lillehammer, Norway, 25–26
Makers: *American:* Barns, Blakslee, 80; Bass, Daniel, 82; Boardman, Thomas D. & Sherman, 265, 267; Bonynge, Robert, 132, 230; Brunston, John Andrew, 91, 215; Capen, Ephraim, 28–29; Chandlee, Goldsmith, 287; Coldwell, George, 180, 284–285; Danforth, John, 159; Danforth, Joseph, I, 159, 223; Danforth, Joseph, II, 133; Danforth, Samuel, 230; Danforth, Thomas, II, 159; Danforth, Thomas, III, 80, 82, 91; Danforth, Thomas, IV, 133; Derby, Thomas S., 133; Dolbeare, Edmund, 75; Dunham, Rufus, 28; Eggleston, Jacob, 80, 82, 133; Fryers, John, 239; Green, Thomas, 132; Griswold, Giles, 133; Griswold, Sylvester, 133; Hamlin, Samuel, 159, 223; Hamlin, Samuel E., 159; Hasselberg, Abraham, 91, 215; Heyne, Johann Christoph, 8, 28, 304; Holyoke, John, 132; Jackson, Jonathan, 230; Johnson, Jehiel, 133; Jones, Gershom, 158–159; Kilbourn, Samuel, 82, 133; Lightner, George, 93; Love touch, 91, 215; Miller, Josiah, 285; Molineux, George, 29; North, John, and Isaiah Rowe, 133; Nott, William, 133; Olcott, James White, 133; Porter, James, 133; Richardson, George, 267, 275; Semper Eadem makers, 132; Simpkins, Thomas, 132; Skinner, John, 132; Stedmen, Simeon, 231–232; Weekes, James, 28; Weekes, James, & Co., 28; Whitmore, Jacob, 82, 91, 159; Will, John, I, 214–215, 273; Will, William, 215, 280; Willett, Edward, 102; Yale, Burrage, 267; Yale, William and Samuel, 133; *English:* Allum, Richard, 84; Aughton, John, 74; Baron, W., 65; Blackwell, Benjamin, 67; Roe, Dx., 53; *English provincial:* Ashberry, Philip (Sheffield), 182; Baldwin, Christopher (Wigan), 57; Banks, Adam (Milngate and Wigan), 55, 228; Banks, Christopher, I (Bewdley), 55; Banks, Christopher, II (Bewdley), 281; Banks, James, II (Bewdley), 281; Banks, Robert (Bewdley), 136; Banks, Thomas (Wigan), 136; Banks, Thomas, III (Wigan), 198–199; Batcheler, John (Bristol), 135; Billings, Samuel (Coventry), 188; Birch, John, & William Villers (Birmingham), 113, 161, 281; Booth, Richard (York), 14; Bourne, Sampson, II (Worcester), 278; Bright, Allen (Bristol and Colwell), 156, 211–212; Burgum & Calcott (Bristol), 156; Burren, Edward (Reading), 218–219; Bush, Robert, & Co. (Bristol), 76, 223, 261–262; Bush, Robert, I (Bristol and Bitton), 76, 119, 156, 214, 223; Bush, Robert, I, & Richard Perkins (Bristol and Bitton), 212–213; Bush, Robert, II (Bristol), 261–262; Carter, A. (West Country), 252–253; Cave, John, I (Banbury), 34; Cave, John, II (Banbury), 34; Coldwell, W. (Sheffield), 284–285; Cox, Stephen (Bristol), 156; Crane, John Carruthers (Bewdley), 279–280; Curtis, James (Bristol), 76, 223; Dixon, Charles (Sheffield), 270; Dixon, James (Sheffield), 271; Dixon, James, & Son (Sheffield), 271; Dolbeare, John (Ashburton), 74–75; Dole, Erasmus (Bristol), 66; Duncumb, John (Birmingham and Wribbenhall), 98, 194; Duncumb, Stynt (Bewdley), 120; Edgar, Curtis & Co. (Bristol), 157–158, 222–223; Edgar, Preston, I (Bristol), 76, 223; Ford, Thomas (Wigan), 34; Fothergill, M., & Sons (Bristol), 245; Frewen, Henry (Reading), 219; Froggart, Coldwell & Lean (Sheffield), 285; Going, Richard (Bristol), 76, 154, 156, 160, 210–211; Greenbank, John, II (Worcester), 54–55, 59, 65; Greenbank, William, II (Worcester), 65, 95; Gregory, Edward (Bristol), 76; Griffith, John (Bristol), 87; Harrison, John (York), 295; Harvey, Edmund (Stockton-on-Tees), 209; Ingram, John, II, & Charles Hunt (Bewdley, Birmingham, and Wribbenhall), 156, 208, 261, 285; Lowes, George (Newcastle), 26, 175–176; Lucas, Francis, I (York), 14; Pennington, John (Tavistock), 85; Sanders, Simon (Bideford), 169; Sandler, Robert (Newcastle), 26; Seegood, Francis (Norwich or King's Lynn), 291; Terry, Leonard (York), 294; Trapp, John, II (Worcester), 278; Tutin, William (Birmingham), 285; Vickers, James (Sheffield), 164, 232–233, 259, 262–263, 265, 269–270, 273; Watson, Jacob (Newcastle), 26, 176; Wilkinson, Daniel Holy, & Co. (Sheffield), 164; Wood, William, II (Birmingham), 98, 187, 194–195, 226–227, 280, 293–294; Yates, John (Birmingham), 181, 183; Yates, John, Thomas Rawlins Birch & Lucas Spooner (Birmingham), 114, 280; Yates, Thomas (Birmingham), 181; *Irish:* Heaney, John, 298, 300; *Jersey, Channel Islands:* de St. Croix, John, 251–252; *London:* Alderson, George, 114; Alderson, Thomas, 110–111, 142; Allen, William, 19; Bacon, Thomas, 103; Baskerville, John, 58; Bridges, Stephen, 84, 168; Burford, Thomas, & James Green, 87, 116; Burton, William, 68; Carpenter, John, 99, 118, 201; Carpenter, Thomas, 201, 219; Carr, John, 241;

Makers *(continued)*
  Chamberlain, Thomas, 125–127, 131, 138–140, 142; Cleeve, Alexander, I, 68, 300; Cleeve, Alexander, II, 95, 97; Cleeve, Richard, 95; Collier, Joseph, and Timothy Blackwell, 151; Compton, Thomas, 112, 143; Compton, Thomas & Townsend, 178; Cooper, Benjamin, 13, 25–26; de St. Croix, John, 251–252; Donne, John, 190–191, 195–196; Drinkwater, Thomas, 40; Duffield, Peter, 187; Durand, James, 46; Durand, Jonas, I, 61, 113; Durand, Jonas, II, 113, 129; Eddon, William, 191, 196, 202–203, 206, 228; Ellis, Samuel, I, 87, 103, 108, 161, 257–258; Ellis, Samuel, II, 87, 108, 129; Ellwood, William, I, 58; Everett, Edward, 47; Fasson & Son, 87; Fasson & Sons, 87; Fasson, John, II, 87; Fasson, Thomas, 87; Fasson, William, 242, 244; Fletcher, Richard, 94–95; Geradin & Watson, 222, 246; Grant, Edward, 66; Green, William Sandys, 138; Grenfell, George, 204; Grenfell, George, & Co., 204; Grunwin, Richard, 108; Hall, William, 68; Hammerton, Henry, 156, 219; Haward, Thomas, 42–43, 48; Heyrich, David, 169; Hitchins, William, III, 282–283; Hitchman, James, 86; Hitchman, Robert, 204; Hurstwaight, William, 46; Inglis, Jonathan, 42; Ingole, Daniel, 43, 56; Jackson, Samuel, 38; Johnson, Charles, 101; Joseph, Henry, 87, 144–145, 149, 160, 257, 297; Jupe, John, 99; Kelk, Nicholas, 68; King, Richard, 87, 120; King, Richard, II, 131; King, Thomas, 62; Langford, John, I, 153, 160; Langford, John, II, 160; Lea, Francis, 13; Leach, Thomas, 176; Leapage, Edward, I, 60, 137; Leapage, Edward, II, 137; Marsh, Ralph, 34; Marten, Robert, 292; Matthews, Thomas, 241; Matthews, William, 48; Maxted, Henry, 132; Munday, Thomas, 278; Munden, William, and Edmund Grave, 246; Nicholson, Robert, 82, 162–163; Perchard, Hellier, 101, 251, 279, 401; Pickard, Joseph, 6; Pitt, Richard, 259, 261; Pitt, Richard, & Edward Dadley, 105; Pitt, Richard, & John Floyd, 204; Porteus, Robert & Thomas, 120; Quick, Edward, 206, 271; Quick, Hugh, 13–14, 16, 19, 25, 145; Quick, John, 152; Raper, Christopher, 43; Ridding, Thomas, 99, 101; Sandys, William, 70; Seare, Robert, 168; Shakle, Thomas, 66–67; Shorey, John, I, 22, 70–72; Shorey, John, II, 72; Smith, John, 197; Smith, Richard, 54, 65; Spackman, James, 66; Spackman, James, and Edward Grant, 296; Spackman, Joseph, 163, 283; Spackman, Joseph & James, 105; Spackman, Joseph, & Co., 112, 119; Spencer, Thomas, 75; Stafford, George, 120; Stribblehill, John, 135–136; Stribblehill, Thomas, II, 136; Swanson, Thomas, 87; Taudin, James, I, 45–46; Taylor, Timothy, 176; Thomas, John, 199; Tisoe, James, 124; Townsend, John, 76–77, 89, 104, 206, 220–221; Townsend, John, & Co., 77; Townsend, John, & Robert Reynolds, 77, 109; Townsend, John, & Thomas Giffin, 77, 106; Townsend, John, and Thomas Compton, 76–77, 79–80, 108, 206; Townsend, Joseph, 257–259; Trapp, John, 25–26; Ubly, Edward, 256; Vaughan, John, 176–177; Waite, John, 154; Watson, Jacob, 26, 176; Watts, John, 114; Webb, Richard, 60; White, Richard, 51; Wiggin, Henry, 65; Withebed, Richard, 13; Wood, Edward, 147; Wyatt, John, 173; Wynne, John, 106; *Scottish:* Rebate, John, 32; Scott, William, 111; Simpson, Thomas, 301; Weir, Richard, 32
Marsh, Ralph: maker, 34
Marshall Field's, 271
Marten, Robert: maker, 292
Martin's Hundred, James City Co., Va., 5
Mary Rose, 234
Mason Collection, 291
Mather, Cotton, 192
Matthew's First Bristol Directory, 223
Matthews, Thomas: maker, 241

Matthews, William: maker, 48
Maxted, Henry: maker, 132
Mays, G. E.: collector, 117
Mazarines, 108
McCarl, Mr. and Mrs. Foster, Jr.: donors, 82, 133, 215, 223, 230, 267, 275, 304
McMahon, George: collector, 148
Measures, 95, 181, 185; baluster type, 245, **245**; baluster type with bud thumb piece, 238, **238**, 239, **240**, 241–242; baluster type with double-volute thumb piece, 239, 242, **243**, 244; baluster type with hammerhead thumb piece, 234, **234–235**, 236–237; bud type, 236; dealer's label on, **244**; decorated hinge pin on, **251**; Guernsey, **250**, 252–253; hammerhead type, 236, 238; haystack type, 245, **245**; initials on, **245**; Jersey, **250**, 251–252; letter about, **236–237**; owner's initials on, **241**, **248–249**, **251**; owners' initials on, 241–242; Scottish, 8, **247**, 248, **248**, 249; trade label on, **248–249**. *See also* ale measures
Meriden, Conn., 133
Michaelis Collection, 147
Michaelis, Ronald F.: collector, 13, 163, 165, 169, 201, 239
Middelkoop, Franz: collector, 114
Middletown, Conn., 80, 82, 91, 133, 159, 223
Miller family, 285, 287
Miller, Josiah: maker, 285
Milngate, Eng., 55
Minchin Collection, 162, 218
Minchin, Cyril C.: collector, 13, 25, 63, 187, 234, 256, 295
Mitchell, Richard, 103
Molds, 3; for basins, **3**; for candles, 277; for dishes, **3**; for spoons, **3**
Molineux, George: maker, 29
Monamy, Peter, 76, 210
Montgomery, Charles F.: donor, 102
Morris House, Stamford, Conn., 91
Moulson, David S.: collector, 36, 273–274, 298, 301
Mount Edgcumbe, Eng., 142
Mount Vernon, Alexandria, Va., 96
Mugs, 5, 7–8, 181, **184**, 185, 215, 218, **218**, 219, **219**, 220, **220**, 221, **221**, 222, **222**, 223, **224**; finishing and engraving on, 220; for religious use, 209; owners' initials on, **218**; skimming marks on, 220
Munday, Thomas: maker, 278
Munden, William, and Edmund Grave: makers, 246
Mundey Collection, 259
Mundey, Richard: collector, 35, 38, 50, 62, 114, 150, 225, 259, 271, 297, 301, 303
Murdoch, Mr. and Mrs. William H., Jr.: collectors, 14, 80
Murphy, Katharine Prentis: collector, 19
Museum of Applied Art, Oslo, Norway, 16
Museum of Barnstaple and North Devon, Barnstaple, Eng., 85
Museum of British Pewter, Harvard House, Stratford-upon-Avon, Eng., 25, 32, 35, 218–219
Museum of Fine Arts, Boston, Mass., 208
Museum of London, 8, 35, 45
Museum of Scotland, Edinburgh, Scot., 32
Museum of Southern Decorative Arts, Winston-Salem, N. C., 287
Mutchkin capacity, 249
Myers, Louis G.: collector, 28, 91, 239

Neish Collection, 25, 32, 35, 108, 218
New England, 20, 154, 158, 223, 231, 239, 285, 287

New Hampshire Historical Society, Concord, N. H., 191
New York, 285, 287
New York Daily Advertiser, 180
New York, N. Y., 28–29, 180, 214–215, 273, 284–285
New-York Historical Society, New York, N. Y., 257
Newcastle Courant, 26, 176
Newcastle, Eng., 26, 175–176
Newport, R. I., 239
Niantic Narragansett tribe, 151
Nichols, Melville T.: collector, 103
Nicholson, Gov. Francis, 192
Nicholson, Robert: maker, 82, 162–163
Nims family, 43
Noggin size, 252
Norborne, Baron de Botetourt, 61, 108
Norborne, Elizabeth, 61
Nordic Museum, Stockholm, Sweden, 13
North Carolina, 3, 79
North Carolina Intelligencer, 82
North, John, and Isaiah Rowe: makers, 133
Norway, 13, 19, 26
Norwegian Museum of Cultural History, Oslo, Norway, 19
Norwich Worsted Weavers' Company, 246
Norwich, Eng., 291
Nott, William: maker, 133
Nuremberg, Germany, 72
Nutmeg graters, 233, 284

O'Connor Collection, 300
Observer, 110
Olcott, J. W. *See* Olcott, James White
Olcott, James White: maker, 133
Order of the Garter, 99
Organ pipes, 277
Oslo, Norway, 19
Oval dishes, 111, 116, **117**, 139, 142. *See also* dishes
Oxford Co., Maine, 242

Palmiter, Robert H.: collector, 76
Pannett, Mrs. Luther: collector, 103
Papboats, 8, 282, **282**
Parish Church of Saint Mary, Martlesham, Eng., 160
Patens, 135, 289, 296, **296**, 297
Pavey, Mr. and Mrs. Jess: donors, 74
Peabody Essex Museum, Salem, Mass., 154
Peal Collection, 26, 168, 188, 246
Peal, Christopher, A.: collector, 295
Pennington, John: maker, 85
Pennsbury, Pa., 154
Perchard, Hellier: maker, 101, 251, 279, 401
Perrin, Mr. and Mrs. Gordon: collectors, 149
Pewter Collectors Club of America, 28, 132
Pewterers' Company, 3, 20, 34, 36, 45–46, 50, 54, 62, 111, 144, 151–152, 176, 187, 204, 219, 227–229, 251, 297
Pewterers' Hall, London, 3, 16, 38, 169, 251
Philadelphia, Pa., 28, 79–80, 91, 108, 154, 215, 259, 261, 272, 280
Pickard, Joseph: maker, 6
Pilgrim Hall Museum, Plymouth, Mass., 20
Pint (OEWS), 241, 244–245

Pint size, 253
Pipes, 8, **276**, 283, **283**, 284
Pitt, Richard: maker, 259, 261
Pitt, Richard, & Edward Dadley: makers, 105
Pitt, Richard, & John Floyd: makers, 204
Plates, 1, 3, 5, 7–8, **30**, 31, 35, 79, 95–96, 98–99, 101, 132, 135, 194, 196; arms on, **45**, **124**; broad-rim type, 37, 43, 44, 45–46, **46**, 47, **47**, 48, **49**, 50, **50**, 95; coat of arms on, **48**, **82**, **95**, **120**, **131**; crest on, **43**, **48**, **96**, **99**, **120**, **127**, **129**; English royals arms on, **45**; fancy-rim type, 70–71, 116, **116**, 120, **121–123**, 124–125, **125**, 126, **127–128**, 129, **130**, 131; for religious use, 300, **300**; multiple-reed type, 51, 62, **63–64**, 65–67, **67**, 68, **69**, 70–71, 95; narrow-rim type, 62; owner's cipher on, **103**; owner's initial on, **101**; owner's initials and tree on, **89**; owner's initials on, **68**, **129**; plain-rim type, 71, 94, **94**, 95–96, **96**, 99, 100, **101**, 101, 102, **102**, 103–104, **104**, 105, **105**, 106, 116; probable owner's stamp on, **89**; single-bead type, 5, 71, 82, 84, **84**, 85, **85**, 86, **86**, 87, **88**, 89, 90, 91, 92, 93, **93**, 116. *See also* cake plates; deep plates; dinner plates; hot-water plates; scale plates; soup plates; spice plates
Platters, 6, 110, **110**, 111–112, **112**, 118, **118**, 119, **119**; coat of arms on, **118**; crest on, **118**, **120**; royal monogram on, **111**
Pleydell-Bouverie, David: donor, 54, 112
Plymouth, Mass., 285
Porringers, 5, **5**, 6, 8, 79, 95, 150, **150**, 151–152, **152**, 155, 156–157, **157**; American, 158, **158**, 159; commemorative, 153, **153**, 154; for religious use, 209
Port Collection, 173, 177
Port Royal, Jamaica, 8, 25, 151, 168
Porter, James: maker, 133
Porteus, Robert & Thomas: makers, 120
Portsmouth, Eng., 234
Pot size, 251–252
Poughkeepsie, N. Y., 28
Prince Charles, 219
Prince of Wales, 8, 225–226
Princess Weuquesh, 151
Proud, William, Daniel and Samuel, 159
Providence, R. I., 151, 158, 223, 267
Prussia, 102
Punch ladles, 231–232, **232**
Punch strainers, 7, 231, **231**

Quart (OEWS), 241, 244–245
Quart size, 251, 253
Queen Anne, 168–169, 196, 220, 236, 239
Queen Charlotte, 177
Queen Elizabeth I, 45
Queen Mary, 168
Quick, Edward: maker, 206, 271
Quick, Hugh: maker, 13–14, 16, 19, 25, 145
Quick, John: maker, 152
Quigley Collection, 273

Race cups, 229, **229**; name and picture of a castle on, **229**. *See also* cups
Ragout spoons, 176. *See also* spoons
Rake's Progress, A, 9
Raper, Christopher: maker, 43
Raymond, Dr. Percy E.: collector, 8, 40, 43, 51, 56–57, 59, 65–66, 87, 93, 98–99, 103, 106, 111–113, 131, 148, 156–159, 191, 203, 221–223, 232,

Raymond, Dr. Percy E. *(continued)*
    241–242, 258, 287, 297; donor, 252
Reading, Eng., 218–219
Rebate, John: maker, 32
Rhode Island Historical Society, Providence, R. I., 151
Richards family, 154
Richardson, George: maker, 267, 275
Richardson, John F.: collector, 294
Richardson, Major John: collector, 234, 236–237
Richmond, Va., 28, 133
Ridding, Thomas: maker, 99, 101
Robinson, Ian D.: collector, 117
Rockefeller, John D., III, Fund, Inc.: donor, 271
Rocky Hill, Conn., 133
Roe, Dx.: maker, 53
Roger Williams Park Museum, Providence, R. I., 151
Rosewater dishes, 32. *See also* dishes
Rowland, Miss Anne: donor, 80
Royal Institution of Cornwall, Truro, Eng., 234

Sackville family, 139
Saffron pots, 257
Saint Nicholas Church, Oxfordshire, Eng., 295–297
Salem, Mass., 263
Salts, 5, 8, 95, 111, 135, 145, **145**, 146, **146**, 147, **147**, 148, **148**, 149; for religious use, 209
Salvers, 8, 135, **135**, 136, **136**, 137, **137**
Sanders, Robert, 76
Sanders, Simon: maker, 169
Sandler, Robert: maker, 26
Sands, John O.: donor, 178
Sandys, William: maker, 70
Sauce ladles, 111, 181, **182–183**
Sauceboats, 8, 111, 144, **144**
Saucers, 5, 35, **35**, 75, 93, **93**, **105**, 106
Scale plates, 60. *See also* plates
Scollay, John, 283
Scotia, N. Y., 76
Scotland, 248, 301, 303–304
Scots pint, 248–249
Scott, William: maker, 111
Scott-Nicholson, F.: collector, 234, 295
Seare, Robert: maker, 168
Seay, Mrs. Thomas H., 146
Seegood, Francis: maker, 291
Semper Eadem makers: makers, 132
Serving spoons, **174–175**, 176. *See also* spoons
Seven Years' War, 102
Seventh Earl of Mount Edgcumbe, 126, 142
Severn River, 98
Shakle, Thomas: maker, 66–67
Shaving basins, 277–278, **278**, 279, **279**. *See also* basins
Sheffield plate, 139–140, 263, 267, 270
Sheffield, Eng., 164, 182, 232–233, 262–263, 265, 269–271, 273, 284–285
Shemmel Collection, 295
Shepherdstown, W. Va., 106
Shorey, John, I: maker, 22, 70–72
Shorey, John, II: maker, 72
Silver plate, 139–140, 164, 263, 267, 270

Silvered brass, 267
Simpkins, Thomas: maker, 132
Simpson, Thomas: maker, 301
Sittig, Charlotte and Edgar: collectors, 89, 206
Skinner, John: maker, 132
Slop bowls, 132. *See also* bowls
Smith, John: maker, 197
Smith, Richard: maker, 54, 65
Snuff boxes, **276**, 284, **284**. *See also* tobacco boxes
Society of Pewterers of New York City, 257
Somers, Conn., 159
Soup ladles, 111
Soup plates, 89, 95, 106, 111, **125**, 126, 139, 142. *See also* plates
Soup tureens, 8, 111, 138, **138**, 139, **139**, 140, **141**, 142, **142**, 143, **143**; coat of arms on, **139–140**, **142**; compared with fused silver plate example, **140**; crest on, **139**, **142**; property stamp on, **143**
South Reading, Mass., 267
South-Carolina Gazette, 108
Spackman family, 66–67
Spackman, James: maker, 66
Spackman, James, and Edward Grant: makers, 296
Spackman, Joseph: maker, 163, 283
Spackman, Joseph & James: makers, 105
Spackman, Joseph, & Co.: makers, 112, 119
Spencer, Thomas: maker, 75
Spice plates, 93. *See also* plates
Spice pots, 149, **149**; crest on, **149**
Spoons, 3, 5–6, 8, 79, 95, 285; baluster-knop type, 165, **166–167**; finial on, **165**; handle end of, 165, **168–169**, **172–173**, **175**, **177**, **180**; Hanoverian type, 172–174, **174**, 175, **175**, 176–179; Irish type, 172; King's pattern type, **182–183**; Old English type, **178**, 179, **179**, 180–181, **182–183**; plain fiddle type, 182, **182**, 183, **183**; probable owner's initial on, **169**; relief-cast initials on, **169**; relief-cast owners' initials on, **172**; round end with ears type, 174–175, **177**; slip-end type, 165, **166–167**; trifid type, 165, **166–167**, **168–169**, 172; wavy-end type, 170, **170**, 171, **171**, **172–173**; with royal portraits, 191. *See also* basting spoons; dessert spoons; ragout spoons; serving spoons; teaspoons
Springfield, Mass., 191, 231–232
Stafford, George: maker, 120
Stands, 60, **60**, 61, **61**; coat of arms on, **61**
Stedmen, Simeon: maker, 231–232
Stills, 5
Stockholm, Sweden, 13
Stockton-on-Tees, Eng., 209
Stratford-upon-Avon, Eng., 26
Strawberry dishes, 162. *See also* dishes
Stribblehill, John: maker, 135–136
Stribblehill, Thomas, II: maker, 136
Sugar basins, 273–274, **274**. *See also* basins; sugar baskets
Sugar baskets, 273–274, **274**. *See also* baskets; sugar basins
Sugar bowls, 255, 285. *See also* bowls
Sullivan's Island, S. C., 238
Sully, Miss Julia: donor, 114
Sundials, 8, 285, **286**, 287, **287**
Sutherland-Graeme, A. V.: collector, 8, 20, 23, 34, 47, 71, 95, 104, 119, 129, 131, 137–138, 142, 154, 156, 165, 169–170, 172–177, 194, 197–199, 201, 203–204, 206, 209–213, 228, 244–245, 248–249, 251–252, 279, 283, 298
Swain Collection, 28, 269

Swanson, Thomas: maker, 87
Sweden, 13, 215
Symonds, Samuel, 296–297

Tankards, 5, 8, 79, 95, 185; American, 214, **214**, 215, **216–217**; baluster-shaped type, 206, **207**, 257; cipher on, **206**; dome-lid on, 197, **197**, 198, **198**, 199, **199**, 201–203, **203**, 209, **209**, 210, **210**, 211, **211**, 212, **212**, 213, **213**, 214; flat-lid on, **186**, 187–188, **188**, 194, **194**, 195, **195**, 196, **196**, 197; for religious use, 8, 187, 209; handle terminal on, **190**; lower hinge plate of, **190**; of small size, 203, **203**, 204, **205**, 206; owners' initials on, **191**; peripheral view of, **191**; rim of cover on, **187**; Scottish, 201, **202**; spire type, **200**, 201; thumb piece on, **187**; touchmark on, **197**; with double-scroll handle, 206, 208, **208**; with inscription on, **187**; with royal portraits, **189**, 190, **190**, 191, **191**, 192; with wriggle engraving, 192, **192**, 193, **193**
Taudin, James, I: maker, 45–46
Tavern pots, 218
Tavistock, Eng., 85
Taylor, Timothy: maker, 176
Tea caddies, **254**, 255, 259, **260**, 263, **264**, 265
Teapot stands, **254**, 259, 262, **262**, 263, **263**
Teapots, 5, 8, 79, 159, **260**, 261, **261**, 262, 271; American, 255, 267, **267**; bachelor size, 257, 265, **265**; cylindrical, 261, **261**; early neoclassic type, **254**, 259, **260**, 262, **262**, 263; early type, 255–256, **256**, 257; neoclassic type, 255; oval, 259; owner's cipher and coronet on, **257**; owner's initials on, 259; pear-shaped type, 255, 257–258, **258**, 259, 265, **266**, 267
Teaspoons, 166–167, 169. *See also* spoons
Terry, Leonard: maker, 294
Thames River, 6, 150, 165, 219–220, 231, 234
The Hague, the Netherlands, 177
Thomas Collection, 85
Thomas, John: maker, 199
Thomas, John Carl: collector, 28, 93, 132–133, 149
Thompson, Peter: collector, 237
Tisoe, James: maker, 124
Tobacco boxes, 8, **276**, 277, 284, **284**. *See also* snuff boxes
Tobacco jars. *See* tobacco boxes
Townsend & Giffin. *See* Townsend, John, & Thomas Giffin
Townsend & Reynolds. *See* Townsend, John, & Robert Reynolds
Townsend and Compton. *See* Townsend, John, and Thomas Compton
Townsend, John: maker, 76–77, 89, 104, 206, 220–221
Townsend, John, & Co.: makers, 77
Townsend, John, & Robert Reynolds: makers, 77, 109
Townsend, John, & Thomas Giffin: makers, 77, 106
Townsend, John, and Thomas Compton: makers, 76–77, 79–80, 108, 206
Townsend, Joseph: maker, 257–259
Trapp, John: maker, 25–26
Trapp, John, II: maker, 278
Trask, Israel, 263, 265
Treaty of Ryswick, 154
Turkington, Dr. Charles: collector, 19
Tutania, 285
Tutin, William: maker, 285
Two-handled cups, 8, 152, 185, 226, **226**, 227, **227**, 228, **228**, 259; owner's initials on, **227**. *See also* cups

Ubly, Edward: maker, 256

United Associate Congregation of Jedburgh, Scot., 303
Upper Marlboro, Md., 102

Van Bergen van der Grijpe, Mr. and Mrs. Derk H. G.: donors, 177
Van Reeth, F. J.: collector, 79, 91
Van Rensselaer, Colonel Johannes, 103
Vaughan, John: maker, 176–177
Vickers, James: maker, 164, 232–233, 259, 262–263, 265, 269–270, 273
Victoria and Albert Museum, London, 152, 177, 226, 279
Virginia State Library, Richmond, Va., 176

Wadsworth Atheneum, Hartford, Conn., 15
Waite, John: maker, 154
Wales, 23
Walpole, Sir Robert, 95, 99
Warner, Roger: collector, 283
Wash basins, 132. *See also* basins
Washington, George, 95–96
Waste bowls, 132. *See also* bowls
Watson, Jacob: maker, 26, 176
Watts, John: maker, 114
Webb, Richard: maker, 60
Weekes, James: maker, 28
Weekes, James, & Co.: makers, 28
Weir, Richard: maker, 32
West Country, Eng., 85, 192, 197, 290
West Roxbury, Mass., 28
Westbrook, Maine, 28
Westerfield, Grace Hartshorn: donor, 87, 89
Western Business Directory, 28
Westminster Hall, London, 110
Wethersfield, Conn., 80, 82, 91
White, Mrs. Miles, Jr.: collector, 77, 80, 87, 89, 104, 164, 231, 239
White, Richard: maker, 51
Whitmore, Jacob: maker, 82, 91, 159
Whitmore, Sarah, 82
Wigan, Eng., 34, 55, 57, 136, 198–199, 209, 228
Wiggin, Henry: maker, 65
Wilkinson, Daniel Holy, & Co.: makers, 164
Will, John, I: maker, 214–215, 273
Will, William: maker, 215, 280
Willett, Edward: maker, 102
Williams, John S., 79
Williams, Thomas D. and Constance R.: collectors, 8, 40, 42, 54, 56, 60, 65–66, 84, 97, 103, 105, 111, 136, 144–145, 190, 204, 208, 210, 214–215, 221, 257, 261, 273, 275
Wilson, Phineas, 16
Winchester, Va., 287
Wine cups, 8, 225, **225**, 226; roundel on, **225**. *See also* cups
Winthrop, Samuel, 283
Wister, Daniel, 79, 259
Withebed, Richard: maker, 13
Wood family, 261
Wood, Edward: maker, 147
Wood, William, II: maker, 98, 187, 194–195, 226–227, 280, 293–294
Worcester, Eng., 54, 59, 65, 95, 278
Worshipful Company of Clothworkers, 161
Worshipful Company of Pewterers of London. *See* Pewterers' Company
Worthington family, 191
Wribbenhall, Eng., 98, 261

Wyatt, John: maker, 173
Wynne, John: maker, 106

Yale University Art Gallery, New Haven, Conn., 91
Yale, Burrage: maker, 267
Yale, William and Samuel: makers, 133
Yarmouth, Mass., 239
Yates family, 181
Yates, Birch & Spooner. *See* Yates, John, Thomas Rawlins Birch & Lucas Spooner
Yates, John: maker, 181, 183
Yates, John, Thomas Rawlins Birch & Lucas Spooner: makers, 114, 280
Yates, Thomas: maker, 181
Yeates Collection, 279
Yeates, Alfred: collector, 152
York Minster Cathedral, Eng., 13
York, Eng., 294–295

Zion Lutheran Church, Middle Smithfield Township, Monroe Co., Pa., 215

Pewter at Colonial Williamsburg

Designed by Helen M. Olds

Composed in Adobe Garamond

Printed and bound in Singapore by CS Graphics Pte, Ltd.